T·H·E
A·N·A·T·O·M·Y
O·F
DISGUST

WILLIAM IAN MILLER

D0879168

Harvard University Press

Cambridge, Massachusetts, and London, England

Library of Congress Cataloging-in Publication Data

Miller, William Ian, 1946–
The Anatomy of disgust / William Ian Miller.
p.   cm.
Includes bibliographical references and index.
ISBN 0-674-03154-7 (cloth)
ISBN 0-674-03155-5 (paper)
1. Aversion.   I. Title.
BF575.A886M55 1997
152.4—dc20
96-35420

For Bess, Eva, Louie, and Hank

CONTENTS

PROLOGUE

DISGUST RAISES SPECIAL PROBLEMS for an author that closely related topics such as, say, sex do not. People are willing to take sex seriously even as they are vaguely titillated by doing so. Convention has come to accord sex and sexuality an almost sacred seriousness— sex because of its occasional link to love, and sexuality because of its supposed role in the definition of personhood and identity. Disgust, however, still demands justification as a serious topic and a permissible one. Disgust invites discussions of unmentionables that tend to undercut certain pretensions and pieties we like to maintain about sex, presentability, and human dignity in general.

There is thus a problem of tone that I have struggled with in this book: how to maintain decorum without seeming prissy. Prissiness runs the risk of introducing the vulgar comedy one is seeking to avoid. But the very mention of some subjects, necessary subjects if we are to face up to the substance and structures of the disgusting, prompts either disgust itself or low comedy. The comic and the disgusting, we know, share significant points of contact. I have tried to maintain decorum without also becoming boring or silly, erring I think on the prissy side.

I do not intend to shock, although I recognize that shocking may not be completely avoidable given the nature of disgust and the disgusting. While one need not be boring to describe boredom, nor confusing to describe confusion, it just may be that the so-called fallacy of imitative form is not completely fallacious when it comes to disgust. Unlike descriptions of boredom and confusion, descriptions of the disgusting have suggestive powers that work independently of an author's will. And so although I have no wish to disgust you, I cannot promise that you will not be at times disgusted. In the end, the subject is a serious one, implicating our moral sensibility, love, politics, and our sense of self.

In many of its forms disgust is not simply aversive, and the content of the disgusting is complex and at times paradoxical. It is a commonplace that the disgusting can attract as well as repel; the film and entertainment industries, among which we might include news coverage, literally bank on its allure. The disgusting is an insistent feature of the lurid and the sensational, informed as these are by sex, violence, horror, and the violation of norms of modesty and decorum. And even as the disgusting repels, it rarely does so without also capturing our attention. It imposes itself upon us. We find it hard not to sneak a second look or, less voluntarily, we find our eyes doing "double-takes" at the very things that disgust us.

It would be disingenuous of me to deny that the disgusting fascinates me for the same reasons it prompts double-takes in everyone else, but I can also claim wholesome warrant for this enterprise. First, I have been interested for some time in the emotions, especially those which rank us in moral and social hierarchies. In my book *Humiliation* (1993) I took the vantage point of the person accepting or resisting reassignment to a lower status in the relevant social and moral ordering. The crucial passions were shame, embarrassment, humiliation, and vengefulness. This book is the flip side. Here I look at the emotions—disgust mostly, but also contempt—that confirm others as belonging to a lower status and thus in the zero-sum game of rank necessarily define oneself as higher. The emotions that constitute our experience of being lower or lowered—shame and humiliation—exist in a rough economy with those passions which are the experience of reacting to the lowly, failed, and contaminating— disgust and contempt.

Both this book and *Humiliation* run counter to some of the dominant strands in Western social thought over the past three centuries, which try to explain most social action by reference to self-interest, greed, or a psychologically thin notion of the quest for power. My own sensibility drives me to a more anxiety-ridden account, privileging defensive and reactive passions, such as humiliation and disgust, at the expense of more offensive and assertive ones. Nevertheless, these lowly passions help preserve our dignity, in fact enable the very possibility of dignity, often at great cost to our more acquisitive and purely egoistic designs.

Second, love bears a complex and possibly necessary relation to disgust. Doesn't love (sexual and non-sexual) involve a notable and non-trivial suspension of some, if not all, rules of disgust? Disgust rules mark the boundaries of self; the relaxing of them marks privilege, intimacy, duty, and caring. Disgust also figures in the attractions and repulsions of the sexual, which from time to time is also an aspect of love. In the sexual setting disgust's relation to love is more complex, involving us in the pleasure that attends the breach of prohibitions. But the connection between disgust and the sexual comes as less of a surprise; the knowledge of such a connection, after all, lies at the core of much of the Freudian enterprise as well as of the traditions of ascetic, Stoic, Christian, and other anti-sexual discourses.

Third, except for the highest-toned discourses of moral philosophers, moral judgment seems almost to demand the idiom of disgust. *That makes me sick. What revolting behavior! You give me the creeps.* Notice that anger and indignation can much more readily make use of the idiom of disgust than disgust can make use of anger's diction. Why is it that disgust figures so prominently in routine moral discourse, even more so perhaps than the idioms of other moral emotions such as guilt and indignation? This is not a recent phenomenon, nor is it confined to English. The entire Latin Christian discourse of sin depended on the conceptualization of sin and hell as raising excremental stenches and loathsome prospects. And recent social-psychological work has revealed disgust's crucial role in the expression of moral judgments across a wide spectrum of cultures.

Fourth, in this book, as in *Humiliation*, I lament the loss during the nineteenth century of the centrality of a certain way of talking about human motivation, a loss that attended the breaking off of a specialized discipline of psychology and psychiatry from moral philosophy, literature, and history. Expertise in psychology came to be claimed by and/or accorded nearly exclusively to formally trained psychologists and psychotherapists. Science brought undeniable gains, but at a heavy cost to a certain depth in psychological (and by extension, moral) discourse. Something very valuable has been lost to us. And in comparison with that pre-professional style of the likes of Montaigne, La Rochefoucauld, or Jane Austen, can we say with confidence that the often dazzling intellectual tours de force carried out in various Freudian idioms are not in the end chillingly restrictive, reducing as they do so much variety to mere veneering on their underlying oedipal master narrative? One suspects the poets, novelists, and moral philosophers of our era must overcome much more to be as psychologically insightful as they might have been had they lived in that earlier age.

This book is thus consciously conceived as a meditation on disgust in the tradition of Robert Burton's *The Anatomy of Melancholy*, written in the early seventeenth century. I see the book as an homage to a time when, in a strange way, psychology was less constricted than it is now. In that time it was about virtues and vices, narratives both fictional and historical, about how one stood with others as much as how one stood with oneself. The psychological was not yet divorced either from the moral or from the social. The book is thus methodologically promiscuous as a methodological commitment, drawing on history, literature, moral philosophy, and psychology. My goal is to develop further the kind of social and micro-political theory that is most often associated with the work of Erving Goffman. By adding emotion—here disgust and contempt—we can enrich the strangely unmotivated world of Goffman's sometimes paranoid social actors.

Fifth, though arguing that disgust can resist culture to some degree, I detail the interpretively rich universe of the disgusting. Here we have the most embodied and visceral of emotions, and yet even when it is operating in and around the body, its orifices and excreta, a world of meaning explodes, coloring, vivifying, and contaminating political, social, and moral orderings. Disgust for all its visceralness turns out to be one of our more aggressive culture-creating passions. This work, however, is manifestly not a body book in the style of that recent and trendy academic genre. Nothing gets "inscribed" on the body here except the tattoos I allude to in my discussion of contempt.

I also make what in the humanities has come to be considered the unthinkable move of taking academic psychology seriously in spite of the limitations of its willfully non-interpretive style. I intend this book to reach across disciplines and even to make some small breaches in the monstrously thick wall that divides the academic and non-academic worlds. In the end this anatomy should engage Foucauldians as well as "normal people." For the former I offer an anatomy which looks remarkably similar to a genealogy of disgust. For the latter I offer the belief that matter matters and that only polemical foolishness will allow us to ignore the fact that some of our emotions generate culture as well as being generated by it. Needless to say there are risks involved in ranging as widely as I attempt to do here, the main one being that I am not formally trained in many of the areas the discussion must engage. My areas of expertise tend toward the literary and historical, but by curious twists the questions that my earlier work on honor and the heroic have raised have pushed me on to terrain that has already been colonized by psychologists, moral philosophers, and political and social theorists. I must ask for some indulgence from the experts in those fields, although I hope not too much will be needed.

The pronoun I, you, one, she, he, we, choose(s) to privilege in exposition is now a matter fraught with political and moral implications. One may wish these matters would go away, but they do not appear likely to do so in the near future. So some remarks are in order. In much of my exposition I adopt what I would like to call an "invitational we." The "we" is not a royal me; it is not me trying to escape responsibility for personal claims or grant my personal claims spurious authority by claiming them the norm. "We" is the voice of attempted sympathy and imagination, of a mediational position of extrapolating from others' and my own observations of the various traditions that have gone into constructing our broad understandings of disgust, of contempt, and of the disgusting and the contemptible. The "we" invites you to suspend local commitments on occasion and entertain what I believe will be a position that, if not exactly yours and not exactly mine, will at least be understandable, conceivable, and recognizable.

One of the big problems with writing about disgust is that sex (and less frequently, sexuality) unavoidably must be part of the exposition. While I seem reasonably confident with the emotions that manage our public selves—shame, humiliation, and embarrassment—Eros and sexual cupidity embarrass me. Furthermore, gender differences, orientations, and individual preferences in the experience of sexuality may pose more of a barrier to sympathetic imagining than areas less politically charged. I do think there is a common ground of recognizability even here, more than it is at present fashionable to admit. Disgust and contempt motivate and sustain the low ranking of things, people, and actions deemed disgusting and contemptible. These emotions are thus blamed more than praised, although the very blame they receive is often motivated by disgust operating in its moral register. Contempt and disgust have their necessary roles to play in a good, but not perfect, social order.

One last preemptive maneuver: the linking of disgust and sex was a central feature of the moral discourse of the Christian world. This discourse's anti-sexuality was informed by a gloomy and foul-spirited misogyny which in turn was driven by a more generalized misanthropy. I wish to distance myself from the misogyny but I am not sure if it is possible to distance myself from the misanthropy. Disgust and misanthropy seem to have an almost inevitable association, for which I call the grand and desperate Jonathan Swift to witness. Humans are most likely the only species that experiences disgust, and we seem to be the only one that is capable of loathing its own species. We also seem driven to aspire to purity and perfection. And fueling no small part of those aspirations is disgust with what we are or with what we are likely to slide back into. As we shall see, ultimately the basis for all disgust is *us*—that we live and die and that the process is a messy one emitting substances and odors that make us doubt ourselves and fear our neighbors.

I have some debts of gratitude to pay. My wife, Kathy Koehler, was my harshest critic and wished me, quite clearly, back in the world of my prior researches, the world of honor, blood, and revenge of the Icelandic sagas where, despite the violence, things were more decorous and my interests were less embarrassing. More than any other, she forces me to clarify my exposition and get it right. My four children aged one to nine years contributed more to this book than they will know for quite some time. My brother-in-law, Eric Nuetzel, a committed Freudian and a practicing psychoanalyst, saved me from several gaffes when my general suspiciousness of and hostility to the reductionism of depth psychology threatened to obscure my better judgment. Liz Anderson, Nora Bartlett, Rob Bartlett, Carol Clover, Laura Croley, Heidi Feldman, Rick Hills, Orit Kamir, Rick Pildes, Robert Solomon, Susan Thomas, Stephen D. White, and Lara Zuckert made useful bibliographic, stylistic, and substantive suggestions. My colleague Phoebe Ellsworth was especially helpful in guiding me through the world of experimental psychology, and her penetrating intelligence saved me several times from errors and sillinesses.

My greatest debt is to my colleague and friend Don Herzog. We share many intellectual interests and also, it seems, certain habits of mind. Much of the substance of this book was filtered through conversations with Don, and his mark is present in more than a few places. In some respects the present organization of the book is his idea; if it is still not to the taste of everyone, it would have been to the taste of even fewer had I not adopted his suggestions. Here form requires that I accept all responsibility for the shape of this book and I do, but the suggestion that Don might be liable for some blame seems to be a necessary correlate to being eligible for praise.

An early and shorter version of Chapter 9 appeared as "Upward Contempt" in *Political Theory* 23 (1995): 476–499; it is reprinted by permission of Sage Publications.

| 1 |

DARWIN'S DISGUST

MODERN PSYCHOLOGICAL INTEREST in disgust starts with Darwin, who centers it in the rejection of food and the sense of taste. Consider his account:

> The term "disgust," in its simplest sense, means something offensive to the taste. It is curious how readily this feeling is excited by anything unusual in the appearance, odour, or nature of our food. In Tierra del Fuego a native touched with his finger some cold preserved meat which I was eating at our bivouac, and plainly showed utter disgust at its softness; whilst I felt utter disgust at my food being touched by a naked savage, though his hands did not appear dirty. A smear of soup on a man's beard looks disgusting, though there is of course nothing disgusting in the soup itself. I presume that this follows from the strong association in our minds between the sight of food, however circumstanced, and the idea of eating it.[1]

Darwin is right about the etymology of disgust. It means unpleasant to the taste.[2] But one wonders whether taste would figure so crucially in Darwin's account if the etymology hadn't suggested it. The German *Ekel*, for instance, bears no easily discernible connection to taste. Did that make it easier for Freud to link disgust as readily with the anal and genital as with the oral zone?[3] I suspect that the English word is in some unquantifiable way responsible for the narrow focus on taste, oral incorporation, and rejection of food in psychological treatments of disgust.[4] Before the word disgust entered the English lexicon in the first quarter of the seventeenth century, taste figured distinctly less prominently than foul odors and loathsome sights.

Disgust undoubtedly involves taste, but it also involves—not just by extension but at its core—smell, touch, even at times sight and hearing. Above all, it is a moral and social sentiment. It plays a motivating and confirming role in moral judgment in a particular way that has little if any connection with ideas of oral incorporation.[5] It ranks people and things in a kind of cosmic ordering.

This book is more than an anatomy of a narrow reading of the word disgust. I use the word to indicate a complex sentiment that can be lexically marked in English by expressions declaring things or actions to be repulsive, revolting, or giving rise to reactions described as revulsion and abhorrence as well as disgust.[6] Disgust names a syndrome in which all these terms have their proper role. They all convey a strong sense of aversion to something perceived as dangerous because of its powers to contaminate, infect, or pollute by proximity, contact, or ingestion. All suggest the appropriateness, but not the necessity, of accompanying nausea or queasiness, or of an urge to recoil and shudder from creepiness.

Disgust, however, is not nausea. Not all disgust need produce symptoms of nausea, nor all nausea mark the presence of disgust. The nausea of the stomach flu is not a sign or consequence of disgust, although, should we vomit as a result, the vomiting and the vomit might themselves lead to sensations of disgust that would be distinguishable from the nausea that preceded it. The nausea of a hangover, however, is more complex, accompanied as it often is by feelings of contamination, poisoning, and self-disgust, as well as shame and embarrassment. On the other side, things or deeds we find disgusting put us in the world of disgust when we have the sense that we would not be surprised should we start feeling queasy or nauseated, whether or not we actually do so. Disgust surely has a feel to it; that feel, however, is not so much of nausea as of the uneasiness, the panic, of varying intensity, that attends the awareness of being defiled.

Let us put that aside for now and look more closely at the passage from Darwin. Is it food and taste that elicit disgust as a first-order matter?

In Tierra del Fuego a native touched with his finger some cold preserved meat which I was eating at our bivouac, and plainly showed disgust at its softness; whilst I felt utter disgust at my food being touched by a naked savage, though his hands did not appear dirty.

In this passage, long before food ever reaches a mouth to raise the issue of its taste, we have suggestions of other categories that implicate disgust: categories of tactility as in cold (meat) vs. hot, soft vs. firm; overt categories of purity such as raw vs. cooked, dirty vs. clean; categories of bodily shame, naked vs. clothed; and broader categories of group definition, Tierra del Fuego vs. England, them vs. us. For the native, it is not ultimately the softness of the preserved meat so much as what eating it means about the person eating it. For Darwin, it is not just that someone touched his food (with clean hands no less), but that the person doing the touching was a *naked savage* who had already offended him. In the first clause the savage is merely a curious native in the two senses of curious: curious because strange and curious subjectively as a dispositional trait that makes him poke at Darwin's food. But once he finds Darwin's food disgusting, Darwin redescribes him downward as a naked savage capable of polluting his food. Before this interaction Darwin could look at the native with the contempt of bemusement or indifference or with a kind of benign contempt that often is itself a component of curiosity. The native, however, gets too close and gives real offense, and the inkling of threat is enough to transform a complacent contempt into disgust.

Would Darwin have been as disgusted by the native touching his food if the native had not insulted it by registering his revulsion? Or had the native already discerned Darwin's disgust for him and decided to use it to toy with him by touching his food? Would Darwin have been less disgusted if the native had touched him rather than his food? Food plays a role here, to be sure, and both actors share a deep belief that you pretty much are what you eat. The native recoils at the idea of what manner of man could eat such stuff, whereas Darwin fears ingesting some essence of savagery that has been magically imparted to his food by the finger of the naked savage. But oral ingestion is put in play here only because food is acting as one of a number of possible media by which pollution could be transferred. The issue is the doubts and fears each man's presence elicits in the other and the little battle for security and dominance by which they seek to resolve it; it is a battle of competing disgusts.

Less loaded with politics is the smear of soup on a man's beard, "though there is of course nothing disgusting in the soup itself." Again it is not food that is disgusting; Darwin's own explanation says it only becomes disgusting by the "strong association . . . between the sight of food . . . and the idea of eating it." But this can't be right. The sight of the man with his beard befouled is disgusting long before any idea of eating the soup on his beard ever would, if ever it could, occur to us. The association of ideas is not of seeing food in a beard and then imagining eating that food. If the soup is disgusting as food, it is so only because beard hair would be in it. Now that *is* disgusting. We could see this, in accordance with the structural theory of Mary Douglas, as a manifestation of things becoming polluting by being out of place.[7] That captures some of the problem but doesn't explain the sense that it is more the hair than the soup, more the man than the food, that elicits disgust. The soup on the beard reveals the man as already contaminated by a character defect, a moral failure in keeping himself presentable in accordance with the righteously presented demand that he maintain his public purity and cleanliness of person and not endanger us by his incompetence. It needn't have been soup or bread crumbs that incriminated him; it could just as well have been bits of lint or even soap residue. No doubt, however, the soup would be more disgusting than either lint or soap. The soup, after all, unlike lint or soap, might have fallen onto his beard from his mouth or from a spoon that had already been in his mouth. It is thus not our fear of oral incorporation that makes the soup disgusting to us but his failure to have properly orally incorporated it.

Yet suppose that it was not a naked savage who touched Darwin's meat but a cockroach that walked across it. Would the issue then be one primarily of ingesting food? Even here I think the matter is more complex. A roach walking across our arm would elicit disgust too and perhaps even more than if it walked across our food, and we are not about to eat our arm. The roach (and the naked savage) is disgusting before it touches our food; its contaminating powers come from some other source.

*   *   *

Disgust has elicited little attention in any of the disciplines that claim an interest in the emotions: psychology, philosophy, anthropology. It is not hard to guess the likely reason. The problem is its lack of decorum. Civilization raised our sensitivities to disgust so as to make disgust a key component of our social control and psychic order, with the consequence that it became socially and psychically very difficult for civilized people to talk about disgusting things without having the excuse of either childhood, adolescence, or transgressive joking. Other negative passions—envy, hatred, malice, jealousy, despair—can be discussed decorously. Talking about them need elicit no blushes, no urges to giggle, no shock, no gorge raising. They do not force upon us the grotesque body, unrelenting physical ugliness, nauseating sights and odors; no suppuration, defecation, or rot. The sinful and vicious soul, in other words, is a lot easier to own up to than the grotesque body and the sensory offenses that life itself thrusts upon us.

One scholar studying disgust recently complained that "contact with the disgusting makes one disgusting. To study disgust is to risk contamination; jokes about his or her unwholesome interests soon greet the disgust researcher."[8] And indeed it is hard to suppress ironic suggestions which seem necessarily to intrude when one commits oneself to a project such as this one. Darwin was the first to risk studying disgust in its own right. Evincing neither overt anxiety nor irony, he nonetheless limited his risk by keeping the discussion very brief, not even five pages. Freud was more expansive; he lumped disgust with shame and morality, treating them as "reaction formations," whose function it is to inhibit the consummation of unconscious desire; indeed reaction formations are part of the mechanism of repression that makes the desire unconscious.[9] Freud did not give disgust much direct attention except generally as a reaction formation. But without disgust lurking about, one suspects, his oeuvre would have been half as long. What else, after all, makes sex so difficult, so frequently the basis for anxiety, neurosis, and psychosis? One might suspect that Freud's theories are themselves grand efforts to overcome a deep disgust with sex.

Until the last decade or so there was little else of much interest except for one superb article, straddling both psychological and psychoanalytic styles, published in 1941 by Andras Angyal.[10] Angyal understands disgust to be directed against close contact with certain objects with the associated fear of becoming soiled. These objects are usually wastes of the human and animal body. These wastes are not contaminating because of any obvious noxiousness but because they signify "inferiority and meanness."[11] Angyal also links disgust to various manifestations of the uncanny. His disgust is richly cognitive and social, not some primitive hard-wired reflex.

It was not until the 1980s that any consistent attention was paid to disgust.[12] And most of that work has been undertaken by the experimental psychologist Paul Rozin.[13] Building on Darwin and Angyal, Rozin has written, in conjunction with several associates, numerous articles on various aspects of disgust. He argues for a core disgust centered on oral incorporation and food rejection. Taste is the core sense, the mouth the core location, ingestion and rejection via spitting or vomiting the core actions. Core disgust, he maintains, is a cognitively sophisticated emotion, depending on well-developed ideas of contamination and contagion. Disgust is organized by laws of sympathetic magic: a law of similarity holds that similarities in appearance mean deeper similarities in substance, and a law of contamination holds that once in contact always in contact. He has proven people reluctant to eat imitation dog feces realistically fashioned out of chocolate or to drink a favorite beverage stirred by a brand-new comb.

Without ever abandoning his notion of a core disgust in food rejection, Rozin has come to recognize that disgust is too rich to be accommodated by such a narrow notion. In later works the core expands beyond food to include bodily products and animals and their wastes[14] and then five additional domains: sex, hygiene, death, violations of the body envelope (gore, amputations), and sociomoral violations.[15] All these are gathered under one new generalizing theory of disgust: a psychic need to avoid reminders of our animal origins.

Rozin's early research was in food and appetite; his interest in disgust followed upon this research, and his theories, not surprisingly, bear the mark of his initial interests. Rozin's work has much to recommend it. His claim about the necessary connection between disgust and ideas of contamination and contagion is clearly right; he also organized the subject and developed clever experiments to prove his claims.[16] Much of my discussion in Chapters 3–5, in which I provide an interpretive phenomenology of disgust, is organized in response to his work. As will be seen, I reject rather more than I accept, especially both notions of a core disgust residing either in food rejection or in anxieties about our animal origins. But I must acknowledge a major debt to Rozin and his colleagues. For one, they have given the study of disgust some small bit of legitimacy. For another, they have provided much empirical work that rescues many of my claims from being dismissed as pure speculation. They are also aware of social and cultural issues in a way one has come to expect academic psychologists not to be. Rozin and his coauthors recognize the complex interaction of disgust with the social and moral situations that engender it. And finally, as is the case with all good work, they raise interesting issues and define an area of inquiry that are suggestive and productive of further work and speculation.

Disgust owes what little acceptability it has as a topic of academic discourse to two main developments, one social and cultural, the other more narrowly intellectual: (1) the general loosening of norms surrounding once taboo topics of bodily functions and sexuality, what we might more tendentiously call the coarsening or pornographization of public discourse; (2) the resurgence across a multitude of disciplines of interest in the emotions. It is hard to imagine that Rozin's work could have taken place much earlier than it did. Let me put aside point 1 as having been adequately dealt with by its mere mention and briefly take up point 2. I am not about to take the space to review the various theories of emotion, but a few general remarks are in order.[17]

Disgust is an emotion. Some may resist this claim because disgust looks too much like a purely instinctual drive, too much of the body and not enough of the soul, more like thirst, lust, or even pain than like envy, jealousy, love, anger, fear, regret, guilt, sorrow, grief, or shame.[18] Such resistance either confuses nausea with disgust or is better seen to evince a claim about disgust's more embodied "feel" than other emotions. Yet the latter claim ultimately depends also on confusing disgust with nausea. As we have noted, disgust's relation with nausea is not a necessary one. Like all the emotions, disgust is more than just a feeling. Emotions are feelings linked to ways of talking about those feelings, to social and cultural paradigms that make sense of those feelings by giving us a basis for knowing when they are properly felt and properly displayed. Emotions, even the most visceral, are richly social, cultural, and linguistic phenomena. How else do we learn to name them? How do we learn the rules governing how to feel, when to feel, whether to feel, and how much to feel in what settings? Emotions are feelings connected to ideas, perceptions, and cognitions and to the social and cultural contexts in which it makes sense to have those feelings and ideas.[19] Emotions also have functions and often are motives for action. They give our world its peculiarly animated quality; they make it a source of fear, joy, outrage, disgust, and delight.[20] They also can de-animate the world by making it a cause for boredom and despair. They even provide the basis for our character and personality traits, our peculiar stances toward ourselves and the outside world.

Disgust is a feeling *about* something and in response to something, not just raw unattached feeling. That's what the stomach flu is. Part of disgust is the very awareness of being disgusted, the consciousness of itself. I find it difficult to understand what it would mean to be disgusted and not know it. Disgust necessarily involves particular thoughts, characteristically very intrusive and unriddable thoughts about the repugnance of that which is its object. Disgust must be accompanied by ideas of a particular kind of danger, the danger inherent in pollution and contamination, the danger of defilement, which ideas in turn will be associated with rather predictable cultural and social scenarios. Even when the source of disgust is our own body the interpretations we make of our bodily secretions and excretions are deeply embedded in elaborate social and cultural systems of meaning. Feces, anuses, snot, saliva, hair, sweat, pus, the odors that emanate from our body and from those of others come with social and cultural histories attached to them.

Some emotions, among which disgust and its close cousin contempt are the most prominent, have intensely political significance. They work to hierarchize our political order: in some settings they do the work of maintaining hierarchy; in other settings they constitute righteously presented claims for superiority; in yet other settings they are themselves elicited as an indication of one's proper placement in the social order. Disgust evaluates (negatively) what it touches, proclaims the meanness and inferiority of its object. And by so doing it presents a nervous claim of right to be free of the dangers imposed by the proximity of the inferior. It is thus an assertion of a claim to superiority that at the same time recognizes the vulnerability of that superiority to the defiling powers of the low. The world is a dangerous place in which the polluting powers of the low are usually stronger than the purifying powers of the high. Rozin quotes a mechanic who captures the point vividly: "A teaspoon of sewage will spoil a barrel of wine, but a teaspoon of wine will do nothing for a barrel of sewage."[21]

Disgust differs from other emotions by having a unique aversive style. The idiom of disgust consistently invokes the *sensory* experience of what it feels like to be put in danger by the disgusting, of what it feels like to be too close to it, to have to smell it, see it, or touch it. Disgust uses images of sensation or suggests the sensory merely by describing the disgusting thing so as to capture what makes it disgusting. Images of sense are indispensable to the task. We thus talk of how our senses are offended, of stenches that make us retch, of tactile sensations of slime, ooze, and wriggly, slithering, creepy things that make us cringe and recoil. No other emotion, not even hatred, paints its object so unflatteringly, because no other emotion forces such concrete sensual descriptions of its object. This, I suspect, is what we really mean when we describe disgust as more visceral than most other emotions.

There are ontological problems regarding the emotions that I do not wish to discuss in detail. Suffice these few remarks. Is disgust really there, or is it just a convenient label that represents the way English speakers happen to carve up their emotional universe? Needless to say people dispute these issues. Some theories of emotion in both philosophy and psychology argue for, or assume the reality of, basic or primary emotions. These emotions, varying from two to as many as eight or nine, meet different criteria for basicness depending on the theory. Some claim an emotion is basic if it, in combination with other basic emotions, can account for all the emotions we understand to make up our emotional experience;[22] others require that the basic emotion itself not be analyzable into other emotions, that it be, in other words, irreducible.[23] Some argue that basicness is defined by whether the emotion has a characteristic universal facial expression and thus can be claimed to be hard-wired, part of our genetic and evolutionary make-up.[24] Others generate a list of basic adaptive behaviors and then argue for a corresponding basic emotion designed to carry out the particular adaptive function.[25]

Whatever the merit of these various theories, most recent ones in psychology have included disgust as one of the basic emotions.[26] It has a characteristic facial expression or expressions. It is claimed to be not analyzable into other basic emotions.[27] And it has the adaptive function of protecting the organism by ridding it of dangerous matter. Others reject the idea of basic emotions and argue that the English word disgust is simply a loose appellation given to a variety of closely related appraisals of the environment and our reactions to it. In this view the word is merely a rough generalizing label that captures the sensation of judging something to have polluting and defiling powers and to be, moreover, too close for comfort.[28]

I am inclined to accept that the English word disgust and related ones like revulsion, repulsiveness, abhorrence describe an emotional syndrome that in its *rough* contours is a universal feature of human psychic and social-psychological experience. Surely, the capacity to be disgusted is a feature of human psychic organization. I can say that and still be agnostic on the question of basic emotions or whether disgust is one of them. But my own hunch is that our folk psychology, the psychology that treats emotions as real and the way we differentiate them as meaningful and descriptively useful, should not be rejected as a way of talking about the emotions because other languages map out the world differently or because psychology has fond hopes that some day it will be able to determine the neuro-biological bases of all emotion.[29]

The differences across cultures are usually matters of the contours of the disgusting and the threshold of disgust, not of whether something sharing many of the features of our disgust works to police certain norms. We have come to suspect that other cultures will normalize some practices that disgust us and that we believe should disgust them (that is often how we recognize their otherness), but we would find it much harder to imagine a culture in which disgust did not figure in some way. Culture, independent of its precise content, strikes us as inconceivable without disgust playing some role in its construction. But it would hardly be surprising that different ways of conceptualizing disgust might push it more in the direction of fear in one culture and more in the direction of hate in another. Different ways of talking about the disgusting will mean that different senses will play the key role in processing the disgusting. We shall see that in the West taste does not become central to our conception of disgust until taste becomes a metaphor for an aesthetic and social sense of discernment.[30] The universality of a syndrome of disgust doesn't tell us much about the precise composition of the disgusting. If disgust is something any human being can (and must?) feel, the content of the disgusting is likely to be open to wide variation across cultures and within cultures across individual persons.

Let us pursue this a bit further after a disclaimer. The discussion in this book is anchored in a specifically Western cultural tradition, and then mostly Western Europe and the United States. The phenomenology of the disgusting that I construct is one meant to resonate with Americans of my social class. That I draw, however, on medieval hagiography, Chaucer, Montaigne, Spenser, Shakespeare, Webster, Tourneur, La Rochefoucauld, Swift, Wollstonecraft, Hazlitt, and Orwell, among others, to make my claims has implicit in it a belief that the account I construct should, in its broadest conception, not be so narrowly limited, at least as to its localization across time. Our disgust maintains features of its medieval and early modern avatars. There are continuities as well as changes.

To feel disgust is human and humanizing. Those who have very high thresholds of disgust and are hence rather insensitive to the disgusting we think of as belonging to somewhat different categories: protohuman like children, subhuman like the mad, or suprahuman like saints. If people simply have different foci for their disgusts we think of them, depending on how far they deviate from our norms, either as foreign or primitive and thus vaguely exotic, or as barbaric and disgusting. How much of our disgust do we come by naturally and how much is thrust upon us by being raised up to it? Darwin and those following him proclaim the universality of the disgust expression and the disgust affect. It may well be that disgust is as singularly human as laughter and tears. No unambiguous evidence indicates that animals experience disgust. Animals find that certain foods taste bad and reject them; they find smells offensive and avoid them; they get sick and vomit and spit out foul substances; but it is not known that these aversions are accompanied by a sentiment like disgust or that animals have any notion (and this to me is crucial) of a category of things that are disgusting.[31] Food-rejection systems don't need disgust, merely the sensation of an unpleasant taste or smell.[32] When something has a taste we do not like, we do not feel contaminated by it unless it also disgusts us; when something disgusts us, however, we feel tainted, burdened by the belief that anything that comes into contact with the disgusting thing also acquires the capacity to disgust as a consequence of that contact.[33] We thus hasten to purify ourselves.

If the capacity to be disgusted comes with being human, actual disgust needs developmental elbow room. Culture and nurture determine some of the timing and a large portion of the precise content and range of the disgusting (subject to equivocations I shall make soon). Any parent knows that one- and two-year-olds show no disgust over excrement and bodily emissions and can remain blissfully immune to the disgust their parents are so eager to instill in them. Rozin and his associates argue that disgust does not break off from mere distaste in children until somewhere between ages four and eight.[34] Since, as they claim, disgust depends on fairly complex ideational notions about contagion, contamination, and similarity, true manifestations of disgust must await the development of the capacity to make such mental discriminations.

Evidence from the few trustworthy observations of "wolf-children," feral humans who have been raised by animals or fended for themselves without human contact, has been read to show that such children had no disgust.[35] The well-documented early-nineteenth-century wild boy of Aveyron had no sense of pure and impure, was extraordinarily filthy, was not "toilet trained," and clearly disgusted Jean Itard, the doctor who supervised him and to whom we owe our knowledge of the case. Itard's evidence, however, is not without some problems. Although the boy would sniff like an animal at everything no matter how malodorous, he would not eat everything. "A dead canary was given him, and in an instant he stripped off its feathers, great and small, tore it open with his nails, smelt it, and threw it away" (100). The boy was not exactly omnivorous. He was initially willing to eat a canary, but this particular canary had an unappetizing odor. Certain odors might indeed have disgusted him, although his aversion might have been more simply constituted, that is, it might have given rise to no thoughts of contamination and pollution. We would surely like to know how he felt about his hands after discarding the bird.

If we accept the conservative notion that disgust becomes distinguishable from mere distaste between the ages of four and eight, it is hardly the case that the category is born full-blown like Athena from the head of Zeus.[36] Nor does it seem to build by slow and steady accretion, but rather appears to descend upon us in large increments which arrive first during toilet training and again around the onset of puberty. These grand accesses of disgust in turn undergo refinement, usually in the direction of being pared back to prevent them from being somewhat disabling, even self-defeating. For instance, the disgust which is the desperate goal of toilet training may finally come on with such force, the revulsion to feces and urine be felt so strongly, that the child refuses to wipe herself or to wear underpants if a drop of urine has contaminated them. One of my daughters felt such a revulsion to feces immediately following her toilet training that she refused to wipe herself for fear of contaminating her hand. And one of my boys at age three not only removed underpants but the pants over them if but one drop of urine dripped out after he went to the bathroom. This could mean several changes of clothing a day. At just about the same time, once-omnivorous little ones start to reject food if it touches any other food on the plate, or if it has touched anyone else's plate or fork, and it is some time before they learn to relax their newly discovered sense of the purity and autonomy of individual foods. Perhaps this is what Orwell was referring to when he declared boyhood to be "the age of disgust," which is the time "after one has learned to differentiate, and before one has become hardened, between seven and eighteen" and during which "one seems always to be walking the tightrope over a cesspool."[37]

Consider adolescence, which is for us a period of aggravated sensitivity to shame, humiliation, and embarrassment and of exceptional sensitivity to disgust, primarily provoked by the vertigo of sexual awakening and bodily changes: menstruation, pimples, voice changes, emissions, unpleasant body odors, and hair in all the wrong places. Pubic hair does not come lightly to our sensibilities; nor does knowledge of the facts of life. As a prelude to normal sexual behavior we must learn to overcome at least some of the initial horror and disgust that attend these discoveries. So it is that disgust does not come smoothly in small accessions that prepare us for the next small acquisition of more disgust rules; it comes in big clumps much in the way grammatical capacities are acquired in language. The emotion kicks in and holds us in its grip right away. That's what it means to be disgusted. It is only later that we learn the kinds of hypocrisies, casuistries, and practical evasive techniques that allow us to suspend or cut back the range of the sentiment. More time and social competence are needed to get the conventions and nuances under control.

This way of acquiring the capacity for disgust also tracks the progress of moral development, to which it is clearly related. First we are grabbed by a rule, then we learn the more precise discriminations of how not to be grabbed in certain circumstances; we learn when to suspend the main rule in the interests of equity and loyalty to the deeper purposes underlying the main rule.[38] We all know people who never quite get past the stage of strictly following the rule. We call such people prigs and associate the style with puritanism and schoolmarmishness. The corresponding character type in the realm of disgust is thought of as fastidious or anal-compulsive.

As we grow older we start to relax our self-monitoring about things that would have nauseated us as adolescents. The scaling back continues apace as we grow into middle age and watch with either bemused contempt or utter despair the transitions in our own bodies. Some of us remember our horror, when younger, of contemplating the sexual coupling of people whose age, we felt, should have worked to suppress their desire, but finding ourselves now at that age we try to kill with self-deception that critical and self-critical capacity, that late-adolescent super-sensitivity to the ugliness of age and slow decay. In the end, it seems, we more and more often have crumbs on our lips that we no longer sense to be there; our children recoil at our breath, and we no longer consider ourselves closely enough in the mirror to trim the hair that grows out of more and stranger places each year. These scalings-back of disgust are different from those which take place in childhood and puberty, when the scaling back occurs in the direction of greater social competence. The scalings-back that attend middle and old age are more a function of a general loss of affect; they represent a giving up in the losing battle against physical deterioration, a general sense that less is at stake, that the game, even if not nearly over, has a determined outcome. Our bio-logical mission has run its course—we either have had kids or will never have them—careers have peaked, and the stakes of failing in the moral and social competences that disgust holds in place are no longer so high.

There is nothing very startling in noting the obvious cultural deter-minants of the disgusting. It is culture, not nature, that draws the lines between defilement and purity, clean and filthy, those crucial boundaries disgust is called on to police. The real issue is not whether nurture raises up the young human to learn what is disgusting; rather it is whether the marking off of some things and behaviors as dis-gusting is a (nearly) universal feature of human society. Incest pro-hibitions, for instance, which in some form are as close to a cross-cultural universal as there might be, are generally maintained by disgust.[39] Moreover, for all the delight which travel literature, an-thropology, history, and archaeology have taken in showing that the substance of the disgusting varies cross-culturally and trans-temporally, there is a noteworthy convergence in just what things and kinds of actions will prompt disgust. Some claim feces,[40] others menstrual blood,[41] as universal disgust substances. There might be and probably are isolated exceptions, but that is not important for they are *exceptions*.[42] That they are exceptions reveals just how constrained cultures are in their choices of what can be excluded from the category of the disgusting; the variation in elicitors of disgust across cultures will hardly look like a random sampling of all things or all actions in the world.

Cultures, it seems, have much more leeway in admitting things or actions to the realm of the disgusting than in excluding certain ones from it. Yet even here there are limits. Some things seem almost incapable of eliciting disgust. Animals and animal substances, we can safely assume, will figure more frequently as elicitors of disgust than plants or inanimate objects. And is snow polluting anywhere? Are stones? And how low are the odds that tears will be? The types of actions that evoke disgust will tend to converge too, even if there are exceptions. Walking, we can safely assume, is less likely to be hedged in with pollution rules than killing is, so that all things being equal walking is unlikely to disgust as much as killing. And we might expect that even the simplest hunter-gatherer cultures will have some notion of disgust-eliciting acts, whether these be breaches of incest rules, murder, treachery, cowardice, or simply eating the wrong food in the wrong season.

I have no great stake in the debate between universalism and particularism, being somewhat mealy-mouthed about it, as the reader may have discerned. As a social historian I incline much more to nurture than to nature to explain social arrangements and human behavior. I have little patience with the easy unthinking assumption of a pre-social, pre-cultural human nature. It is impossible to contemplate the "human" nature of a woman or man deprived of such socially generated things as language, history, and culture. Not even Hobbes's brute with the short, nasty life was pre-cultural or pre-social. He had a keen sense of honor and he spoke; he had language. But when I had children, who seemed to arrive with a good portion of their character already impressed upon them, I was pushed a little more toward nature, so that I now probably lie at the divide between it and nurture, with my heart, however, still in the nurture camp. Silly things get said in favor of the extreme social constructionist position and even sillier things in favor of the social-biological extreme. But in the humanities the sillinesses are of a relativistic sort that claim no common ground, no mutual bases for understanding or comparing experience across gender, class, race, or culture. This has to be wrong given the speed with which we can learn to talk and commiserate, sympathize and understand, even across gulfs as wide as those which separate man and woman, anthropologist and native, black and white.

Our present obsession with difference is motivated by the politics of diversity. This politics has a stake in favoring difference over similarity. But even before identity politics gathered steam, anthropology had a built-in bias for difference. It was differences, after all, that attracted the attention of the traveler and the anthropologist. Differences generated romance and danger; they captivated and enticed, or repelled and disgusted, but they did not leave us neutral. Disgust shocks, entertains by shocking, and sears itself into memory. Incredible that those Sambian boys must fellate the men regularly, that the Nuer wash themselves in cow urine, that the Zuñis have rituals in which they eat the excrement of humans and dogs.[43] But it is not as noteworthy that they tend to seek some semblance of privacy to fornicate or defecate.

If there are broad convergences in the content of the disgusting, that doesn't mean there aren't also important variations. The category of the disgusting is constrained by its dependence on the prior existence of the emotion disgust, an emotion common to humans by age six; but the constraints leave to culture a large field to play in. The content of the disgusting varies across cultures and changes within cultures through time. Not only the content of the disgusting but the overall threshold of disgust is subject to change. Some cultures feature disgust more prominently than others, just as some people are more sensitive to disgust than others. Presumably the more rule dense a culture is about food, hierarchy, class, and bodily comportment, the lower the threshold of disgust for violations of norms within those ruled areas.

We will return to these matters when we try to assess the shifts in levels of disgust with changes in notions of cleanliness and with the appearance of the idea of good and bad taste as a faculty of aesthetic and social discernment. For now let us simply declare that although disgust is not conceivable without ideas of contamination, pollution, and defilement, it is culture constraining as well as culturally constrained. Disgust seems intimately connected to the creation of culture; it is so peculiarly human that, like the capacity for language, it seems to bear a necessary connection to the kinds of social and moral possibility we have. If you were casually to enumerate the norms and values, aesthetic and moral, whose breach prompts disgust, you would see just how crucial the emotion is to keeping us in line and minimally presentable.

In this book I argue for the importance of disgust in structuring our world and our stance toward that world. I seek to demonstrate disgust's powerful image-generating capacities and the important role it plays in organizing and internalizing many of our attitudes toward the moral, social, and political domains. The book does not begin in such aery regions, however, but amid the dankest matter where disgust arises from the fetid ooze of what I call life soup, the roiling stuff of eating, defecation, fornication, generation, death, rot, and regeneration. Yet even in the midst of unpleasant sensation, of bodies and their wastes and orifices, the larger cultural and moral orderings intrude and animate the ooze with spirit, which spirit is in turn embodied in images of the rankest matter.

The ideas of pollution, contagion, and contamination are not constrainable to the body; stenches begin to arise from sinful deeds and also from lowly positions in the social hierarchy. The socially low do not smell good to the high, and the high feel the social and political orders are threatened by the polluting powers of the lower orders. Disgust, to be sure, paints the world in a particular way, a distinctly misanthropic and melancholic way. But disgust is also a necessary partner in the positive: love, as we know it, would make little sense without disgust being there to overcome. Our own commitment to virtues of moral and bodily cleanliness, to the loathing of cruelty and hypocrisy, depends upon it. My central mission in this book is to demonstrate that emotions, particularly ones like disgust and contempt, make possible social orderings of particular stripes, and that it behooves social and political theory to care about these emotions and how they structure various social, moral, and political orderings.

Let me provide a brief roadmap to the exposition that follows. The next chapter does the necessary preliminary work of marking off disgust from closely related emotions and concepts. I treat disgust's relation to contempt, shame, hatred, indignation, fear, horror, the uncanny, *tedium vitae* (disgust with life), boredom, and fastidiousness. The phenomenon that we commonly designate by disgust and related terms, I hope to show, is meaningfully and productively distinguishable from its near kin, in spite of certain overlaps that make, say, a particular subset of contempt indistinguishable from disgust.

Chapters 3–5 plunge us into the nitty-gritty, the sensual phenomenology of disgust and the disgusting. In Chapter 3 I pose various oppositions—inorganic vs. organic, plant vs. animal, animal vs. human, us vs. them, me vs. you, outside of me vs. inside of me—and examine how well they organize the disgusting, where they generate ambiguity, and where they fail. It is precisely at the points of ambivalence and failure that the oppositions are most instructive about the nature of the disgusting.

Chapter 4 tracks the conceptualization of disgust and the disgusting as it varies by virtue of the sense doing the perceiving. Touch, smell, and even vision occupy the terrain long before taste gets involved. Touch is the world of the slimy, slithery, viscous, oozing, festering, scabby, sticky, and moist. Smell brings us to Freud, Swift, and Lear, who were obsessed with the barriers to sexual desire created by the unfortunate placement of our genitals and by the mere fact that humans are a source of odors. Vision forces us to face the ugly and the horrific. Only hearing is relatively exempt from disgust, and even it, via its remarkable sensitivity to annoyance and irritation, can lead us by slow degrees to disgust.

Chapter 5 focuses on the body's orifices and the wastes and emissions that emanate from them. The mouth and anus, the endpoints of a tube that runs through the center of the body, are crucial to the conceptualization of the disgusting, as indeed is the vagina to the extent that it gets assimilated to both mouth and anus. The anus and excrement are the great reducers of human pretension. Disgust is as married to the genitals as it is to the alimentary canal. I argue that semen is perhaps the most powerfully contaminating emission. Semen has the capacity to feminize and humiliate that which it touches. And it just may be that the durability of misogyny owes much to *male* disgust for semen.

The book then moves away from the visceral, grotesque, and material to the way disgust organizes wider domains of experience. In Chapter 6 I take up the difficult issue of the relationships of disgust to desire and desire to prohibition. I argue that on the basis of function we can divide disgust into two distinct types. One works in the manner of Freudian reaction formation as a barrier to unconscious desire; its purpose is to prevent indulgence. The other works after the indulgence of very conscious desires; this is the disgust of surfeit. Both types of disgust call into question the trustworthiness of the alluring. One type suggests that foulness is an illusion that hides beauty beneath; the other suggests that fairness is a disguise hiding inner foulness. Both types force us to face up to the ultimate overindulgence, sexual pleasure itself. In this chapter I also tackle the intimate connection between love and disgust, proposing that love is the suspension of certain important disgust sensitivities and rules. Love as we know it involves a very particular relation to certain aspects of the disgusting.

But was it ever thus? What about disgust in the world before the civilizing process? In Chapter 7 I give an episodic account of the changing styles of disgust and the disgusting through time. I compare the disgust of the heroic ethic with that of the world of medieval sanctity as it copes with lepers and embarks on a competition for ever greater mortification of the flesh as evidenced by the pus drinking of St. Catherine of Siena. In this chapter I also examine the lexicon of disgust before the word disgust came into English in the early seventeenth century and suggest that it undergoes a shift in orientation with the development of the notion of good and bad taste as a faculty of discernment. Disgust also has a key role to play in the civilizing process, working as it does to internalize norms of cleanliness, reserve, and restraint so as to help create the desire for a private sphere distinct from the public world of shame and humiliation.

Chapter 8 deals with disgust as a moral sentiment. Disgust figures centrally in our everyday moral discourse: along with indignation it gives voice to our strongest sentiments of moral disapprobation. It is bound up intimately with our responses to the ordinary vices of hypocrisy, betrayal, cruelty, and stupidity. But disgust ranges more widely than we may wish, for it judges ugliness and deformity to be moral offenses. It knows no distinction between the moral and the aesthetic, collapsing failures in both into an undifferentiated revulsion. Is this a necessary cost of a sentiment which does so much of the work of keeping us sociable and preventing us from being sources of offense and alarm?

The final two chapters focus on disgust in the political and social realms, where it confronts democracy and the idea of equality. In Chapter 9 I argue that key shifts in the styles of contempt had a constitutive role in the formation of democracy as we know it. I see democracy as based less on mutual respect for persons than on a ready availability of certain styles of contempt to the low that once were the prerogatives of the high. The high begin to suspect anxiously that they are often seen as contemptible and utterly disattendable by the low. The high fall back on disgust for the low. When the high are securely high the low are objects of contempt or pity. Once the low rattle their chains or are granted political equality the high's complacent contempt gives way to a disgust prompted by a horror of the low. Thus the final chapter examines Orwell's discussion of the bad smell of the working class.

The last several chapters make the larger points implicit in the roiling ooze of life soup presented in the earlier chapters. Disgust is an emotion that has large political and social theoretical consequences. This book is an attempt to map out a political and social theory of disgust and related sentiments. I have no simple reductionist claim to make, but argue rather for a way of looking at the social and moral order that privileges the emotions in general and certain emotions in particular. Still, one simple motif provides a frequent refrain: disgust seems to be a necessary consequence of our consciousness of life itself—fat, greasy, teeming, rank, festering, viscous life.

Back to Tierra del Fuego for an instant, since Darwin's account raises one more key issue: Can there be any doubt that the disgusting is central to cultural anthropology? Stephen Greenblatt has noted the existence of a "haunting phenomenon . . . the role of loathing and disgust in the development of the human sciences."[44] The West searched for stories that would elicit an incredulous "You mean they do that?" Among academics, anthropologists had a kind of macho cachet, whether they were women or men, simply because they lived in the field with those disgusting natives. They were courageous in the face of the contaminating; they endured life without toilet paper. Darwin's account reveals, however, that the naked savage was staring back at him with many of the same emotions.

It is not just anthropology that seeks out the loathsome and disgusting and delights in it. We needn't travel abroad to find the disgusting. Right at home we have criminal law, criminology, studies of pornography, the entire trendy field of "the body" throughout the humanities, and, above all, Freudianism with its befoulment of childhood innocence with sexual and excremental desires. What is psychoanalysis, after all, but an attempt to make the journey inside us reduplicate the horrors and disgusts of an anthropological expedition into the heart of darkness? My first love—the Middle Ages—is if nothing else a compendium of stories that shows our cultural predecessors to have been as barbarically loathsome as anthropology has revealed the distant other or as psychoanalysis claims to show ourselves to be. And the Middle Ages cannot compare with the disgusting spectacle the Roman emperors provide even the stuffiest of classicists. Who of us who engage in these studies would deny the added appeal luridness gives to the more wholesome fascinations of the subject matter?

Again we cannot avoid one of the most troubling aspects of so much of the disgusting: it attracts as well as repels. The disgusting has an allure; it exerts a fascination which manifests itself in the difficulty of averting our eyes at a gory accident, of not checking out the quantity and quality of our excretions; or in the attraction of horror films, and indeed of sex itself. But this is a trite observation. We all know it. And we also know that not all disgust is ambivalent. Sometimes we simply are repelled and the repulsion is in no way at the horror of our own desires but is lodged firmly in a kind of essential revulsiveness of the disgusting object. Yet we must take care to note that the emotion disgust and that which we find fit to label disgusting may not be perfectly congruent. The disgusting is a broader category, including as it does not only that which does disgust us but also that which we judge should do so. To begin to understand this we need to consider the domain of the disgusting and how we talk about those things we deem to be in it.

| 2 |

DISGUST AND ITS
NEIGHBORS

OUR FOLK PSYCHOLOGY has it that individual emotions have kinships with other emotions. The kinship might exist along an axis of intensity as in the linkage of annoyance, irritation, anger, rage, and fury. The kinship might be a functional or stylistic one, as when we link shame, humiliation, embarrassment, and guilt as emotions of self-assessment or self-attention. Other emotions exist in social pairings so that the appearance of one in person A will elicit a predictable second emotion in person B. Thus it has been proposed that justified anger elicits guilt,[1] that contempt and disgust elicit shame and humiliation. We, however, do not consider guilt to be anger's opposite, or shame to be contempt's opposite, merely because they exist on two sides of a competitive encounter, one responding to the other. We think of emotional opposites from the perspective of one person feeling either the one passion or the other. The opposition of these passions is within the psyche, in which they are understood to war with each other or to embody antithetical claims toward the same object. Thus love is paired with hate, anger with fear,[2] joy with sadness, pride with humility[3] or shame. And disgust? Our normal diction of emotions doesn't provide us with a ready opposite for disgust. R. Plutchik, who considers being paired against a polar opposite a necessary feature of primary emotions and who considers disgust primary, opposes it to acceptance.[4] That is hardly a compelling opposition in the manner of pride and shame or love and hate. Disgust can kill love and friendship, but its relation to such "accepting" states, as we shall see, is more complex than can be captured by a simple notion of polar opposition.

Disgust surely has some close affinities with other sentiments. In routine speech we use contempt, loathing, hatred, horror, even fear, to express sentiments that we also could and do express by images of revulsion or disgust. Some of the imprecision in our ways of talking about emotional experience is an homage we pay to the fact that we rarely experience one emotion unaccompanied by others. Emotions flood in upon us as we respond emotionally to our own emotional states. We are guilty about our anger, embarrassed by our grief, disgusted by our fear.[5] Hatred and disgust often assist indignation in doing the moral work of vengeance. Certain emotions almost bear necessary companionate relations with other emotions. Can pity not be accompanied by a certain kind of contempt? We also can experience nearly simultaneous contrary emotions, thereby confirming that the oxymoron is a psychological fact, not just a rhetorical figure.

Some have argued that emotions are mixable, although it is not clear exactly what such an image suggests: is the mixture the simultaneous experience of several emotions or rather the experience of one emotion newly compounded out of basic elemental emotions?[6] As will be discussed shortly, loathing has connections to both disgust and hatred, horror to disgust and fear.[7] Whatever the status of mixes and blends, and granting considerable imprecision in our ways of speaking about emotions, we can articulate features and a style to disgust that marks it off from closely related emotions, some of which are often co-experienced with disgust and some of which are best understood as shadings of one emotion by degrees into another much in the manner of color perceptions.[8] In the discussion that follows I will extract the distinctive features of disgust that distinguish it from emotions that it borders upon or overlaps with or is co-experienced with to produce what can be seen as hybrid sentiments.

Fear and Horror

Like fear, disgust is a strongly aversive emotion. It is usually supposed that fear leads to flight and disgust more to a desire to have the offending item removed. Flight, of course, can also serve to remove the disgusting object from one's presence, but flight to escape the disgusting is not easily confused with fear-impelled flight. It has been proposed that the difference is that fear is a response to harms threatening the body, disgust to harms threatening the soul.[9] That contrast strikes me as implausible. Many of our fears are not about our bodies. The panics that accompany midnight insomniacal heebie-jeebies are not fears about the body, but about one's self, that amalgam of body and soul that we present to others in the world as the thing we call us. One fears contamination of one's soul not much less than the bruising of one's body, and part of the fear of bodily bruises is that we are not sure they do not also damage the soul.

At the core there is an easy distinction in feeling that we are not likely to confuse. We know when we are disgusted and we usually know when we are afraid. But the two are frequently co-experienced: thus the easiness and justness of the collocation "fear and loathing." To the extent that we ever experience a pure emotion unmixed with others it seems that the pure experience of intense fear is more likely than a pure experience of intense disgust. Intense disgust invites fear to attend, for contamination is a frightful thing. Fear without disgust sends us fleeing to safety and to a sense of relief, but disgust puts us to the burden of cleansing and purifying, a much more intensive and problematic labor than mere flight, one that takes more time and one at which we fear we may not have quite succeeded. Pure fear decays much more rapidly than the slow-decaying, always lingering disgust.

We have a name for fear-imbued disgust: horror.[10] What makes horror so horrifying is that unlike fear, which presents a viable strategy (run!), horror denies flight as an option.[11] And it seems to deny fight as an option too. Because the threatening thing is disgusting, one does not want to strike it, touch it, or grapple with it. Because it is frequently something that has already gotten inside of you or takes you over and possesses you, there is often no distinct other to fight anyway.[12] Thus the nightmarish quality of no way out, no exit, no way to save oneself except by destroying oneself in the process. Horrifying things stick, like glue, like slime. Horror is horror because it is perceived as denying all strategy, all option. It seems that horror is a subset of disgust, being specifically that disgust for which no distancing or evasive strategies exist that are not in themselves utterly contaminating. Not all disgust evokes horror; there are routine petty loathings and gorge raisings which do not horrify. Disgust admits of ranges of intensity from relatively mild[13] to major. But horror makes no sense except as an intense experience. Mild horror is no longer horror.

The uncanny also bears a close relation with fear, horror, and disgust. The eerie and unsettling need not and often does not involve disgust, but the uncanny can unsettle us in a way that produces disgust, and disgust itself can raise the specter of uncanniness.[14] The aspect of disgust that makes the disgusting contaminating and infectious means that disgust behaves somewhat magically in having extraordinary powers of invasiveness and duration.[15] The disgusting can possess us, fill us with creepy, almost eerie feelings of not being quite in control, of being haunted. Disgust, horror, and the uncanny also figure in the unsettlingness of the effigy, the mock-up felt to have magical powers to harm and to mock the entity it represents. Have you not seen dolls that disgust simply by being almost too good a likeness? Effigies are not just dolls and figures, but are understood in the world of the uncanny to include the deformed, the mutilated, corpses, and madmen, those poor souls who remind "normals" just how fragile, transient, and partible they are.

There are few things that are more unnerving and disgust evoking than our partibility. Consider the horror motif of severed hands, ears, heads, gouged eyes. These do not strike me as so many stand-ins for castration. Castration is merely a particular instance of severability that has been fetishized in psychoanalysis and the literary theoretical enterprises that draw on it.[16] Severability is unnerving no matter what part is being detached, castration merely being one instance of many and not especially entitled to stand as an emblem for any instance of separation. Even Freud cavils on this in various places by making parturition or defecation as foundational an experience of our partibility as the fear of castration.[17] Part of death's horror is that it too is a severance of body and soul and then, via putrefaction, of the body's integrity.

If for Freud horror is intimately connected with female genitalia,[18] it should be noted that the uncanny also seems to inform stories in which the male organs are the source of horror. How many archetypal narratives have as their central theme male repulsiveness and embody a (male) belief that women would never suffer slimy male intrusions voluntarily, but only by abduction and rape (Hades and Persephone);[19] or if endured voluntarily then only because of the woman's uncanny and rarest of disgust-overcoming powers (Beauty and Beast, Mina in the Dracula stories)? Is it an accident that so much of the horror genre involves a distinctly disgusting, cadaverous, bestial, or slimy man competing for the central woman against her decent, handsome, Apollonian fiancé? One senses that the monster and the proper man are related as Mr. Hyde to Dr. Jekyll, different manifestations of the same male principle. The view ultimately is that male sexuality, embodied in an organ reminiscent of a slug that emits viscous ooze, makes every man, in men's view, unimaginable to women except as a source of horror, a monster.[20]

Tedium Vitae

The notion of disgust with life itself implicates disgust with a set of dispositions, moods, and psychological states that are variously described as *tedium vitae,* despair, boredom, depression, melancholia, ennui, or, reaching back deep into the Middle Ages, *accidie* or the deadly sin of sloth.[21] Disgust with life comes in a variety of styles depending on the particular moral order and the historical moment. It can manifest itself in the morbid hatred of the flesh and all its joys, as in the grim ascetic traditions of the early and high Middle Ages. In the style of the Jacobean melancholic it appears as a kind of misanthropic moral fury, marked by a barely suppressed delight in its own shock value and in its own substantial wit and intelligence. Hamlet, the character, is a case in point, and Tourneur, Webster, and Ford provide many more instances in their plays. Disgust with sex and women, with generation, with mutability and transience prompts a black humor, both in our sense of the term and in theirs as the black bile of melancholy. And that melancholic style is considerably more attractive to us moderns than the grimmer style of the Christian despairing of his own salvation. Dispense with the wit, some of the misanthropy, and we can describe the style of *tedium vitae* captured in the posturing of French existentialists of the 1930s and 1940s. There is still irony but it languishes in pretense and self-congratulation.[22]

The disgust we meet in these malaises is an attitude, a stance toward the world. And the self-conscious style that in part causes the malaise and in part is an effect of it makes the sufferer somewhat of a poseur too. Orwell, in typically biting and uncanting fashion, expresses his own mixture of indignation, contempt, and disgust at the pose in the particular form in which it was adopted by the leading writers of the 1920s: " 'Disillusionment' was all the fashion. Everyone with a safe £500 a year turned highbrow and began training himself in *taedium vitae*. It was an age of eagles and crumpets, facile despairs, backyard Hamlets, cheap return tickets to the end of the night."[23] Such is the nature of that stance, however, that it is often accompanied by the emotion disgust. Posing can in the end produce the real thing. Indeed faked expressions of an emotion are known to produce the emotion.[24] Sartre's Roquentin is not merely using disgust metaphorically when he describes his condition as nausea.[25] He feels it and finds everything around him to elicit it.

This disgust with life is surely more than the easy predisposition to be disgusted comprehended in traits like fastidiousness or squeamishness. Fastidiousness is a fear of disgust; whatever *tedium vitae* and melancholia are, they hardly fear disgust at all, but indulge it whenever they can. Disgust with life seems to be experienced more consciously, more intellectually, more self-consciously than fastidiousness. Fastidiousness when obsessional can be every bit as pervasive as *tedium vitae*. But fastidiousness is characterized by a certain triviality, a certain foolishness that is excessively concerned with the very particular, whereas the disposition that produces disgust with life colors all things generally and makes loathsome what the fastidious person might find acceptable. The one makes a prig; the other often makes a philosopher, moralist, scholar, or genius, even if something of a poseur. Melancholic persons experience a perverse satisfaction when the universe obliges their disposition by showing all existence to be as infected as they believe it to be. For them, existence itself is contaminating; for the fastidious person only specially nominated contaminants are. Nothing escapes disgust with life, for when appearances suggest there is no cause for despair the melancholic disposition has the talent to expose the pleasant and desirable as a set-up or a sham.

My description of disgust with life is closer to melancholia in the Jacobean style than to modern clinical depression. The former has always been associated with increased levels of mental activity and superior critical judgment; it was both the spur to intellectual activity and its consequence; it perversely underwrote a claim to moral as well as intellectual superiority.[26] Modern depression does not take such pleasure in itself even though it has been shown that depressives tend to be more mentally acute than "happy" people.[27] Yet I suspect that disgust, a genuine sense of the sickening quality of being, is present in both. Depression, despair, and boredom in the large sense of ennui share then a common ground with disgust, especially self-disgust or self-loathing. The Renaissance melancholic for all his talents disgusted himself too. Hamlet is again the easy example. But disgust with oneself does not prevent a sense of one's own peculiar talents. The melancholic is no less disgusted for having what it takes than for not having what it takes. In the latter case there is no action, in the former futile action. Hamlet curses his habit of thinking too precisely about things to engage in heroic action, at the same time that he cannot disguise his contempt (even though it is tinged with admiring envy) for the willingness of young Fortinbras greatly to find quarrel in a straw. If the melancholic loathes himself, he does not thereby lose the means of feeling superior to those others who in their happiness he deems to have the sensibility of a stone. Consider in this vein how the modern insomniac both envies and is disgusted by a certain insensibility that she feels distinguishes the good sleeper from herself.

Boredom, it has been claimed, is the name we give to a less intense form of disgust. By this argument boredom stands in relation to disgust as annoyance does to anger or maybe as pensiveness or wistfulness does to sadness.[28] Surely, however, something other than degrees of intensity is at stake here. It is easier to understand annoyance as a less intense form of anger than it is to feel the rightness of boredom as a less intense form of disgust. Even then annoyance seems to have a life of its own so that it makes sense to think of an intense annoyance that is not the same thing as anger; annoyance embodies a sense of distraction that distinguishes it from anger's intense focusing effects. Lowering the intensity shouldn't produce a different beast, but in fact we collapse a lot of different claims rather shoddily into the notion of intensity. Does less intensity mean the object of the emotion becomes harder to identify or simply that the feeling directed toward the same object is less gripping? The fact is that once we name an emotion it takes on a life of its own and boredom is thus something much more complex than merely fading disgust. Crank up boredom's intensity and we get intense boredom, not disgust.

Let me briefly distinguish two kinds of boredom. There is the kind we have been talking about: *tedium vitae* in its various manifestations. There is another: the kind of boredom that results from being bored *by* someone. We all know people who are boring, whose mere Hello sets our minds to wandering between the Hell and the O, sets us to hasty strategies of escape and extrication. Being bored by a consummate bore is an intensely aversive experience, and it borders on panic at times, but not really on disgust. The boredom that is ennui can be exceptionally intense also, but ever more so the less it is able to focus on one particular object. The more intense it is the less differentiable anything out there seems to be. This lack of differentiability is unnerving and can easily end in a generalized "nausée," a kind of self-congratulatory self-disgust. Being bored by a bore, however, focuses intensely on a particular object, the bore, who is vividly differentiated, a highly individuated source of aversion. Strange it is that English should have not better differentiated lexically the very different experiences of being bored by someone and the boredom that is ennui.

Contempt

The distinctions between disgust and contempt will be of some consequence in this book and especially in the last two chapters, in which we deal with the social and political effects of both of these crucial hierarchizing emotions. In the interests of making the exposition as accessible as possible I postpone more detailed treatments of these distinctions to those settings in which they will appear more urgently motivated and more richly textured. For our present purposes I wish only to make a few broad claims. There is no doubt that the most intense forms of contempt overlap with disgust. Darwin called this extreme contempt "loathing contempt."[29] But through most of their usual ranges these two emotions are readily distinguishable. I will simply list some points of distinction now, reserving others to be treated more fully later.

Both contempt and disgust are emotions that assert a superior ranking as against their objects. But the experience of superiority based on the one is quite different from that based on the other. We can enjoy our feelings of contempt, mingled as they often are with pride and self-congratulation. Contrast disgust which makes us pay with unpleasant sensation for the superiority it asserts. Whereas disgust finds its object repulsive, contempt can find its object amusing. Contempt, moreover, often informs benevolent and polite treatment of the inferior. Disgust does not. Pity and contempt go hand in hand, whereas disgust overwhelms pity.

Consider in a related vein how differently the two emotions intersect with love. Not only are love and contempt not antithetical but certain loves seem to be necessarily intermingled with contempt. What is the judgment that some persons or animals are cute but a judgment of their endearing subordinance and unthreateningness? We love our pets and our children and we find them cute and adorable. Even love between equals is less a matter of admitting constant equality than of taking turns at being up or being down, so that even "true" adult love can admit judgments of cuteness and adorableness, as long as they don't run in one direction only. Where there are rankings there is contempt doing the work of maintaining them. I do not mean my claim of the unavoidable mingling of contempt and some genuine kinds of love to be all that contentious, yet it is just the kind of claim that will elicit resistance. But contempt has a light side as well as a dark one; and though we might not wish to admit it, there is good reason to suspect that contempt can be as complex and varied as love itself. Why not admit that helplessness and need may be elicitors of love as much as strength and autonomy? Perhaps one of the most adaptive traits of humanity is that we find some kinds of helplessness endearing, or feel that it raises a duty in us to help and succor. How else do parents bond to their infants no matter how colicky or obnoxious they may be, whether related by blood or adoption? Contempt is more than just a sneer of hostility. The notion of looking down is consistent with softer and gentler sentiments: pity, graciousness, and love.

Whatever disgust's relation to love, it is not the one we have just constructed for contempt. If some forms of contempt are in fact love itself, disgust opposes love. It operates as an antithesis to love as much as hatred does. We can love and hate the same object at the same time, but we cannot love and be disgusted by the same object in any non-deviant, non-masochistic sense of love. Disgust does not have a pleasant warm side like contempt. Disgust is what revolts, what repels; it is never benign. Unless it is pardoned, excused, or overcome by desire, disgust terminates love, while contempt often maintains and sustains it.

Contempt often moves in the ironic mode, thus its frequent appearance with wry grins or sardonic smiles.[30] Disgust does not have such a felt connection with abstract bemusement. Its very visceral nature keeps it from being experienced as ironic even though, as we shall see, disgust has more than its share of structural and conceptual ironies. It is just that the felt sense of irony does not inform revulsion in any consistent way as it does our experience of contempt. In some of its ranges contempt marks a genuine complacency that all is right with the world and one's position in it; disgust, by contrast, never takes a rosy view of the world even though it may perversely at times delight in the stenches it uncovers, in the imperfections and decay it discerns.

There are other very telling differences which I postpone; here let me briefly mention one more that will be taken up in detail in Chapter 9. Contempt is in one of its avatars indistinguishable from indifference, which may be understood as a particular instantiation of complacency. Indifference is that particular kind of contempt which renders its object nearly invisible. Disgust can never treat its objects that way. Disgust is always very present to the senses, arguably more so than any other emotion. The disgusting forces us to attend to it in a way that the contemptible does not unless it is also disgusting. In drawing these contrasts I do not deny significant areas of overlap between the two emotions.[31] But they ultimately have different styles, different feels, and through broad ranges of their respective domains are readily distinguishable.

Shame and Hatred

Disgust, contempt, shame, and hate all join hands in the syndrome of self-loathing. Shame marks a failure to adhere to communal standards one is deeply committed to; it is the consequence of being understood to have not measured up.[32] It means loss of honor and hence loss of the basis for self-esteem. Disgust with oneself is hardly improper given the circumstances and may even help motivate one to do the work of reestablishing dignity. Your shamefulness justifiably elicits the disciplining actions of derision and mockery (contempt) or shunning (disgust) in others. Shame is your response to others' disapproval. Whether the disapproval is manifested as contempt or disgust will depend on variables of context, the nature of the norm not adhered to, the identity of those harmed by your failings, and the egregiousness of the violation.

Shame's frequent link with modesty and sexual propriety suggests another connection with disgust, a connection recognized by the Freudian understanding that they share the function of inhibiting unconscious erotic desire. In this setting the shame doing the inhibiting is not the emotion shame, but the sense of shame, the sense of modesty and propriety that keeps us from being shamed. In fact this sense of shame is largely constituted by disgust. One feels that if the disgust barriers are too weak one's sense of shame must suffer correspondingly. Disgust works first and if it fails shame will be the consequence unless the offender is shameless.[33]

In disgust we wish to have the offensive thing disappear by the removal of either ourselves or it; in shame we simply want to disappear.[34] Shame is experienced as "psychological" and intellectual, involving us in complex judgments about our standing relative to others and the quality of our character, even though it can be accompanied by a sinking feeling that is indistinguishable from the sick feeling of disgust. In fact, it may be that, to the extent that shame can be understood as disgust with oneself, the physical sensations of shame and disgust are indistinguishable. Like guilt, shame is felt to have its seat in the conscience. Disgust, in contrast, whether elicited by bodies or not, is understood and experienced as something noxious to our senses rather than as a matter of conscience.

Disgust and hatred also overlap through some of their ranges. The chief connection is marked by the notion of loathing, which carries a sense not only of the mixing of hate and disgust but of the intensification that each works on the other. What disgust adds to hatred is its distinctive kind of embodiment, its way of being unpleasant to the senses. It also subjects hatred's volatility to disgust's slow rate of decay. Though slow to dissipate, disgust is quick in onset; hate bespeaks a history. Hate wishes harm and misfortune on the object of hatred but is very ambivalent about wishing the hated one gone; disgust merely wants the thing relocated and quickly. Hatred can combine in the commonly lived oxymoron of love-hate, whereas disgust and love have a much more complex though largely antithetical relation. Disgust, we have noted, creates and is witness to a claim of moral (and social) inequality, while hatred tends to embody the resentment of an unwelcome admission of equality. Hatred can be quite positively energizing; disgust, by contrast, sickens and often enervates.[35]

Other Disapproving Moral Sentiments

Disgust is a mode of disapprobation. It thus takes on some of the work that could fall to sentiments such as dislike, resentment, anger, indignation, and outrage. I only note the issue here because it will be much of the subject of Chapter 8. Suffice it to say that disgust has its special areas of competence. Some of these it shares with indignation, but indignation tends to be more precise in its manner, focusing on particular wrongs, whereas disgust is a more generalizing moral sentiment casting blame on whole styles of behavior and personality traits. Disgust plays both extremes of the moral: it can occupy itself with what, in the judgment of other moral sentiments, is deemed utterly trivial, such as failings in the rules, say, of bodily carriage or volume of voice. Or it can be the appropriate mode in which to disapprove of cruelty. In the first instance indignation is too selective to get involved. In the second, indignation, as furious as it can be at times, seems inadequate to the moral claims cruelty raises.

Indignation, as an especially righteous form of anger, operates in the bright light of the day.[36] It is raised by actions that need to be avenged but that are in themselves often understandably part of strategies of competition and aggression that have a kind of business-as-usual quality to them. We expect people to quarrel, to fight, even to kill those they hate under some claim of their own right to do so. These are the bread and butter of indignation. The harms must be paid back or paid for and indignation impels us to do justice, to do the work of setting the balance right.[37] Disgust, however, operates in a kind of miasmic gloom, in the realm of horror, in regions of dark unbelievability, and never too far away from the body's and, by extension, the self's interiors. Disgust deals with harms that sicken us in the telling, things for which there could be no plausible claim of right: rape, child abuse, torture, genocide, predatory murder and maiming. Sadism and masochism belong here too, including those practices deemed within the prerogative of "consenting adults" whose pleasure still depends on the moral illegitimacy of what they are consenting to. Indignation seems too innocent for this realm and must be supplemented by disgust.[38]

Indignation is organized around metaphors of reciprocity, of debit and credit, of owing and paying back. Indignation prompts revenge. Disgust is conceptualized in a totally different way. No core metaphor controls it, not even the image of vomiting, not the feeling of queasiness. What the idiom of disgust demands is reference to the senses. It is about what it feels like to touch, see, taste, smell, even on occasion hear, certain things. Disgust cannot dispense with direct reference to the sensory processing of its elicitors. All emotions are launched by some perception; only disgust makes that process of perceiving the core of its enterprise.

Disgust, we have seen, is distinguishable from its kin and neighbors, even though they get involved with boundary disputes every now and then and share some common ground. The others have their unique styles and feels; disgust has its own. Our folk psychology has already given us a glimpse of disgust's integrity and extraordinary richness even before we embark on the particular organization and substance of the domain of the disgusting. That other languages and cultures might carve this up differently is of no particular moment to our enterprise for now. Disgust has more than enough conceptual integrity to warrant the enterprise that follows. The next three chapters are not for the squeamish. They take us down into the circles of disgust's inferno and examine the very material, very visceral side of disgust:

> And therefore, whoso list it nat yheere,
> Turne over the leef and chese another tale;
> For he shal fynde ynowe, grete and smale,
> Of storial thyng that toucheth gentillesse,
> And eek moralitee and hoolynesse.
> Blameth not me if that ye chese amys.
> The Millere is a cherl, ye knowe wel this.[39]

| **3** |

THICK, GREASY LIFE

HOW IS THE DOMAIN of the disgusting structured? Consider these oppositions, some of which are more central to disgust and the disgusting than others, but all of which impinge upon the concept to some degree:

inorganic vs. organic
plant vs. animal
human vs. animal
us vs. them
me vs. you
the outside of me vs. the inside of me
dry vs. wet
fluid vs. viscid
firm vs. squishy (compare hard vs. soft
   and rough vs. silky)
non-adhering vs. sticky
still vs. wiggly
uncurdled vs. curdled
life vs. death or decay
health vs. disease
beauty vs. ugliness
up vs. down
right vs. left
ice-cold/hot vs. clammy/lukewarm
tight vs. loose
moderation vs. surfeit

one vs. many (as in one cockroach
    vs. ten million)

These oppositions involve considerable overlap and exist at different
levels of generalization. Some implicate disgust more readily than
others. They also reveal incoherencies and contradictions. Nor is it
the case that every term on the left is immune from disgust, nor
every term on the right solely devoted to it, especially, as we shall
see, in the opposition of animals and humans. Non-adhering things
are not disgusting when opposed to stickiness, but when non-
adhesion is bought at the price of wiggliness or slitheriness we have
another matter. Water can be purifying, but wateriness a sign of
disease and suppuration. Dry will usually be less contaminating than
wet except when the benchmark expectation is of moistness or sup-
pleness; so scabs, skin flakes, and crust, though dry, are securely in
the realm of the disgusting. But these pairs, nonetheless, quite clearly
exhibit tendencies and probabilities. Notice too that I did not list
oppositions that largely reproduce the category, like fragrance/
stench, delicious/nauseating, cleanliness/filth, and others that seem
too tendentious given my drift, like virtue/vice, moral/immoral,
benevolent/cruel.

Out There

INORGANIC VS. ORGANIC   The inorganic is seldom disgusting
unless it comes to bear features that remind us of organic disgustingness. It is not dead, having never lived. When inorganic substances
undergo transformation via erosion or transition from solid to liquid
or vice versa there is no disgust. Large tracts of desolate non-life
whether it be tundra or desert may fill us with sensations of awe,
sadness, or fear, but not disgust. Inorganic substances are not utterly
immune to contamination, although they seem to clean up faster once
polluted. And then once our imaginations imbue the never-having-
lived with metaphorical life the inorganic might suggest disgust. Take
rust and slag heaps for example. But we imbue rust and slag with a
mild capacity to disgust, if any, only because man has already intervened in transforming the iron ore into an iron artifact and its waste

products; it is because of the peculiar relation of iron to civilization that its oxide can suggest decay and, with decay, disgust. Iron oxide in the soil or in a rock loses its evocative power. In folk belief rust suggests contamination with tetanus; but again rust is more contaminated than contaminating. Such is the cost to iron's purity when it makes contact with the organic world, particularly the world of human industrial culture.

PLANT VS. ANIMAL; ANIMAL VS. HUMAN   Disgust operates in the organic world, but not evenly throughout its ranges. It is much harder for plants to disgust than animals, much harder for certain animals than others. And we must descend pretty far down the plant phyla before plants become as disgusting as animals.[1] When Poor Tom drinks the "green mantle of the standing pool" (*King Lear* 3.4.125), we are disgusted by the image of the cloak of algae scum even without reference to drinking it. In those lower phyla primitive plant and primitive animal merge into slime, ooze, and murky quagmire, fens, bogs, and swamps with their odors of decaying plant life, and whether the creatures making for the fetid "pondness" of the setting have chlorophyll is not all that crucial to their capacity to make the environment in which they thrive disgusting. Rotting vegetation can be nearly as gorge raising as rotting flesh, and we are still wedded to folk beliefs that such vegetable muck spontaneously generates the worms, slugs, frogs, newts, mudpuppies, leeches, and eels we associate with it. From it come some of the most piquant ingredients of our witches' brew: "Fillet of a fenny snake, / Eye of newt, and toe of frog."

Here is our first view of a string of images that will form as consistent a theme as there is in the world of disgust. What disgusts, startlingly, is the capacity for life, and not just because life implies its correlative death and decay: for it is decay that seems to engender life. Images of decay imperceptibly slide into images of fertility and out again.[2] Death thus horrifies and disgusts not just because it smells revoltingly bad, but because it is not an end to the process of living but part of a cycle of eternal recurrence. The having lived and the living unite to make up the organic world of generative rot—rank, smelling, and upsetting to the touch. The gooey mud, the scummy pond are life soup, fecundity itself: slimy, slippery, wiggling, teeming animal life generating spontaneously from putrefying vegetation:[3]

> As when old father Nilus gins to swell
> With timely pride above the Aegytian vale,
> His fattie waves to fertile slime outwell,
> And overflow each plaine and lowly dale:
> But when his later spring gins to avale,
> Huge heapes of mudd he leaves, wherein there breed
> Ten thousand kindes of creatures, partly male
> And partly female of his fruitful seed;
> Such ugly monstrous shapes elsewhere may no man reed.
> (*Faerie Queene* 1.1.21)

Further up the hierarchy of plant forms, ferns and seed-bearing weeds are still suspect, capable of generating images and suggestions of disgust. They indicate rankness, excessiveness, a certain kind of disorderly productivity and reproductivity that passes beyond lushness into the rankness of surfeit.[4] If we do not think of weeds as disgusting they seem to have been so in the Jacobean world: thus melancholy, disgust with life, and thoughts of his mother's unconstrained sexuality draw Hamlet to images of weeds:

> How weary, stale, flat and unprofitable
> Seem to me all the uses of this world!
> Fie on't, ah fie, 'tis an unweeded garden
> That grows to seed. Things rank and gross in nature
> Possess it merely. (1.2.133–137)

The ghost, his father, has the same imagistic propensities combining death and fat rankness: "duller shouldst thou be than the fat weed / that roots itself in ease on Lethe wharf" (1.5.32–33). And the poison in the play within the play is a "mixture rank, of midnight weeds collected" (3.2.247). Note that rankness bears the sense not only of overgrowth but also of the bad odors of which ripeness is the harbinger and overripeness and rot the conclusion.[5]

Higher plants participate in the world of disgust as emblems of surfeit, as sources of poison, and hence serve as a source of metaphors that imbue moral discourse with the sense of disgust that so often drives it. That even higher plants should have the capacity to disgust means that other sources of disgust are overwhelming the non-sliminess of trees and most weeds. Moss, for instance, is not particularly disgusting because it is dry and of a pleasing softness (not all softness is pleasing). And a single weed or a single fern is unlikely to be disgusting; but a host of them is a different matter, much as in the difference in affect raised by one cockroach and a thousand, one social inferior and a convocation of them. Plants in groups, like any large assembly of the low that has not been authorized by the high, have the capacity to generate uneasiness and on occasion even to disgust. (Must I indicate that they also have the capacity to attract and please?) Trees when grouped as forests become sites for the uncanny, the location for witches' covens and Satanic rites in which mixtures very much like the weird sisters' concoction are brewed.

Above all, plants can become the vehicle for expressing horror and loathing of generation, of fecundity and fertility itself. Lush greenness can only too easily pass from the basis for wealth, health, and well-being to disgust, rot, and nausea from surfeit:

> He and his brothers are like plum-trees that grow crooked over standing pools; they are rich and o'er-laden with fruit, but none but crows, pies, and caterpillars feed on them. Could I be one of their flattering panders, I would hang on their ears like a horseleech, till I were full, and then drop off. (*The Duchess of Malfi* 1.1)

While caterpillars and horseleeches might evoke disgust singly and without much assist beyond their mere mention, this passage clearly shows that the generator of disgust is generation itself, surfeit, excess of ripeness. It is the innocent plum, which in large groups on over-laden branches deforms the branches and redefines what might have been a beautiful reflecting pool into a stagnant breeding ground which in turn, by poetic license, generates carrion-eating birds who find plums indistinguishable from rotting flesh. It is vegetable excess that draws the loathsome creatures of the animal world and redefines everything downward. Humans, albeit flattering panders, become horseleeches, who sate themselves to death falling like overripe plums down into the ooze. And the imagistic circle comes full round when the horseleech dropping off like a plum from its host turns plums into figurative horseleeches that leech from the tree. The passage, however, does not pretend to be a description of nature but of corrupt and vicious humans ("he and his brothers" and the panders who attend them). Surfeit and gross feeding, sucking blood, leech-infested ponds, these are tropes for moral and social corruption. Food again is implicated, not because food is at the core of disgust so much as because it is feeding that prompts rankness and overripeness and the excessive generation of fat, greasy life whose thriving necessarily implies something else's failing and decay.

Rich fruit-laden trees, hardly disgusting in themselves, draw carrion eaters, bloodsuckers (caterpillars suck the juices of fruit, as horseleeches do those of mammals) to surfeit themselves to death and thus further the production of more fruit. The plant world does not escape the disgusting in spite of arguments that disgust is a function of our anxious relation to animals, a relation which we are so eager to repress and deny.[6] The animal kingdom, broadly conceived, surely figures more insistently than the plant kingdom in our basic organizing notions of disgust. But not all animals; as was the case with plants, the contaminating powers of animals increase as we descend through the phyla. It is remarkable that the disgust-producing capacity of things is so intimately tied to their position in a rank-ordered hierarchy with one significant exception: humans. As a general matter it is the low, the contemptible, that are contaminating; it is inferiority itself that tends to disgust no matter whether it be the inferior position in a classification system of plants or animals or in our own social and moral hierarchies.[7] Does scientific classification write our social arrangements large upon the natural world?

Like all general statements this is only a rough organizing principle, and it does not account fully for all instances in the complex conceptual schemata of disgust. According to Mary Douglas's well-known structural theory of pollution and purity, the polluting, and by extension the disgusting (she does not talk about disgust), is utterly contingent on the conceptual grid that structures the particular domain.[8] The dangerous and contaminating are those things which don't fit within the ordering structures. The anomalous thus becomes polluting. "Dirt then, is never a unique, isolated event. Where there is dirt there is system. Dirt is the by-product of a systematic ordering and classification of matter" (35). "There is no such thing as absolute dirt" (2); it is nothing but "matter out of place." Social and cognitive structures create dirt less by assigning something to play that role than as a consequence of categorization itself.

There is much truth in this, but as we shall see it is not the whole truth. As noted earlier, cultures don't quite have free rein as to what to exclude from the polluting, although they have enormous leeway as to what to include. Menstrual blood, human sperm and excrement, and other excreta of the human body seem to resist being innocuous substances except in very limited roles, specifically understood to be exceptional. Like powerful masses in space these substances have a gravitational attraction that bends social and cognitive structures along their lines of force. They make their own grids or twist the grids they are admitted to in the direction of their own images.[9]

In Douglas's scheme it is the anomalous, the things that don't fit the classificatory principles, that pollute. Thus people look to Douglas to explain why rats and bats disgust or why food prohibitions take the form they do. Bats just don't fit most folk classification systems; mammals that fly are freaks, uncanny, spooky night creatures.[10] Rats seem to suffer by identification with sewers[11] and the excremental, by starring in tales of bubonic plague, and by having tails that look like a contaminating lower-phylum animal attached to their backside. Like bats they suggest teeming nocturnal multitudes; in this they recall insects and pond creatures.[12] "Every swarming thing that swarms upon the earth is an abomination."[13] But why are swarming things anomalous? And aren't we really pushing it for rats and even bats? It can't be that they don't fit. They give us the creeps for reasons that have little to do with mammalian classifications. If bats stand condemned in Douglas's scheme because mammals shouldn't fly, then why shouldn't dolphins and otters be equally distressing for swimming?

The risk to this kind of structuralism is that it ends in reduction and tautology. If something pollutes, it doesn't fit; if it doesn't pollute, it does fit. We then can only pretend to get at the structure through the very thing we need the structure to explain. My sense is that the idea of anomaly does quite well for explaining rather explicit classification systems, that is, those in which the rules are spelled out and an object of official cultural knowledge. Douglas's theory thus does rather well in the area of food-prohibition rules and it is largely in that context that she presents her theory to advantage. The real problem is with the notion of fit itself. There are things that are uncanny or disgust because they don't fit, like deformed people. But most things that disgust fit rather well. Excrement is hardly anomalous; it is a necessary condition of living. It is not that things don't fit; it is that they fit right at the bottom of the conceptual grid. Yet this doesn't explain everything either, for not all lowness is polluting, as long as it knows its place and behaves. And that is precisely it: the low by virtue of being low are always a risk to threaten and misbehave, to harm and contaminate the high who know they are high because the low are there to provide the necessary contrast.

I have strayed from my own grid to make a detour for Douglas. Some argue that our relation to animals is the key to unlocking the structures of disgust. These arguments focus on two main lines of inquiry, both of which are put forward by Rozin: (1) the evidence of food-prohibition systems; and (2) Rozin's particular view that we are anxious not to be reminded of our close connections to the animals.[14] We humans, no matter what our culture, are rather reticent about eating most of the possible nourishing things we could eat and digest. And we are generally more inclusive with regard to vegetable matter than animal calories. Even the least restrictive culture excludes most of the possible edible animal calories available to it. The Orthodox Jewish and Brahmin restrictions are thus only slightly more demanding than those of the loosest regimes when compared with all that in fact could healthily be eaten.[15] In the West we still eat only a very few animal species and of the ones we eat we have come to rank their bodies into favored and disfavored portions, either rejecting most of the animal or assigning the valued parts to valued people, the disvalued parts to the lower orders.[16]

The fact is that with very little exception all animal flesh from slug to human is nourishing; the same is not true for plants, of which relatively few can be digested by humans. Nature breaks down plants into edible and inedible,[17] and culture is distinctly less intrusive in erecting prohibitions among edible plants than it is in erecting them among animals. The plants which are inedible, oak for instance, do not elicit disgust at the thought of eating them because eating them is not so much unthinkable as foolish. Only things that we know we could profitably eat or that have the consistency of edible things can elicit disgust (notice that this includes excrement). Thus all soft animal matter is on the table, so to speak, of our imaginations.

I have already argued that the plant world participates in the realm of the disgusting by virtue of lushness, excess, and surfeit; in general, however, plants are notable for only weakly figuring in being disgusting as food even as to those plant substances that are ingestible. The thought of eating seaweed might disgust some, but the disgust elicited by prohibited edible plants is less gripping than that elicited by prohibited organs or species of animals. The person who says he is disgusted by broccoli is most likely indicating distaste not disgust: the broccoli is very unlikely to be seen as contaminating unless it is serving as an unconscious proxy or fetish for some other substance that is more fundamentally bound up with the disgusting, such as the usual gang of disgusting things one might find in the genital region.

Animals are indeed another story. But why? Is it because we feel ambivalent about killing animals in a way we do not about harvesting plants?[18] Food-prohibition systems are so restrictive with regard to eating animals that one could argue that these systems are but superficial manifestations of deeper, more generalized conceptual structures which define our relation to the rest of the animal order. Is it that we are nervous about being an animal and also eating animals? Is all meat-eating understood to be simply a weaker version of cannibalism? Is this the basis of our anxiety about our relation to the animals below us? But then one would suspect the animals that look the least like us to be the least disgusting, and that is manifestly not the case.[19]

Food-prohibition systems could occupy us for pages, indeed for chapters. I will limit myself to a few suggestive remarks. A principle of rather wide-ranging applicability is that it matters what the animals we eat eat.[20] This principle informs the Levitical prohibitions against eating birds of prey, mammalian predators, and carrion eaters.[21] In Leviticus land animals must be vegetarian to be edible: more narrowly, they have to chew their cud (and part the hoof).[22] Fish however could eat other fish and still be acceptable. They only had to meet the standard of being a canonical fish in the Douglasian sense, which in Leviticus meant having fins and scales. Leviticus objected to swarming and teeming things that slithered and crawled, but not to locusts, grasshoppers, or crickets, which hopped. The inclusion of these insects reveals by its deviation from middle-class American and Western European practices just how little we have strayed from the Levitical ordering. We have added pigs, shellfish, and a horse or two, but little more. This gives some credence to Samuel Driver's view, expressed near the turn of the last century, that the dietary restrictions of Leviticus were less prohibitions than confirmations of what the Hebrews, as pastoralists, were eating anyway.[23] And since we have added very few species to those that were already domesticated for their meat and/or milk in biblical times it should not be surprising that the Levitical prohibitions still do not seem all that strange. Moreover, by favoring the eating of herbivores over that of carnivores, the Levitical scheme codified certain sensible matters of efficiency and safety. Cloven-hoofed cud chewers made life easier for man by conveniently clumping themselves in herds rather than ranging about alone, and they had the pleasing trait, in stark contrast to carnivores, of having no desire to return the favor of eating those who sought to eat them.

But why then prohibit beasts of prey or other foods the people were not likely to eat anyway? Prohibition has a way of suggesting the possibility of conduct that would have seemed unthinkable without the prohibition to hint of forbidden delights. Assuming Driver is right, the pastoralist Hebrews were eating exactly what they wanted to and not longing to eat what pastoralists did not eat. But the prohibitions soon made them think that the grass was greener where they were not allowed to tread. Thus Philo of Alexandria's explanation for the Levitical restrictions (c. 40 A.D.) already assumes that God was denying his chosen the opportunity for a richer cuisine rather than wishing them bon appetit as per Driver: "The lawgiver sternly forbade all animals of land, sea or air whose flesh is the finest and fattest, like that of pigs and scaleless fish, knowing that they set a trap for the most slavish of senses, the taste, and that they produced gluttony."[24]

No single-dimensioned scale explains satisfactorily all the cultural distinctions we make in constructing the category of edible animals.[25] Nor does disgust figure in a simple straightforward way in the scheme of prohibitions. Some prohibitions are backed by guilt and shame, rather than by disgust. In those backed by disgust, disgust may work differently in different settings. Contrast these five situations: (1) The person eats the forbidden food, enjoys its taste, but thinks he is eating a permitted food. Upon learning what he has really eaten, he experiences overwhelming disgust. (2) The person knowingly eats a forbidden food, loves it, and later experiences guilt for having eaten it (or in a variation experiences shame or guilt for not experiencing guilt or disgust for having eaten it). (3) He eats a favorite permitted food to excess and gets sickened by surfeit. (4) She tries to eat a food she knows is forbidden and immediately retches, spitting it out and shuddering periodically when considering what she has done. (5) He is tempted to eat a forbidden food and recoils at the thought. This is hardly a complete list of the possible ways the emotions may figure in violations of food prohibitions, but it does suggest that the association of disgust and food prohibition may be as much a matter of our relation to prohibition in general as of our relation to animals. The problem of disgust and prohibition is something I will return to in Chapter 6.

What makes one animal disgusting is not what makes them all disgusting, nor is what makes the disgusting ones disgusting merely the thought of eating them.[26] We distinguish readily between finding an animal disgusting and finding eating its meat disgusting. Nevertheless, there is something that begs for explanation of the fact that we eat so little of the possible array of animals. I will leave it unresolved, merely suggesting that our disgust may be a manifestation of some primordial guilt, not so much for killing the father as for eating him. The fear and disgust, as I suggested above, may be of cannibalism. This would help account for a greater reluctance to eat carnivores, and especially carrion eaters, who may have actually feasted on Dad or some other human carcass, whereas the herbivore proceeds more discreetly and indirectly by eating the grass that grows on graves.

Rozin, as I have mentioned, proposes that the deep principle driving disgust is a universal human desire to avoid reminders of our own animal origins. I do not wish to deny that fears of falling back into a culturally constructed notion of "bestiality" inform some aspects of disgust, but that principle cannot explain all disgust. The story cuts two ways. For all the concern to claim ourselves superior to animals and our horror that we are assimilable to them, there is a countervailing admiration and envy of them, a desire to live *up* to them. Their bodies do anything ours can do better and they do it "clothed." We have patches of hair; they have fur and feathers; if they aren't so clothed we are more likely to find them disgusting, they are more likely to remind us of us. Thus it is often easier to compare ourselves to worms, mole rats, pigs, and plucked chickens than to tigers. Human bodies are doubly damned. We disgust as (bad) animal bodies and as human bodies. No one is disgusted to think his or her body is gazellelike or tigerlike. Yet it is generally the case that the more hair covering our bodies, the more disgusting we are likely to be. This supports Douglas as well as Rozin: "fur" on us is matter out of place and its absence is a key category marker distinguishing us from the beasts.[27] But it is not just a matter of our falling back into bestiality, it is also that when we do we make a rather pathetic animal.

Surely we do not need the example of the animals to remind us that our bodies generate, fornicate, secrete, excrete, suppurate, die, and rot. True, the fact that animals fornicate works to undo our self-deceptions regarding the transcendence of the sex act. But we can blame the animals for little else. It is not that animal bodies decay, excrete, suppurate, and die that makes these processes sources of disgust to us: it is that ours do. The animals that disgust us do not disgust us as animals but because they have characteristics that are disgusting: sliminess, slitheriness, teemingness. Moreover, the fact that the higher animals experience many emotions that we value (and some that we do not), such as love, jealousy, sadness, anger, concern, fear, and joy, and virtues that we admire, such as courage, steadfastness, industriousness, and loyalty, does not affect the valence these passions and virtues have for us. It is just as likely that we are disgusted by how badly we measure up to animals as that we fear being like them. Note too that animal wastes do not disgust as intensely as human wastes. We hold no animal's feces as disgusting as human feces. Some animal feces, the kind we call dung or manure, barely disgusts at all. Our bodies and our souls are the prime generators of the disgusting. What the animals remind us of, the ones that disgust us—insects, slugs, worms, rats, bats, newts, centipedes—is life, oozy, slimy, viscous, teeming, messy, uncanny life. We needn't have recourse to the animals for that reminder; all we need is a mirror.[28]

US VS. THEM; ME VS. YOU   These are crucial oppositions to a full theory of disgust. Us vs. them we have already touched upon in our discussion of Darwin's interaction with the native. Disgust, along with contempt, as well as other emotions in various settings, recognizes and maintains difference. Disgust helps define boundaries between us and them and me and you. It helps prevent *our* way from being subsumed into *their* way. Disgust, along with desire, locates the bounds of the other, either as something to be avoided, repelled, or attacked, or, in other settings, as something to be emulated, imitated, or married.

But I want to put this aside for now to return to later when we take up Orwell, smell, and class in Chapter 10. I will also be brief with me vs. you, which I will treat more fully when we deal with the relation of love to disgust in Chapter 6. Suffice it to say that as between cultures, so between individuals. Disgust helps mark boundaries of culture and boundaries of the self. The boundaries of the self extend beyond the body to encompass a jurisdictional territory, what Erving Goffman calls a territorial preserve, which may be defined as any space that if intruded upon would engender rightful indignation or disgust in us.[29] The size of this jurisdiction varies by culture, age, gender, class, and status. Generally the higher a person's status, the larger the space within which offenses against that person can take place. In contrast, some people's jurisdiction may not reach beyond their skin, may not even include it: thus in some instances prisoners, slaves, prostitutes, and infants.

Me, in other words, is not just defined by the limits of my skin, although it is clear that disgust will be most readily triggered by those infringements of our jurisdiction that are nearest to our bodies. The closer *you* get to me without my consent or without readily discernible justification or excuse, the more alarming, dangerous, disgusting you become, even without considering your hygiene. I understand your violation as a moral one, knowing it to be so precisely by the moral sentiments it evokes in me. Contamination, pollution, and the capacity to disgust are inherent in your youness. You are dangerous simply by being you and not me, or by being you and not yet having been defined as privileged to do disgusting things without disgusting me by doing them; that is, you are not yet loved or my doctor. I have, however, no great reason to feel superior to you on account of your ability to disgust me; for I should know that I am as contaminating to you as you are to me. This mutual knowledge should engender a certain respectfulness, a willingness to mind the other's territory and claims to inviolability.

It is not just the other who can offend and violate our territorial jurisdiction. We can become the other to ourselves and engage in various forms of disgusting behavior that are understood as violations of the self. The set of self-violating actions is smaller than that of actions that would disgust and offend if done by another. I can without self-defilement touch parts of my body in ways that would be defiling if impermissibly done by another. These self-touchings, however, must be carried out with decorum, usually with the excuse of hygiene or necessity, even though they are in some sense permitted. I can't just grant myself any kind of permission. Masturbation, for instance, even by our present liberated standards, is still self-defiling; and it would seem that the pleasure of it would require that it remain so. Some people are recognized as experts at self-violation: the mentally ill and saints are often both preternaturally astute in the techniques of awing and offending others by offending against themselves. If coprophagia is peculiar now to the insane, the eating of bodily discharges was an exercise in mortification of the flesh made popular by certain kinds of saints. Self-befoulment, self-mutilation, are motivated by a complex mingling of desires to disgust oneself with desires to disgust others by such displays. Nothing assists self-loathing quite as well as having your unflattering views about yourself shared by others.[30]

At Home

INSIDE OF ME VS. OUTSIDE OF ME   If the more inclusive oppositions of organic/inorganic, plant/animal, left us humans on the side of the disgusting we could solace ourselves with the enormous size of the class that we were part of. Once in the narrower midst of humanity we could put off the inevitable by deflecting disgust onto other humans with them/us and you/me. We can no longer avoid looking in the mirror or simply within. We must face disgust right at home with our own bodies (and later on, our souls).

Consider the skin. It figures in folk physiology as an organ of sense, the place where we conceptualize the location of touch. Arguably, touch shares with smell (and both more than taste) the honor of being the sense that is most intimately involved in sensing the disgusting. It is the skin that gets the creeps from contact with contaminating substances long before we would ever think of putting them in our mouths. Skin defends us from the outside and it seals within a lot of unpleasant sights and smells. It is also somewhat magical and bears a heavy symbolic load: its color often determines initial positions in many social hierarchies, and as a covering for the deeper self inside it allows us to entertain the illusion of our own non-disgustingness to others, if not quite ourselves. Skin not only covers our polluting and oozing innards but also allows us the illusion that the heart can be a seat of love and courage rather than just a pulsing slithery organ. Moralists of a certain stripe considered the skin doubly insidious: it deceived by making others think superficial beauty was more important than "inner" beauty and then perversely by preventing us from seeing that the inner was nothing but excrement and slime; the image of the skin as a sack loaded with excrement was indulged in with great verve by moralists from Heraclitus onward.[31] Skin, especially in young women, was held to be the chief contributor to beauty, and its exposure always evoked the erotic and the sensual. But its fragile and transient attractiveness made it a locus of some of the worst forms of the disgusting. There is nothing quite like skin gone bad; it is in fact the marrings of skin which make up much of the substance of the ugly and monstrous.

If skin covered the disgusting matter inside, the festering inside might write itself large upon the skin, desecrating it by erupting to the surface. Diseases that attack the skin in especially grotesque ways often come to be understood as allegories of the moral condition of the inside: leprosy and syphilis (like AIDS today) were thus seen as moral afflictions and the wages of sin. The skin also harbors glands that secrete sweat and oil; but of all the polluting substances the body produces perhaps the most polluting (at least of the non-sexual substances) is associated with breaches in the skin. For the skin is where suppuration takes place. Pus, running sores, skin lesions, which were a regular feature of medieval life and helped define the pariah status of lepers and syphilitics, have only very recently come to be rare sights in the West, confined not so much to lazar houses as to a few rough years around puberty.

Skin is dangerous because we load it with so much meaning. We constrain under a complex web of rules just how much of it can be shown by whom to whom, when and where. Skin threatens or promises (depending on the context) the prospect of nakedness. In the Middle Ages and the Renaissance period, and still in many ways today, too much skin, too hairy, too old, or too male, produced the frightening image of the wild and savage, the insane, and disgust for the pathetic image of "unaccommodated man," that "poor, bare, forked animal" in the imagery of Lear.

Skin also prompted desire, but mostly as a function of its being covered and prohibited. We testify to skin's dangerousness by having a general rule that, except for hands and face, most of it must be covered unless excusing settings like the beach or privileged statuses like infancy and early childhood provide exception. The suppression of skin means clothing, that surcharged emblem that marks us off from savage and beast and from one another by rank and status, gender and age. Without clothing, man and woman were unaccommodated, unfit, unlocatable in the cultural order, neither man really nor beast, nor all that desirable either. Clothing still makes the man and woman but not in the total way it did in the West as few as seventy-five years ago. In that older order (to a lesser extent now, we are told) the amount of skin discernible through gaps in cloth raised grave moral matters. The calibration was very finely honed, especially for women, whose skin was more powerfully dangerous than men's: hers endangered the morals of others and revealing it implied a laxity, if not in chastity, then in a commitment to the norms of modesty and propriety. As such it could disgust as well as titillate.

Skin means hair, except for the palms of the hands and the soles of the feet.[32] Like skin, hair is overdetermined with meaning.[33] The hair on the head and face carries meaning by its texture, length, color, and style of cutting. Culture often places great significance on whether women's hair is bound or loose,[34] and in men on whether it is even there to be cut. It has sex, race, and age attributes. Hair on the face in males and in the pubic region and under the arms for both sexes often figures as the juridical marker of the transition to majority.[35] Hair can hardly be divorced from gender and the sexual, and it always has been, in the West at least, charged with erotic significance. Beards meant something about male virility and female head hair was fetishized, more consistently than legs, skin, feet, into one of the chief markers of the erotic.[36] On the top of the head or on the face (for men) it is critical to the judgment of a person's beauty, especially for women. When a woman is said to have long flowing tresses the speaker need add nothing further to the judgment of her attractiveness. The very word tresses is clearly gendered and bears a not-so-subtle erotic charge. (With the eroticism borne by tresses compare the Eros-killing effect of a description of a man as bald or, worse yet, as balding.)

Hair's connection with disgust may be even more complex than skin's. Like skin, because a powerful constituent of beauty, it is vulnerable to the disgust of desecration. Hair, however, need not be desecrated by something else; it desecrates itself quite well on its own. Hair just can't seem to obey the rules of modesty and propriety, having an uncanny habit of growing in places of darkness, places which contaminate anything coming in contact with them. Pubic hair is unsettling to the adolescent and earlier eyed with disgust by young children who catch a glimpse of their parents'. Hair, they seem to think, is what belongs on heads; nature got things turned upside down when it put hair below, or on men's chests and backs.[37] And such views do not die with childhood. The discovery that women, whom he did not know very well, were not graced as the pubic-hair-less Greek statues of women he did know well filled John Ruskin with such disgust that he was unable to consummate his marriage and forever after focused his (innocent) attentions on prepubescent girls.[38]

Hair's refusal to stay where it started means that it has a problematic relation with our conception of innocence. Hair is generally innocent only when it is pure and that is only before it starts to invade territories beyond the scalp. Once embarked on its colonization of other regions it becomes everywhere a source of danger, either because seductive or because repellent. It is perhaps impossible to be decorous about the subject of pubic hair; in this it is even more contaminating than excrement and other bodily emissions. The dry language of scientific euphemism is helpless against it and cannot prevent the contaminating power of the mere thought of it. What is it that Americans most remember about the confirmation of Clarence Thomas to the Supreme Court? That pubic hair on the Coke can is branded on our consciousnesses and Justice Thomas himself forever polluted and trivialized because of it.

Hair's problem is not only that it is mixed up with sexual desire, or that it is contaminated because it grows in nefarious places or in comical ones like the nose and ears, or that it appears as a centerpiece on moles; hair also marks the areas where sweat is most odiferous in the armpits and groin. But mostly consider what it means to have a hair in one's mouth or to find a long scalp hair in one's food. That it is long proves that it comes from the head and not from the groin, but that does not seem to lessen one whit its disgust-generating powers once it gets in your food or in your mouth. Even innocent hair, that is, hair from the top of the head, possesses its purity only as a consequence of being collective, of being a "head" of hair. Extract one and that single hair contaminates as much as a clump of it would. In this hair runs counter to the disgust of swarming animals, in which one individual can be tolerable or even cute but a multitude literally defines plague, horror, and revulsion.

Some of my children's earliest facial expressions of disgust—wrinkled nose, protruding tongue, a shudder, and spitting—were elicited by hairs in their mouths as early as four months of age.[39] Long before the smell of feces, the feel of a hair in the mouth elicits an expression of disgust. Could it be that hair, not feces, is at some level the universal disgust substance? In one experiment to determine just where children under two years of age would draw the line as to what, if anything, they would not put in their mouths, 62 percent ate imitation dog feces realistically crafted from peanut butter and smelly cheese; 58 percent ate a whole, small, dried fish; 31 percent ate a whole sterilized grasshopper; but only 8 percent would tolerate a lock of human hair.[40] This doesn't show much except that before age two all but the slowest of kids know that hair is not food, something they could know without disgust figuring in the calculation. But how did they come by that information and not acquire it with regard to grasshoppers and dog feces? I suppose that like my children they know from prior experience that it is unpleasant to feel a hair in the mouth, and that once they acquire notions of contagion and pollution the sensation will come to elicit disgust as well. The issue, however, is more one of tactility than of taste, even if we recognize that tactility is an important aspect of palatability, if not quite of taste as narrowly conceived.

The beauty of skin and hair depends then on the value of location. It also depends on imprecise vision. Too close a look can render what was enticing disgusting or horrifying. Thus Prufrock:

> I have known the arms already, known them all—
> Arms that are braceleted and white and bare
> But in the lamplight, downed with light brown hair! [41]

Gulliver found Lilliputian skin extraordinarily fair, but a different view was afforded him in Brobdingnag, where he observed a wet-nurse giving suck to an infant:

> I must confess no object ever disgusted me so much as the sight of her monstrous breast, which I cannot tell what to compare with so as to give the curious reader an idea of its bulk, shape and colour. It stood prominent six foot and could not be less than sixteen in circumference. The nipple was about half the bigness of my head, and the hue both of that and the dug so varified with spots, pimples, and freckles that nothing could appear more nauseous . . . This made me reflect upon the fair skins of our English ladies, who appear so beautiful to us only because they are of our own size, and their defects not to be seen but through a magnifying glass, where we find by experiment that the smoothest and whitest skins look rough and coarse and ill-coloured. I remember when I was at Lilliput the complexions of those diminutive people appeared to me the fairest in the world. (*Gulliver's Travels* pt. II, ch. 1)

Later among the maids of honor at the Brobdingnagian court, who showed no shame in dressing before such an insignificant creature, he observed a sight that filled him with "horror and disgust:"

> Their skins appeared so coarse and uneven, so variously colored, when I saw them near, with a mole here and there as broad as a trencher, and hairs hanging from it thicker than packthreads; to say nothing further concerning the rest of their persons. (ch. 5)

Swift anticipates the even more unflattering revelations of the microscope and what it reveals about skin. A trip to the encyclopedia shows us illustrations of sweat glands that look like worms or viscous ooze, sebaceous glands, hair shafts, subcutaneous fatty tissue, pores like craters. Enlarged cross-sections do for us what Brobdingnagian proportions did for Gulliver. Swift did not need such aids to disabuse himself of the illusions of the beauty of fair skin, and lamplight sufficed for Prufrock.[42] One of the reasons that big-screen cinema is so powerful a fantasy-creating and fantasy-sustaining form is that it allows us to see Brobdingnagians with the skin texture of Lilliputians. The magnification of projection contrasts greatly with magnification of microscopy, for the former magically enlarges without making pores, follicles, moles, hairs, and blotches more perceptible. Skin and the hair of the scalp remain lustrous, pure, and alluring. No wonder we love those film stars.

Now it need hardly be mentioned, so obvious it is, that hair is more defiling to women than to men, in direct proportion to the fact that it is more alluring with regard to women than to men. It is simply more charged sexually either positively or negatively for women than for men. Men can have hairy arms and chests and may even be thought more attractive for having them as long as the hair is not excessive, but the light brown hair discernible in lamplight was enough to unsettle Prufrock. Americans are especially obsessive about denying the hairiness of women, who remove it from legs, upper lip, chest, and armpits, and now with bathing suits cut in the way they have been for the last decade, from the pubic region also.[43] Men are given much greater leeway and tend to prompt disgust only when backs and the backs of arms get hairy or when appropriate levels of chest hair are exceeded and it forces itself out of shirt collars and up the neck or out of noses and ears.[44]

I started this section with the intention of contrasting the outside of me (less contaminating) with the inside of me (more contaminating), but showed instead just how variegated a surface the outside is with its capacity to disgust, to allure, and to contaminate. Not all parts of the outer body are of equal moral or ritual value. Some parts are easily contaminated and contaminating, like the sexual organs. Others have little power to contaminate or be contaminated, like the shoulders and elbows. The latter are thus serviceable as spacers and clearers of the way, able to make and suffer contact in elevators and subways without risking the disgust that using the hands might elicit;[45] the sexual organs, in contrast, can only be allowed to touch or be touched under very specially negotiated conditions; they are what the spacers mean to protect. We could scarcely endure society or ourselves if some parts of us couldn't serve as protection for other parts.

The inside of us is not without variegation either. The inside, of course, is polluting because it is a mess of gooey, oozy, slimy, smelly things.[46] The ascetic tradition treated the entire inside as a mass of undifferentiated excrement, allowing excrement to stand as the appropriate symbol for all the stuff within. Yet the inside is also where that same tradition locates the soul and character and virtue. It is where the undulating flesh of the heart muscle is also a metaphorical seat of courage; where the convolutions of the brain are the seat of mind and thought. The inside, while disgusting in its physicality, is somehow honest by not alluring us with false fronts. Only the outside can play the hypocrite. The inside, when sealed, provides us with the location of the immaterial, the spiritual, the characterological; it is the space in which the metaphors and images associated with the positive value of "depth" get played out, while the beautiful surface is home to images of shallowness and superficiality.[47]

The disgust that arises when the body is sliced open with a knife or pierced with a bullet is more than just a function of the muck that pours out, it is a function primarily of the inappropriateness of destroying the integrity of the body's seal. But the body's seal is already broken at various orifices, and these orifices must bear the bulk of the weight of the opposition between inside and outside because they are where the danger of unclarity and disorder is. They are the holes that allow contaminants in to pollute the soul, and they are the passageways through which substances pass that can defile ourselves and others too.

Some of these holes—for instance, the eyes, ears, nose, mouth— are also the loci of reception for sensory perception. The senses, some more so than others, are crucial to the phenomenology of disgust, and it is in the idiom variously of touch, smell, and other sensation that many of the qualities of the disgusting are developed and conceptualized. For instance, it is in the context of the sense of touch that oppositions like moist/dry, viscid/fluid, sticky/non-sticky, squishy/firm are perceived. We will thus postpone the orifices as particular points of danger and vulnerability until after a discussion of the role individual senses play in the constitution of disgust.

| **4** |

THE SENSES

SINCE DARWIN, as we have already observed, the non-Freudian literature on disgust has focused on disgust as an affect linked originally and functionally to the sense of taste. I have attributed this focus to the unintended effects of the etymology of the English word disgust. If we list those qualities that we tend to associate with disgust-eliciting things, however, we find that attributes of taste figure no more saliently than those of smell or touch.

Touch

The qualities of consistency and feel provide the bulk of our lexicon of disgust. Thus the oppositions squishy vs. firm, moist vs. dry, sticky vs. non-adhering, scabby vs. smooth, viscid vs. free flowing, wriggling and slithering vs. still. Add further certain qualities without easily paired opposites, for which the opposite is simply the absence of the trait: oily, filmy, curdly, gooey, slimy, mucky. All these qualities deserve some special comment. For one thing, it is easier to come up with words to describe disgusting sensations when these are moist, viscid, pliable, than when they are dry, free flowing, or hard. For every disgusting scabby or crusty thing there are tens of disgusting oozy, mucky, gooey, slimy, clammy, sticky, tacky, dank, squishy, or filmy things. And even the scabby and the crusty borrow their disgustingness from the fact that they are formed from the coagulation of viscous substances. Note how hard it is to find non-pejorative terms to describe some of these consistencies, primarily those which are characteristics of what I earlier called life soup. Just how is it possible to name slime or indicate something that slithers without the term taking on a heavy negative moral and aesthetic baggage?

Consider the case of oil, which shares with slime a slippery smoothness and similar viscosity. Oil is as good as the slimy can get; it has the capacity to lead a life of ritual purity, being transparent and having the capacity to make things shine. When from olives it anointed kings and Homeric heroes or when blessed it served in the sacrament of extreme unction. In this role it was not only pure but purifying. But oil came soon to have a less exalted life.[1] Not initially disgusting in the material world, it came to be infected by the meaning it acquired in the moral world. The same capacities that made it useful as a lubricant, its slipperiness, smoothness, and adhering characteristics, when applied to moral traits served to describe a particularly vile character. Glib, oily, unctuous, greasy. It is in the moral world that oil sinks to the slimy; and once morally infected it loses its pristine quality in the world of matter.[2] Oil also suffered from its religious pretensions. Unction was made unctuous and slimy by the human capacity for fawning and hypocrisy.

The diction governing tactile disgust reveals certain presumptions and tendencies about the way we conceptualize disgust; these are captured by the oppositions I noted at the beginning of this section. Even if we discount for the bad associations that come with the words themselves we are still left with the distinct sense that things that are slimy, sticky, slithery, wriggly, oily, or viscid are more likely to elicit disgust than those without such qualities. Again, I am not saying that the category of disgust cannot be constructed differently, only that it exhibits certain tendencies and probabilities. Presumably rice farmers have long been acclimated to muck, eel fisherman to slimy slitheriness, nurses and doctors to evil-smelling and decaying bodies. And because we are dealing with probabilities and presumptions, these presumptions can be overcome by context and the kinds of expectations context generates. That which should be moist can disgust by being dry, that which should be supple can disgust by being hard, that which should be thick or viscous can disgust by being watery, the very word watery being a pejorative of concepts like clear, fluid, limpid, or pellucid.

But the presumptions are there and one wonders if they are themselves solely generated by culture or if they work to constrain cultural choices. As mentioned in Chapter 1, I suspect that more cultural work is needed to make slitheriness non-disgusting than to make it disgusting.[3] We might discern here two categories of tactile disgustingness. In the first are those things that disgust by failure to accord with expectations. Such would be the disgustingness of human skin that feels like a reptile's, or, for that matter, a reptile's that feels like a human's. In the second category expectations of disgust are met in full by disgust unless love or inurement prevents it. This is the realm of the slimy, oozy, sticky, squishy, wiggly, and slithery. What draws the disgusting to these qualities? Douglasian structuralism doesn't give a non-reductive answer;[4] with a little ingenuity it could provide an answer for each culture, but it would still not account for the tendencies of so many different cultures to converge in agreement that slime and ooze, feces and menstrual blood, are on the polluting side of the equation.

Might it be that disgust itself has a structure which it imposes on cultural orderings? This is hardly an outrageous proposition. Cultures surely vary in the degree to which they call on disgust to back their moral ordering, but to the extent that they look to disgust (or something like it) rather than, say, guilt or fear, certain things must follow. Even here culture can override the tendencies that come with the disgust affect, but it has to work harder to do so. Once a culture erects the classification pure/impure the clear and free flowing will be valued as against the slimy and viscid. Another constraint imposed on the category of the disgusting may well come from certain broadly shared ideas of what purity means. Here the influences work in two directions. Disgust constrains the possible attributes of the pure, while the idea of the pure, in turn, supplies precise content to the disgusting. Purity seems necessarily to involve a certain sense of the discreteness of a thing, of its inviolability, and its disconnectedness with other things. If this is so things that stick will be presumptively contaminating. Then what of slippery, slithery things that are impossible to get a grip on? These surely don't stick but they leave filmy, clammy, or oily substances that do. Slime is slime because it doesn't flow away quickly.[5] Clear free-running things will thus be presumptively pure. A culture could override these presumptions or even stand them on their head. But it would take more work, a longer story, to do so than to go, so to speak, with the flow.

Purity must be defined against the impure and the impure against it; purity cannot exist as a concept without creating its contrary. Culture is stuck here with the nature of certain mental concepts, which can exist only as oppositions and contrasts.[6] Black needs white, good needs evil, virtue needs vice, or the first term makes no sense. And in the strange way that qualities give rise to their contrary or are reducible to a common underlying concept, so the word cleanness itself may owe its origins to stickiness. In one of those uncanny etymologies[7] that shows a word meaning itself and its opposite, the OED notes that some philologists believe *clean* to derive from an Indo-European stem meaning "to stick," "with the suggested connexion of sense that sticky things, such as oil, give a clear surface, or 'make the face to shine.' "[8] I think it may be less the luminous shine than the sticking itself. Water and clear, free-flowing liquids clean by washing away, by rinsing. Oil, unlike water, must be understood to purify not by rinsing but by adhering and bonding. In this it behaves quite like a pollutant, which with its extraordinary powers of contagion has the ability to adhere to or mingle with anything it touches. In order to do battle with the impure the purifying agent must itself be able to stick to what it touches so as to shield it, as with oil, or mingle with the pollutant so as to wash it away, as in purification by ablution. Whether water or oil, the purifying agent must give itself up for the general cause of purity. The pure thus borrows from the impure its disgusting qualities to fight against it. The fear is, of course, that pollutants stick only too well whereas it takes a heady dose of wishful thinking to believe purity to be as contagious as pollution.[9]

The skin is our chief organ of touch and, strangely, some of the things we least like to touch parody the form if not quite the function of skin. Take the skin on heated milk for instance. Some, like Julia Kristeva, find this the *pièce de resistance* of the disgusting.[10] Part of its loathsomeness is the feel of it in the mouth, not unlike the disgust that a hair produces.[11] It seems that crusts, skins, and films covering fluid interiors have a special ability to elicit disgust. The phenomenon of coagulation, of curdling, unites ideas of bubbling, seething, generative surfeit, with ideas of fermentation and rot. It is the green mantle on the standing pool again. The curd, the milk scum, thus reproduce the central themes of disgust elicitation: the eternal recurrence of viscous, teeming, swarming generation and the putrefaction and decay that attend it. It is as if the milk, when heated, spontaneously generates a loathsome image of gestation itself: a membrane appearing to cover warmish fluids. Life must be packaged just right not to make us cringe when it touches us.

A subsystem of the sense of touch processes temperature. Coldness couples with clamminess to mimic death, heat couples with hellfire to produce sulfurous stenches. Yet, as a general rule, extreme temperatures do not elicit disgust. (Pain, not disgust, is the specie of the extremes.) The cold clamminess of death is no less than 60°F; once we get below 32°F we are in the world of crystalline purity. And well before we get above 212°F we enter a world purified by fire. Fire does not disgust unless accompanied by foul odors, but lukewarmness, or body temperature, might well do so. We will sit on a public toilet seat with less upset when it is cold than when we discern that it is warm from the warmth of a prior user. Body heat is in some way as polluting as more material pollutants in that setting. Temperature, it seems, disgusts precisely in those ranges in which life teems, that is, from the dank of the fen to the mugginess of the jungle; this is the range in which sliminess exists, for slime ceases to be when frozen solid or burnt to a crisp. The temperature must be sufficient to get the old life soup bubbling, seething, wiggling, and writhing but not so great as to kill it. The boiling and seething of life, the coagulating of blood, the eruption of suppurating sores, the teeming of maggots—disgust itself—operate in what we call the comfort zone.

We do not need to swallow things to be contaminated by them. A taste-based conception of disgust cannot account for the fact that most contamination takes place simply by contact rather than by ingestion and not just contact with the skin but with the extended covering that includes our clothing (even clothing we are not wearing but intend to put on) as well as the space we claim as our immediate bodily preserve. The approach of disgusting things causes us to cringe, shudder, or recoil in anticipation of offensive touchings. We have seen that some areas of our surface are more at risk, more sacred than other areas, and that all the orifices, although in different degrees, are points of serious vulnerability. Those places which are likely to cause disgust by being touched are also likely to cause disgust when they are used to touch another. Touching with or being touched by a shoulder or elbow is far less problematic than touchings involving hands, tongues, or genitalia.

Being touched by another under certain predictable circumstances elicits disgust. Take first the case of the person whom our sentinel senses of sight and smell, or our moral sense, already reveal as disgusting. Touchings from this person will disgust if they are attempts at greater intimacy, and will both disgust (because of what he is) and raise indignation (for what he did) if the touching is not a request for intimacy but takes the form of non-sexualized aggression. Disgustingly ugly people are given very little leeway. We tend to impute intentionality to their disgustingness, and thus we are unlikely to excuse their accidental touchings as accidents. They are blamed for not attending to the special duties to avoid contact that their pariah status imposes on them.

Even people who are not perceived as initially disgusting can quickly become so by getting too close without our permission. When they touch us impermissibly we treat them to a mix of disgust and indignation similar to that we direct toward the pariah. The difference is that these people are allowed the opportunity to plead their lack of intention. A ritually apt "sorry" will prevent offense being taken, or remedy any offense already taken if the excuse is reasonably plausible and sincere. Plausibility regarding such "accidents" usually depends on not having to raise the plea of accident more than once and on the relative triviality of the offense being excused. These not unattractive people are also given another benefit: they are often granted the privilege of having their unpermitted touchings processed as if they were proper requests for permission for the touching taking place. Such a touching is the first escalation in the ritual of courtship, and it directly involves disgust. For the touching is a request to consider the prospect of the ultimate sexual touching and whether that touching from the person in question would be disgusting. That first touching, that first gesture in the course of conversation when one lightly touches the other's arm, is thus raising only one serious question: Do I disgust you?

Smell

In the diffuseness of the location of its sensors touch differs radically from sight, taste, smell, and hearing, all of which are centered at orifices and localized organs devoted to receiving those inputs. But though touch is diffuse in the location of its receptors the contaminating toucher is usually quite identifiable and localizable. Smell works just the other way, with a highly localized receptor, the nose, but often emanating from unlocalizable and diffuse sources. Smells are pervasive and invisible, capable of threatening like poison; smells are the very vehicles of contagion. Odors are thus especially contaminating and much more dangerous than localized substances one may or may not put in the mouth. Before germ theory existed nauseating smells bore the burden of carrying disease, while good smells were curative. Germ theory did little to undo this belief, as makers of home cleaning products well know. The aseptic must have a smell that accords with our beliefs about the smell of asepsis. And detergents must produce suds and be perfumed or they won't sell even though the suds and odorants pollute rivers and have no cleansing action whatsoever.

Smell combines with taste to give us the rich array of flavors we love and loathe. But smell gets there long before taste and we might wonder why, if our sense of smell were attuned, we should ever put nauseating foods in our mouth. The problem seems to be that even though smell is a powerful component of flavor the smell of things outside the mouth is very different from the olfactory effect they have once in the mouth.[12] Smell is thus not constructed to give a perfect indication of what might taste good. Any lover of strong cheeses and fishy fish knows this to be true. If smell alone were to control access to the mouth we would not only miss cheeses but repent of drinking perfume and eating flowers. Even a coffee lover has to feel that twinge of vexation in the falling off between its alluring aroma and its taste.

Whatever defensive role disgust plays for the biological organism would seem to be of little value if it had to wait until the sense of taste was engaged. Taste operates as a defense of last resort; it is meant to catch only those things that get by the outer sensory defenses. The eyes can be fooled by pleasant exteriors, as the nose can be by hypocritical aromas. But taste is no more foolproof a defense than touch or vision, for there is no guarantee that harmful things will taste bad. Taste can be tricked too. Poison may not be identifiable by taste, and otherwise unharmful things can taste too good, giving rise to the harms of addiction and surfeit. The bulk of the ingestive defense work is accomplished by smell not taste. We follow an easy rule regarding ingestion to which we admit a few carefully delineated exceptions: do not stick foul-smelling things in the mouth unless they are members of the limited class of items culture and experience identify as smelling bad but as being nonetheless nutritional and good tasting: thus cheese, fish, or cooked cabbage-family vegetables (there is also an exception for sex which will be dealt with in a general and abstract fashion later).

We saw that touch provides a rich lexicon of terms to describe revolting tactile sensations and that the gradations in sensation are measured along qualitative axes of temperature, viscosity, texture, movement, adhesion, and so on. The lexicon of smell is very limited and usually must work by making an adjective of the thing that smells. Excrement smells like excrement, roses like a rose, rotting flesh like rotting flesh. Sometimes we attempt description by saying that rotting flesh smells like feces, or that a perfume smells like a rose.[13] What is missing is a specially dedicated qualitative diction of odor that matches the richness of distinctions we make with the tactile as with squishy, oozy, gooey, gummy, mucky, dank, and damp. Odor qualifiers, if not the names of things emitting the odor, are usually simple adjectives and nouns expressing either the pleasantness or unpleasantness of the smell, most of which merely mean bad or good smell: fetid, foul, stink, stench, rancid, vile, revolting, nauseating, sickening. Routine tactile sensation spurs language to inventiveness, while the olfactory and gustatory reduce us to saying little more than yum or yuck.[14] One qualification: if perception of pain is considered a subset of tactile experiences and not the separate system of sensation it is, then to the extent that the tactile produces pain it abandons lexical richness for screams, moans, groans, sighs, grunts, and little more.[15]

Our inability to describe smell other than by naming the thing that gives off the odor does not however make smell any less central than touch to the way we conceptualize disgust. Without the odors of feces, urine, decay, and sweat, neither they nor life itself would be so disgusting. It is precisely the odor of these things which strikes the moralist of the ascetic stripe so deeply. Even in the bloom of youth our bodies produce reeking substances daily. Swift in his typically self-destructive way catalogues the sights and smells that greet the lover reconnoitering in his lady's dressing room and to his horror discovering her close stool. The poet is moved to a culinary simile in the mock heroic style:

> As Mutton Cutlets, Prime of Meat,
> Which tho' with Art you salt and beat,
> As laws of Cookery require,
> And roast them at the clearest Fire:
> If from adown the hopeful Chops
> The Fat upon a Cinder drops,
> To stinking Smoak it turns the Flame
> Pois'ning the Flesh from whence it came;
> So Things, which must not be exprest,
> When plumpt into the reeking Chest;
> Send up an excremental Smell
> To taint the Parts from whence they fell.
> The Pettycoats and Gown perfume,
> And waft a Stink round every Room.
>   Thus finishing his grand Survey,
> The Swain disgusted slunk away.[16]

Swift makes clear that odors have the power to contaminate; for him they irrevocably destroy all desire and poison his overly sensitive consciousness. The simile of the stench of burning fat (notice this seems to be an odor barbecuists have long since reevaluated) suggests that the stuff we eat begins to mimic the process of its transformation into foul-smelling excrement even as it is being prepared for consumption. Everything man (and especially woman) touches turns to shit and then that same excrement comes back to stew us in our own juices. Or more precisely the vision is of us cured in our own smokehouse, in which we provide both the smoke and the meat to be cured. The smells of excrement rise up to taint the parts from whence it fell, which in a paranoiac vision of contagion then fill all the room and all thought with stench.

The primordial scene for Swift was not coitus but defecation, and the horror of the latter was a function of the stench.[17] The thought of defecation and its smell was the one thought whose power no other thoughts could resist. It made beauty a fraud and sexual desire a function of sustained and insistent self-deception. For Swift desire could not survive the close stool. If Swift's obsessions end in misogyny, the thought that men must defecate too could lead to the heresies of doubting Christ's divine nature. Freud's Wolf Man, tormented by the thought of Jesus defecating, solved the problem with the subtlety of a schoolman: "Since Christ had made wine *out of* nothing, he could have made food *into* nothing and in this way have avoided defecating."[18] We get an inverse miracle of the loaves. Swift was not as resourceful as Wolf Man or, more likely, was unwilling to allow himself such facile self-deceptions. For him, the loss is not just the snuffing of desire but the loss of the sublimity that attends it, the loss of an illusion, which loss brings not wistfulness but the feeling of having been rendered a fool, hoodwinked by one's own desire and woman's mysterious abilities to aid one's self-deception. Thus the well-known lines: "Nor wonder how I lost my Wits; / Oh! Cælia, Cælia, Cælia shits."[19] The comic despair masks real bitterness that is not suppressed in other places: "Should I the Queen of Love refuse, / Because she rose from stinking Ooze?"[20]

Desire requires that we suppress entirely thoughts of beginnings and endings. Gestation and decay are all condensed into the primal odor of feces. Its stench expands to capture the odors of sex, desire, generation, and decay. It poisons us by smoking our flesh on the outside and recorrupts the inside by being inhaled as vapors. Lear, soon to make an appearance, could imagine that an ounce of civet might sweeten his imagination befouled by the odors of copulation. Swift's imagination, however, gives him no possibility of relief: the daily recollection of the smells of the close stool banish sweet thoughts and fix themselves permanently to guard against the return of desire-creating illusion. "For fine Ideas vanish fast, / While all the gross and filthy last."[21] The smell of feces, its vapors, produces thoughts which follow Gresham's law no less enthusiastically than money does. And thus it is on a suffusion of nasty excremental odor that Swift anticipates Freud's formulation of the anal character type with its linking of money, excrement, and cultural production itself.[22]

The linking of olfaction to the sexual has a long history to which we will return later. The ascetic monkly literature meditated on bad odors in an attempt to kill desire; Swift and Freud can be seen in some respects as continuing the tradition. The unrelenting misogyny is still there; it is always the odors emitted by women that kill male desire. (It seems men are much more likely to confuse anuses and vaginas than women are likely to confuse anuses and penises.)[23] We never hear much about female abhorrence for male odors, which is little wonder given that with rare exception men were doing the writing. Even then, these crabbed men, in their hagiographies of female virgin saints, did not fail to indicate female revulsion for male bodies.[24] The difference between the monks and Swift and Freud, however, is not their misogyny, but that the monks never came close to killing desire, while Swift and Freud were much better at rendering it vile by wishing it not to be.

Freud, like Swift, is not quite able to wrest the nose away from the excremental. In a long and famous footnote in *Civilization and Its Discontents* he supposes great consequences for the sense of smell that attended man's arising from all fours to walk erect. Standing up changed the placement of the nose relative to the genitals of others, but more precisely the relation of men's noses to women's crotches.[25] He expounds at some length on the theme:

> The organic periodicity of the sexual process has persisted, it is true, but its effect on psychical sexual excitation has rather been reversed. This change seems most likely to be connected with the diminution of the olfactory stimuli by means of which the menstrual process produced an effect on the male psyche. Their role was taken over by visual excitations, which, in contrast to

the intermittent olfactory stimuli, were able to maintain a permanent effect. The taboo on menstruation is derived from this "organic repression," as a defense against a phase of development that has been surmounted . . . This process is repeated on another level when the gods of a superseded period of civilization turn into demons. The diminution of the olfactory stimuli seems itself to be a consequence of a man's raising himself from the ground, of his assumption of an upright gait; this made his genitals, which were previously concealed, visible and in need of protection, and so provoked feelings of shame in him.

The fateful process of civilization would thus have set in with man's adoption of an erect posture. From that point the chain of events would have proceeded through the devaluation of olfactory stimuli and the isolation of the menstrual period to the time when visual stimuli were paramount and the genitals became visible, and thence to the continuity of sexual excitation, the founding of the family and so to the threshold of human civilization.

The footnote continues by discussing the increasing cultural concern with cleanliness, which originates not in hygienic considerations but "in an urge to get rid of the excreta, which have become disagreeable to the sense perceptions." Nonetheless children have to be socialized into being disgusted by excreta:

Upbringing insists with special energy on hastening the course of development which lies ahead, and which should make the excreta worthless, disgusting, abhorrent and abominable. Such a reversal of values would scarcely be possible if the substances that are expelled from the body were not doomed by their strong smells to share the fate which overtook olfactory stimuli after man adopted the erect posture.

The story is of the transformation of the sense of smell from the sense that excited periodic sexuality in times of rutting or with humans in times of menses to a diminished and devalued sense once man stood up. As the nose moves up, the olfactory stimuli diminish in their powers to excite, less it seems by diminishment of the sensitivity of the sense of smell than by a reversal in the valence of the stimuli it receives from below.[26] What once attracted now repels; hence the broad acceptance of menstrual taboos. Man (and man means man in the restricted sense) is compensated for the betrayal of the nose by being given the power to stare and get excited all the time, not just once a month. Vision on high from a distance replaces closely sniffing around down below. Now man wants a woman around all the time; hence family organization begins and then civilization built upon the family model takes off from there. And what of woman? She had better stay with the man if she wants to protect herself and her children from other men who are now looking for sexual objects to control continuously, rather than sniffing around once in a while for periodic violent contacts.[27]

Standing up does more than reverse the value of menstrual odor; it paves the way for the devaluation of everything in the genital region. The first stage in this process is one of "organic repression." This repression owes nothing to culture or society, being solely, according to Freud, the consequence of standing up, and it is directed toward the odors of menstruation. The second stage of devaluation of the olfactory is social, and it is directed toward feces. The "merely" social impetus behind the second stage means that we remain more ambivalent about excrement than about menses, the aversion to which Freud supposes to be part of our biological make-up. Very young children find their excrement "valuable to them as being part of their own body which has come away from it," and we consequently never quite learn to loathe our own excrement with much intensity: "The existence of the social factor which is responsible for the further transformation of anal erotism is attested by the circumstance that, in spite of all man's developmental advances, he scarcely finds the smell of *his own* excreta repulsive, but only that of other people's" (emphasis in the original).

The *social* inculcation of disgust for feces recapitulates in the life of the individual male the progress of the entire male half of the species' *organic* development of disgust for the odors of menstruation. Yet in each case—the organic disgust with menses and the socially originating disgust with feces—more primitive aspects of the erotic are repressed and olfaction, formerly the engine of desire, now founds the very capacity to be disgusted by those things once desired. So it comes to be that disgust keeps us on our feet and out of bed. But it is more than just a tale of feces and menstruation. In yet another footnote following fast on the one we have been dealing with Freud notes that man's assumption of erect posture and the depreciation of the sense of smell threatened not only anal erotism "but the whole of his sexuality . . . The genitals, too, give rise to strong sensations of smell which many people cannot tolerate and which spoil sexual intercourse for them."[28]

Freud's story ultimately depends for its intelligibility on whether we accept his account of repression and sublimation, which in turn depends on our devaluation of down as opposed to up. Like most of Freud's accounts, this one provokes, engages, and seduces in its confident reductionism and suggestive possibilities. It is not without its problems though. One wonders, first, about the distinction between disgust with menstruation and that with excrement, the one wired in organically, the other barely holding on by the socially constructed thread that tells us we must find it disgusting. To the extent that Freud's argument plays with the notion of ontogeny recapitulating phylogeny, it is horror of feces that should precede horror with menstrual blood in the development of the species. Consider that we are hardly born with a loathing of menstruation, nor does the infant acquire it when he stands up and learns to walk. Unlike excrement, most of us don't even learn what menses is, let alone confront it, until years after we have confronted feces and learned to be disgusted by it. The two disgusts, it turns out, are not distinguishable by virtue of their putative organic or social origins.

The varying intensity and difference in treatment of the two may well lie in the fact that only half of us menstruate but all of us defecate. And the half that menstruate are not men. Freud stacks the deck unfairly here. He compares the weaker disgust of a man with "his own" excrement with the implacable disgust of man for *another's* (woman's) menstruation. The appropriate comparison would be if a man is as disgusted with another's feces as with another's menstrual blood. Which disgust is stronger would be a nice empirical matter which I imagine would be subject to wide variation across individuals and cultures. But assuming with Freud for the moment that disgust for excrement is not as firmly in place as disgust for menstrual blood, could this difference not more satisfactorily be accounted for by the fact that among us the socialization regarding menstruation takes place at a later stage of development, long after the disgust mechanism has been primed, prepped, and fashioned by its interactions with excrement? Toilet training precedes sex education even today. Freud's account again depends on its purporting to describe only male disgusts and desires.[29]

The account seems to war with itself in another way. Just what happens to the sense of smell in this account? Does it grow weaker? Or does it simply change functions? Freud is clear that olfaction loses its capacity to impel sexual desire and suggests that the sense of smell is generally weakened, losing strength and function to vision. Yet perversely smell, because now associated with the vile and revolting, seems to be much stronger than when it was unambivalently a sense of desire. Freud abandons his usually non-adjectival style to pile up adjectives in an effort to capture our (and his?) panic in the face of excrement; feces is not only "worthless" but "disgusting, abhorrent, and abominable." Smell may no longer occupy the glorious role that vision assumed, but when it comes to the power to disgust it is no contemptible weakling. One wonders whether the attractive is ever quite as moving as an equal quantity of the loathsome (the teaspoon of sewage vs. the teaspoon of wine again). Or is it more appropriate to ask whether culture reinforces many more aversions than it does attractions? It may not be the case that desire must merely overmatch the specific aversion opposing it before achieving fulfillment, but rather that once it overmatches the disgust opposing it, it still must confront other scruples before it can lead to action.

To gloss Freud's footnote adequately would lead us too far astray, but I want to make a few quick observations regarding it. Freud draws an analogy between the displacement of the olfactory by the visual and the process by which new deities replace the old: "This process is repeated on another level when the gods of a superseded period of civilization turn into demons."[30] The old do not disappear; they simply change their valence. Once gods, they are now devils and demons. Vision, the sky god, banishes smell to Hell where it becomes the god of the underworld. This conforms rather nicely to the conventional Christian cosmology in which Light is associated with salvation, the proper end of desire, and Hell is a place of darkness visible, where fire gives no light but only loathsome evil stenches, a mixture of sulfur and excrement whose source is the bowels of Satan, who in his incarnation as Mephistopheles takes his name from the Latin word for pestilential odor.[31]

Smell ranks low in the hierarchy of senses. That there are bad sights and bad sounds does nothing to undermine the glory of the "higher senses" of vision and hearing; and that there are delightful fragrances does nothing to raise smell from the ditch. So low is smell that the best smell is not a good smell but no smell at all. And this sentiment predates the twentieth-century American obsession with not smelling. Montaigne in the sixteenth century cites classical authors to the same effect: "The sweetness even of the purest breath has nothing more excellent about it than to be without any odor that offends us."[32] Whenever a devil or the damned appear in medieval hagiography they give proof of their condition by stinking. Vision and hearing belong on high. They are the proper entrances to intellectual and contemplative pleasures; smell (and taste) and surely touch in the form of pain sensation are the senses of Hell, perhaps because they get closer to our core and are the senses of our bodily vulnerability.

The high/low opposition invariably makes disgust the domain of the low, whether that be genitals and anus or the dark and primitive. That the nose is on the face gives it no claim to credit. Its position, in fact, makes it dangerous in the extreme because the sense located there risks bringing us low on all fours with our eyes cast down on the ground.[33] In the Western tradition smell ends up associated with the dark, the dank, the primitive and bestial, with blind and subterranean bestiality that moves in ooze. We are back with Freud and the association of smell with the (primarily female) genitalia. The imagery of *King Lear* plays on this theme insistently. Moral blindness and real blindness are understood to be consequences of vaginas. Says Edgar to the bastard Edmund regarding the blinding of their father: "The dark and vicious place where thee he got / Cost him his eyes" (5.3.173–174). And without eyes one can only smell things out: "Go thrust him out at the gates, and let him smell his way to Dover"

(3.7.93). The blind world of *Lear* is a world of hopelessness, randomness, moral chaos, and despair. Only smell thrives, and that is why the atmosphere is so poisoned and depressingly frightening and filled with utter disgust with life. Smell thus exists in a kind of moral war with vision, with vision representing the forces of light and smell the forces of darkness.[34]

In its war with smell, vision depends for its virtue on its looking up or out or metaphorically in or within but manifestly not down. When Lear starts to hallucinate visions of copulation everywhere—"The wren goes to 't, and the small gilded fly / Does lecher in my sight"—images of sight are soon transformed into ones of olfaction. Disgust, for Lear, means bad smells, bad visions being bad to the extent that they suggest bad smells. For him disgust is primarily a matter of procreation, of life itself—the production of filial ingratitude and father-killing children—and that means we end up in that dark and vicious place which cost Gloucester his eyes. Strange, but no woman in the play is fertile; all procreation either has taken place prior to the play by women now dead or is enacted in the imagination. But that is more than enough, for the mere thought of it poisons imagination. Lear not only anticipates Freud in this matter, he pushes further:

> But to the girdle do the gods inherit
> Beneath is all the fiend's.
> There's hell, there's darkness, there is the sulphurous pit, burning, scalding, stench, consumption; fie, fie, fie! pah! pah! Give me an ounce of civet; good apothecary, sweeten my imagination.
> (4.6.125–130)[35]

The interjections tell us this is no weak disgust. Lear is retching at the mere thought of the dark place. Memory produces disgust. The memory of smells (and tastes and touches) differs from memories involving the so-called higher senses of hearing and sight. When we remember a sight we resee it; when we remember sounds we rehear them; we also can will such memories, conjure them up on purpose; or they can come unbidden triggered by nothing special. What does it mean, however, to remember a smell, taste, or touch? We cannot conjure up the memory of a smell like the memory of a face.[36] Nor do the tastes or smells of previously experienced things simply occur to us unbidden without molecules of that thing actually being perceived by our senses. If I desire to recall an odor that made me retch five years ago, or the taste of that bad meat that gave me food poisoning, I cannot do so. What I can remember is how I felt; I can recall the disgust, even reproduce it. I can remember gagging, retching, and a generalized sense of unpleasantness, strong enough to make sure I never will knowingly eat that food or put myself in a place to smell that smell again. But I am not doing this by imaginatively resmelling the smell or retasting the taste in the way we can imaginatively reconstruct sounds and sights. Memories of taste and smell can only be triggered by a real experience of the same smell or taste. That present sensation seems to give memories triggered by olfaction and taste their peculiar generative power: would a visual memory of Swann and Odette have had the evocative power that actually smelling and eating a madeleine pastry had for Proust?

Reconsider Lear. He would have us believe as part of a grand rhetorical gesture that he is at present smelling the smells of female sexual arousal. But there are no women present. Actually to smell such smells would manifestly be an hallucination, and Lear has been hallucinating quite actively during this scene. His hallucinations, however, are visual, not olfactory. That crazy he is not. Even he knows that the ounce of civet he requests from the apothecary is to sweeten his imagination, not the air he breathes. The civet is figural and he knows it is. What Lear is reproducing in himself is not an actual reexperience of sexual smells but the aversion he feels when he smells such smells. That sensation he can re-create; it is in fact the essence of how disgust works to keep us from doing again that which disgusted us before. Lear may not then be resmelling vaginas and sulfurous pits, but he is reexperiencing a most profound loathing and disgust. The gesture of disgust indicated by the fies and pahs is not faked. And even if it were, such faking has a peculiar way of generating the feelings it is expressing. Imitating retching can, if one is not careful, lead to vomiting.[37]

Lear and Swift (and even Freud can be read in this way) show that it is nearly impossible to keep bad smells out of the moral domain. The language of sin and wickedness is the language of olfaction gone bad. Vision and hearing, the higher senses, do not play this role in the articulation of our moral sensibility. "Do you smell a fault?"[38] Bad smells are evil, evil smelling; and bad deeds stink to heaven because they smell like Hell: "O, my offense is rank, it smells to heaven" (*Hamlet* 3.3.36).[39] If bad touch gives moral diction a number of axes of measurement to categorize moral action, smell gives only bad and good smell. But that is apparently all that is needed.

As a parting observation on smell note that the word stink has a forcefulness that makes it not quite proper in polite conversation. One usually avoids it by using softer formulations such as "smells bad." Or one uses stink while suffering a small anxiety regarding its likelihood of breaching decorum or of typing oneself as vulgar in a way that any number of words we would describe as "swear words" would not. No word dedicated to the disgustful sensations of the other senses has this power. It is hard to date exactly when stink gets so powerful as to become somewhat improper. It is frequently used in the public language of moral condemnation in the sixteenth and seventeenth centuries, evidencing its power but not its vulgarity. The OED shows it to have become not quite proper at least by the late nineteenth century.[40]

To what might we attribute the change? Its impropriety is clearly another step in the march of the "civilizing process." But perhaps it is something more concrete. One of the great accomplishments of the nineteenth century was ridding cities of the ubiquitous stench of feces and decaying animal matter by massive public construction of underground sewers. When man began walking upright he did not rise all that far above the stenches he emitted below. It just might be that Freud's theory of the final devaluation of smell depended on putting sewers under ground as much as on raising man's nose above it.[41] It might even be claimed that the placement of sewers underground is a necessary precondition for and enabler of Freudian theory. Underground sewers were not an emblem of the repressed but the repressed itself, a burying of dangerousness. The sewers become the new Hell, the lower gastrointestinal base for the civilization resting upon it, as captured in the free verse of Francis Newman, brother of the better-known John Henry:

Thus underneath our cities, by curious and perishing art,
A new city is built, of Tartarean loathsomeness,
A network of brick-bowels, which perpetually decay.[42]

Vision

For the anti-sexual and misogynistic tradition of asceticism disgust
was a function of odors, the odors of sex, generation, putrefaction,
and defecation. I have suggested that Swift and Freud, in some way,
can be understood as very much in continuity with this tradition. For
Freud, smells are what ruin sex, the very sex the eye drove us toward
once we learned to walk erect. Vision in Freud's world is the first-
order sense of desire. Sight gives us the distance desire must have to
operate, back far enough so that smells can be masked and shameful
things alluringly covered.

Sight, unlike smell, needs distance to operate properly. Get too
close and things blur out or darken under the very shadow we cast;
get too far back and vision fails to discern enough to desire. In
between, in the range of desire, however, the eye can be tricked by
myopia, by wishful thinking, and by strategies of the object, like
cosmetics and clothing. In this middle distance, out of the reach of
smell and within focusable view, sight works to impel desire to levels
sufficient to overcome disgust that the odors of proximity may well
evoke before the pleasures of touch work to justify sight's desiring.
The mid-range also allows the construction of a competing truth to
counter the truth of microscopic vision that revolted Gulliver in
Brobdingnag. And the masking of the sources of odor behind clothing prevents us from observing the very organs activated by the
desire that vision prompted. What strange trick has made the attraction that beauty engenders end in organs that look like penises, scro-
tums, and vaginas? Is it any accident that the sense of shame forces
us to cover up?[43]

Or if, say, sexual coupling were accomplished by kissing, or by
an exchange of glances, would we then find lips and eyes as unsightly
as we now find the genitals? Milton's Adam pursued this line of
inquiry with the angel Raphael, getting an angelic blush and an eva-

sive answer in response (even incorporeal beings, it seems, must know the blush of embarrassment and shame and with shame the prospect of disgust):

> Bear with me then, if lawful what I ask;
> Love not the heav'nly Spirits, and how thir Love
> Express they, by looks only, or do they mix
> Irradiance, virtual or immediate touch?
>   To whom the Angel with a smile that glow'd
> Celestial rosy red, Love's proper hue,
> Answer'd. Let it suffice thee that thou know'st
> Us happy, and without Love no happiness.
>
> (*Paradise Lost* 8.614–620)

For us, no less than angels, that which might evoke disgust in others when seen by them is that which should be protected by shame. The observed one should cover up and the observer should cover his eyes. Eyes, exhibitionism, and shame run together in the Freudian world and implicate disgust only because what is shameful is also often disgusting.

The world is filled with disgusting sights only a small fraction of which have to do with copulation. Any action which ought to elicit shame in the doer can elicit disgust in an observer. Any serious breach of norms of modesty, dignity-maintenance, and self-presentability can be disgusting to behold. In this sphere disgust operates as a moral emotion, a motivator of discipline and social control. Not all visual disgust is directly involved in this kind of policing of norms; some of it piggybacks on disgusts generated by smell and touching. The sight of an unflushed toilet in a public facility, of a giant slug, of eels, of maggots slithering and writhing can disgust quite intensely. In these settings we recognize that sight works by suggesting the prospect of unnerving touches, nauseating tastes, and foul odors or by suggesting contaminating processes like putrefaction and generation. These things offend because of their contaminating powers; they offend not because of what they look like, but for what they are, for their moral failings if you will. In some instances we are even prepared to admit an abstract beauty in form and proportion, color and sinuosity as in caterpillars, salamanders, jellyfish, and such, but that only serves to make their contaminating powers more uncanny, more unnerving.

Vision is the sense through which much of horror is accessed. The movies that define the horror genre horrify and disgust without taste, smell, or touch (although we should not underestimate the power of music to evoke terror and uneasiness). Vision activates our sympathetic imaginative powers, but note that sympathetic sensing does not extend to smell. Smell plays virtually no role in the horror genre. Things abhorrent to the touch can get us cringing sympathetically by the mere sight of the offensive thing; likewise watching someone have to eat decayed matter, human flesh, or excrement produces strong sympathetic sensations, but watching people smelling vile smells does not reproduce in us the corresponding sympathetic response. Bad-smelling things are experienced in film because they look bad, or because we see that they would be disgusting to touch.[44]

The reason smell does not translate well via a visual medium is that the visual presence of an object is not necessary for its smell to disgust. In fact we usually think of odors as sneaking up on us from some hidden source or leaking out through an orifice which should be properly closed. Nice-looking things can emit bad odors; that is what drove Swift to distraction. Things that taste bad may look attractive too, but then our horror is not triggered by the sight of them but by the sight of someone eating them. We see the thing chewed on and swallowed; we have, in other words, muscular actions that can be sympathetically triggered by the sight. Bad smell gives us no such means to sympathize with the person suffering the odor. And slimy things, writhing things revolting to the touch, are processed instantly as dangerous and repulsive; their touching someone else triggers shudders and cringings but they usually disgust long before that.

The visual can horrify in its own right independent of suggestions from the other senses. It is sight that processes ugliness, deformity, mutilation, and most of what we perceive as violence: gore, indignities, violations. The difficult question about the horror of visual ugliness and deformity is whether these ugly things or beings are horrific independently of the prospect of intimate contact with them. Are grotesquely hideous persons disgusting only to the extent that we imagine them sexually, or in some sort of intimacy with us or others? I think the answer is no, in spite of the rich medieval romance theme of the loathly hag which has continued in various reincarnations unto the present. We find the hideously ugly disgusting and horrifying quite independently of sexual fantasy or fears of intimacy. The visual has its own aesthetic and consequent moral standard which if breached can evoke horror, disgust, pity, and fear. It is not that we fear intimacy with them or their intimacies with others; it is that we know how we see them and could not bear to be thus seen. The horror then is not in being intimate with them (though that too), but in *being* them.

Deformity and ugliness are further unsettling because they are disordering; they undo the complacency that comes with disattendability; they force us to look and notice, or to suffer self-consciousness about not looking or not not looking. They introduce alarm and anxiety by virtue of their power to horrify and disgust. Yet there still seems to be an intractable psychological terror that ugliness and hideousness present just on sight independent of social problems of how to manage ourselves in their presence. Some sights simply evoke disgust: gore and mutilation, the effects of violence on the body, especially when these are inflicted cruelly without justification. Something pre-social seems to link us to a strong sense of disgust and horror at the prospect of a body that doesn't quite look like one, either grotesquely deformed by accident or disorganized by mayhem.

Hearing

Hearing is the sense that plays the smallest role in processing disgust, and then it mainly disgusts because of prior associations with bad visions, nausea, or loathsome touchings. The sounds of someone vomiting or gagging can prompt a sympathetic contagion of nausea. Grinding of teeth also elicits sympathetic jaw tightenings and disgust. The noises that accompany any disgusting bodily emission are themselves tainted: the sounds of defecation, throat clearing, nose blowing, even nail clipping for some sensitive souls.[45] The sounds of other people's lovemaking, although they are mostly absurdly comical and embarrassing, can be revolting too. And either the comedy or the revulsion is often sufficient to induce alterations in the volume of our own noisemaking. If contagion operates in that setting it does so by way of arousal for some, but to others the violation of norms of modesty and decorum and restraint evokes disgust. For some, such noises make it harder, as does the idea of animals "doing it," to sustain the sentimentalist fictions we construct about the transcendence of sex and lovemaking.

Certain qualities of voice disgust us because of the personality traits they indicate or partially create. Whining, wheedling tones are of this sort, as are, I have been informed, my own unriddable northern Wisconsin nasal vowels. Class and regional accents may disgust because of a judgment about their ugliness and vulgarity, but that judgment is always more than just a matter of some essential disgustingness of the sounds. Judgments about the beauty of an accent and the sounds of speech are very much mixed up with prior judgments of class, rank, ethnicity, nationality, and ancient rivalry. But then the difference in aesthetic appeal, for instance, between Dublin English and the English of the Boston Irish can't just be owing to that.[46] We clearly prefer language sounding one way rather than another independent of social variables. Certain speech defects and disorders can disconcert, embarrass, and even disgust. Here class, region, ethnicity are not involved; the simple failure to fall within the range of the normal and the intelligible is sufficient to stigmatize and marginalize.

In this vein consider laughter. The sounds of certain styles of laughter condemn those who so laugh to being loathed.[47] Laughter, to be sure, can annoy and disgust for reasons independent of what it sounds like. The nicest-sounding laughter can prompt disapproval and disgust if it is improperly directed. The person may be laughing at something we think evinces depravity or callousness; or it may simply be that the person mistimes his laughter or laughs too long or too frequently. Laughing habits turn out to be one of the crucial clues we use to get a fix on a person's moral and social competence.

Our judgment is not just a matter of the laughter's motivation, its timing and duration; it is also caught up with judgments as to the appropriateness of the *sound* of a person's laughter. Some laughs simply sicken by their sound. Manifestly it is not always the case that we find the laughter loathsome because we find the person laughing hateful and disgusting. The style of laughter itself can trigger the kind of annoyance and predisposition that will lead to finding the person irritating. Irritation is not disgust, but continuing annoyance can evoke a kind of aversiveness that ends by using the idiom of disgust and so ends up metamorphosed into it. Disgust is not an infrequent accompanier or consequence of annoyance.

I am not sure I can capture just what it is about certain laughing sounds that elicits such aversion. Nervous tittering, hyena-like-yelpings, suggest that laughter is disgusting when it can be described as an animal sound. Laughter, after all, is one of the few things that distinguishes us from animals; could it be that we resent blurring of the distinction by what we perceive as a vulgar attempt at imitation, demeaning both to us and the animal? Is this why humor that makes use of animal noises is typed as either infantile or irredeemably vulgar and usually succeeds in embarrassing rather than entertaining? I doubt the adequacy of such an explanation (it does not account for the disgust cackling evokes, for instance), but it should be noted that it accords quite well with the Douglasian theory that disgust is a matter of category violation and of anomalies in structural systems of meaning.

We surely have a code of gender-appropriate laughters; women are not to laugh like men or vice versa. But exaggerated styles within each gender can be disgust-evoking also. The kind of hyper-male raucous laughter over things not very funny that seems to be a frequent ritual of male bonding (for an example see the use made of the hardy-laugh motif in *The Wild Bunch*) can disgust no less than female titters or giggles. But these examples are less about laughter being disgusting than about the kinds of masculinity or femininity they represent being disgusting. Let that suffice, although the subject merits more attention than I can justify giving here.

Like sights, sounds figure very much in generating the disgust that we use to recognize violent action. Screams and shrieks partake of the uncanny, and although they are unlikely to disgust they surely can disconcert and raise the specter of actions that will disgust. The sound of a leg or an arm breaking can sicken quite quickly. The dull thud of my daughter Eva's head smashing into the backyard deck as she tripped running full speed raised my stomach to my throat (though she, tough as nails, merely stamped her feet in indignant rage at suffering an unsightly goose egg). There is only the most attenuated notion of self-violence in the sound of knuckle cracking, but that does not prevent it from disgusting many people.[48]

Hearing's minor role in disgust is compensated for by its being the primary sense (with a healthy assist from touch) for processing the niggling and annoying. Taste, vision, and smell play more limited roles in that domain. It is the sound of gnats and mosquitoes, of dripping faucets, of whining complaints, of the self-satisfaction that informs the tone "I told you so"; and though eventually these may lead to disgust, they can only do so with assists from associations borne by the other senses, including our sense of propriety.

Taste

I have been engaged in a mild polemic against the psychological literature that supposes the core of disgust to be a function of taste and food rejection, of bad things in the mouth. I am thus dealing with taste last after having shown just how much disgust is bound up especially with touch and smell but also with vision. The importance of the sense of taste I think has been gained at the expense of two confusions. One, noted earlier, is that the etymology of English disgust forces taste to the fore by linguistic suggestion. The other is that the sense of taste is made to stand as a metonym for the fact that disgust is often indicated by facial expressions and interjections that denote spitting, vomiting, or rejecting contaminants that have gotten past the lips. Etymology, facial expression, and interjections have thus combined to mislead researchers into overemphasizing taste in the phenomenology of disgust. We don't only get nauseated and vomit from bad tastes. Foul smells, appalling sights, and repulsive touchings can have the same effect. This fact makes the facial expressions used to denote bad taste also quite serviceable to indicate disgust from whatever sensory source. We spit when we have something bad-tasting in our mouth; yet Lear uses "pah," a front plosive sound which mimics spitting, to represent a bad smell; we wrinkle our noses or curl our lips not only at bad smells but also at disgusting tastes and sights.

In short, the facial expressions for disgust do not all focus on taste; some do, but others feature smell. If we include gestures of the hands and entire body as Darwin did and do not just focus narrowly on the face as so many present researchers do, the somatic lexicon of disgust expands to include recoils and cringes.[49] These are primarily touch focused, but they are also used to mark aversions to the prospect of bad tastes and foul smells. Disgust never was solely a matter of taste, but embodied (and I mean em*body*) the species' means of making rather broad judgments about likes and dislikes, good and evil, and what and who's in and what and who's out. I find it more plausible as an evolutionary matter to believe that disgust found its way to taste rather late in its developmental process. I would guess both smell and touch got there first. And this would make perfect adaptive sense.[50] We would surely want some sense or senses to warn us of foul things *before* we put them in our mouths. Rejection by taste is a defense of the last resort.

Of the taste sensations as narrowly construed in the folk under-standing of taste—bitter, sweet, salt, sour—none seems even to be a presumptive indicator of a disgust response. Bitter and salt have no real role in the disgust complex. Bitter, as any beer lover knows, is a taste that is not itself distasteful. Excessively bitter or salty foods may be distasteful but not disgusting. Sourness, in the sense of the processing of acidic tastes, has little to do with disgusting tastes either. Sour things may make us pucker, a gesture of sucking in rather than spitting out. The puckering of sourness is often prompted by the sourness of unripeness, the premature fruit, and this rarely evokes disgust; nor should we be surprised, since, as we have seen, it is ripeness and overripeness that invite disgust, not unripeness.

But sourness does double service semantically. In matters of taste it marks the tartness of the unripe or the acidic; in this context it is viewed as an opposite of sweet, contrasting unripeness with ripeness. But as the process of ripening continues past ripeness into rottenness we resurrect the notion of sourness to describe that too, but not for the same food items that were described as sour when unripe. Thus we get sour milk and sour towels and sour breath. Here sourness is synonymous with rancid and is manifestly not the same concept as the sourness of unripeness.

Sour's problem is not a matter of what acidic things taste like, but that it has suffered more than a millennium in English for its alliterative contrast with sweetness. As a result sour ends up also meaning unpleasant traits of character that represent the absence of sweetness of disposition: the peevish, morose, sullen, and bitter. And maybe sour also suffers because the facial expression that marks it when eating unripe or very acidic fruit is one that habitually marks the face of the peevish and smallminded person even though the taste that leads to the expression may in fact be enjoyed.

Sweetness has an interesting relation to disgust because sweetness attracts as an initial matter and then repels as it begins to cloy. I will take this up in more detail when I deal with surfeit in Chapter 6. We have all suffered the attractive and seductive power of the taste of sweetness. It is the one thing that regularly overcomes the powerful wills of young children by rendering them bribable. Or more precisely, those monumental young wills are mobilized to attain the pleasures of sweetness, to which is added the spice of knowing that a parent's will must be broken to get to it. But even children experience surfeit and cloyingness, albeit at extraordinarily high thresholds of sweetness. Few things disgust quite as much as excessive sweetness, but rarely does that deter the next assault on the candy jar. One's desire rises Antaeus-like from the fall.

Once sweetness moves beyond taste and into the small lexicon of smell descriptions, it tends to serve equally to describe attractive odors, say, of flowers, and rank offensive odors of a certain nausea-inducing type. Thus the disgusting smell of urine in public lavatories, or of those many kinds of odors we feel best described as nauseatingly sweet. As a description of character, however, sweetness is mostly positive, except even here the notion of cloyingness can make some styles of sweetness disgusting. As social actors we are rather good at distinguishing a real sweetness of character that is always a virtue and never cloying from a certain kind of saccharine sweetness that suggests shallowness, bubbliness, or yet another kind that often drags solicitousness and intrusiveness in its wake.

If taste proper doesn't figure as prominently in our construction of disgust as touch and smell do, the process of eating surely does, and this provides yet another reason why disgust has been misread as a taste-based emotion. Food and disgust are intimately related because so much of the divide between purity and danger, purity and impurity is staked out over food. But issues of purity are just as intensely raised at orifices other than the mouth. The issue here is less a matter of taste as narrowly construed than as a violation of a vulnerable orifice, the mouth, and the mouth is just one of several vulnerable orifices each of which raises its own particular problems for disgust. We take these things up next.

| 5 |

ORIFICES AND
BODILY WASTES

THE DISGUSTING is marvelously promiscuous and ubiquitous. It is what is strange and estranged but threatens to make contact; it is also the utterly familiar guest who threatens to remain or to return again soon. When our inside is understood as soul the orifices of the body become highly vulnerable areas that risk admitting the defiling from the outside. But when our inside is understood as vile jelly, viscous ooze, or a storage area for excrement the orifices become dangerous as points of emission of polluting matter, dangerous both to us and to others. Not all of the orifices are equally dangerous in their power to pollute or vulnerable in their capacity to admit pollution, nor are they the only sources of secretions that are polluting: the skin is home, after all, to glands producing sweat and oil, which have varying capacities to elicit disgust.

We can divide the orifices into two groups by virtue of their function in disgust. The first is the Freudian trio of erogenous zones—genitals, anus, and mouth; the second the locations of key organs of sense—eyes, ears, and nostrils. Note that this division accords with whether the disgusting is understood to involve the admission of raw matter—liquids and solids—or whether it is understood to be formed of revolting visions, sounds, smells, more gaseous and spiritual invaders. Take the eyes, ears, and nose first, those orifices most susceptible to spiritual invasion.

Eyes

The eye—which, I think, we must consider an orifice—is usually viewed as the most valuable of all our organs. Oedipus, it should be remembered, chose to blind, not castrate himself, and he was not pulling punches when he did. He was thinking in terms of the only thing he had of sufficient value to expiate his wrongs; he manifestly was not making his eyes a symbol of his testicles, nor making them a scapegoat for the faults of the sexual organs.[1] His eyes suffered for their own commissions and omissions.[2] The eye, though jelly, is the only orifice we think of as leading not to muck and slime but instead to the spiritual inside; it is a window, even a portal, to the soul. The eyes are also the only orifice from which a non-disgusting secretion flows: tears, which owe their privileged position to their source, their clarity, their liquidity, their non-adhering nature, their lack of odor, and their clean taste.[3]

But that doesn't mean the eye cannot be disgusting. Conceived as a severable body part it is lusterless "vile jelly" in the arrestingly brutal image of the Duke of Cornwall, and nothing is more horrifyingly disgusting than to think of poking it out, of actually penetrating the eye. Even when the eye is in place and intact, mucous, that "thick amber and plumtree gum" in Hamlet's disgustfully inspired image, can ooze from it (2.2.198). And the eye can surely horrify; precisely because it is a mirror to the soul, it is dangerous in the extreme, for if that soul is evil, the eye may well be too. The association of the eye and the uncanny, the stare of the dead, the blankness of idiocy, the possession of madness, all these have the capacity to horrify—horror being, we recall, a peculiar blend of fear and disgust.

We expect so much from the eye aside from its capacity to see; we expect it to signal our intentions to others, to make known our views of them (as when we glance, glare, stare, or look askance), and even more than that, to signal just who we are. But that is risky because the eye reveals us when we may not want to be revealed; we fear as a consequence of it being a window that it tells truths when we would be better served by lies. Take the smile. We all can make the mouth fake a smile; it is the eyes that resist. They don't join in convincingly in the fake smile without enormous effort. The eye, in other words, is seen as well as sees and in fact must endure visibility as the price of its vision.[4]

The eye, then, as an orifice, as a window, is a site fraught with danger. It can be penetrated figuratively by the vision of others, which is a source of fear and uncanny uneasiness; it is also at risk of physical penetration, which like the unconsented physical penetration of any orifice is disgusting in the extreme. The looks of others can disgust us in both senses of the word looks: we don't like what we see looking at them, and we fear what they might be seeing when looking at us. Their penetrating vision is very much a part of the genesis of our self-consciousness, with the shame and self-loathing to which it can lead.

Ears

Compared to the eyes, the ears and nose are less dangerous. Folk psychology and physiology do not rank the ear as high as the eye. Ears are funny looking; their beauty is a negative beauty, the beauty of not being ugly. Ears give no special pleasure for lying close to the head, only relief that they are not sticking out like jug handles. When decorum stipulated that more of us be covered, however, people invested the few visible parts with more capacity for attractiveness. The shell-like ears of nineteenth-century heroines are a case in point. Moreover, we are not as horrified by deafness as we are by blindness. Blindness almost seems to cancel the soul, deafness just makes it obtuse.[5] When blindness or near blindness comes with old age we pity the person; when, however, the old get hard of hearing we get annoyed with them or think them comical. The ear suffers the indignity of producing earwax, a substance which though generally less threatening than other bodily wastes is disgusting nonetheless.[6] Consider that earwax disgusts no matter how and where we think of it, whereas urine, feces, snot, are relatively innocuous when safely inside. Why? Because earwax is not tears? Because of other more fundamental qualities, like odor, color, taste, or feel? It seems that the governing principle is that all secretions and emissions at orifices are tainted except for tears. Tears, not ear wax, require explaining.

Nor is the ear sacralized for being spoken into as the eye is for being looked into. But ears are still portals and as portals they can admit dangerous substances. One such incident has become a suggestive part of our cultural heritage:

Upon my secure hour thy uncle stole
With juice of cursed hebona in a vial,
And in the porches of my ears did pour
The leperous distilment, whose effect
Holds such an enmity with the blood of man
That swift as quicksilver it courses through
The natural gates and alleys of the body,
And with a sudden vigor it doth posset[7]
And curd, like eager droppings into milk,
The thin and wholesome blood. So it did mine,
And a most instant tetter barked about
Most lazar-like with vile and loathsome crust
All my smooth body. (*Hamlet* 1.5.61–73)

A theory of disgust is contained in this passage: poisons working inside of us causing inwardly the curdling of blood, like vinegar in milk, and erupting on the outside by blasting their own way through a once-smooth skin to bark it about with running sores and scabby crust.

Nose

To the extent that the nose is implicated in the sense of smell it figures crucially in disgust, especially in sexual and excremental disgust. As an entryway for matter it seems less charged with danger than any orifice except, perhaps, the ears; yet we shudder in horror at the thought of, say, a long needle being inserted up the nasal passage[8] or down into the ear, but not when contemplating a similar intrusion into muscle tissue. We suspect, quite rightly, that the pain in the first two cases would be beyond description and that except for the justifying context of surgery and anesthetic no such intrusion could ever be justifiable.[9]

But the nose disgusts not because of what can go in but because of what comes out. Snot is contaminating. I don't wish to go into excessive detail because of the reader's likely difficulty in allowing the topic any chance of seriousness. I restrict myself to vague suggestions. Not all snot is equally disgusting. Its relative clarity, viscosity, hardness, and color all figure in the calculus. Our own snot does not defile us as long as it stays within; once outside it must be disposed of discreetly. We can even contemplate sniffing and swallowing it without too much pause. Other people's snot is a different matter, and when they call it to our attention by snuffling, sniffling, even by blowing their nose, we are not pleased.[10] Certain advocates of celibacy in the early church thought it a sovereign remedy for intrusive sexual desires to meditate on the presence of snot inside beautiful female exteriors. Thus John Chrysostom, writing in the fourth century:

> If you consider carefully what things lie hidden under the skin which seems so beautiful to you, what is concealed within the nostrils and within the throat and stomach, these seemly external features (filled within with all kinds of vileness) will proclaim the beauty of this body to be nothing else but a whited sepulcher. And if you could see the phlegm under its cover, you would be horrified. Or if you could touch it with just the tip of your finger, you would be revolted and run from it. How is it then that you love and desire the horrid dwelling place of this phlegm.[11]

Mucus is one of those substances that embarrass as well as disgust and as such fuels enormous amounts of childhood humor and wit. Medieval theologians found it so contemptible that it, along with sweat, was theorized to have become our lot only after the Fall. Semen and feces were begrudged their place in Paradise, but mucus was banished utterly.[12]

Mouth

The mouth is next to the nose and shares certain functions and features with it. Both are used for inspiration of air, both are used to expel mucus from the nasal passages, and both, by synergies of smell and taste, are necessary to construct flavor. Yet the affinity between mouths and noses was never as salient as that between them and the orifices below. We need not blame Freud for dragging the mouth and nose down there or pulling the "down there" up. He is at the endpoint of various folk and learned traditions that saw homologies between mouths and anuses, mouths and vaginas, and noses and penises. Vaginas borrow from the mouth the nomenclature and concept of lips (and teeth); and like mouths they engage in oral activities: it is common for them to talk in the bawdy medieval fabliaux and other low-humor forms.[13] Anuses talk too: the notion of farts being a kind of speech is a common one: " 'Spek, sweete bryd, I noot nat where thou art.' / This Nicholas anon leet fle a fart" ("The Miller's Tale," A3805–3806).

The penis was always thought to be a nether nose, the length of one supposedly corresponding to the length of the other, both spewing contaminating substances of similar consistency. The correspondence informs a good deal of the whimsically prurient suggestiveness of *Tristram Shandy*:

> For by the word *Nose*, throughout all this long chapter of noses, and in every other part of my work, where the word *Nose* occurs,—I declare, by that word I mean a Nose, and nothing more, or less . . .
>
> Fair and softly, gentle reader!—where is thy fancy carrying thee?—If there is truth in man, by my great grandfather's nose, I mean the external organ of smelling, or that part of man which stands prominent in his face,—and which painters say, in good jolly noses and well-proportioned faces, should comprehend a full third,—that is, measuring downwards from the setting on of the hair.
>
> —What a life of it has an author, at this pass! (vol. 3, chs. 31, 33)

(What a life indeed!) The pre-Freudian symmetries moved more in the direction of assimilating the anal and genital to the oral, rather than the oral to the anal and genital. The issue is one of priority. Is eating more salient than fornicating? Each ultimately leads to the other, but where one starts the process has conceptual consequences. The medieval and Renaissance view starts the cycle with ingestion.[14] Mouth first, not as a sexual orifice, but as the devourer of food. The account can be valenced in a life-celebrating fashion as in Rabelais and some of Chaucer or it can prompt melancholic and bitter musings on the loathsomeness of generation. Musings of this sort give Jacobean tragedy its particular aura of sexual disgust and *tedium vitae:* feast, food, gluttony, and drunkenness are seen as dulling the sensitivity to disgust sufficiently to prompt fornication, which then engenders amoral beings who eat and grow, reproduce again in stealth, luxury, and drunkenness, then rot and die, leaving other reprehensible beings to continue the process:

> I was begot
> After some gluttonous dinner; some stirring dish
> Was my first father . . .
> The sin of feasts, drunken adultery!
>
> (Tourneur, *The Revenger's Tragedy* 1.2)

As an historical matter eating and drinking have been understood to lead more quickly to sex than sex to eating and drinking. Sex runs to the quick beat of lust, eating to the slower rhythms of growth and development. Food first, then lust, just as the story of Adam, Eve, and the apple would have it, or in the more rousty imagery of the Wife of Bath: "For al so siker as cold engendreth hayl, / A likerous mouth moste han a likerous tayl."[15]

Whether we pose the genitals as prime movers or confer that priority on the mouth and eating is a point of emphasis that suggests fairly important underlying cultural concerns. A vulgar materialist might note that in the West during those centuries in which famine was always a distinct possibility and food production abysmally low, food occupied more space in consciousness and culture than when it came to be taken for granted. The conditions of our taking sex to be so foundational to personhood and character thus may depend, in a strange way, on the potato. More plausibly we would want to think about how a culture conceptualizes social existence. Does whom you eat with bear more social and symbolic weight than whom you sleep with? It surely did throughout the long expanse of the Middle Ages. One might reasonably wonder whether the centrality of sexuality in character formation depended on the development of privacy and private spaces free from noise and rousty conviviality. Surely rousty conviviality led to sex, but it was more how much and what you ate than whom you lay down with in a drunken stupor that defined who you were.

The mouth and the anus bear an undeniable connection. They are literally connected, each being one end of a tube that runs through the body. No great feat of metaphorization or cultural imagination was needed to show that what went in at one end came out at the other. Among us, both ends are highly vulnerable to contamination and are highly dangerous contaminators. And the one often represents the other. Chaucer's Pardoner can thus envisage that those who drink excessively make their throat their privy.[16]

Once food goes into the mouth it is magically transformed into the disgusting. Chewed food has the capacity to be even more disgusting than feces. The person who routinely checks the production of his bowels does not have the same type of interest in looking at well-chewed food he has spit out of his mouth: there is no sense that masticated food can be looked on with the pride of creation that feces can. The sight of chewed food, either in the mouth or ejected from it, is revolting in the extreme. Some parents who have no trouble changing their children's diapers still have to steel themselves before touching masticated food. Even those few foods which by rule are allowed to be withdrawn from the mouth after entering it or acceptably licked by the tongue are dealt with charily. Even lovers must overcome some small resistance to lick an ice cream cone that the other has licked. Some people experience anxiety about returning olive pits to the same plate that they are eating from. Separate plates are often provided for such contaminated refuse, and when there are none the pits are piled neatly in a corner of one's own plate so as not to touch foods still to be eaten.

Although saliva is clearly contaminating and disgust-evoking, chewed food owes its contaminating power to more than just contact with saliva. The chewing itself, the reduction of formed things into gooey things, also plays into it, but it is the simple fact of entry into the mouth that transforms the substance.[17] That which is spit out can never be the same again.[18] The true rule seems to be that once food enters the mouth it can only properly exit in the form of feces.[19] This helps account for why vomit may be more disgusting than feces (only feces is playing by the rules). Even spitters, who though they surely disgust non-spitters, and probably mean to do so, recognize that spittable substances are limited and constitute special exceptions from the general rule of non-spitting: tobacco juice, saliva, phlegm. The rest of us are allowed to spit seeds and shells, but these are marked as acceptable because though contaminated by saliva they are not chewed and thus retain a certain pre-ingested integrity.[20]

With the possible exception of earwax, which simply must be removed upon the knowledge of its presence, other dangerous bodily excreta are benign if in their proper place inside the body. Saliva in the mouth, snot in the nose, blood in veins, feces in the colon, urine in the bladder are basically not present, being safely where they belong as long as attention is not called to them. The magical transformation that happens once any of these substances leaves its natural domain can be illustrated by a thought experiment Gordon Allport proposed more than forty years ago:

> Think first of swallowing the saliva in your mouth, or do so. Then imagine expectorating it into a tumbler and drinking it! What seemed natural and "mine" suddenly becomes disgusting and alien. Or picture yourself sucking blood from a prick in your finger; then imagine sucking blood from a bandage around your finger! What I perceive as separate from my body becomes, in the twinkling of an eye, cold and foreign.[21]

Once outside, out for good. But anyone with children knows that it takes a lot of social labor to inculcate the disgust that keeps us from orally reincorporating various kinds of excreta, snot, earwax, fingernails and the dirt beneath them. Rather large quantities of socializing and civilizing energies are called on to suppress these temptations. Some perverse reflex gives people the urge to sneak these things as a kind of food: cannibalism and auto-cannibalism? Or just the remnants of the conventional infantile oral manifestation of curiosity by gumming rather than by looking? Indeed we might see the Real Presence in the Eucharist as a concession to the urge (we will return to this in Chapter 7). Or maybe, like cats who lick their fur, we still instinctually use the mouth to groom our bodies.

Notice too that the eye, ear, and nose are not blamed for or polluted by the fact that they constantly take in bad sights, evil words, or vile smells. This bespeaks a deep-seated materialism in our fears of pollution as they relate to the orifices. It is the taking in or penetration by liquids and solids that puts an orifice at risk. Sights, sounds, most gasses, and intangible spirits can surely pollute but not in a way that places blame on the orifices for taking them in. The "ingesting" organs—mouth, vagina, and anus—all of which in various symbolic schemes, not just the Freudian, come to represent one another, are put at risk more by matter than by spirit.

It is not just oral incorporation that drives disgust; it is also anal and vaginal incorporation. Ingestion, because crucial to beliefs about purity, is more important than the precise portal of ingestion, although, clearly, some orifices are deemed more appropriate than others for certain substances. When dealing with the alimentary canal, as we are now, oral incorporation will appear most salient, but the other end of the canal, as we are about to see, gives no quarter when it comes to linking incorporation and disgust.

Allport asked us to consider that the central contextual criterion regarding the dangerousness of a bodily fluid is whether it is safely inside its generating body or outside it. And he supposed the way of proving the disgustingness of these substances was to contemplate oral *re*-incorporation of them. Allport's point, however, does not depend on the fluids being our own; drinking our own saliva from a tumbler is hardly less disgusting than drinking someone else's. He merely used our own fluids to bring the point home harder about the magical and irreversible transformation wrought in them by expulsion. Not all bodily excreta pose the same risks; they are ruled differently and backed by passions of different intensity. Some must come out (feces, menstrual blood, urine, semen). But when these remain inside beyond their time that does not prompt disgust, but variously annoyance, nervousness, enervation, or despair. Some excreta cannot be re-ingested without defining the madman or saint; some merely define the boor. Disgust is implicated in each instance, but with different consequences.

Anus

The anus is the end of a tube; the mouth is the beginning, although the Pardoner reminds us that "at either ende of thee foul is the soun."

One is properly ingress; the other egress. The mouth routinely risks contamination simply by carrying out its role as entry point. Its job is to admit things and make the final judgment about their swallow-ability. The anus is not at risk from so many sources. While a multitude of taboos rank the food substances that enter the mouth, those substances are all leveled by the time they are expelled at the anus. The anus as endpoint of the reductive digestive process is a democratizer. It not only levels food, but reminds us (and horrified Swift) that we the eaters of that food are not immune to its leveling powers. The odors that issue from it destroy the sublime illusions constructed by vision and hearing, by class and rank. If John Chrysostom meditated on snot to rid himself of desire, others offered meditations on the lower contaminating orifices: *inter urinas et feces nascimur*. Some, however, were not so delighted at the desire-killing destructiveness of the vision. Swift, we have already seen, was traumatized by it:

> O Strephon, e'er that fatal Day
> When Chloe stole your Heart away,
> Had you but through a Cranny spy'd
> On House of Ease your future Bride,
> In all the Postures of her Face,
> Which Nature gives in such a Case;
> Distortions, Groanings, Strainings, Heavings;
> 'Twere better you had lickt her Leavings,
> Than from Experience find too late
> Your Goddess grown a filthy Mate.[22]

Excrement and the anus bring down the whole body, making it subservient to the anal. The body is not just a passive partner in the process. Even the purest regions—the face, voice (Distortions, Groanings)—join in. The contemplation of coprophagia (offered hypothetically: "'Twere better you had lickt her Leavings") is preferable to the disgust attendant upon shattered illusion. Her Leavings, in any event, are not masked tricksters: they appear as they in fact are and thus provide no basis for self-deception as to taste and smell, or character. The licking, therefore, unlike the marriage, would never take place: unless of course a person delighted truly in turning himself and the world upside down, taking his pleasure from total indulgence in self-defilement.

I need not spell out just how contaminating, how disgusting, the anus is. It is the essence of lowness, of untouchability, and so it must be hemmed in with prohibitions. The anus is to be properly only an exit for foodstuffs that first entered via the mouth. Of course it can be penetrated and therein lies the danger. Even those penetrations consented to and not forced lower the status of the person so penetrated. This works in a way that has something paradoxical about it. Most cultures, and surely ours, understand that the anus is not as contaminating as it is contaminatable. For the penetrator of the anus does not lose rank to the extent the penetrated does if he loses it at all. The penetrator is engaging in an act of domination, desecration, and humiliation of another and in doing so he remains relatively untainted.[23] This suggests that the anus is in fact very sacred, even more so than the mouth. Mouths are already rather wide-ranging as to what they will admit, and things going through the mouth in the wrong direction, like vomit, do not taint the mouth for more than hours; but anuses are not to admit anything and if admitted the taint can endure for a lifetime. Mouths are also armed with teeth; the anus is rather pathetic in its defenses although the advent of AIDS effectively has transformed it into *anus dentatus*.[24]

Yet more than any other orifice, it is the gate that protects the inviolability, the autonomy, of males and indirectly of females too. Only feces and gas are to pass through. This fact makes it indelibly the lowest-status place on the body, rendered disgusting by feces and buffoonish and comical by gas. It is at the bottom, which word— bottom—serves euphemistically to refer to the area of which it is the center. More anciently it is the fundament, the foundation.[25] Fundament, like bottom, is a relational term and thus requires that which lies above it for its own completion. It implies the function of holding up, of supporting, of providing the basis for. The fundament may be the lowest but what rests on top of it needs its grounding, needs its support or it cannot be above. The higher regions are thus conceived as beneficiaries of the lower, not only sustained by it, but requiring the presence of the low so as to enable the very possibility of highness and superiority. The foundation is surcharged with significance. By virtue of this extended metaphorization the anus is seen as the footing on which our dignity depends. It must be secured or everything else built upon it crumbles. For this reason, however, the anus is also a temptation. It can be seen as the gateway to the most private, to the most personal space of all. It signifies the removal of all barriers of otherness.

Clearly this linking of ideas is a cultural matter and within cultures will play itself out differently by gender. If one of the key notions underpinning the feminine is accessibility via penetrability, and the corresponding notion for the masculine is inviolability via impenetrability, then the female anus may not bear the surcharge of significance the male one does. Women expect a certain amount of penetration as coming with the territory of femaleness. It is a necessary condition of the most definitive female action: parturition. Because women's bodies are penetrable by design, the issue about where the penetration is to take place is one about the propriety of location rather than about the issue of penetrability per se. The female anus can never be her vagina; it is at best a backup, a second stringer, but a male's anus is his only vagina: penetrable and capable, in a sense made thinkable by Freud, of giving birth, with feces as the baby.[26]

The anus is thus the center, the eye, from which genderbending possibility radiates. What is the fundament but the foundation of, not just personhood, but manhood? Yet this works the other way too, for femaleness is also on the line here. If penetrating a man's anus feminizes him, then penetrating a woman's does more than brutally drive home her penetrability as a woman; it shows rather that she is penetrable as a man. He feminized, she masculinized after a fashion, for his anus is a figurative vagina, but her anus is an anus being used as if she were a he being used as a she.[27] In either case, to the extent that gender is so thoroughly subsumed into personhood, the foundations of personhood are shaken, he is degraded in one way and she in another.

Genitals

The genitals, female and male, are also highly dangerous and vulnerable. I will return to the subject of sex, love, and disgust in more detail in the next chapter. Suffice it to say here that both male and female genitals produce highly polluting substances: menstrual blood and semen.[28] Urine though contaminating is not nearly as much so as the clearly sexualized substances are (it is also assisted by its liquidity and clarity). The organs themselves are also highly contaminatable, although culture puts the female organs more at risk than the male. With the vagina goes the cultural baggage of virginity, of who controls sexual access to the female, of the entire misogynistic tradition which blames male desire for females on females, even male desire for males on females. The vagina is a gateway inside, the gate to the woman's soul by which act of entry property in her body is claimed, whence the notion of possessing and knowing a woman meaning having intercourse with her.

Men desire access to the vagina, but also fear it and are disgusted by it. They see it as a gaping maw, at times toothed, frighteningly insatiable. At other times a literature of seduction blames the woman for being too reticent or scrupulous about making her vagina available. The argument is the well-known gather ye rosebuds while ye may, which alternates flattery with the threat of horror and disgust that ultimately attends such scrupulosity. An honorable vagina (quaint Honour) eventually must admit a wormlike creature, like it or not:

> then Worms shall try
> That long preserv'd Virginity:
> And your quaint Honour turn to dust.[29]

Even amid desire for access the argument for access cannot forgo imagery that invokes horror and disgust. But the disgust is not of vaginas but of decay. It is when vaginas are accessible that they evoke disgust and horror in their own right.[30] It is then that male fears make them monstrous, hellish, and vile, disgust-evoking places. Recall Lear's image:

> Beneath is all the fiend's.
> There's hell, there's darkness, there is the sulphurous pit, burning, scalding, stench, consumption; fie, fie, fie! pah! pah!

But I suspect that the reason vaginas are capable of evoking disgust depends on something more than that "Love has pitched its mansion in the place of excrement" or that they are surrounded by pubic hair, or that they secrete viscous substances, or that they are victim of centuries of misogyny. It is not only what they secrete or what they look like, but that they are receptacles for that most polluting of male substances, semen.[31] Semen pollutes in a number of ways. First, by fertilization. It makes the vagina the site of rank fecundity and generation that assimilates it to the constellation of images that makes teeming, moist, swampy ooze a source of disgust. Second, semen has the extraordinary power conferred on it by patriarchy to feminize whatever it comes into contact with. In a sense, semen is more feminizing than the vagina itself. Whatever receives it is made woman. The feminizing power of semen can reduce men to women, even lower than women in some moral orderings since as biological men they had the option not to become sociological women. Semen is dangerous to oneself as well as to others, self-defiling as well as defiling. Ascetic communities that feared the contaminating powers of women felt that nocturnal emissions were contaminating also. Penitentials frequently required penance for nocturnal emissions.[32]

Still today men are trapped between competing fears with regard to their semen, fears that manifest themselves in ancient medical literature as well as the literature of virtues and vices. Retaining semen sent poisonous vapors to the brain and heart (and feminized the male so retaining it); releasing it risked enervation and desiccation; and both were seen as causes of melancholia.[33] Semen evokes disgust not only because it is slimy and viscous, "nasty slime" in the words of the Earl of Rochester,[34] but also because its appearance is accompanied by a little death, an orgasm, which is a loss of self-control accompanied by facial expressions as undignified as those that revolted Swift when he imagined a woman defecating. Or as Rousseau noted regarding the facial expressions of a man who had been aroused to ejaculation by desire for him: "And I really know of . . . nothing more revolting than a terrifying face on fire with the most brutal lust . . . If we appear like that to women, they must indeed be fascinated not to find us repulsive."[35]

I am of the view that semen is of all sex-linked disgust substances the most revolting to *men:* not because it shares a pathway with urine, not even because it has other primary disgust features (it is slimy, sticky, and viscous),[36] but because it appears under conditions that are dignity-destroying, a prelude to the mini-shames attendant on post-ejaculatory tristesse. The appearance of semen signals the evanescence and the end of pleasure. Male disgust with semen also bears no small connection with misogyny. The crabbed moralist's fulminations against womankind often suppose the loathsomeness of semen and the defiling power of male sexual contact (which women are then blamed for taking in): "What are you but sincks and privies to swallow in men's filth?"[37] Men can never quite believe that women aren't as revolted by semen as men feel they should be. Such lack of revulsion or such overcoming of revulsion bespeaks the power not only of women's insatiability but of their inchoate drive to spawn, teem, and wax thick with fecund life no matter what the cost to their purity.[38]

As a general rule in Western folk beliefs the vagina is more contaminated by ejaculant than the penis is by having penetrated to ejaculate. Part of this is a reflex of the metaphors of invasiveness, of penetrator and penetrated, that organize the usual conception of the mechanics of coitus. Even the competing, less conscious conceptual construct which sees the vagina as a devouring and engulfing mouth has the vagina bear more risk of contamination by what it ingests than is borne by the engulfed one for being ingested. The risk the latter runs is of annihilation, not of pollution. The metaphor of penetration is in a way a desperate male defense against the male fear of being engulfed, a different sort of fear I think than the usual castration anxiety. Since penises penetrate, they, like knives, do much less damage to themselves than they do to the other. And the belief is that they clean up more easily, it being easier to clean the outside of the penetrating instrument than the inside of the penetrated "victim."[39]

That such images still hold us in their grip is reconfirmed by the enormous expenditures on pharmaceuticals, personal "hygiene" products, and advertising designed to cleanse the whole terrain. Consider too the difference in importance accorded to female virginity as compared with male chastity. Only in ascetic communities is male virginity prized to the same extent as female virginity, with the consequence that in that world penises are put more at risk by vaginas than vaginas by penises. Outside such communities, in the routine social world, female virginity (unto this liberated day) carries enormously more social and moral significance than male virginity, the latter almost disqualifying someone as a male, whereas one's femaleness still survives virginity quite well.

The penis, though penetrable itself under dignity-challenging medical circumstances, is the original image of the contaminating, defiling, and dominating penetrator. Though dry, it emits ooze, and it is condemned by location to suffer the ignominies of pubic hair and the general disgust that its location elicits. But the danger to the penis and testicles is not penetration, since its orifice seems too small to entice other organs of penetration.[40] It is excision, and that is a topic I have no wish to embark on because it seems everyone else has, castration underlying as it does so much academic discourse in various Lacanian and Freudian idioms. I allow myself only a few observations.

I suggested that the horror of semen is that it has the power to feminize, but then so does a scalpel. The castrating blade "deforms" the male into female, making him bleed from his genital region in a parody of menstruation. The misogyny that drives this conceptual order is what raises the stakes for castration as against other maimings, mutilations, and deformities which do not require misogyny to account for their uncanny and disgusting qualities. Women, after all, as well as men, can be deprived of eyes, nose, and limbs. Castration, however, does not need misogyny to make it disgusting. It only needs misogyny to explain why it is more disgusting than either men or women losing arms, legs, and noses or women suffering clitorectomies. Maiming disgusts and horrifies quite well without any psychosexual theory informing it. Semen, however, disgusts because it is sexual, fertilizing, and reproductive. Its way of feminization is rather different from castration's way, but it need be no less sadistic for all that.

We first viewed the terrain of the disgusting in Chapter 3 by adopting the lens of various categorizing oppositions. Some of these classified on the basis (1) of large abstractions—inorganic vs. organic, plant vs. animal, animal vs. human, us vs. them—others classified on the basis (2) of sensation, mostly tactile—soft vs. firm, wet vs. dry, wiggly vs. still, viscid vs. fluid—and so on—and a third (3) classified hierarchically, morally, socially, and aesthetically—high vs. low. In the first group we found that though the general opposition of inorganic vs. organic captured an uncontroversial truth about disgust, as the oppositions narrowed their range their ambiguities increased. Plants were surely less likely to generate disgust than animals, but since both plants and animals could decay, smell foully, and participate in the uncanny, and were virtually indistinguishable in the lower phyla, the opposition could only be relied upon to support probabilities of greater or lesser likelihood. When animals opposed humans the boundaries were even more porous and became most porous of all when we descended to ourselves and the difference in contaminating powers between the inside and outside of us.

The second type of opposition captured qualities that though owing something to contextual expectations seemed to transcend context, or rather to mold context along its lines. These kind of oppositions—ones that produced the slimy, the gooey, the squishy, the viscous—were rather powerful predictors of the disgusting. Those qualities were abstracted from a deep structure that found life itself fraught with anxiety-provoking and ultimately disgust-generating processes: eating, fornicating, excreting, dying, and decaying. Life soup, seething, roiling, oozing, in dankness or lukewarmness, is what disgusts. Not because all ends in death, but because there is no fixed point. All is flux and in flux, eternal recurrence. Nothing stands still. Christianity thus invents a Heaven in which bodies are static and immutable to escape disgust; and on earth immutable, crystalline purity has no immediate disgust-generating powers at all. The problem is not the Douglasian one of things being out of place; it's that there is too much flux for fixed structures to get a grip on all the turmoil.[41]

The third opposition—high vs. low—overrode all the others and, as we have yet to examine, imbued all manifestations of disgust with a moral dimension. It could hardly be otherwise since disgust was intimately involved with the determination of the pure and impure, the contaminating and contaminatable. This means culture will figure greatly in determining what is disgusting, as well as set general disgust thresholds by the extent to which purity is an important value. Yet cultures had much freer rein in deciding what to include in the category of the disgusting than what to exclude. No matter where and when, it is harder to make the squishy and slimy non-disgusting than the non-squishy and non-slimy. Disgust, peculiarly human and one of the emotions that enables culture itself, thus imposes its ambivalences and values on the world.

Disgust's connection with purity is itself complex. It defends against the impure and it punishes for our failures to be pure. But not all purity rules or rituals are backed by disgust. Some are maintained by shame, guilt, a sense of duty, or by mere habit. So that where there is disgust there will be a corresponding notion of pollution, but where there is purity the prospect of its defilement need not always engender disgust. Yet despite the fact that other passions can support purity rules, no single one seems as qualified for the job as disgust is. Disgust may not be absolutely necessary to the maintenance of purity, but it would seem that purity's grip will be less to the extent it is not supported by disgust.

In Chapter 4 we observed that the grammar, lexicon, and particular quality of disgust varies with the sense via which the disgusting was perceived. That the precise conceptualization of disgust can vary so much depending on the sense engaged is, with the partial exception of fear, not a feature of other moral sentiments. The different senses play no especially distinctive role in guilt, indignation, anger.[42] Yet we felt that no matter what sense was alerted to the disgusting and no matter what the qualities that evoked disgust were, all disgusts were linked by a common function (defense of body and soul against pollution) and a common feel and reaction (the feeling of disgust, violation, and contamination and the desire to be rid of the offending sensation). We saw that disgust was much more than a defense against oral incorporation centered in the sense of taste. Touch and smell processed disgust as much or more than taste and not simply as a surrogate for taste but in their own right as a first ordering. Touch, it was observed, provided the rich lexicon of tactile sensation that went to make up the oppositions of category two. Even as a defense against oral incorporation, both touch and smell were more efficient defenders of purity than taste. Taste made its judgments dangerously close to the brink or, given that the judgment was made in the mouth, already over the brink.

If disgust changed its style by virtue of which sense was engaged, this chapter has shown that disgust took on different social and psychological significance depending on which part of the body (and by implication the soul) was engaged. Disgust that was a defense against oral incorporation did not raise the same issues as disgust that was a defense against anal incorporation. The different bodily substances, though all contaminating, did not contaminate in precisely the same way. Semen worked differently from snot which in turn worked differently from feces. Yet despite the differences there was an overriding sense that the disgust category sensibly bound all these disparate things together as dangerous, as contaminating, as sources of magic and the uncanny.

The story up to now has been sunk in matter; we have dealt with disgusting *things*, and barely touched at all on disgusting actions or characters. The moral, the historical, and the social are yet to come. We now turn our attention to the central paradox of disgust: the allure of the disgusting.

FAIR IS FOUL,
AND FOUL IS FAIR

THE REALM OF THE DISGUSTING is a remarkably inclusive one. It contemplates disgust at all kinds of offensiveness, whether these have their origins primarily in touch, smell, or taste; or whether they be understood as more complexly moral and aesthetic. We recognize all such disparately originating disgusts as belonging to the same syndrome. They all end in a feeling state we recognize only too well. I want to distinguish two main types of disgust nonetheless. Both types are utterly familiar, but only one, because backed by the Freudianism which underwrites so much of our thinking, gets any serious attention. The other gets virtually no attention except in diet books.

Two Types of Disgust

The first type, the Freudian kind, acts as a barrier to satisfying unconscious desire. This is the disgust, as I mentioned earlier, that Freud called a reaction formation, in which role disgust joins with shame and morality to work as a dam (the image is Freud's)[1] to hold back the sexual instinct. Disgust makes the genitals of the other smell bad and look ugly and one's own appear as a source of shame. Disgust is there to prevent the activation of unconscious desire, or, more precisely, disgust is part of the very process of repression that makes such desires unconscious.[2] In any event, disgust so conceived acts to prevent indulgence in the deeds or things that prompted the disgust. It tries to keep us from getting too close by making us turn away holding our noses. Just how unconscious these desires are is something we will puzzle ourselves about further below, but if desire is perhaps too strong a notion for the attraction most disgusting things hold for us, curiosity about or fascination with the disgusting is something we are often quite conscious of even as we turn away in disgust.

The disgust that works as a barrier to unconscious desires, barely admitted fascinations, or furtive curiosities is only one part of the disgust story. There is also the disgust I alluded to in Chapter 3 that has its origins in the notion of surfeit. No unconscious desires or furtive attractions there. The overindulgence in any number of foods, drinks, and activities, sexual or otherwise, for which the desire is completely conscious and acted upon, leads to disgust also—the nausea and sickness of surfeit. Here disgust is not a barrier to imbibing but either a punishment for having done so or, less ominously, simply a time-activated barrier that judges (usually too slowly) when enough has been enough.

Both types of disgust suggest that fair is foul and foul is fair, but they structure the confusion of opposites in somewhat different ways. The first type of disgust suggests that foulness is an illusion; the second suggests that fairness is. In this second category—disgust originating in surfeit—that which initially appears fair is revealed to be only fragilely so. The initial fairness suffers the possibility of several kinds of downward reevaluation. One is that fairness might lead to the pains and anguish of the diminishing pleasures of addiction; imbibing simply increases the desire for further consumption to the inevitable illness and self-destruction of the desiring agent. Another reevaluation might attend satisfaction itself, which transforms the once desirable into the now loathsome:

> There lives within the very flame of love
> A kind of wick or snuff that will abate it,
> And nothing is at a like goodness still,
> For goodness, growing to a pleurisy,
> Dies in his own too-much. (*Hamlet* 4.7.113–117)

Claudius captures, in the idiom of excess, rottenness, and disease that so characterizes the world of *Hamlet,* the sense of choking in excess of the good that transforms the good, the desired, into the disgusting. Desire dying in its own too-much suggests that disgust has a kind of inevitable connection with the satisfaction of desire, whether these desires be openly admitted or whether they fester only in denial.

The disgust that operates as an initial barrier must operate that way because of a necessary admission that what lies behind the disgust is not foul at all but fair. In this view, disgust is not a feature of the object desired but stands detached from it and is interposed between it and the curious agent or is superimposed on it as a kind of veneer.[3] The images of dams, barriers, and veneers have one nice consequence; they save us from the definitional absurdity of calling the aversive attractive. These images allow the attractive to remain distinct from the loathsome barrier of disgust behind or under which it resides. But what if we dispense with the images of barriers and veneerings? Suppose instead that we take the comminglings and confusions of "fair is foul and foul is fair" seriously, which force upon us the idea that the disgusting itself has the power to allure. By this view the fair does not lurk behind a wall of disgust; the disgusting is precisely what is fair.

If the loathsome attracts then is it properly loathsome? It doesn't make much sense to make aversive mean attractive, but it might very well make sense to understand that the emotion we call disgust does not give rise only to aversive actions.[4] The complex of judgments that are embodied in disgust, the way disgust in fact works, means that it has to get its hands dirty. How could it be otherwise?[5] To the extent that disgust defends us against pollution it must be alert to the polluting; it has to study it and know it well. It may even have to be curious about it or fascinated by it to do its job really well, carouse with it after a fashion.

Disgust must always repel in some sense or it is not disgust.[6] Repulsion, however, might bring in its train affects that work to move one closer again to what one just backed away from. These affects could range from curiosity, to fascination, to a desire to mingle. Repulsion also can raise resentment for having been repelled and a consequent desire to reclaim lost territory. And that too draws one forward again.

Ultimately, however, whether the disgusting is fair only hiding behind a disgusting barrier or whether the disgusting is itself alluring does not make all that much difference. In either case the disgusting must still be understood to repel and overcoming it is a big part of the story. It is just that in one instance the barrier can be envisaged concretely as an obstruction and in the other the barrier becomes more abstract. Barriers (or resistances) we have either way; what changes is how we conceive of what is lying behind the obstruction: objects of unconscious pre-social and pre-cultural desire or messier desires that are not quite unconscious and obtain some of their force from the knowledge that what culture declares forbidden might become desirable for that fact alone.[7]

Whether the disgust that provides an initial barrier works in the way of a Freudian reaction formation or simply as a repulsive component in a more complexly conceived emotion of disgust, it can be distinguished from disgust as a consequence of surfeit. The two main styles of disgust—the one that attempts to deny access, the other that kicks in after glutting—reinforce each other in significant ways and join to reconfirm that the deep structure of the disgusting centers on key life processes like eating (and its consequences) and fornicating (and its consequences).

Are there no simple, purely disgusting things that do not involve us in "a vortex of summons and repulsion" as Kristeva puts it,[8] that do not implicate attraction, desire, fascination, or allure either unconsciously, as in disgust as reaction formation, or consciously, as in disgust as the consequence of surfeit? We surely tell ourselves there are; they are almost too vulgar to name. Entry into a stall of a public restroom always entails anxiety that one will have to see the unflushed leavings of some thoughtless reprobate. Inspect we must as a necessary task of monitoring danger in the environment; yet is there an unconscious desire beyond the conscious work of such monitoring? Even here, isn't there a small twinge of a double-take reflex, not of desire but of the fascination of disbelief? Something makes us look at the bloody auto accident, thrill to movies of horror, gore, and violence; something makes porn big business and still draws people to circus sideshows. Is there no moral offensiveness that doesn't by some dark process elicit fascination, if in no other way than in the horror, wonderment, and befuddlement such depravity evokes? Is the disgust that is connected to the comic, to the Rabelaisian delight in the excretory, the emissive, the fecund, part of the thrill of overcoming the disgust that prevents desire or part of the risk in courting

disgust by surfeiting desire? Disgust motivates an aversiveness that
is more complex than that caused by pain (even though the aversiveness of pain is often no easy psychological matter either), for
disgust implicates more complex social and moral judgments than
pain does.[9]

How are we to understand the strange association of desire and
disgust? Though I will focus mostly on sex here, we could also
choose violence, gore, or horror, which although they may overlap
with sex neither are congruent with it nor march to its beat. The
allure of violence, gore, and horror is an allure that gets indulged
mostly, but not exclusively, via facsimile and fiction: we are more
likely to watch than do. It is supposed to be the opposite in sex, where
we are expected to do more than we watch; in fact, we are expected
to do much more than watch or find ourselves labeled abnormal. The
contrast with violence couldn't be starker. Enough said. Because we
cannot escape Freud on this topic even if we wanted to, we must
make his hobbyhorse ours too. Sex it is.

First, we might not want to oppose so-called unconscious desire
(and I use desire here to include motivating states like curiosity and
fascination) to disgust at all, but see them as necessary to each other,
part of one complex syndrome. Freud recognized, for instance, that
disgust and the other reaction formations were not just there to prevent pleasure but were needed to heighten it, even to create the
conditions for it. The damlike barrier, in other words, works both to
obstruct access to the desired object and to provide the means for
storing quantities of desire sufficient to overcome the barrier:

> Some obstacle is necessary to swell the tide of the libido to its
> height; and at all periods of history, wherever natural barriers
> in the way of satisfaction have not sufficed, mankind has erected
> conventional ones in order to be able to enjoy love. This is true
> both of individuals and of nations. In times during which no
> obstacles to sexual satisfaction existed, such as, may be, during
> the decline of the civilizations of antiquity, love became worth-
> less, life became empty, and strong reaction-formations were
> necessary before the indispensable emotional value of love could
> be recovered.[10]

Sexual pleasure was a function of overcoming disgust as much as it was of the mere satisfaction of an instinctual drive: "The sexual instinct in its strength enjoys overriding this disgust."[11]

The disgust that works to make desire possible by making the desired thing rare and inaccessible is very different from the disgust brought on by surfeit. The disgust of surfeit makes the once alluring now disgusting, while the disgust of reaction formation uses disgust to create desire, or if not precisely to create it, then surely to augment it to those dam-breaking levels. More than make the once disgusting now alluring, it makes the now disgusting now alluring. The argument is largely economic. Disgust helps create conditions of scarcity which build up demand and increase value.

But not all pleasures march to laws of supply and demand. Nor is it simple scarcity that prompts all high evaluations of pleasure. It matters just how that scarcity is created. If things are simply under-produced, that is one thing; but if the scarcity is created by the intervention of a prohibition, that is another, for the overcoming of prohibition is itself a pleasure independent of whatever pleasures may lie in the acquisition of the object so prohibited. A witty twelfth-century bishop could thus suggest to a woman who sought his advice about her husband's impotence: "Let us make him a priest and his potency will immediately be restored."[12] Breaking rules has its un-deniable attraction, but it is a complex pleasure at best and a pleasure that is often rewarded by punishment. We are in quite a fix. So much pleasure is tied up in the violation of rules we are committed to, the very commitment providing the basis for the pleasure in violation. And then we are punished; sometimes by external authority, but most often internally by such painful sentiments as shame, guilt, or disgust.

No doubt there is some economizing here too. We weigh the like-lihood of the pain of punishment against the likelihood of attaining the pleasures of violating the rule and of acquiring the thing gained by the violation. Anyone but an economist will object to such a purely rational and unemotive account. Some social and cultural norms hold us so strongly in their grip that we cannot bear to do the calculation; we are prevented by the norm from even doing the calculation, even from fantasizing about it except under very rare and special condi-tions. Some rules we just don't violate; nor would we get pleasure out of doing so. And what are those? The ones backed up by strong negative emotions of the most moral sort: guilt, shame, and, yes, disgust.

Yet we remain intractably curious about and fascinated by those who overcome such restraints. These violators of deeply held norms populate our myths, books, and movies, either as gods or as criminals. The defining trait of both gods and criminals, it seems, is being able to offend against norms of moral and social decency that successfully keep us normal middling sorts normal. Gods are accorded higher status than the criminals they resemble by virtue of offending against more serious norms (they betray as well as prey) and by virtue of having done it long ago in a way that defies most standards of proof. Those who violate the norms that hold us in their grip are objects of fear, loathing, awe, precisely the emotions that drive tragedy, horror, suspense, and some religious devotion.

What strange creatures we are! We require social and cultural rules to provide order and give meaning to our lives, yet we are so constructed as to chafe under the conditions that enable our thriving. It is not hard to see that there are adaptive advantages to this quirk that compensate us for the disorders it provokes. The desire to press against our restraints and our limits is what makes us strive, improve, and create. We recognize this about ourselves and make it the subject of foundational narratives that account for the actions of Eve, Satan, Prometheus, Faust, even Oedipus, on one side, and the despair of Don Juan on the other. Satisfaction dissatisfies and disappoints and thus pushes us to more striving and desiring. We encapsulate the thought in homely sayings that make the whole tragic matter of the unattainability of satisfaction less threatening. Thus the grass is greener on the other side of the fence. The same thought can become infinitely more despairing in the grimness of Baudelaire's formulation: "The world is a hospital in which each patient is driven by a desire to change beds ... It seems to me that I would be content, there, where I am not."[13]

Folk wisdom in its delphic way never gives us one view, but makes the opposite view look equally convincing. If by the Faustian account we must strive, if by the Don Juanish account we are driven in despair to seek satisfaction that eludes us as soon as we get to the other side of the fence, we have an opposing story that is less grand: the fox and the grapes. When we can't have what we want, by a nice self-deception we cease to desire the unattainable by redefining it as disgusting. The grapes that looked so good when the prospect of attaining them was plausibly entertained now become sour and the mere thought of them puts our teeth on edge.

Sour grapes implicates distaste and disgust.[14] Like Freud's disgust the aversion defends the self by constraining its range of activities to the permissible or realizable.[15] But sour grapes is not Freud's account. Sour grapes doesn't repress desire and put it behind a barrier of disgust so as ultimately to enhance the pleasure of attainment. It makes the desirable thing disgusting in itself; it kills desire completely; it shrinks the world of possibility, even eliminating the desire to contemplate the grapes—consciously at least. Here we seem to have stumbled on part of the mechanism by which desire becomes unconscious and so in the end we can do some small service on behalf of the Freudian story. The mechanism of sour grapes, however, achieves repression via resignation rather than via the fear of castration. Sour grapes is what enables the virtue of prudence, prevents us from striving excessively, so that we can live to love: a bird in the hand is worth two in the bush explains as much about the repression of desire as Oedipus does.

I have been indulging a kind of romantic sentimentalism here in a Byronic style—Fausts, Don Juans—which embarrasses me. Things just aren't all that tragic, for the whole process of finding pleasure and fascination in the violation of norms that exposes us to disgust enables a good portion of the comic too. It is trite to observe that much of the comic depends on transgressive irreverence, a kind of feast of misrule in which, if not the violation, at least the mockery of certain norms is given a privilege. No sooner is an aspect of the capacity for disgust acquired than the very substance of that disgust becomes material for joking. My children never thought feces funny until they were toilet trained, never thought snot comical until it disgusted them or, more precisely, until they could feel what it meant for it to disgust their parents.[16] Sexual jokes, which come much later than "poop" jokes, depend on the acquisition of sexual disgust and sexual desire. And the real sick joke, the sin against norms about the sanctity of human life or about the concern that should be manifested in the face of human misfortune, depends on subscribing to moral norms the breach of which elicits disgust. Disgust, then, is involved in more than just the styles of comedy that feed on the Rabelaisian grotesque body. With guilt, indignation, and shame, disgust also helps sustain the higher and less corporeal moral order.

Some small insight into why norms supported by disgust are so suitable to comic transgression can be obtained by noting one significant contrast between disgust and shame. In the Freudian account both shame and disgust operate to inhibit the libido, repressing desire and rendering it unconscious, but they involve different risks should they be triggered. The experience of our own shame is never entertaining to us; the experience of disgust, however, can be, and especially, as is commonly the case in comedy, when it is elicited by *another's* shamelessness or ineptitude. Disgust allows us to play at violating norms in certain restrictive settings; shame does not. Shame can only be felt as the very unpleasant recognition of our moral or social failure,[17] although it is surely possible for some masochists to seek such unpleasantness. Disgust, in contrast, can be indulged playfully for rather low stakes. And this is true not only for comic transgression but also for the entertainment derived from genres that truck in violence and horror.

Transgressions against disgust norms are entertaining as long as they are in some sense authorized.[18] In an earlier age permitted transgressions were largely confined to formally inaugurated feasts of misrule or made the daily task of licensed court jesters. For us, authorized transgressions are less formally institutionalized; instead they are permitted by other norms that define the domain of the laughable and ridiculous; these norms demand that mockery take such a form that it reveal its limits and thereby pay homage to that which is mocked. When the transgressions are not authorized, they are acts of rebellion or insanity. But why should such permitted charades amuse? If transgression releases the energy that yields laughter and comic pleasure, how do we trick ourselves into thinking we are transgressing when in fact such transgressions are allowed us?

I suspect that the norms we mock have such a strong grip on us that even playing at transgression is sufficient to energize us and that Olivia is somewhat less than half right when she says "there is no slander in an allowed fool" (*Twelfth Night* 1.5.89). Notice how tame disgust humor is. People do not eat feces as a joke, even as a sick joke; what they do is talk about eating it or ridicule people who do eat it. The transgression is limited to suspending the rules of decorum regarding *talking* about such things.[19] So powerfully do the norms against coprophagia hold us in their grip that it is more than enough of a transgressive release just to imagine such actions. We thus ward off revulsion by laughing in disbelief when we hear of a child or lunatic who feasted on feces.[20]

The fascination and curiosity, if not quite desire, we evince toward the disgusting often arise very close to home, not just in spectacles of humiliation or Dionysian violence. There is no doubt that our own snot, feces, and urine are contaminating and disgusting to us. If they weren't we would hardly be so fascinated by or curious about them. We are proud of our production and quite pleased if especially large amounts are expelled in one effort. We are further pleased if the cleaning process after the fact quickly restores our prior purity. We look at our creations more often than we admit, or if we don't look we imagine with pleasure our extraordinary productive capacities. We have private classification schemes for consistencies, odors, colors, and quantities. I am always struck by how common it is for people to check their Kleenex or handkerchief after blowing their nose, allowing themselves at least a quick glance. We, in other words, do not just suffer our excretions but take active interest and pride in successful productions, and suffer chagrin, anxiety, and disappointment for our less successful ones or for ones that promised much but produced little. These things are common subjects of conversation during childhood and adolescence, after which they become less appropriate and a more private concern, but more central to our private meditations than we will generally admit, even to ourselves.

For all this interest in, even love for, our own excretions there can be no doubt as to their polluting power. It is not that other people's excreta are harmful and ours are safe. As we saw in Chapter 5, ours are very dangerous to ourselves as well to others. What distinguishes my excrement from yours is my pride in mine, not my aversion to being touched by it. Nor is it true as Freud and others have said that our own excrement doesn't smell.[21] If it didn't we could hardly be as interested in it as we are. Recall that it is the fact that our feces is disgusting that gives it its power to fascinate. True, we do not find the smell nearly as dangerous as if it were someone else's, but this is largely a function of its familiarity, not of some unconscious remembrance of infantile desires. Even though the smell does not disgust we understand ourselves to be in the presence of the disgusting and thus we are alert to danger and aware of the need to take special care with the enterprise at hand. Change our diet and we can become rather estranged from the odor, which can be disconcerting if not quite disgusting.

Freud's account that has feces variously signify babies and penises helps explain some of the fascination with feces,[22] though I am suspicious of the automatic priority conferred on the sexual and the reproductive. It is production, as well as reproduction, that impresses us. We have just transformed and impressed with our own stamp the dangerous stuff we ate. As in those orgiastic feasts, eating comes before fornicating. Caroline Bynum constructs a brilliant account showing priority of the nutritive and productive to the sexual and reproductive in medieval devotion. Could it not be argued that we have returned to that model (or never left it)? Consider the quasi-unconscious calculations we do to compare the mass ingested with the mass excreted and secreted, and for weight-conscious persons the calculations will be quite conscious indeed. Production—not reproduction.

We have just dealt with that type of disgust which works as an initial barrier to desire or works by making that which is unconsciously desired disgusting so as to drive us away and prevent any sampling at all. I have also supposed a differently functioning disgust, the disgust of surfeit, which pays us back for getting just what we thought we wanted. The two styles of disgust contrast in the ways they involve the conscious or unconscious status of desire. The first deals with barriers to barely admitted desire, if admitted at all. The second is a consequence of conscious desiring. The first is felt before imbibing and works to prevent it; the second is felt after imbibing and works to prevent further indulgence. The two can join hands, as when transgressing the barrier itself produces the sense of excessiveness that provides pleasure as well as disgust and shame for it, all felt in some strange simultaneity, pleasure and aversion augmenting each other in a kind of ecstasy. The two basic types of disgust have similarities of function. Both work to curb appetite.[23] And once the disgust of surfeit has been felt it has the capacity to work as an initial barrier to future instances of consumption or indulgence. In such cases disgust 2 (surfeit) converges with disgust 1 (initial prohibitional barrier). But that these two disgusts can converge occasionally does not undo their real distinctiveness.

The disgust of prohibition, we saw, has a paradoxical relation with desire. By prohibiting, it actually augments, even helps create, the desire it wishes to prevent. Disgust 2, the disgust of surfeit, also has a paradoxical relation with desire, but the paradox is a cruel joke instead of an ironic attraction. It treats us to the dismal realization that pleasure often ends in pain, either because desire itself can never be satisfied and leads to frustration or addiction, or because satisfaction itself has a downside. It can leave us without purpose, or embarrassed by our prior desire, or saddened by its conclusion, or simply sickened by a sense that the ecstasy of satisfaction, were it to have more than its brief duration, would lead us to the sickness of surfeit. I am exaggerating the dark side. Exaggerations, however, are not inventions; we recognize the unfortunate truth upon which they are built. Yet we often find those uncomplicated satisfactions that we think have no dark side, whether they be gustatory or sexual, leading to the oblivion of sleep; one wonders if that is by way of the pleasure of exhaustion or as an escape from the letdown brought on by satisfaction's fade to black.

The disgust of surfeit succeeds in killing desire once and for all because it doesn't operate by desire-provoking prohibition but by punishment, by the actual infliction of pain. If we were to analogize the two disgusts in terms of legal process, the initial prohibiting disgust would be the statute and the surfeit-produced disgust the sentence and punishment. The distinction begins to collapse, as noted earlier, when the memory of the punishment works as a barrier to the next infraction, a barrier which looks not very different from the barriers imposed by disgust 1. But the two disgusts do not have the

same ranges of competence. Surfeit has a narrower range of operation, more clearly associated with food, drink, and sex; disgust 1 is
involved with the entire physical and moral order. Nor do the memories of the disgust induced by surfeit work in the same way throughout the range of all surfeiting experience. Surfeit has its own com-
plexities.

Let us distinguish two broad kinds of surfeit. One kind is to take
too much in in one sitting, leading thereby to hangovers, nausea, and
other disgust-related sensations. The other kind is the habitual indulgence in what are perceived as merely sensory delights, a kind of
surfeit of repetition; this kind is the compulsion to re-experience the
same sensation in ways that people understand to involve excessive
imbibement, but with no one indulgence being especially excessive.
This second sense is considered surfeit only when the indulgence can
be justifiably looked upon with disapproval.[24] Both surfeits, however,
are inveighed against by moralists; both offend against some idea of
moderation and temperance. The former involves the intense consumption we associate with the vice of gluttony; the second involves
a somewhat different weakness of will we associate with the concept
of a habit (usually a bad one). This is the vice of non-denial of fleshly
pleasure, closely akin to sloth and laziness.

In the first kind of surfeit we must also note that not all overin-
dulgences have the same consequences and that some things are much
more likely to produce long-standing aversions than others. A hangover on good wine or beer is blamed less on the wine or beer than
on our own failure to adhere to norms of moderation and health.
When we get sick on beer or wine we experience nausea and self-
disgust, but the sense of contamination has a very short half-life.
Alcohol gets the benefit of its fluidity and purity, of its non-disgusting
consistency. The sight of a beer bottle the next day may do us in,
but two days later it won't. At some level we believe that our system
is efficiently self-purifying with regard to the poison that is alcohol
and that the process of purification is the nausea and headache of the
hangover.

Contrast the disgust inspired by overeating greasy foods and
sweets. Unlike alcohol, these substances are contaminating by virtue
of their consistency even as we are unable to resist their taste. Fat,

oil, and syrupy sweetness structure the concept of cloying. Alcohol does not cloy unless also sweet and syrupy. We believe our system not to be particularly efficient as a self-purifier with things that cloy, the very word attracted by alliteration to sister concepts of "clinging" and "cleaving unto" that make things hard to get rid of. Fat and sweet stick like glue and like the host of other nauseating things we think of as greasy and sweet: "honeying" in a greasy bed in Hamlet's grim imagination. Grease and fat conjure up images of indolence, otium, weak-willed lethargy, sliminess, unctuousness. Sugariness does not fare much better. For all the moral energy that went into American teetotaling, the fact is that greasiness and sugariness offend us morally more than alcohol.[25]

Yet the greasy and the sweet continue to allure with their taste. They have the capacity to make us eat more of them than we wish; they are will-weakening or will-deviating. The taste somehow makes us eat beyond our needs until disgust enters to put a stop to it, that is, until cloy finally outweighs joy. Certain other tastes can prompt overindulgence too, but they do not cloy and hence they do not disgust: fresh raspberries, for example. Overindulgence in raspberries means something different from overindulgence in french fries or chocolate. The latter involves a feel, a sensation of disgust that is the sign of overindulgence. Overindulgence in raspberries, however, is more likely to be figured in notions of eating more than your share or eating substantially more than is prudent given their expense or simply eating more than it is decorous to eat. The mark of overindulgence with them is purely social; with grease and sweet it is physiological and moral as well.

We need to distinguish one more disgust after the fact, one that by generous extension of the notion of surfeit can be understood to belong here: the aversion to foods that we believe caused us to vomit. It is rare that we can ever eat again with the same gusto any food that gave us food poisoning. Even vomiting induced by the onset of the flu, if mistakenly believed to have been caused by a food, will often cause that food to suffer in our estimation long after the falseness of the belief has been revealed. In this case no desire, unconscious or otherwise, impels us to reexperience a newly forbidden pleasure, for there was no pleasure to forbid. The experience of disgust, not having been a consequence of pleasure, cannot now provide the basis for a barrier that prohibits a pleasure never experienced. This is an instance of aversion pure and simple. We have at long last uncovered an example of disgust in which there is no curiosity, no fascination, no allure whatsoever. The memory of prior overwhelming sickness stops desire dead in its tracks with present disgust.

The second sense of surfeit, that of repetitious indulging of the senses in which no individual instance of indulgence need lead to hangover or illness, has a different sociology and psychology but is part of the anatomy of disgust nonetheless. If one is in the habit, say, of having intercourse with the same partner, we call that a virtue if it is exclusive, but it is the kind of virtue that makes a virtue of what might be seen as a self-indulgent vice. The loyal copulation of others can disgust almost as much as disloyal copulation. It is the disgust that Lear manifested in the famous passage I quoted in the previous chapter at the thought of copulation run rampant. Jacobean drama is filled with melancholics revolted by lechery, even loyal lechery within the bounds of wedlock, and in such revulsion they merely continue what theologians had been advancing throughout the Middle Ages.[26] Recall the substance of Hamlet's upbraiding of his mother in the famous scene of Act III. It was not just the thought of her living "in the rank sweat of an enseamèd bed / Stewed in corruption, honeying and making love / Over a nasty sty" (3.4.93) with the usurper Claudius, for Hamlet was only a little less sickened by the thought of the avidity with which she and his father went at it:

> Must I remember? Why, she would hang on him
> As if increase of appetite had grown
> By what it fed on. (1.2.143)[27]

The worry is that such avidity is less a demonstration of love for the other than a blind drive that must find an outlet somewhere. The love is of sensation, not of a person. The ghost discovers, in a selfserving reference, that Gertrude's avidity to his person was indeed more generalizable:

> So lust, though to a radiant angel linked,
> Will sate itself in a celestial bed
> And prey on garbage. (1.5.55)

Hamlet's revulsion at sex, as unsettling as it may be to our ro-
manticizations regarding its beauty and attractiveness, pales beside
that of the hero in Tourneur's *The Revenger's Tragedy*, who, like Lear,
imagines a world in which copulation never dies so that even skele-
tons go to it. In that somber and disgustful world bawds are "bone
setters" setting bones together, and an "old surfeiter" thus dies by
kissing the poisoned "pretty hanging lip" of a skull made up to look
as if it lived.[28] Much of this epidemic of fornication is driven by food
and drink, the surfeit of gluttony, but this luxury is distinguished by
the fact that it is never described as raising disgust in the actors
themselves, only in observers sickened by thought of so much indulgence.

The failure of others' surfeiting to inhibit their future indulgences
raises a disgust in the melancholic observer that functions as disgust
1, the disgust that works to keep him from acting on his unconscious
desires. So then disgusts 1 and 2 figure in a kind of moral economy
in which the imagined failures of surfeit to limit desire in other people
work to construct inhibitory barriers in the melancholic observer who
now must see his own desires polluted by images of unseemly sex in
epidemic proportions. Incest, mismatches between old and young,
"bloat kings with reechy kisses,"[29] "grey-haired adultery," "hollow
bones stuffed with damned desires,"[30] poison his thought and pollute
his fantasies. It is also the case that his inhibitory disgust makes him
susceptible to finding others' indulgences disgusting. In other words,
he is projecting. That is the usual tale we tell to dismiss such railing.
Is it just projection that makes the surfeiting of others revolting?
Hardly. Passion and desire suspend our critical faculties when we
copulate and carouse, but when we look with the cooler eye of the
third-party observer we have no such veils to our judgment, the
success of porn notwithstanding.

The surfeit of habituation and addiction plays itself out in different
ways in different domains. Freud discusses the symbiotic relation of
desire and its frustration and whether "the mental value of an instinct
invariably sinks with gratification of it":

One thinks, for instance, of the relation of the winedrinker to
wine. Is it not a fact that wine always affords the drinker the
same toxic satisfaction — one that in poetry has so often been

likened to the erotic and that science as well may regard as comparable? Has one ever heard of a drinker being forced constantly to change his wine because he soon gets tired of always drinking the same? On the contrary, habit binds a man more and more to the particular kind of wine he drinks. Do we ever find a drinker impelled to go to another country where the wine is dearer or where alcohol is prohibited, in order to stimulate his dwindling pleasure in it by these obstacles? Nothing of the sort . . . Why is the relation of the lover to his sexual object so very different?[31]

Freud underestimates the degree to which scarcity can enhance the pleasure of those wines and beers that geography and price make a rare treat. That, however, does not dismiss the larger point he is making about the difference between wine and women. His answer is that men are loyal to their favorite wine because it is the real thing, the very thing they desire; no taboo prevents them from getting the exact one they want. But with sexual objects it is different. Satisfaction with the same sexual object cannot be attained because that object is only a substitute for the real love object to which access is barred by incest taboos. Anyone or anything else is but a frustratingly inadequate surrogate for the real object of desire.

Is this quest for the unattainable an adequate explanation for the satisfactions with the same wine and the dissatisfactions with the same woman, for why surfeiting in love often means Don Juanism while surfeiting in drink means delighting too much in the same thing?[32] The relation of drinking to disgust is not quite the same as the relation of sex to disgust. There are no strong norms that tell us to be loyal to wines; nor are we in the habit of getting pleasure out of seducing wine, the very idea being absurd. The pleasure of wine is mostly in the physical pleasure of drinking, tasting, and smelling and in the attendant liberating intoxication. The pleasure is sensual. Yes, there is the wine aficionado's elaborate ritual that adds the pleasure of claiming expertise to the pleasures of conviviality that attend some wine drinking, but my rough point still stands. Once one comes of age, wine drinking offers no real opportunity for the pleasures of violating prohibitions that sexuality constantly offers.

Moreover, the stakes with wine are much lower morally, socially, and psychologically than they are with women so that the pleasures of wine and women become largely non-comparable. The pleasure of sex is only partly sensual because that pleasure can never quite extricate itself from the dense array of norms and prohibitions that govern sexual matters. Many find the gamesmanship, the risk and excitement of seduction, the flattery to one's self-esteem that comes with the favor bestowed (since expounding Freud here I assume the male as seducer), much more pleasurable than the clumsy mingling of bodies that is its goal.

Unless love intervenes the mere sensual pleasures of sex tend to cloy in a way that wine does not. And it seems to make no difference whether the sex is all with one unloved person or with many unloved persons. In either case despair is the risk that attends the repetitiveness of the deed. Don Juan can keep going because he can still get pleasure from seduction, but even that begins to bore him. Either he discovers as does Byron's Don Juan that he is as much hunted as hunter, his pride in his strategic abilities and in his seductive powers maintained by a thorough self-deception as to the lack of similar abilities in the women who are his targets; or he in fact is such an accomplished seducer that the nth seduction holds no surprises and no pleasures beyond the merely physical. A game with a foregone conclusion can hardly be as interesting as one whose outcome is in real doubt. The "unless love intervenes" is crucial, however; for when it does intervene something is added to the merely physical that, though not providing the pleasure of strategy and flattery that inheres in seduction, comes to be something more. Sleeping with mother could be no better either, unless love intervened. And indeed Freud assumes that love has intervened both with mother and with wine, but not with any other woman.

There are other crucial differences. The pleasure curve of wine, for instance, has a less abrupt decay rate than sex has. Wine lets us down very gently if we drink in moderation. Sex has orgasm; wine has nothing quite comparable. Wine's gently sloping pleasure curve on both the ascending and descending sides means wine holds the possibility of pleasure in moderation. It offers the opportunity for pleasure without surfeit, even though there is the danger of surfeit and addiction.[33] One of the peculiar features of sexual satisfaction, however, is that indulgence becomes indistinguishable from surfeit and overindulgence. Orgasm is by definition excessive. And this is partially the reason its decay rate is so abrupt.

It is thus not unusual for people to accompany sex with wine for two reasons: wine helps desensitize our disgust receptors, deaden our self-critical capacity, undo our commitment to norms of decorum and our sense of shame so that we can overcome the inhibitory disgust that would prevent sexual indulgence; and then, post coitus, it helps smooth out the letdown, helps assuage the disgust that comes with the surfeit that is orgasm which leaves one rather at loose ends for what do to, panicked, empty, disgusted with one's own having desired. Wine helps us confuse lassitude with a sense of well-being. When there is no love to intervene we ask wine to do love's work to make sex less daunting and the aftermath less an occasion for despair.

The pleasures of wine do not put us to this kind of confusion unless we sicken ourselves with overindulgence. Wine gives us the choice of pleasure in moderation. Freud's explanation of why the same wine satisfies and the same love object does not ignores the very different pleasure curves of each and the subsequent consequences. Wine can be indulged in pleasurably without engaging disgust and only holds the threat of the disgust if we overimbibe; sex, in contrast, must deal with disgust on the trip up and on the trip back down as a necessary aspect of its orgasmic pleasure. If wine produced orgasm or if orgasm had the gentle sloping moderate pleasures of wine, in the manner medieval theologians imagined the decorous rational sex of prelapsarian Adam and Eve,[34] then Adam would be as content with Eve day in and day out as Freud was with his Bordeaux.

What do we make of the fact that so much (male) sexuality is constructed around the desire to indulge disgust, to roll in the mud so to speak?[35] Sex is perceived as dirty, bestial, smelly, messy, sticky, slimy, oozy, and that is precisely, for many, its attraction. I suggested that sexual satisfaction means excess and thus involves the disgust that surfeit entails. There is also the problem alluded to earlier of how to understand the Freudian reaction formation. Is it a barrier behind which the fair object lies or is the fair object in fact foul and does that constitute its attraction?

In *Three Essays on the Theory of Sexuality* (1905) Freud envisaged reaction formations as dams of disgust, shame, and morality that worked to repress desires for forbidden objects. By the time of "The Most Prevalent Form of Degradation in Erotic Life" (1912), the disgusting has itself become an object of desire.[36] Why, he wonders, are men often psychically impotent with the women they respect and admire yet quite successful at performing with "a sexual object who in their estimate is degraded and worth little?" Men need a degraded sexual object to find pleasure. Hence they find mistresses among women who are "ethically inferior" and "to whom [they] need ascribe no aesthetic misgiving" (210). Men, in other words, look for those undiscerning women who do not seem to be revolted by the ugliness of the sexual organs. As Freud puts it with deadpan understatement: "the genitals themselves have not undergone the development of the rest of the human form in the direction of beauty" (215).[37]

Freud's account may seem to us to be a localized ethnography of the sexual desire of Viennese bourgeois men, for whom sexuality was never separable from the images of the lower-class serving women, nurses, maids, and nannies who raised them.[38] Freud, however, claimed a wider applicability for his observations. The prevalent form of degradation of the sexual object was not a localized pathology but a characteristic "of the erotic life of civilized peoples" (209). The origins of this urge to degrade, he says, are to be found in the split of "two currents of feeling"—"the tender, affectionate feelings and the sensual feelings," the latter not being especially tender (204). The former remain attached to members of the family, namely mothers and sisters, while the sensual feelings are diverted from their desired object choice (mothers and sisters again) by the barrier of the incest taboo and the disgust, shame, and morality that sanction it.[39] The consequence is that the "sensual feeling that has remained active seeks only objects evoking no reminder of the incestuous persons forbidden to it" (207). Those who remind him of mother and sister, that is, women of his own (respectable) social class, will be loved tenderly but not sensually; those who are nothing like mother will get sensuality devoid of tenderness. Sexual pleasure is thus divorced from tender feelings and tender feelings kill sexual desire (207).

Sensuality thus seeks degraded objects or objects that are accept-

ably degradable. But which is it? Is the pleasure dependent on the
prior degradation of the object or does the pleasure depend on degrading the object through sex? Freud is never quite clear on this
point and seems to want it both ways. The sexual act is felt to degrade
its object, to pollute it. But the desire for that object is already a
function of its being low.[40] It is already degraded. The degradation
of intercourse then could be understood to work as a ratification, a
confirmation, of a ranking already in place by virtue of sociological
determinants like class, ethnicity, and educational level. But that
seems insufficiently forceful to explain the problem. Just how can
satisfaction reside in desecrating that which is already desecrated?
Freud does not, in this essay, suggest that the pleasure lies in the
man's self-degradation; the pleasure is in degrading someone else.[41]
As Freud has it, the "full sexual satisfaction" that these lower women
provide is not unrelated to the fact that one does not love them, that
one can walk away with one's soul intact and gratified, for she "cannot criticize him" (210).

Freud cannot mean to suggest that the lower-class women are
alluring simply because they themselves are disgusting; it is more that
they have high thresholds of disgust and hence will do or suffer things
respectable women won't. There is the lowness that allures and then
there is the lowness that prevents desire. He would admit a difference
between relations with a young wench and relations with a loathly
hag. His account still depends on what some might consider to be a
conventionally sexist notion of the violability of these low women,
or there would be no possibility of degradation upon which to base
the pleasure.

One suspects the lower-class women serving this role for upper-
class men are attractive independent of their vulgarity. A third-party
observer, in other words, would understand what is drawing the man.
This is not the kind of indulgence in disgust that finds men seeking
the ugly, the deformed, the diseased, the old, for sexual release. Aesthetics still matter; the "most *prevalent* form of degradation in erotic
life" is not about sleeping with lepers. It is about doing dirt to someone who still is deemed to have some kind of innocence or purity
(youth, beauty, and vulnerability) that can be polluted, but who possesses an inferior ethical disposition that sees no point in not making

herself available for such pollution; that is, her inferior ethical nature makes her sensual.

Freud's story is of men who seek women who are morally and socially contemptible, not physically disgusting. Not that there aren't souls who will indeed seek out the ugly, ill, and deformed for sexual pleasure—but that is not what Freud is talking about.[42] He and we recognize a difference between the "social deformities" of low-class taste and vulgarity and the bodily ugliness that bears no special connection with class once we discount for the effects of class on physical health. And one even suspects that those who do indulge what are generally thought to be perverse preferences for the unhealthy and deformed do so either by the transforming powers of genuine love or less nobly, with an unavoidable, almost avant-gardiste irony for indulging in the violation of such powerful prohibitions.

If the act of degrading one's partner were the thrill, presumably men would have more fun desecrating women from the class of their wives, mothers, and sisters. Freud says love and tender feelings interpose to prevent that. That might account for sparing one's own wife, sisters, and mother, but why should tenderness spare the wives, sisters, and mothers of one's social equals? It is not the incest taboo that saves these women from degradation, nor love. Freud suggests indirectly that they mostly save themselves by being frigid (211) or are saved by the same impotence that first brought their husbands in to visit Dr. Freud. In fact they seem saved by class alone, which is so controlling that every woman of mother's social class resembles her sufficiently on that sole basis. The mere femaleness of the lower women is, however, not thought to make them resemble mother so as to spare them. Class drives this story more than Oedipus, the sociological beating out the psychological in a rather un-Freudian way.

One wonders how the social economy works to fund Freud's view that the desire to degrade is a part of all civilized male sexual life. Where do working-class men find women to desire who are not their mothers and sisters? Presumably they are not civilized and are thus excused from the application of this form of prevalent sexual practice. Or is it that once down at those levels being a woman is all the lowness that is needed for a man to delight in wallowing in the moral mud she provides? The prevalent degradation that Freud is discussing is dependent on class hierarchy for its specialness, not on gender hierarchy, nor on Oedipus for that matter; it seems then that men of the lower classes must have their desires to degrade their sexual objects structured differently or forgo completely the erotic gratifications available to men of the higher classes.

Instead of finding lower women to degrade, mightn't these lowly men simply look upward? Upper-class men in fact feared that lower-class men might be doing just that. A long literary tradition dating from courtly love in the twelfth century, through the well-hung footmen of the seventeenth and eighteenth centuries, and continuing well beyond Lady Chatterley suggests that these lower men were believed to be delighting the upper-class women whom their men held too dear to get dirty with. But then who was degrading whom? The story was never told (until the nineteenth century) in a way that depicted the lower men acting on desires to degrade.[43] In courtly love they sought to be elevated by the woman, not to degrade her. And the story is seldom told in a way that gives the lower man any real say in the matter. He merely did the behest of his mistress, who felt he would be more avid than her enervated husband. This was the degradation that upper-class men believed their women engaged in. The wives of the upper class degraded their husbands by sleeping with the footmen as they indulged their own fascination with the contemptible and the disgusting, while their husbands were degrading their serving women whose lowness in turn degraded them. What a world of mutual battlings of contempt and disgust!

Freud tells a different story about women. "Women"—that is, either the bourgeois women he treated or the mothers, wives, and sisters of the professional or bourgeois men he treated—"show little need to degrade the sexual object" (211). The division between the tender and the sensual is resolved for them by repression of the sensual. Frigidity thus corresponds to the psychic impotence of their husbands. This is a grim picture indeed. Sex is either too disgusting to engage in, or when engaged in not disgusting enough to be gratifying, unless one can make use of one's servants and maids. Disgust does triple duty: First it tries to prevent coupling, but in so doing constitutes almost a dare to try. Once overcome it joins in the fun and enhances it both by having been conquered and by having itself become a participant in the proceedings by providing the muck and goo which makes the sexual process so momentarily liberating. And then it comes stumbling in afterward accompanied by shame to punish for such surfeiting indulgence. Disgust has a busy life in the sexual world.

This is a simplistic summary which states a strong case in the context of sex in which the stakes are high and the particular pleasure curve of sex, with its abrupt decay rate, complicates matters. Things will play themselves out somewhat differently when the transgressions take place in contexts in which the stakes are lower, such as food, or when the moral issues are merely different. This is not the whole story with sex either; I have had to append a frequent and untrivial qualifier to this discussion: "unless love intervenes." Love changes the whole economy of sexual disgust and also many of those disgusts which arise from failures to maintain a presentable and non-polluting public presence. Love conquers almost all.

Love and the Suspension of Disgust Rules

I want to spin a somewhat brighter tale now. This is a tale of love more than sex, of changing diapers and caring for sick family members, of loyalty as well as of sexual love. It is one of tolerance for bodies and a willingness to excuse their foibles as well as to indulge their dangerous and polluting qualities. This tale works as much socially as psychologically, with sex being only one of many areas of behavior that are at stake.

One way of describing intimacy (and/or love) is as that state in which various disgust rules are relaxed or suspended. Consider the following rough and sometimes overlapping stances toward the disgusting capacities of another: in one we pardon or suffer deeds or things that are still felt to be disgusting; in the second we come not to be disgusted by things that would otherwise disgust, but these things afford no special pleasures or attractions for not disgusting and are still recognized as belonging to the realm of the disgusting; and in the third we understand the disgusting behavior or substance to be a privilege of intimacy which would be a grave offense if it were not understood that it was privileged; this last often involves the intersection of disgust and sexual pleasure (but need not).

Of the first sort, those things that must be pardoned or endured and still disgust, consider bad breath. Bad breath in a stranger is often processed as a kind of low-level moral failing; it can outweigh many virtues and kill desires for continued relations that would bring us within smelling range. Bad breath in a loved one will be pardoned, borne with, or negotiated by postponing closeness with the knowledge that the distancing is temporary and of no import at all beyond the momentary avoidance of a discomfort that no one, including the person so distanced, would expect you to bear. If the breath is not pardoned or cannot be negotiated then I would suspect love is at an end or will soon be. Bad breath is one of those disgusting problems that is not given special weight as a marker of status relations. It cannot be seen by third parties and the first party often is without a clue that he has it, so its power to signal to the couple or to observers the specialness of the relationship is reduced to nil. It does not, for instance, have the signaling power of permitted touchings. Bad breath is a cross for the second party to bear without any benefit except perhaps a small twinge of satisfaction in the private knowledge that one is suffering in silent nobility and is thus conferring a gift in the sufferance. And to the extent that competition is a part of intimate relations it allows one to indulge in the little contempts that provide momentary relief from the sanctified burdens of love and devotion.

Of the second type—those things which by virtue of a special status come to lose their disgusting aspect without affording any special pleasures or attractions for being overcome—the prime examples are intergenerational acts of caretaking and devotion: changing diapers, cleaning up regurgitated food, and otherwise caring for sick and infirm kin. Unlike enduring bad breath, changing diapers partly defines a status, parental status. But changing diapers is something more than just part of the territory of parenthood. As an act it is so fundamentally emblematic of the type of commitment involved in the relationship as to bear a symbolic and constitutive significance. Parents are those who will care no matter what; will cart away the excrement; risk getting it on their hands and clothing; suffer being shat upon. Parents thereby engage in humbling actions which are simultaneously status-enhancing in that the parents assert and acquire by such actions the right to care in addition to the burdens of the duty to care.

To love as a parent means humbling oneself before a mere baby (as preparation no doubt to the final breaking of the parental will that attends the puberty of one's children). This ritual (and often real) humbling of the powerful in love is easily recognizable as the model of a special kind of devotion. Christianity constrained God himself to love humanity in this way. Before the ultimate self-abasement of humiliation and crucifixion he engaged in small acts of self-effacement and self-degradation by washing the feet of his in-feriors. Most of us recognize such self-abasements as clever strategies in the assertion of superiority. Gandhi and Jesus knew this well. Do the worshipful make the same move of asserting a claim for domi-nance under the guise of conceding it? In this light consider the homage paid to the *infant* Jesus at Christmas time. Just how threat-ening can God be in the form of baby? Or might such worship be a sign of our knowledge that our will and claims to autonomy are as much inhibited by our children as they had been by our parents?

Not all love of the strong for the weak takes the form of self-abasement, of serving the low by cleaning them of their dirt and self-befoulments. One can love from a cool distance and delegate the dirty work; this in fact often distinguished father-love from mother-love until only recently, if that.[44] It seems that it is precisely the overcoming of normal disgust that makes mother-love the model of all selfless love, whereas the general reluctance of fathers to do the same is part of what makes father-love an ambivalent thing that a child might often rather do without.[45]

Changing diapers, overcoming the disgust inherent in contami-nating substances, is emblematic of the unconditional quality of nurturing parental love. Without such overcoming, the act would have no such emblematic significance. Love means a kind of self-overcoming in this context, the overcoming of powerful aversions, and the suspension of purity rules that hold you in their grip. It means that your fastidiousness, your own purity of being, must be subor-dinated to the well-being of the next generation.

The reader may suspect, from the significance I attach to the act, that it was no small effort for me to overcome my disgust at changing diapers. These things, admittedly, come easier to some than to others, and their larger meanings get lost for the actors in the routinization and repetitiousness of the chore. (One's sensitivity, however, though dulled by the daily bout with excrement, remains marvelously intact in the face of the rarer demand to clean up the vomit of one's sick child.) But the larger meaning of dealing with a child's bodily wastes, though obscured by routine, is still there. It is often confirmed more by third parties who pay an involuntary homage to the symbolic power of such disgust-overcoming devotion than by the hardened principal actors. The childless often look on in awe, horror, and/or disgust, and many can barely envisage parenthood at such a price. For observers who are already parents the act bears no such significance, having become coded for them as routine, except when they are rudely reminded of the disgust they overcame with their own kids by having to deal with the excrement of someone else's child. The self-overcoming, though unconditional with regard to your child, is still largely conditional on its being your child. Without love and devotion disgust is still there; a labor of love becomes a mere thankless task.

Nature is accommodating to the fastidiousness of new parents by making a newborn's excrement relatively uncontaminating, neither sticky nor especially vile smelling and even unrecognizable as the thing itself by color and shape. The very distinctiveness of infant feces confirms their special status as infants and is perhaps partially constitutive of that status. If a certain uniformity in offensiveness in human feces is a great democratizer, erasing distinctions among us, the special quality of infants' feces separates them from the offensive human mass. There may be an interesting evolutionary story here, but I do not know how to tell it. Is it about the selection of a particular kind of milk or about the selection of a particular kind of disgust mechanism? If disgust was already in place then the change would have to come in the constitution of the feces, favoring those mothers whose milk produced feces that didn't trigger violent disgust. Or is it that the disgust reflex developed so as to make a partial exception for the feces of infants?

Intergenerational love of parents toward children and of children toward aging parents is bound up with the putting aside or overcoming of disgust, which putting aside is itself defining of caring and caring for. The confrontation with disgust unlocks no special pleasures lurking within the disgusting. Some intragenerational love takes the same form. Friends in need make this kind of demand at times, as do lovers. When one is lying sick from food poisoning on the floor of a restaurant restroom, do the pain and nausea of the illness even begin to outweigh the humiliation of having to be so seen and cared for by one's friends? Will the others, we fear, ever be able to think of us as a dignified being again? And no matter how much solicitude they show, will we ever again trust the way they look at us? If they love us already this puts love to a test; if they do not love us, then we fear they will never be able to. This is why we admire animals who have the grace to crawl off and lick their wounds or die by themselves. Only children have an absolute right to make demands on us to dispense with disgust; others must earn this right, or pay for it in some way by recognizing a reciprocity in the relation: I have cared for you, now you for me; I have seen you as you should not have been seen, now you must suffer the return.

The claim that love is the suspension of disgust rules can mean several things. As already indicated, love means a willingness to pardon normal failings of the other's body, such as bad breath or the uglinesses that attend puberty and growing old. It also means overcoming disgust in favor of caring and concern. Here I want to take up the notion of privileging another to see, touch, or otherwise experience you in a way that would be disgusting, shameful, or humiliating to you if that person were not so privileged. It is not just the intimacies of sexuality that are at issue but rather the entire range of behaviors and practices that go to defining intimacy between rough equals. For lack of a better name I shall call this love.

The intimacy of love is different from that of simple proximity and cohabitation in which we become inured to the disgusting habits and normal bodily functioning of a mere roommate. The inurement to disgust that leads to the toleration of roommates is not deemed a privilege of intimacy but a burden which often ends in contempt, sometimes even loathing, for the other. This contemptuous inurement is similar to the kind doctors and nurses acquire in order to manage the disgust that the diseased and aging bodies they deal with would normally elicit. This inurement manifestly does not arise by positive commitment but by a familiarity that breeds contempt. It is quite a different matter with love, where the overcoming of disgust is necessary (but not sufficient) for the maintenance of the relationship and where mutual indulgence in some kinds of the disgusting marks a privilege and provides some of the crucial means for demonstrating and proving love.

We have already dealt with the ways in which sexual desire depends on the idea of a prohibited domain of the disgusting. A person's tongue in your mouth could be experienced as a pleasure or as a most repulsive and nauseating intrusion depending on the state of relations that exist or are being negotiated between you and the person. But someone else's tongue in your mouth can be a sign of intimacy *because* it can also be a disgusting assault. The marks of intimacy depend upon the violability of Goffman's "territories of the self." Without such territory over which you vigilantly patrol the borders there can be nothing special in allowing or gaining access to it.

This takes us back to the paradox of the permitted transgression with a new wrinkle. Consider that the boundary of the self is manned at its most crucial and vulnerable points by disgust. Consensual sex means the mutual transgression of disgust-defended boundaries. But whence the violative thrill amid all this permission? Earlier, in another context, I suggested that disgust so holds us in its grip that even permitted transgressions still retain their punch. Now I suggest we look not so much at the authorized transgressor as at the permission giver. To the thrill of transgressing another's boundary is added the thrill of granting the permission to be so transgressed upon. Somewhat strangely, it is the granting of permission that may be more transgressive than the transgression it authorizes, for it is the permission that suspends the disgust rule, not the boundary crossing that is thereby allowed.

The thrill of permitted transgression thus ends up being one of complicity with the permission giver. The permitted transgressor aids and abets the authorizer in a violation of the authorizer's most strongly held, disgust-manned defenses. But the true offender against the all-powerful rules of disgust is the permission giver. It is that person who authorizes the violation of the disgust rules by redefining the violation of him or herself in a disgust-transfiguring experience. Generally in sex the boundary crossing and permission granting are mutual, so both partners get the same disgust-related thrills and offend the gods of purity equally—a pure feast of misrule. We simply will do things or let things be done to ourselves in love and sex that violate all the norms the violation of which would trigger disgust if unprivileged, if coerced, or even if witnessed.[46] And to do such and to have such done to us is much of what sexual intimacy is.

I don't, however, want to make this an issue of sex. I am claiming that *love* means the suspension of disgust rules, not just that sex does. On the contrary, sex, as we have seen, does not quite suspend disgust; it indulges it. Love is something less dramatic. When I say love means the suspension of disgust rules I am speaking about much more mundane intimacies that really mark out the terrain of familiarity and the occasional contempts that it can breed. Contrast our public self and the energy we devote to self-monitoring and to the monitoring of our surroundings with the monitoring of self and one's own behaviors when alone, or when in the presence of intimates, whether these be formally classified as family or friends. Imagine if we let ourselves be seen in public as our family and especially our spouses or partners see us. Imagine seeing others that way. It would be shameful to be so seen and disgusting to have to see others so without the privilege having been granted.

Sex is only one kind of boundary crossing, involving one kind of nakedness. There are other strippings, exposures, and knowledges upon which intense intimacies are founded, the intimacies of prolonged, close, and loving contact. One thinks of sharing and revealing doubts, worries, concerns; of admitting aspirations, confessing shortcomings and failures; of simply being seen as having warts, weaknesses, and needs. That is the touching picture. We could recast it. We could define friends or intimates as those persons whom we let whine to us so that in return we may whine to them, with both parties understanding that such whining is the privilege of intimacy which our dignity and disgust would prevent in the absence of the privilege.

These privileges are often not in themselves pleasurable except to the extent that they mean intimate commitment. Intimacy has its costs as well as its benefits. Some costs include seeing the other and being seen oneself as ugly, unpresentable, cowardly, boring, hot-tempered, peevish, affectless, fearful, sick, failing and having failed, pretentious, foolish, and so on. It means suffering the relaxation of certain civilities we accord to mere strangers, and this reimplicates Swift: it means the inability to deny much of the body's gas, excrement, odors, secretions, and assorted misbehavings.

We must not go too far. At some point the private relaxation of our commitment to public norms of reserve, restraint, cleanliness, disattendability, and simple manners of propriety will be deemed excessive and disrespectful to the intimate. If we were to do no self-monitoring at all, it is unlikely that love could ever endure such an implicit judgment of the other's "taken for grantedness." Some manners can be relaxed, but not all can be dispensed with. We may be able to eat out of the serving bowl and not thereby acquire the right to chew with our mouths open or belch without any attempt at stifling the sound. There are norms of civility which should so hold us in their grip that we could not conceive relaxing them even when alone, let alone in the presence of our loved ones.

Love, we see, is hardly the suspension of all disgust rules. What certain kinds of intimacy necessarily entail is not so much a relaxation of defenses as the near impossibility, short of obsessional behavior, of maintaining them under the constraints of constant surveillance in close quarters. The work that goes into producing our public selves takes place off stage, invisible to the public audience. Close quarters means selected others are behind stage watching the rehearsals and preparations.[47] This kind of privileged access backstage can be understood as an honor when it is indeed conferred. But the presence of another imposes some minimal demands to maintain some dignity under conditions in which it is very hard to do so. Intimates still demand respect and are entitled to it. So it is not that all disgust barriers are thrown to the winds with intimacy. Some disgusting behaviors are allowed (and we know roughly what they are) and function as confirmations of intimate status, while others would seem to indicate a contemptuous indifference for the other, and still others, like most of the foul odors we emit, simply cannot always be helped. These last are the unavoidable costs of intimacy, not the confirmations of it, nor are they meaningfully construable as privileges.

It is not a privilege of intimacy to endure bad breath in the way it can be a privilege to see someone with his or her guard down, to see someone weak, vulnerable, sick, fearful, and ugly, conditions which if manifested publicly would elicit contempt and disgust in the viewer. It is a very narrow line that separates the things that disgust from the things that elicit concern, love, pity, and affection. Some of these privileges are conferred voluntarily as by confession and avowal. Some are revealed in spite of ourselves.

Consider the pain of seeing a person whom one loves behave so as to humiliate himself and disgust others and of understanding that those others have some justice in their disgust. One then comes to know oneself as loving a fool. Can love survive such visions? Hume, as we shall see in Chapter 8, says only parental love can survive such knowledge, all other forms of love are killed by it.[48] Yet are no vulgar fools loved by people who are neither their parents nor themselves vulgar fools? True, to witness one's beloved elicit justifiable disgust in others forces one to face up to the great costs of the commitment, but people maintain such commitments nonetheless. Does witnessing painful ineptitude put the loving one to the burden of informing the fool so as to allow him to amend; does it demand repressing the vision so as to reestablish a certain blindness that loving this kind of person requires, or does loving this kind of person mean one has come to love this person for the fool he is? One sees dignified women attached to foolish men whom they appear to love, much more than one sees the gender relations reversed. One is tempted to explain this by recourse to a dark desire on the part of the women to love men who are in every way beneath them so as to relish the contempt they feel. Is this contempt a particularly prevalent feminine form of degradation of the love object? But contempt is the observer's explanation, desperate to account for the misalliance; in fact the woman may well be devoted to the disgusting boor. This must be what it means for love to conquer all.

In sum, love, as we know it, privileges another to see us in ways that would shame us and disgust others without the intervention of love. Not all norms backed by the sanction of disgust are up for grabs in love. We can, nonetheless, accept the weak claim that love often manifests itself by its special stances toward the disgusting and by special undertakings either to lower one's sensitivity to disgust through certain ranges of activity or, as in sex, to find in the disgusting itself a source of pleasure.

A stronger claim would be that the suspension of disgust is so central to love that love is parasitical on and secondary to a prior domain of the disgusting. This would suggest that a certain kind of love depended on the achievements of the civilizing process. (Earlier I offered the view that our obsession with sex might owe something to the potato; could it possibly be the case that those potatoes also needed to be eaten with forks and napkins to support the obsession?) The stronger claim, as one rightly suspects and as we shall observe in the next chapter, is ultimately not sustainable.[49] Yet it seems likely that high thresholds of disgust will have some discernible consequences for the sense of one's individuation and thus also for what we think of as love.

I have perhaps overemphasized the boundary-breaching aspects of love, taking the process and meanings of achieving intimacy and love for the rather different set of expectations and arrangements that reflect an achieved state of intimacy and love. We might, for instance, ask ourselves what the suspension of key rules of disgust might mean for individual identity and autonomy within love or under conditions of intimacy over time. The legal vocabulary of rights, privileges, and grants that I have been using requires grantor and grantee to remain distinct and autonomous beings, for these grants and privileges can be revoked and must be frequently reconfirmed. In this view love simultaneously dissolves and confirms boundaries of self. Love thus individualizes the loved one well beyond the individuation one concedes to any other person.

But suppose we used a different organizing image, seeing the suspension of disgust as a weakening of each individual's sense of self so that they merge into one being: the Pauline image of two fleshes made one. In this construct disgust dissolves boundaries of the self not via grants and regrants of privilege but by weakening the separation of self and other so that the whole idea of granting privilege ceases to make sense. No wonder divorce is forbidden in the Pauline regime; the idea of two fleshes made one makes it a conceptual impossibility.

One might hazard the idea that in their early stages relations of intimacy and love seem more governed by the regime of rights and grants, but with the passage of time and the routinization of permitted boundary transgressions, the loved one passes eventually from an intimate autonomous other to something more akin to one's own vital organ, from lover to liver, if the word play can be endured. So in the end two fleshes are made one. This may help account for the frequently noted occurrence in long-married couples for the death of one spouse to follow shortly on the death of the other.

| **7** |

WARRIORS, SAINTS,
AND DELICACY

HOW MIGHT DISGUST have been constituted in a world of un-speakable poverty, high mortality, rampant disease; where privacy was attainable with difficulty if at all, where love, sex, death, defe-cation, almost always took place within ear and nose shot, if not within the sight of others? A world in which only the wealthy had a change of clothes, in which washing more than the hands and face was unusual; in which teeth rotted and disinfectants were generally unknown? We will pursue three avenues of inquiry. The first will be to look closely at several medieval and Renaissance texts that will provide departure points for discerning how disgust might fit in a world in which bad smells, loathsome sights, disease, and deformity were unavoidably present in a way they are not now. The second will immerse us in the English lexicon of disgust. How was disgust discussed before the word disgust (before, that is, such puns were possible)? Third, we will confront the crucial and fertile work of Norbert Elias, the theorist of the civilizing process, as it bears on the anatomy of disgust.

Historicizing Disgust

I begin with what I know best: heroic culture. Heroic cultures are inevitably presented as ur-cultures, as something not so much lived in as looked back upon. The heroic books of the Bible—parts of Genesis, Judges, and all of Samuel—are thus in the *Old* Testament which in turn is organized so as to have the books of a distinctly heroic cast fall in its first half, the early portions of the timeline.

Heroic cultures are cultures of honor, of bloodfeud, of weak or non-existent central authority, so that when these cultures finally acquire the means of writing down the stories of their own exploits the very technology of writing usually coincides with the political and cultural developments that spell the end of feud and the heroic style. Thus the stories of the *Iliad*, the Icelandic sagas, *Beowulf*, *The Song of Roland* circulated orally for some time before being reduced to their final written form in a world in which they already had a certain antique air.[1] Our finest productions in the heroic style, though often tough-minded themselves and remarkably astute at identifying and criticizing the dysfunctions of heroic culture, are never quite divorced from a sense of nostalgia, a sense of a nobler world since lost.

We think of heroic cultures as belonging to a ruder time, with ruder manners; as cultures in which people had relatively few material things to occupy their time and so occupied it with worrying about how they were looked upon by others, whether they were feared, respected, esteemed.[2] Among those in contention for honor the concern about where one stood relative to others was all consuming; there were very few spaces in which one could relax, out of the judging eyes of jealous and envious others. People were edgy and sensitive; conversation hovered on the edge of insult. A person's honor was fragile and easily violated; its state of health was closely monitored by his (and even her) sense of shame and a keen ability to discern whether others envied him more than he envied them. The key emotions in this culture are shame and envy. Shame is the emotion of self-monitoring; it maintains the ethic of "face" and courage; envy motivates the competitiveness that is the very competition for scarce honor. Disgust, by this account, has very little public life in a culture in which there was very little life that wasn't public. But we can't dismiss it that easily.

With such a hasty caricature of a psychologically and sociologically complex moral regime let me introduce you to two short vignettes recorded in the family sagas of medieval Iceland. In the first, from *Laxdæla saga*, Kjartan and his followers, as an escalating move in a dispute, surrounded the farmhouse of the people of Laugar and denied them access to their outhouses for three days. "In that time," says the saga, "it was the custom for the privy to be located quite a way from the house . . . Kjartan blocked all the doors and refused anyone exit and they had to relieve themselves inside for three days" (ch. 47). Kjartan then returned home. The people of Laugar were none too pleased and said they "thought it to be a much worse dishonor, greater even than if Kjartan had killed one or two of them instead."

The second requires a little more detail in the telling. Egil and his companions, after surviving freezing cold and a massive blizzard, arrive exhausted at the farm of a prosperous man named Armod Beard, who invites them to stay for the night and serves large amounts of a yogurt-like substance called skyr. Armod expresses his disappointment that he has no ale to give them. After Egil and his men have consumed considerable quantities of skyr, Armod's wife sends her eleven-year-old daughter to tell Egil to save some room for better fare. Egil refuses to take another mouthful of skyr. After reprimanding his daughter with a slap, Armod treats Egil and his men to some better food and to as much strong ale as they can drink. The drinking, not untypically in the Viking world, is competitive. Once embarked one loses face by not continuing. Egil drinks his rounds and drinks his men's as they fall by the wayside. Finally even Egil can't go on. He then gets up and

> goes across the floor to Armod. He put his hands on Armod's shoulders and pushed him up against the post. Then Egil heaved up so much vomit that it poured over Armod's face, in his eyes, his nostrils, and into his mouth. It ran down his chest so that Armod couldn't breathe. Once he managed to get his breath again, he then began heaving all over. Armod's servants, all of those present, said that Egil was the most vile of men; only the worst would do something like this, not go outside to vomit, but do such an appalling thing in the drinking hall.
>
> "Don't berate me about this," said Egil, "I am doing nothing more than what your master is doing. He's vomiting with all his might, no less than I am." Then Egil went back to his seat and asked for more drink. (ch. 71)

Hard to believe, but in spite of Egil's behavior the sagas themselves are remarkable for their decorousness and reticence about what we today would consider embarrassing or disgusting bodily functions. There is surprisingly little vulgarity or ribaldry. When vulgarity enters it does so by way of conscious insults that are part of the give-and-take of the acquisition, testing, and reclamation of honor. Men and women thus impugn men's and in a rare instance a woman's sexual orientation; occasionally a man mocks another by claiming to have slept with his wife, but these insults are generally issued in the obscurest verse and very seldom in comprehensible prose.[3]

The routine saga account is characterized by a decorous reserve in which bodily functions are mentioned only when a character puts the subject into play via insult. The thousands of pages of the Icelandic saga corpus, for instance, show very little concern with contaminating body fluids. Mentions of smells, tastes, and loathsome touchings are rare, and when they occur they are again assimilated into the exchange of insults, so that a person's bad breath can become a cause for making insulting verses about his condition.[4] A few farts are mentioned but these are, as is usual with farts, less matters of disgust than of comedy.[5] Even pain, despite the amount of killing and battle in heroic literature, gets virtually no mention. Bodies pile up, limbs are severed, without any mention of agony. The mayhem of violence is either glorified in an almost cartoon way or simply there as a fact of life, a given in a world in which the defense of honor is the driving force. The heroic world is a world of action more than of sensation, and the emotions that figure most prominently in it are ones elicited by public action, its successes and failures.[6]

What does it mean that disgust and the usual domain of the disgusting play so little role in this style? Does it indicate that the threshold of disgust is so high as virtually to banish body-originating disgust from the emotional economy? Or is it that disgust is so assimilated into the mechanisms and structures of shame that it doesn't have much of a separate existence apart from shame? Or might it simply be that disgust over bad odors, bad tastes, the connection between disgust and desire, are luxuries that depend for their articulation on a minimal pacification of the society and the reliable provisioning of food, clothing, and warmth? Could it be that these astute strategists of personal interaction may simply have been too hard pressed to be able to indulge the very special kinds of miseries that produce Swift, Proust, Freud, and musings on desire and close stools?

I have found only two examples in the entire saga corpus of lock-
ing people in so as to force them to excrete indoors. Yet one of these
instances indicates that the mere phrase *dreita inni*, which in English
means literally to make dirt inside, to defecate indoors, is sufficient
in itself to describe the action with no further detail necessary: "and
they made Markus make dirt inside." This means that the term is a
technical one, a quasi-legal one of known content, that indicates a
possible, even if infrequently attested, move in the feud, the rules of
which are given in the fuller *Laxdœla* account: block the doors, hold
a limited three-day siege solely for the purpose of making the people
inside live amidst their own excrement, and then depart, leaving them
to be the objects of ridicule. The ritual has a perverse wit to it. It
lasts three days, just the number of days Icelandic custom permits a
guest to stay who shows up uninvited.[7] The attackers pose as uninvited guests, playing on the ambivalence always lurking in the guest,
as friend or foe, delight or burden, an ambivalence captured in the
etymology of the word guest, which is derived from an Indo-European root that gave us the word for enemy as well: guest/host/
hostile.[8]

This tactic suggests that disgust is there, but is so enmeshed with
the politics of shame as to have no real idiom separate from shame.
Clearly defecation is degrading and contaminating. It is hedged in
with rules about appropriateness as to place.[9] And to violate those
rules is a cause for disgrace and shame, so disgraceful that it is better
to lose a few members of one's group in an affray than to suffer such
an indignity: they "thought it to be a much worse dishonor, greater
even than if Kjartan had killed one or two of them instead." We
might query as to just who would be willing to lose his life rather
than defecate inside for three days. The sentiment is attributed to a
group. One suspects that no individual in the group would volunteer,
only that in the calculus of shame the dishonor accruing to all of
them is worse under one course of events than under the other. Still,
the hyperbole captures just how indignant and humiliated the men
of Laugar were.

Disgust and shame work in tandem here. To defecate inside is
shameful because it forces people to violate disgust norms in a setting
where such violation shames them. The shame is twofold: it is the
shame of being coerced and beaten in the give-and-take of feud, and

it is the shame of being forced to do something disgusting. The latter is what makes it worse than losing a man or two, which is simply the normal kind of shame suffered in the feud. Note however that their disgust is not quite ours. The taboo is not so firmly in place that violations of it have passed into the realm of the unthinkable. This is an acceptable strategy in the feud; Kjartan need feel no shame for making someone else violate these disgust norms. He gets the credit for shaming others fair and square. The move may be tough, mean, comical, and hence especially humiliating to his opponents, but it is decidedly not considered perverse and sadistic behavior, as it would be if someone coerced others into befouling themselves in our world. Kjartan is playing a mean and vulgar joke, but the cost of the joke is borne solely by the people of Laugar.

Egil's episode fills in the sketch a little more. Egil clearly shows that even Viking drinking halls had rules of delicacy, though they were pretty minimal: don't cheat in the drinking bouts and don't vomit indoors, especially on your host. The episode also reveals that vomit was disgusting, for being vomited on is so nauseating as to elicit a like return. Disgust is there but the thresholds are quite high, although Egil is able to scale the heights so as to disgust Armod thoroughly and his servants too. They find Egil to be revolting, vile, bestial, no proper man at all. They call him an *undr*, a wonder, which in this setting means a most appallingly disgusting man. Disgust is thus prompted by contact with a contaminating substance, and, more important, by witnessing shameful and disgusting behavior. Disgust is, as among us, a social and moral emotion that enforces norms of proper behavior. The shameful and the disgusting again walk hand in hand.

As in the previous vignette, disgust is also subsumed into the give-and-take of honor and insult. Armod doesn't treat his guests with the dignity they feel themselves entitled to and so they don't treat him with the dignity a proper host deserves. Egil takes the norms of hospitality a little more seriously than most. His reaction is excessive. But as with Swift, who is also extreme in his responses, the basic direction of the response is understandable and very recognizable. Egil, by the way, still did not think himself sufficiently avenged for having been originally served skyr instead of ale. He gouged out Armod's eye the next morning before leaving. Disgusting to us, indeed. Disgusting to Egil? There is more to this scene, but it would take us too far afield. One might note that the norms of hospitality outweighed in the mind of Armod's wife and daughter the obligation to obey the head of household, their husband and father.

Vomit and feces are dangerous and contaminating in the Old Norse world even if they are more present and less hidden than they are among us. Familiarity is not guaranteed to inure us to the disgusting. Urine defiles also, which is why those opposed to Bishop Gudmund would urinate in the wells he had blessed.[10] With Gudmund we escape the Norse world and return to the more "civilized" and Christianized continent where the decorum of the heroic gives way to the morbidness of disease both spiritual and physical. The intersection of saintliness and the disgusting bears looking into briefly. In the *Life of St. Anselm* written by Eadmer, a monk who had first-hand knowledge of his subject, we find the following account (c. 1090):

> There was then a certain nobleman, an active and important man, in the country between Ponthieu and Flanders. His body was afflicted with leprosy, and this caused him the more sorrow as he saw himself despised and deserted even by his own men, despite the dignity of his birth ... Then one night a man appeared to him in a vision, and advised him, if he wished to regain his former health, to go to Bec and to persuade abbot Anselm to give him water to drink, with which he had washed his hands during Mass. He put his trust in the vision and went as he had been advised, without delay. He told Anselm privately why he had come. Anselm was astonished at his words and emphatically admonished him to desist from such a plan. But he persisted in his entreaties, and begged him all the more to have mercy on him and not to suffer him to be deprived of the medicine whence he believed that God had promised him a speedy cure. And what was the result? Pity prevailed over humility, and in the morning Anselm celebrated a private Mass to offer prayer to God for the sick man, who was allowed to be present and received from Anselm's hands the water which he sought. He drank it on the spot, and it restored him from sickness to the most perfect health.[11]

Let me put aside for the moment the revulsion that lepers evoke, which is perfectly understandable to us, and look instead at the one detail that gives us moderns pause. The leper, in a vision, is told to go to Anselm and drink the water in which he has washed his hands during Mass. Anselm is taken aback, astonished at the request. Not because he can't imagine assisting someone doing something so degrading if not quite disgusting, although there is a suggestion that that might be part of the response, but because his request raises a perplexity of inconsistent demands on Anselm's virtue. Pity is at war with humility. The wretched man's condition evokes pity; but how is Anselm to grant his request without claiming sanctity for himself, without succumbing, that is, to the flattery inherent in the request? Norms of modesty, the commitment to humility that drives his particular kind of holiness, drive Anselm to refuse. To accept is too much to play the saint. Imagine the presumption in thinking your body has magical powers solely by the force of the virtue of your own soul.

The healing power of sanctity doesn't operate exclusively in the world of spirit. It requires matter, bodily effluvia, real touching, real ingestion. Cure and purification mimic exactly the disgust-evoking processes of pollution and contamination, except that one heals, the other destroys. Medieval people showed no hesitation in using water others had washed in to wash themselves;[12] but they were not in the habit of drinking the water others had washed in. The leper, in other words, is asking to do something that would degrade himself, hence in fact its healing power. The magic in the ceremony, then, is not just Anselm's to provide. The leper has to debase himself, has to do something disgusting (even if only minimally so) to show he has the proper stance toward Anselm and the miracle he is requesting. So it is not that disgust plays no role here; on the contrary disgust is part of the magic. There is a connection of two beliefs: the holy can heal because the disgusting can pollute. Both owe their magic to the powers of contagion and the surge of emotion—disgust, fear, awe—that such powers evoke.

The holy man to be holy has to worry about his humility and pay it its due before allowing his pity its reign. The leper provides him with the perfect way out: he is disgusting and asks the holy man to participate in a ceremony the latter finds somewhat off-putting.

Whatever flattery there is in the request is balanced by the humbling experience of simply having to deal with this disgusting wretch. Notice, however, that the leper's vision does not require Anselm to touch him. The vision accepts certain limits on the extent to which Anselm's pity will be taxed. Let the leper mimic the style of self-befoulment by drinking the water, so that Anselm can avoid befouling himself by touching the leper. There is no laying on of hands here.

Anselm's holiness maintains a certain decorum; it does not manifest itself in the style of certain disgust-welcoming, self-befouling ways that we associate with St. Francis and the pus-drinking saints of whom more anon. Nor does he make a spectacle of the miracle: he celebrates a private Mass for the leper. Even the leper's self-degradation is decorous, a mere shadow of the performances that would become more general two centuries later. He is not drinking the green mantle from the standing pool but water used to wash the hands of one holy person at a Mass.

Norbert Elias paints a caricatured view of the Middle Ages in which civility was at a minimum and shame and disgust over bodily functions pretty much nonexistent. The vignettes we have examined show that picture is not entirely accurate. Though ubiquitous, excrement was still defiling. And if the omnipresent foul odors of excreta and decay must have led to some inurement to them, inurement was never so complete as to prevent stench, and primarily the stench of excrement and decay, from becoming the defining essence of sin. Sin stank; and therefore hell was imagined as an enormous privy: "What stynk and what corrupcioun, what filthe and what abhominacioun is there [in hell]."[13] Feces is not so familiar as to have its odors cease to appall; familiarity hardly makes it less disgusting for us and we should not expect it to have done so completely for them either; it still was an emblem of foulness and vileness. Nor is it entirely true that this rude age had no shame about the excremental. The virulent and almost panicky attacks on lust, sin, and fleshly vice could hardly have dispensed with the intensification and passion that the language of disgust provided; without recourse to foul odors sermonizing would have been bland fare indeed. And using excrement as part of the diction of cursing makes sense only if it was vile and powerfully magical in its powers of degradation. A notorious example from the late fourteenth century captures the energy that could inform the strange mix of excrement and sacrament in cursing (see the endnote for a translation):

> Thou woldest make me kisse thyn olde breech,
> And swere it were a relyk of a seint,
> Though it were with thy fundement depeint!
> But, by the croys which that Seint Eleyne fond,
> I wolde I hadde thy coillons in myn hond
> In stide of relikes or of seintuarie.
> Lat kutte hem of, I wol thee help hem carie;
> They shul be shryned in an hogges toord.[14]

Excrement was implicated in sin and punishment precisely because it was vile and because it was shameful. Consider Guibert of Nogent's description of a monk whose lethal dysentery comes as punishment for unconfessed sin (c. 1085): "At the moment the abbot came, however, the monk had yielded to the call of nature. Since he could not walk, a cask had been brought for him, and the abbot saw him, in a disgusting condition, sitting on it in pain. After they had stared at one another, the abbot was ashamed at meeting the man in such circumstances."[15] Guibert indicates also that for all the ubiquity of excrement and excreting, that despite the unavailability of privacy, one was to avert one's eyes when confronted with someone answering nature's call. Delicacy may not be quite the word to describe this modest level of aversiveness and circumspection, but the abbot shows some small socially appropriate fastidiousness, as indeed does Guibert himself in his recourse to the euphemism "call of nature."[16] Euphemism shows that we are in the presence of taboo and the danger and disgust that attend it. What Guibert does not feel, however, is that this little story itself shows a certain lack of delicacy. We are still a long way from the time when mere talking about excrement would be deemed inappropriate.

No, they were not just like us about these matters. People were plainly not as circumspect about excretion as we are. Some five hundred years after this account we see that delicacy regarding excretion had a somewhat uneven progress. Elias, quoting passages from handbooks on manners, shows that even sixteenth-century people were tempted not to take great care about such matters. From 1589:

> Let no one, whoever he may be, before, at, or after meals, early or late, foul the staircases, corridors, or closets with urine or other filth, but go to suitable, prescribed places for such relief.[17]

Most surprisingly from 1558:

> It does not befit a modest, honorable man to prepare to relieve nature in the presence of other people, nor to do up his cloths afterward in their presence. Similarly, he will not wash his hands on returning to decent society from private places, as the reason for his washing will arouse disagreeable thoughts in people. For the same reason it is not a refined habit, when coming across something disgusting in the street, as sometimes happens, to turn at once to one's companion and point it out to him. It is far less proper to hold out the stinking thing for the other to smell, as some are wont, who even urge the other to do so, lifting the foul-smelling thing to his nostrils and saying, "I should like to know how much that stinks," when it would be better to say, "Because it stinks do not smell it."[18]

This is not the behavior of eleventh-century gothic benightedness, but takes place in the brilliant lighting of the late Italian Renaissance. Anselm and Guibert were much more decorous. The sixteenth-century instances reveal that there were proper places to go to do one's duty, even if people occasionally had to be prodded to undertake the inconvenience of finding them and accepting them as the *only* permissible indoor places for it. The second passage reveals remarkable warrings of sensibilities. We have people so fastidious that it was better not to wash one's hands after excretion than to remind such people of what one had just been doing by washing them.[19] But we also have people actually picking up disgusting things, presumably turds, in the street and thrusting them under their friends' noses. This behavior already has the air of a studied ironical boorishness, parasitical on prior notions of its social unacceptability. The person doing this is trying to shock and he succeeds, shocking the author of the tract and us too who find such facts illusion-shattering about ages romanticized for us in novels and film.[20]

Remarkable to us is that the jokester's desire to shock has not been sublimated further into verbal jokes, rather than remaining mired in the broad physical comedy that is portrayed in this passage. Feces, for all its presentness, is still worthy of being pointed out in the street; it fascinates and draws attention. No one takes it all that much for granted; Guibert already had felt it necessary to use euphemism to describe it; by Chaucer's time nearly three hundred years later, the word privy means a latrine, a telling euphemism that suggests that some kind of privacy and discretion in these matters was to be striven for. But whatever delicacies are in place they do not prevent certain late-fifteenth-century pilgrims on a sea voyage to Jerusalem from throwing their brimming chamber pots at the candles of their companions whose chattering keeps them awake at night.[21]

Let us return to Anselm. Even in that earlier age of minimal amenity, excrement, vomit, and urine, though omnipresent, were contaminating substances. Feces, and the foul odors associated with excretion, are associated with the stench of sin, but we have also seen that people did not recoil from them in the way we do; contaminating they were, but so unavoidable as to make it impossible to maintain too delicate a stance toward them.[22] The social organization of disgust as it related to bodily substances was mostly subsumed into the moral and social economy of shame and honor, but we can begin to discern it taking on a life of its own. Anselm's miracle involved more than just the difficulty of maintaining saintly humility when being flattered as a saint, it was also about what it meant to be a leper. In the world of the high Middle Ages disgust, in some contexts, grew so large as to break away from the shame that organized it in more routine settings. Intense disgust in this period is not focused on vile substances like excrement but on people who inspire horror, fear, and loathing: the leper, the Jew, the heretic, and, for monks and priests and hence much of the official discourse, women. Let me confine myself to an unconscionably brief treatment of a complex topic and touch on only a few matters concerning lepers and Jews.[23]

Lepers were the most polluting of beings; unlike Jews, who could pass unless identified with special badges and apparel, they disgusted on sight. Even high rank did not save the leper who sought out Anselm from being abandoned by friends and kin. Regulations required lepers to put themselves downwind of those they spoke to; they were forbidden to go into narrow lanes lest others be forced to pass close to them; they were not allowed to touch children or give them anything; they were banned from all company except that of other lepers. The English jurist Bracton, writing in the thirteenth century, indicates that a leper can be denied his claim for inheritance if "he is so deformed that the sight of him is insupportable."[24] Their grotesque appearance and the stench of their rotting flesh made lepers disgusting and horrifying, uncanny in the way of cadavers. These were the living dead and in fact were ritually separated from the community by a ceremony that mimicked the rite for the dead; yet because they still walked they were compelled, hauntingly, to announce their approach with their mandated bell or clapper.

If not excrement then lepers, and if lepers couldn't give the requisite amount of disgust to provide the contrast so as to distinguish the pure from the impure, then leprosy could be extended to include Jews and heretics. "Jews were also held to resemble . . . lepers in being associated with filth, stench and putrefaction, in exceptional sexual voracity . . . and in the menace which they presented . . . to the wives and children of honest Christians."[25] In France in 1321 Jews were alleged to have joined with lepers in a conspiracy to poison wells.[26] The association between Jews and lepers was still alive and well in the eighteenth century, when Voltaire could write that "the Jews were more subject to leprosy than any other people living in hot climates, because they had neither linen, nor domestic baths. These people were so negligent of cleanliness and the decencies of life that their legislators were obliged to make a law to compel them even to wash their hands."[27]

But one might distinguish a difference of emphasis between the disgusts and styles of loathing prompted by Jews and those prompted by lepers. More than lepers, who were associated with rotting flesh and cadavers, Jews were associated with excrement and menstrual blood. Such was the Christian demonization of the Jew—and the uncomprehending Christian horror of circumcision—that the Jewish male was believed to menstruate.[28] Jewish men were thus feminized and all women were thus Judaized to make both more disgusting, more dangerous than they had been before. Without pushing the distinction too far one might notice that physical disgust at appalling sights and odors of lepers led to a belief in their moral loathsomeness; whereas the Jew's assumed moral loathsomeness led to a belief that his body must then be as disfigured as his soul. So the Jew was believed to stink.[29] He smelled of the excrement that was the true substance of the money he lent;[30] he smelled of sex and women because of his diabolical desire for Christian flesh and blood. He was Dracula before Count Dracula, that eastern European with hooked nose, was ever embodied in the Western imagination.

Disgust figures in the hatred of Jews in ingenious ways. In 1215 the Church declared the doctrine of transubstantiation—the belief that Eucharistic bread and wine are transformed into the Real Presence of Christ—to be dogma. This doctrine continued to meet resistance throughout the medieval period and was centrally at issue in the Reformation. With the doctrine came new grounds for attacking Jews, who were now accused of desecrating the Host, the very body and blood of Christ. They were said to have shat on it, spat on it, burned it, driven nails into it, among other things. Lester Little points out the Christian projection onto Jews of their own doubts regarding the doctrine.[31] These were more than mere doubts, for the doubts informed an almost hallucinogenic disgust. The disgust is with cannibalism, with having to eat and drink human flesh and blood to be a good Christian.[32] This is not my projection but their thoughts on the matter: "If thou [were to] see in liknesse of fleisch and blood that blessed sacrament, thou schuldest lothen and abhorren it to resseyve it into thy mouth."[33] If the doctrine of transubstantiation compelled Christians to eat a Jew and drink his blood then Christians repaid the favor by imagining that Jews were doing the same to Christians.[34] The doctrine also puts each communicant in the self-befouling condition of the leper in Eadmer's story of Anselm. One must ingest holy contaminants—blood and flesh—to be cured and saved. One must eat that which no one would eat in his right mind, or right state of health. The materialism of the doctrine is remarkable in its implicit admission of the doubtfulness of purely spiritual cures.

In a moral and spiritual regime in which humility was a virtue and in which suffering had moral value in its own right, the leper could actually be envied. Precisely because he revolted you, because he raised your gorge, because he smelled and was grotesquely ugly, you feared he stood well ahead of you in the race for future bliss. His hell, or at least his purgatory, was in this life. Yours was still to come unless you could degrade yourself as fortune had degraded the leper. His condition was a goal to strive for because he was so offensive to your sensibility. One monk in order to expiate his sins prayed for leprosy. His prayer was answered.[35] Inevitably, God seems more willing to grant our prayers requesting victory in negative lotteries than in positive ones. And if God didn't give you the disease you could immerse yourself in the horror of the disgusting by caring for lepers, by kissing them and washing and dressing their running sores. No one, however, envied the Jew or prayed to become one. The loathsomeness of the Jew gained him nothing but pogroms and death; the leper's got him eternal life.

Humility is a virtue that can't work its way out of a psychological paradox it always finds itself in. If the granting of rewards is based on how humble you are, then you find yourself in a system in which the attainment of humility provides the means for being looked up to by others and thus for knowing yourself superior to those who are looking up to you. You become proud of your humility and enjoy the payoff of winning the humility contest. Anselm was already painfully aware that sanctity put humility at risk, and also that it was humility that brought sanctity. But Anselm was restrained and decorous. As a person who had to administer abbeys and eventually episcopal sees, he knew that virtues sometimes compromise one another.

The quest for humility, however, eventually led to an escalating competition for greater humility because an easy humility was inevitably suspect as not being enough of a test of virtue. And when you could look with loathing at lepers you knew in your heart that you were not cast down as they were, that you were not looked upon as they were, and that nothing could ever be more humiliating than to be seen as you had seen them. The quest for humility, the struggle to show oneself with absolutely no pride in one's wealth, beauty, rank, made for some strange behaviors and perverse incentives. Above all it led to a cultivation of the disgusting, to that behavior which if successful would so revolt those who might be tempted to admire your humility as to send them running away with their hands over their mouths. Without the notion of the disgusting firmly in place, the strategies for humility and self-abasement which we are about to discuss would have made no sense.

Let me present rather fully an incident from the life of St. Catherine of Siena, c. 1370, some two and one-half centuries after Anselm. A sick nun had a cancer on her breast that put forth such an awful stench that no one would attend her in her sickness. Catherine volunteered to care for her but one day "when she was about to open the sore to dress it there came out such an horrible stench, that she could hardly bear it, but that she must needs vomit."[36] Catherine was upset at her own squeamishness and resolved to overcome it. "She bowed down and held her mouth and nose over the sore so long until at the length it seemed that she had comforted her stomach and quite overcome the squeamishness she felt before." The sick woman was quite disconcerted by this behavior and begged Catherine to stop inhaling the "infectious savor." From this point on the sick woman began to dislike Catherine. At first just annoyed, she came to loathe her, slandering her and believing that whenever the "holy maid was anywhere out of her sight . . . that she was about some foul act of fleshly pleasure." The loathsomeness of the patient's suppuration tested Catherine in one way, the slanders in another: one to overcome her disgust, the other to overcome indignation at such ingratitude and false accusation.

Catherine persevered and the woman literally saw the light and begged her forgiveness, but the devil was not yet finished. He still had some say in the reactions of her stomach. On another occasion when she was dressing the old woman's sore the stench again overpowered her and she vomited. Catherine, seeing that it was the work of the serpent, nonetheless took "an earnest displeasure against her own flesh," which she addressed as follows: "I shall make thee not only to endure the savor of it, but also to receive it within thee. With that she took all the washing of the sore, together with the corrupt matter and filth; and going aside put it all into a cup, and drank it up lustily. And in so doing, she overcame at one time, both the squeamishness of her own stomach and malice of the Devil." That night Christ came to her in a dream, and in reward for drinking pus, by which she "despised the delight of the flesh, cast behind [her] back the opinion of the world, and utterly subdued [her] own nature," he drew her mouth to the wound on his side and let her drink her fill.[37]

How does one explain this kind of devotional exercise? Part of it is the ratcheting up, in the manner of an arms race, of the moves in the competition for humility: "You did that? Well, match this!" Part of it is the unnatural end of an obsession with fleshly mortification when it meets the grimmer suggestions of the doctrine of transubstantiation: drinking and eating the body.[38] And part of it is the consequence of desperately seeking to overcome the bind inherent in the virtue of humility: indulge a loathsomeness so mortifying, so shamefully degrading that no pride in the attainment of humility could ever rationally compensate for the misery endured to attain it. And so she "cast behind [her] back the opinion of the world."

Catherine positively courted the disgusting because in the pursuit of humility it was the last barrier to test the level of one's commitment, to test just how far one would go in giving up on the deepest held, most fundamental norms of bodily dignity, inviolability, and self-respect. Even in the Middle Ages, with its presumably high thresholds of disgust, disgust-backed norms were the hardest to violate. One simply did not drink pus, even back then.[39] One can fornicate in spite of strictures of disgust and shame because pleasure is the draw and everyone knows that pleasure and disgust battle back and forth, now one, now the other gaining the upper hand and sometimes even colluding in joint ventures. But licking suppurating sores?

What must one really do if one wanted to overcome the claims of the body? Celibacy was the usual strategy, but too many people were celibate and they had cheapened the currency of that virtue. Celibacy, in fact, raised the stakes of the kind of bodily violation that enticed Catherine. Celibacy obsesses on the purity of the body, on valuing it so highly as not to let it come into contact with the contaminating bodily emissions of sex. Moreover, a rational calculator of one's own interest could figure that eternal life was worth a life of sexual denial and seek support in communities that would keep one tied to the mast of the vow. But the sexual urge was nothing compared to the aversive reflex of drinking pus. And who could ever be claimed to have pursued such a policy rationally? One does not do such a thing by rational calculation.[40] One has either to be inspired or to have a gun to one's head. And even if Catherine's behavior was hardly disinterested, such an egregious violation of disgust rules seemed to purge interest of its dross. Catherine devised a strategy that only the elect few could ever have the commitment to adhere to; for the time being at least its currency had not been debased (it eventually would be, as even this kind of devotion became old hat).[41] The difference between us and the Middle Ages is not the capacity to feel disgust. Catherine's behavior is intelligible only if disgust is a very active part of her and everyone else's life. She hit on the one bodily substance that few if any had ever thought of as a source of pleasure. Yet for her, paradoxically, it was a pleasure. It got her what she wanted and she knew it: "she could not remember that she had ever eaten or drunk such a pleasant or delicate meat or drink."

She was striving for sanctity, no small honor indeed. And she was successful in her own lifetime at attracting attention and honor. She gathered disciples and lectured popes. Not everyone, in other words, was appalled by her actions, or more precisely, not all those who were appalled thought that a reason to condemn her; many thought it a basis for praise. Yet the sick women dying of repulsive diseases whom she cared for were quite frequently tempted by the devil to chafe under Catherine's care and sorely resent her. Although they benefited from her attention they apparently were able to discern that she had more on her mind than caring for them, that they in fact had become props in her play. They also doubted whether anyone so able to overcome disgust could ever be as sexually chaste as she purported to be: it was hardly unreasonable for Catherine's patient to think the "holy maid was . . . about some foul act of fleshly pleasure" whenever she was out of her sight, considering the manifest pleasure Catherine learned to take in the odors of her patient's rotting flesh and diseased body. Even a very flattering hagiography can't quite eliminate the just bases of her enemies' suspicions of her motives. They sensed the self-dramatization and they knew that her effacement of the flesh meant a most willful obsession with it.

Jesus too remarks on her will, but praises her for it: "thou hast ... utterly subdued your own nature." Jesus apparently understands nature to reside in the human gag reflex and the instinctive recoil in the face of the disgusting. It takes no mean act of will to overcome that, and Catherine's vision seems to suggest that Jesus indeed recognizes that her action was more demanding than his passion. Note that Jesus did not command her to drink pus. That was her own idea; she did it out of anger and disgust for having vomited when she was putting on a show of sufferance and endurance. He only ratified her behavior afterwards.

Catherine was remarkable in her day and her story is remarkable in ours, but not quite for the same reason. Both to us and to her contemporaries her story makes no sense without a keen sense of disgust. On that point we and her contemporaries agree. The difference is that our rules for the appropriate violation and overcoming of those norms are different. Both cultures found pus loathsome and gag inducing. Only one had a theory of sanctity or was committed to a notion of humility in which it could even remotely make sense to drink it. We would send Catherine to a mental institution. Many in Catherine's own time would concur and others were very suspicious of her motives. But there was an official ideology which could give sense to Catherine's actions and link her behavior to other behaviors—self-flagellation, self-denial, self-mortification—that were more mainstream or at least part of well-known saintly narratives set in different times and different places which were supposed to elicit awe in the faithful, even though they were not quite meant to give them a pattern for rote imitation. Pus drinking is something we are not prepared to do even in the name of love, while most other bodily fluids have some place of varying respectability in love. Love will drive us to care for the ill, even a professional calling will do that, but some things remain beyond the overcomable for the sane. We might say that Catherine simply drinks pus out of love of God and thus her behavior confirms our view of love as a suspension and in some cases an overcoming of disgust.

With lepers, Jews, and Catherine's self-befoulments, disgust, though still bound up with shame, comes to take on a life of its own, ex-

panding greatly the bit part it played in heroic culture. Shame, as
before, remains public and organizes relations, among the respectable.
It is about honor in public life. Disgust works to support shame in
public settings but it has a more private and secret life, working in
darker places. Disgust, in effect, starts to make the private possible.
It extends beyond the arena of social ranking and public presentation
of self to include one's stance toward life, death, one's own body,
relations between the sexes, and God. Disgust, as embodied and visceral a passion as there is, comes to support a metaphysics of the
physical in a way shame did not, in spite of shame's connection to
female sexuality and bodily decorum. Disgust is at home with the
politics of pollution and purity, and so it is hardly surprising that
Christianity, with its obsessive anti-sexuality and great ambivalence
toward the body, should have made disgust central to the faith by
adopting the doctrine of the Real Presence in the Eucharist; or that
devotion should have taken leave of reticence and decorum and produced a Catherine, who nonetheless remained enough immersed in
the world of honor and shame as to wish to make her devotions awe-
eliciting public spectacles.

Catherine concocted her witch's brew of the most vile and gorge-
raising ingredients more than two centuries before the weird sisters
announced to the world their own special recipe. Rather than *Mac-
beth*, our text is a variant version from Webster's *The Duchess of
Malfi*, in which the stage melancholic berates an old woman for being
old and for painting herself so as to disguise it:

Bosola. You come from painting now?
Old Lady. From what?
Bos. Why, from scurvy face-physic. To behold thee not painted in-
clines somewhat near a miracle . . .
Old Lady. It seems you are well acquainted with my closet.
Bos. One would suspect it for a shop of witchcraft, to find in it the
fat of serpents, spawn of snakes, Jews' spittle, and their young
children's ordure; and all these for the face. I would sooner eat a
dead pigeon taken from the sole of the feet of one sick of the
plague than kiss one of you fasting. Here are two of you whose
sin of your youth is the very patrimony of the physician . . . I do
wonder you do not loathe yourselves. (2.1)[42]

The theme of the loathly lady here unites witches, Jews, sloughs, vermin, excrement, leprosy, syphilis, and sex. Face painting turns out to be a perverse reenactment of Catherine's self-befoulments with all the meanings inverted. What Catherine is willing to swallow as self-mortifying contaminants, more worldly women resort to smearing on as cosmetic cures and disguises.[43] Medieval and Renaissance disgust, if not completely driven by unrelenting misogyny, surely is never very far from it. Leprosy gives way to syphilis and both diseases were felt to be linked with sexual voracity and thus with women and Jews.[44] There rages a veritable epidemic of disgust, loathing, and self-loathing: hatred of sex, of growth, of ripeness and aging, hatred of life itself, all of which is vile and loathsome because it must truck with decay, putrefaction, and death. But because sex and reproduction are at the core of this depressing economy of disgust, women bear the brunt of it.

It takes a lot of wishful thinking to see women as carving out their own productive and positive spaces within this poisoned atmosphere. Catherine may be engaging in a specifically female type of devotion, but at what cost? The price is the destruction of her body. She eats so little as to be amenorrheic (she eventually starves herself to death), winds an iron chain so tightly around her hips as to score and inflame her skin,[45] and parodies maternal caring by making the indulgence of disgust the desired end, not an unavoidable cost, of nursing the sick and dying. The witch's brew the more worldly women paint with, even in the eyes of a misogynistic preachy melancholic moralist, is never more than a means to an end. Worldly women's forays into the realm of the disgusting are purely rational given the shallowness of the men they seek to deceive. Yet both Catherine and the worldly women, each in their way, seek to escape nature's sentence by a kind of mithridatic indulgence in substances marked as disgusting. How much more refreshing the aggressiveness of heroic culture.

The Lexicon of Disgust

Shakespeare does not use the word disgust. Yet his tragedies are incomprehensible without a very strong notion of it. Hamlet's self-reproaches and reproaches, Lear's rages, Poor Tom, the weird sisters, Yorick's skull, and Lear's, Hamlet's, and Iago's misogyny and sexual loathing are all disgust-driven and disgust-producing, but without the word. The witches' brew, a grossly comic indulgence in the horror of disgust and the uncanny, mixes up a recipe of the disgusting that needs little translation to trigger the sentiments in us that it was meant to trigger back then. It rounds up what for us are the usual suspects: the foreign, the Other, gruesome images of birth, death, growth, and decay; suggestions of sexual surfeit, standing water, cloacae, sliminess, dismemberment and deformity, bodily orifices, even a Jew who desecrates the Host:

> Liver of blaspheming Jew
> Gall of goat, and slips of yew
> Slivered in the moon's eclipse,
> Nose of Turk and Tartar's lips,
> Finger of birth-strangled babe
> Ditch-delivered by a drab. (*Macbeth* 4.1.26–31)

But disgust without the word disgust is not quite the same; the words we have and the words we choose to describe things help structure our world, help constitute the very thing spoken of. It thus makes some difference whether the concept at issue is designated as the disgusting rather than the foul or the loathsome or the abominable. A caveat: I am looking for differences between pre-disgust disgust and our disgust and in fact there are some, but it may be that these differences pale beside the continuities observable in the broad category of the disgusting as it developed in the last thousand years in the West. St. Catherine and Anselm were not insensible to things we would find disgusting, and the relatively late witches' brew has little to teach the modern maker of horror films.

First let us consider briefly the specific vocabulary of disgust before the word disgust. The words used to describe reactions to the disgusting break into two main groupings. The groupings reflect the two broad types of disgust I delineated earlier: that of Freudian reaction formation with disgust working to obscure desire and to prevent indulgence, and that of surfeit with disgust following upon thoroughly indulged desires. In the first group are the notions of abomination, abhorrence, fastidiousness, squeamishness, loathsomeness, odiousness, and irksomeness. In this group I would also include early interjections like pah, fie, fut. In the second group are rankness, surfeit, fulsomeness, cloyingness, and the late mawkishness, among others.

It would be too taxing of the reader's patience to give a full picture of each of these words, but a cursory account is in order. Take abomination. To us, this word conjures up biblical fulmination against sodomy and other things that exasperated and disgusted that eminently exasperable God of the Old Testament. In Middle English abomination is used as a medical term to mean nausea: "The pacient feleth abhominacioun . . . and ache in the mouth of the stomak."[46] It is then generalized to refer to loathsome, odious, or disgusting actions that would trigger such responses.

As is often the case, the etymology has a story worth telling. Abomination comes from Latin *ab* + *omen*, registering horror at a bad omen, which when spelled with an h, abhominable, as in Middle English, was incorrectly understood to have derived its sense from "away from man," meaning inhuman. The misunderstanding underscores the intense sense of aversion and repulsion indicated by the word.[47] The spelling is put in issue by Shakespeare in *Love's Labour's Lost:* "I abhor . . . such rackers of orthography as to speak . . . 'det' when he should pronounce 'debt'—d, e, b, t, not d, e, t . . . This is abhominable, which he would call 'abominable' " (5.1.17–21). Like abomination, abhor was used to register the type of aversion we associate with the physical cringe and recoil of disgust. Recall the passage quoted earlier from Wycliffe on transubstantiation: "If thou were to see in liknesse of fleisch and blood that blessed sacrament, thou schuldest lothen and abhorren it to resseyve it into thy mouth."

To loathe and abhor: the first is the common, the second the more learned word for disgust. The conception of disgust was primarily formulated around loathing and loathsomeness. The notion of loathing narrowed its range once the word disgust came to occupy some of its turf. But for the English speaker of the thirteenth through sixteenth centuries, it captured all the things that elicit yucks from us. Unlike disgust, however, loathing was not as an etymological matter partial to any one sense. In fact taste was rather less likely to trigger loathing than ugliness. Even sounds could be loathsome.[48] Loathsomeness united all that was ugly, foul, hateful, hideous, and centered it in the visceral sensation of recoil, cringe, and regurgitation.

Abhor, abominate, loathe are not all that surprising to us. They have changed their registers or their range, but they still cut across significant areas of disgust to this day. Other words have had a different course; some simply faded into oblivion. By the end of the fifteenth century few if anyone still understood what the word wlate meant, but it too could refer to nausea or more generally to those moral failings which generated loathing and abhorrence.[49] The word irk had as its core sense in the fourteenth century the notion of tiresomeness, boredom, annoyance, much as today, but it also was used to gloss Latin *fastidium*, that is, nausea. From one cookbook of the late sixteenth century we have that overeating medlar pears will "extremely irck, and loath you,"[50] with both irk and loath meaning nauseate. If irk's range of reference shrank, fastidious virtually began to mean its opposite. In the sixteenth century it referred to the sensations of nausea and disgust, but by the eighteenth century it had come to mark the trait of being too concerned to avoid the disgusting and the nauseating.[51]

Interjections, such as Lear's pahs and fies, and Hamlet's pah at smelling Yorick's skull, give us a nice way of recognizing the presence of the visceral aspects of disgust even in the absence of a rich discussion of the sensation. One pah is worth a thousand words and tells us just how serious Hamlet's observation regarding Yorick's skull is: "And now how abhorred in my imagination it is! My gorge rises at it" (5.1.175). Yet even with rising gorge he still bothers to lift the skull to his nose! Have we here another instance of ambivalence toward the disgusting, another tale of aversion and allure, or rather evidence of the culturally conditioned higher disgust thresholds of an earlier time, in which the aversive, though unambivalently aversive, could still be endured for the sake of speechifying on the pointlessness of human existence? Hamlet is consciously engaging in a broad vulgar comedy when he sniffs at Yorick's skull, vulgar comedy not unlike that of the nameless man in the street we met above who lifted "the foul-smelling thing to his friend's nostrils . . . saying, 'I should like to know how much that stinks.' " Hamlet is mocking his own sententiousness while still continuing to make the point he mocks. There is not much doubt that the smells of rotting flesh horrified people in the Middle Ages as today; but these foul odors were not easily avoidable given the locations and manner of maintaining graveyards, to say nothing of the smells of animals and animal slaughter.[52]

Interjections bear meaning. One would like to know the socio- and psycholinguistics behind our using yuck rather than phew or ach or various other expressions that have no convenient orthographic representation.[53] In Shakespeare, the pah seems less studied, more visceral, almost involuntarily extorted by the disgusting thing. The fie, in contrast, serves to admonish as well as to register aversion; it is more consciously controlled and thus somewhat less interjectional than pah. Fie serves at shame's altar first; but it knows disgust too in the same way that shame does. By doubling and redoubling pahs and fies Lear can posture as being so disgusted as to be beyond speech, the interjections serving to buy time in order to recover his diction: "Fie, fie, fie, pah, pah."

The disgust that comes of surfeit has always prompted rich diction from moralists inveighing against gluttony and luxury and enraged at the pleasures of others or from melancholic souls chagrined at the costs of pleasure. Medicine and morals mix as the word surfeit comes to indicate both excessive indulgence and the morbid condition that is the effect of having so excessively indulged. Rankness, which begins non-pejoratively by indicating force and vigor in growth, soon comes to indicate excessive growth and then the smell of such excessiveness and the rot and decay that are its consequence. The history of the word rank mimics the biological processes it eventually found to be foul and loathsome. Just like life itself, the sense of the word is born in vigor, health, and forcefulness, flourishes, and then begins to choke itself in luxury before it sickens amid odors of rot and decay.[54] The history of fulsome is somewhat different from that of rank. It begins in abundance and after a very short time comes to mark all the miseries of surfeit and rankness: nauseating, cloying, foul-smelling, disgusting, loathsome. But these unhappy meanings are pruned back so that among us fulsome survives in the less gorge-raising sense of marking a certain style of bad taste: the overdoing of a good thing.

Taste figures rather differently in this older lexicon of disgust than it does in ours. What makes food a matter for disgust in their world was not its foul taste but its good taste; and the same inversion holds for touch, where it was that sense's pleasures, not its displeasures, that prompted disgust.[55] Touch, like eating, got enmeshed in the disgusting as a consequence of too much of a good thing: to the physical woes of the always tardy disgust of surfeit were added the spiritual woes of deadly sin. So closely connected were the vices of gluttony and lust—the former, as we have seen, leading to and assisting the latter—that Aquinas could understand gluttony to be about the "pleasures of touch."[56]

The medieval and pre-modern emphasis is rather different from ours. To be sure surfeit of food and sex generates disgust for us as it did for them, but their disgust is for failures of the spirit in the face of pleasures of the flesh; our disgust is for failures of the flesh to be pleasured as advertised. They worried about mistaking the mere means necessary for maintaining life—food and fornication—with the proper end of life, usually understood to be the love of God or salvation. We worry more about the disgusting look and feel of human fat that might interfere with more feeding and fornicating. I do not mean to suggest that they were deeper for having their disgust regarding taste and touch conceptualized differently than ours. We might, for instance, have good cause to suspect that their concern with salvation was not always much less self-indulgent than the sins of the flesh that stood in their way to it.

Oral incorporation was, undeniably, a significant feature of pre-modern disgust, but not in the way disgust theorists following Darwin would have it. Oral incorporation raised the moral issue of gluttony more than it raised the bodily protective issue of rejecting foul-tasting substances. I do not want to overstate the case; medieval people expressed keen aversion to the idea of putting certain things in their mouths. Neither Catherine of Siena nor the resistance to the doctrine of transubstantiation would make sense if the quality as well as the quantity of what was being ingested were not a crucial part of the disgusting. It is not that pre-modern people did not recognize the gorge-raising capacities of various substances in the eating as well as in the looking at or the smelling of them; it is simply that they conceptualized disgust without privileging foul taste.

One cannot help noticing, however, an increasing concern with taste that begins to make itself felt in the seventeenth century. Can it be coincidence that the word disgust appears roughly contemporaneously with the expansion of the meaning of the word taste to name a newly recognized general capacity of refinement, a discernment for style? And doesn't this new sense of good and bad taste depend on a correlative notion of disgust, which turns out to be true "taste" itself? Such a view would track rather closely Bourdieu's reading of Kant which claims that "pure taste," that is, the aesthetic capacity, is "purely negative in its essence." It discerns what is to be refused and avoided; it is above all a "disgust that is often called 'visceral' (it 'makes one sick' or 'makes one vomit') for everything that is 'facile.' "[57] Disgust is thus the pure aesthetic taste, the capacity to judge and recognize the tawdry, the cheap, the fulsome. It rejects the easy pleasure of the senses, the taste of the tongue, preferring instead the more demanding.

A distinction is made then between the taste of reflection and the taste of sense, the former being rare, a talent, a cultivation, the latter being easy and tending to excess and surfeit. The vulgar are those given to the excessive, the cloying, the fulsome and facile; the refined are those who can discern vulgarity and reject it in advance by the mechanism of good taste, which is disgust. Taste thus manifests itself by refusing, by turning away in disgust, by recoiling at that which bears the marks of the vulgar, easy, cloying, and cheap. The disgusting is that which poses no resistance; it is the easy, that which just happens unless we cultivate and train to avoid and to reject it; it is the path of least resistance, the allure of sinking back into the belly. More precisely, the disgust of the refined, their good taste, is a revulsion at other people's lack of taste; it is revulsion, in other words, toward the unrefined who are able to indulge and not experience disgust. This resembles the horror of surfeit that the Jacobean melancholic had for the epidemics of copulation that took place before his eyes.

Let me sketch this out a bit further. The word disgust is a seventeenth-century entrant into English, which follows fast on the heels of its appearance in French in the mid-sixteenth century.[58] There was no shortage of words at the time devoted to the various manifestations of disgust, as we have just seen. Shakespeare did not appear to miss the term. But the importation of disgust seems to be part of the general trend that saw the sixteenth century extend the meanings of words like rank, fulsome, surfeit beyond their benigner sense of excessiveness into the more malign sense of nauseating, cloying, and loathsome. It seems that the disgusting was becoming more a matter for refined articulation during the course of the sixteenth century so that by the mid-seventeenth century English would have a surfeit of terms to indicate these particular kinds of displeasures and aversions.

There is a certain attractiveness to the suggestion that the notion of taste as a capacity for refined discernment gave rise to a taste-based word to describe its "negative essence," that is, disgust. The gust in disgust was very early on, in both English and French, not a narrow reference to the sense of taste as in the sensation of food and drink, but an homage to the broader, newly emerging idea of "good taste."[59] The new expanded taste was about distinction, class, education, wealth, talent; it was the ability to reject the ugly in art, architecture, speech, and dress, to disapprove of glib music and poetry; in short the new taste was no less promiscuous than the old way of conceptualizing disgust had been as far as its capacity to engage all the senses.[60] With the emergence of good taste disgust was called on to police ever more refined distinctions as the civilizing process claimed new turf for matters of propriety, civility, and privacy.

The Civilizing Process

It is a trait of great works to be able to be proven wrong in particulars and still manage to offer a truth about the larger picture that would not have been achievable if all the particulars were right. Many feel such is the case with Freud and Foucault, and such is indeed the case with Norbert Elias's *The Civilizing Process*. Medievalists resent the caricatured picture of a vulgar uninhibited childlike medieval people that Elias takes as his starting point, and medievalists can prove it to be a partial and flawed account.[61] All my examples from the first section of this chapter show more disgust, euphemism, and delicacy in the Middle Ages than Elias would allow, and more is evident in Anselm in the eleventh century than in Catherine in the fourteenth. Other cultural historians may wonder that Elias's entire two volumes barely mention the church or religion except to dismiss their effect in the civilizing process.[62] Yet despite these gaps and shortcomings his work remains a powerful account of a process by which an emotional economy changed over the course of six hundred years, from one in which embarrassment and disgust played a small role to one in which they dominated the inner life of the courtly and upper bourgeois orders.

Elias's story is one in which changes in social structure, primarily in the structures of dependence and relationship among people, have necessary consequences for emotional life. The refashioning of medieval warriors into Renaissance and seventeenth-century courtiers, he claims, makes them less labile in their moods, less prone to great swings in emotional display, more moderate, restrained, and "civilized." Elias writes the Freudian developmental story of the individual psyche onto a social and historical process in which the childlike exuberance of medieval man is metamorphosed into the decorous repressed style of the contemporary bourgeois adult. Sanctions that once relied on public ridicule and the actual presence of disapproving others become internalized so that the social is transformed into the psychological. The outer restraint becomes an inner restraint with the effect that it ceases to be perceived as convention and is felt as the workings of nature itself. As regards exposure of the body and performance of natural functions he writes that first

> it becomes a distasteful offense to show oneself exposed in any way before those of higher or equal rank; with inferiors it can even be a sign of benevolence. Then, as all become socially more equal, it slowly becomes a general offense. The social reference of shame and embarrassment recedes more and more from consciousness. Precisely because the social command not to show oneself exposed or performing natural functions now operates with regard to everyone and is imprinted in this form on the child, it seems to the adult a command of his own inner self and takes on the form of a more or less total and automatic self-restraint. (139)

This development has far-reaching consequences; for one, much of the teaching of social control moves from public spaces into the home. The entire civilizing process represents a shrinking, a cramming back in, so that what was once publicly performable and pub-licly sanctionable becomes only privately performable (and some-times not even that) and internally sanctioned by conscience, by guilt, embarrassment, and disgust. One interesting effect of this process that Elias recognizes is that childhood becomes psychologically dis-tinguishable from adulthood, since adulthood comes to be marked by the repression of precisely those behaviors that are now understood to be sufferable only in children. One can see an intriguing impli-cation in Elias's theory. Rather than childhood, the cult of the child, being an invention of the eighteenth century as the common story runs, in Elias's scheme it is adulthood which is invented. Adulthood is the new state, characterized by new repressed behaviors. Medieval people had all been undifferentiated children in their lack of restraint.

Elias stresses that his account is one of emotions affected by social structure. The civilizing process witnesses grand changes in the emo-tional economy of court society. Civilization requires the lowering of the thresholds of disgust and embarrassment, that is, it requires the easier triggering of these emotions. But civilization requires more than just greater amounts of disgust and embarrassment; it requires that these emotions govern specific domains that heretofore were ungoverned by them. Eating, blowing the nose, farting, excreting, become areas subject to embarrassment and disgust. Complex rule-governed behavior starts to emerge around eating and care of the nose.

Consider the nose. From a fifteenth-century conduct book we have "It is unseemly to blow your nose into the tablecloth" (144). By the sixteenth century the counsel governs the proper disposition of hand-kerchiefs: "Nor is it seemly, after wiping your nose, to spread out your handkerchief and peer into it as if pearls and rubies might have fallen out of your head" (145). By the end of the seventeenth century it becomes difficult for conduct books even to talk about a topic now deemed too embarrassing to discuss in graphic detail. Instead the advice focuses on the proper euphemisms for indicating the behavior: "As this expression 'blowing the nose' gives a very disagreeable im-pression, ladies ought to call this a pocket handkerchief, as one says neckerchief, rather than a handkerchief for blowing the nose" (146). By the late eighteenth century all details are avoided: "You should observe, in blowing your nose, all the rules of propriety and clean-liness" (148). The process has not stopped. Handkerchiefs have now given way to Kleenex. What once was to be put back into the pocket, washed and reused, became too disgusting for some to endure and so arose the disposable handkerchief named Kleenex so as to reference the purity norms its marketing success would depend upon.

Different emotions play their parts at different stages of the norm-internalizing process. First social control depends upon public sham-ing and the instillation of embarrassability: Don't blow your nose on the tablecloth; that is what peasants would do. Next come more re-fined rules of practice so as to avoid embarrassment. And at the end of the process the code of conduct is held in place not by embar-rassability so much as by disgust, which makes the entire subject too upsetting even to be talked about. The process is less one of a move-ment from shame to guilt than one of the replacement of shaming sanctions by internalized disgust rules. Shame pushes the expulsive back inside and disgust holds it there under lock and key. Shame is crucial to gaining the next piece of turf, disgust secures it, keeping it repressed. The move from shame to disgust tracks exactly the move from public to private, from external to internal, from child to adult, from expulsive to repressive. It also is a story that supports the de-velopment of good taste, which, as we saw, was a function of a refined and generous application of the disgust response to the behaviors and preferences of others. Note also that once the disgust mechanism is firmly in place people come to understand the practices they recog-nize as conventional as being wisely hygienic. The "argument by hygiene" obviously does not account for the origin or selection of these practices; it is simply a reflection of the success of the psycho-logical and social mechanisms upholding them. The hygiene argu-ment is a way of decorously discussing disgust.[63]

There are several ironies that inform Elias's account. The first is that he can tell the story at all. The repressive mechanisms that made it impossible to discuss the details of bodily behaviors that had been discussible in the sixteenth century were not such as to prevent Nor-bert Elias's book. There are ways within the rules of the repressive regime that disgust maintains to let the repressed return to see the sunlight. One way is via low comedy and dirty jokes, which allow some release but are not acceptable to people of taste like Elias. For him, the form of release is the quotation mark. This is the refined scholar's safety valve. And then there is simply the dispassionate tone of the scholarly style that seeks a flat, authoritative, clinical tone, without the flatness taking on the charm of deadpan wit. Elias never breaks with decorum which shows that we have rules even amid repression that allow us to speak of these things in certain subcultures as long as certain criteria are met.

Even then some subjects remain taboo. Women, for instance, are barely present in Elias's account except as early guardians of the civilized style. He simply cannot imagine women blowing their noses on the tablecloth or spitting on the floor and rubbing out the spit with their shoes. No mention is made of the process of privatizing the handling of menses; or had women already subjected themselves to a civilizing process in that regard long before the men ever managed to restrain their own bodily behaviors? Elias seems too embarrassed to take these issues on.[64] Thinking of women in this way is too disgusting. Women can therefore only enter the account once the civilizing process has feminized men enough so that the general level of deportment for men *and* women is such that women's table manners and nose care can be talked about without embarrassment. Women thus only appear when we reach the seventeenth century.

The concept of good and bad taste, as we have seen, necessitates a correlative concept of disgust structured in a certain way, a disgust conceived of as a faculty of the most refined discernment. Disgust, however, does not necessitate the concept of good and bad taste. But it does have a necessary relation to the concepts of cleanness and purity that holds across cultures and time. When by Elias's theory disgust thresholds become lower and disgust is thus more easily triggered we should expect some corresponding movements in the applicability of the notions of purity and cleanness. Purity and cleanness were expanding their domain into regions which had not raised the specter of impurity before. These areas were by Elias's account those which had to do with table manners and the public presentability of the body.

But I want to examine Elias's notion of the *expansion* of disgust and embarrassment and the necessary correlative expansion of notions of cleanness and purity. Is there some kind of conservation of cleanness at work here? Does the new expansion into areas of bodily cleanness mean abandoning other areas which now become ritually insignificant? It is not as if ascetics in the style of St. Catherine who mortified the flesh by drinking pus or by wearing lice-infested hair-shirts were not concerned about bodily purity; they were obsessed with it. They just understood cleanness in a way we would judge to be more abstract or more spiritual than we consider it. Theirs was an inner purity, a spiritual purity that still was very materialistically manifested in demands made upon the body, its desires, and the be-haviors it was allowed to engage in. They could say without irony that they were adhering to the true meaning of the proverb which we take to mean a scrubbed face and washing behind the ears: "Cleanliness is next to godliness." Nor should we think that when David Hume lists bodily cleanliness as a virtue he means something that would pass our test of squeaky cleanness.[65] For him it is a con-dition that "renders us agreeable to others" which thus must be a relative standard indeed. Hume was not expecting a bath a day, but, most likely, clean linen, clean face and hands, with a wig that fit and was properly powdered.[66]

Elias's story could be retold not as one in which cleanness ex-panded but in which it merely changed its style and meaning. In the earlier regime it was the risks imposed by bodily desire, primarily sex, that were at stake. Cleanness thus meant chastity first and then was extended to comprehend freedom from other vices as well. In the subsequent civilized order, the body is seen less as a locus of desire than a source of offense because of the kinds of things it does, only some of which implicate sexual desire. Sweating, defecation, spitting, and chewing in such a way that is noisy and unsightly put cleanness to the test on a daily basis, whereas the cleanness of chastity posed less frequent tests although at higher stakes and of much greater intensity. The civilized order did not dispense with the virtue of chastity, but redefined its relation to the new understanding of clean-ness. Failures in cleanness were punished by undesirability and chas-tity by default. There was no virtue there. The virtue lay in chaste-ness coupled with desirability. Marriage, not a lifetime of virginity, was the virtuous end.

In both the Christian and civilized regimes the body was still very much at the center of cleanness, but the cleanness shifted its style and quality, if not its quantity.[67] In both regimes cleanness ranked people in hierarchies. In the Christian one the low were styled as sinners and the damned; in the civilized world the low were styled variously as peasants or nouveau riche bourgeois.[68] The high in the civilized regime gain recognition for not making scenes, for poise and tact, for confirming expectations regarding the social ordering of the world. In the medieval Christian order the quest for humility led to scene-making, to self-abasement so garish as to call attention to one's separateness and one's election; it desired to upset and provoke, to disconcert and unnerve, to upend normal social expectations.

To tell the story this way can be seen as a strong claim arguing for a conservation in the amount of purity (and hence disgust)[69] available to a culture, or as a weaker claim arguing that changes in the levels of disgust in a culture can be reconceived as changes in the distribution of disgust across different cultural domains, as, say, from the religious to the secular, from *what* gets eaten (as in the taboos of ritual prohibition) to *how* things get eaten (as in having proper table manners). Still, I think Elias is largely right on the big issue; the amount of disgust is not invariable over time.

Although the claim for conservation I have just been presenting cannot survive in its strong form, we must not lose sight of the fact that some of what looks like changing threshold levels of disgust is better understood as the consequence of different ideas of cleanness and purity, different applications for cleanness and purity rules. It seems strange to us to think of our age as more bound up in rules of purity and cleanness than more religiously inclined cultures. Yet such must be the case; for disgust is necessarily linked to corresponding rules of cleanness. We have secularized cleanness, by making it so much a matter of soap and water, but no less magical for that.[70] For us too, cleanliness is next to godliness; it is an issue of ranked purity, not of scientifically valid rules of hygiene. The generally higher sensitivities to disgust ushered in by the civilizing process work to re-enchant the world disenchanted by bureaucratic rationality. Disgust helps make our world a magical place, uncanny, and dangerous, not quite in the way of religion but sufficiently comparable so that in the end violation of purity rules means contamination and defilement and some mixture of fear, loathing, and disgust.[71]

The rules of disgust, the kind that are the very substance of the civilizing process, change their density and not always in the direction of greater prohibition and more disgust. Societies, like individuals, learn to modify and suspend the range and subject of certain disgust rules once acquired. The greater acceptability of foul language, sexual explicitness in the arts and in the "not so arts," are cases in point. These may even bear some complex sociological connection to increasing moral disgust for sexism and racism, but the connection is palpably not a hydraulic one in which rises in one area require declines in the other. It is rather remarkable how much variation in disgust norms we learn to accommodate over the course of a lifetime, with more or less shock and resistance. Not all disgusts, however, are equally overcomable.

In Elias's story, disgust must grow at the expense of some emotions the display of which comes to be viewed as inappropriate and disgusting. Disgust warred with the expressions of anger, rage, sexual and bodily urges, and gluttony, and won great gains for civilization and repression. But some people feared civilization had not been discriminating enough so that it ended by making all emotional display, even the display of positive and sociable emotions, a disgusting breach of decorum. Thus George Orwell: "One of the effects of safe and civilized life is an immense oversensitiveness which makes all the primary emotions seem somewhat disgusting. Generosity is as painful as meanness, gratitude as hateful as ingratitude."[72] We may read this narrowly as a reserved Englishman noting the costs of a peculiarly English reserve or we can read it as expansively as it asks to be read. Orwell is plainly not willing to count disgust among the primary emotions, but he, contemporaneously with Elias, notes the effects of an expanded disgust on the emotional economy. Repression is not quite as discriminating as we would wish it to be.

One final point about Elias's theories. The civilizing process, according to Elias, means the expansion of the private sphere at the expense of the public. The new norms demand private spaces in which one prepares, grooms, and does the things that would disgust others if they were to be witnessed. But the two spheres, public and private, interpenetrate. The private arises as a necessary space for the production of civilized behavior. It is the staging area where unsightly preparation takes place, which once having taken place is granted invisibility in public by all except those like Swift, who cannot rid their tortured consciousnesses of the images of what has taken place in the staging area. Private space enables a civilized public space.

On the other side, the public intrudes into the private. The behaviors put on in public spaces become harder to suspend in private space. Once we learn to eat with our mouth closed we usually do not begin to chew with it open when catching a midnight snack by ourselves. My father, a product of a more formal generation, still wears wool pants on the weekends. Not all norms hold us so tightly in their grip, and we may judge that some breaches disgust only in public and not in private, while some disgust in both places. What constitutes the safe domain of the private will also vary with the practice at hand. People will blithely pick their noses in the car next to you at the stoplight, who would not do so in a convertible or even with their windows down. For some reason being enclosed in one's car works to make the space private enough to sing, to talk to oneself, and to pick one's nose, despite the transparency of the glass enclosure. For these activities the glass is felt to be opaque, but it would regain its transparency for other behaviors which even when alone we monitor as if we were in public.

Not all civility norms, in other words, are locked into our consciousnesses or unconsciousnesses with exactly the same force or in exactly the same way. Some norms trigger embarrassment, others trigger disgust. The former we think of as the domain of manners in the light sense of manners;[73] the latter we think of as the domain of the moral or the unthinkable, that is, the area of moral space the violation of which renders one not just uncivil but shameless and a pariah. This brings us to the subject of the next chapter, in which I will address more systematically the implicit claim underlying most of my account so far: that disgust is central to moral discourse and to the construction of our moral sensibility.

| 8 |

THE MORAL LIFE
OF DISGUST

IN RAMBLER NO. 4 Samuel Johnson offers his advice on how vice should be treated in fictional narration:

> Vice, for vice is necessary to be shewn, should always disgust; nor should the graces of gaiety, or the dignity of courage, be so united with it, as to reconcile it to the mind. Wherever it appears, it should raise hatred by the malignity of its practices, and contempt by the meanness of its stratagems; for while it is supported by either parts or spirit, it will be seldom heartily abhorred.[1]

For Johnson our moral capacity depends on the proper activation of aversive sentiments and passions, primarily disgust and abhorrence, supported by suffusions of hatred and contempt in particular circumstances. Moralists like Johnson stop short of defining vice as that which disgusts, because for moralists of that stripe our disgust mechanisms are never as sensitive as they should be. Our will to disapprove is too dull or we are too amiable, too willing to forgive. Mix in graces like gaiety or virtues like courage, and vice will not be properly abhorred, to say nothing of those for whom unvarnished vice is the unabashed attraction. A newer style of moralist, however, one for whom tolerance and respect for persons are fundamental virtues, might wish our disgust sensitivities lowered so we would be less susceptible to finding difference and strangeness sources of disgust. Nonetheless, whether we be Puritan or not, we express many of our bread-and-butter moral judgments in the idiom of disgust. The argument is not whether disgust operates in the moral domain, but about its proper scope, its proper object, and its reliability in that domain.

Consider how hard it is, in normal conversation, to give voice to moral judgments without having recourse to the idiom of disgust or reference to the concept of the disgusting. About persons and actions we say, as noted earlier, things like these: *He gives me the creeps. He makes my skin crawl. Yuck! That makes me want to puke. You're revolting (repulsive, disgusting)!* In a higher register we speak of vile, odious, abhorrent, and loathsome characters and deeds. Johnson, of course, need have no cause for pleasure unless we were making those aversive judgments about the genuinely vicious. He knew what vice was and it was to be met with disgust;[2] our discourse seems to invert the order. We perceive what disgusts and tend to imbue it with defective moral status for that reason alone.[3] Authors have frequent recourse to this moralizing capacity of disgust when they direct our moral judgment against entire social orders by circumstantial descriptions of a city's sewers, the rankness of a river, or the filth and foulness of a boarding school: "London, thou art the seeded Garden of sinne, the Sea that sucks in all the scummy chanels of the Realme."[4] Johnson's annoyance is that disgust doesn't come as easily for the things he knows to be vicious as he would wish; vice is often too alluring, as indeed it must be to constitute a temptation and a threat to social and moral order. Yet I suspect he is asking for too much, for surely disgust does admirable action against some vices, just not all of them.

By being so much in the gut, the idiom of disgust has certain virtues for voicing moral assertions. It signals seriousness, commitment, indisputability, presentness, and reality. It drags the moral down from the skies toward which it often tends to float, wrests it from the philosophers and theologians, and brings it back to us with a vengeance. The day-to-day nitty-gritty of moral decision, moral policing, moral education, and morality talk is more likely to involve reference to the disgusting than to the Good and the Right. Our moral discourse suggests we are surer of our judgments when recognizing the bad and the ugly than the good and the beautiful. And that's at least partly because disgust (which is the means by which we commonly feel the bad and the ugly) has the look of veracity about it. It is low and without pretense. We thus feel it trustworthy, even though we know it draws things into its domain that should give us pause. The disgust idiom puts our body behind our words, pledges it as security to make our words something more than *mere* words.

I want to take up three main issues in this chapter. First, are there particular vices and moral failures that seem routinely and appropriately to elicit disgust? And if so, what does that say about those particular vices? We will focus on stupidity and hypocrisy, especially as the latter figures in the kinds of necessary evils and moral compromises that are often viewed as giving the professions of law and politics their somewhat distasteful moral cast. The second issue involves us in an attempt to discern the mechanisms by which disgust does its moral work. With Adam Smith as our guide we will focus on the readiness with which disgust can be experienced vicariously and sympathetically. Third, we will deal with disgust's moral failings as a moral sentiment. Disgust tends to be a little too zealous in its moral work. It wants to draw things into the moral domain that we feel in our better judgment should be left out. Here the discussion will center on the Goffmanian moral duty of maintaining disattendability, of being safely ignorable, in certain social orderings.

Disgusting Vices

What kind of vices tend to elicit disgust rather than indignation, or at least prompt disgust as much as outrage? In some instances we need not name a vice; we instead name the role or office which comes to stand for particular vices: thus the lawyer and the politician. Certain personality traits tend to elicit disgust.[5] Hume finds "disgustful and contemptible" a general abjectness of character. He goes on to describe this person more particularly as the kind who "crouches to his superiors" and is "insolent to his inferiors."[6] Servile to those above, cruel to those below: of what Judith Shklar called the ordinary vices, surely that defect of character is one of the most disgusting. Unfortunately it is also the kind of defect which is not rare, and we all have had occasion to suffer the presence of such people or to experience self-loathing for having showed evidence of the defect in ourselves. There is of course the boor, but some might also find the excessively fastidious person disgusting,[7] perhaps because the fastidious call attention to the disgusting by being so zealous to avoid it. The goal of civilizing manners is to repress the disgusting, to put it out of mind or at least out of mind in public spaces. This requires a fine calibration of behaviors. The fastidious person calls attention to himself with regard to just those facets of life which decorum requires that we must publicly pretend do not exist.

Many of the ordinary vices in Shklar's and Montaigne's sense elicit disgust: cruelty, betrayal, hypocrisy, gluttony, lust. Hume would include the ordinary vice of foolishness and aggressive stupidity:

> Business, books, conversation; for all of these, a fool is totally incapacitated, and except condemned by his station to the coarsest drudgery, remains a *useless* burthen upon the earth . . . Except the affection of parents, the strongest and most indissoluble bond in nature, no connexion has strength sufficient to support the disgust arising from this character. Love itself, which can subsist under treachery, ingratitude, malice, and infidelity, is immediately extinguished by it, when perceived and acknowledged; nor are deformity and old age more fatal to the dominion of that passion.[8]

Humean disgust is reserved for those who make for dull company or whose ineptitudes destroy the bases for good conversation. Nothing quite disgusts, he says, like the fool.[9] One would prefer, he claims, to be known for injustice and for appalling moral failings than to be thought a fool. Only parental love, locked in by nature herself, can survive the powerful disgust the fool evokes.

I noted in Chapter 6 that Hume is being somewhat hyperbolic; yet he rightly identifies just how much work must be done by self-deception, wishful thinking, or other forms of blindness to overcome the mutual incompatibility of love and the disgust a fool generates. The kind of disgust that stupidity breeds destroys desire[10] and undoes the stupid person's claim for virtue in general: "Who did ever say, except by way of irony, that such a one was a man of great virtue, but an egregious blockhead?"[11] Hume is making stupidity more than comically contemptible. When one defines virtue and personal merit, as Hume does, as being either useful or agreeable, stupidity must needs be a vice. One senses that it is distinguished from other vices because it is also an offense against a very precisely formed notion of taste in matters of wit and conversation, but that does not mean that stupidity, in Hume's eyes, is not properly a moral issue.

Hume's disgust strikes us as excessive.[12] Disgust seems to be a hyperbolic shorthand for the short-term annoyances, embarrassments, and frustrations the fool (and perhaps the fastidious person) evokes. This is a far cry from the direct assault on our disgust sensitivities intended by Poor Tom drinking pond scum or St. Catherine quaffing a cup of pus. We often speak of being disgusted by little things, styles of self-presentation or minor behaviors that merely "turn us off." For some they may include the general style of frat boys or sorority girls or the obliviousness to others that makes a person write a check for three dollars worth of purchases in the express line of the grocery store. In such instances we feel that the idiom of disgust is consciously being used figuratively, that it is meant to exaggerate. A kind of intended comedy, a certain self-mockery, accompanies the assimilation of such peeves, often designated, as "pet peeves," into the idiom of disgust. These are marked as trivial; they are the annoyances and irritations that buttress the usual kinds of contempt that inform so much of social existence. These contempts help define our character; they go to making up our personal politics of everyday life; and they present fairly loose claims to a relative and momentary moral superiority. These are not informed by disgust except in a consciously ironic vein, the very irony of which places us more squarely in the world of contempt, which so frequently adopts the ironic register to express itself: the roll of the eyes in impatience and annoyance, the "tsk" of disapproval, the one-sided smile all capture the ironic style that so often characterizes certain avatars of contempt.

Nevertheless, these comic rankings are part of the moral ordering, and that is just what the disgust idiom claims to accomplish; we are judging what someone is and according him or her a lower place in the moral and social order because of it. Still, despite Hume's and our use of the diction of disgust to register our opinion of fools, we are easier on fools than Hume is. Hume barely distinguishes between knaves and fools, both meriting intense disapprobation in the form of disgust. Most of us distinguish between knaves, like lawyers and politicians, on the one hand, and fools on the other, the former meriting indignation, fear, wariness, disgust, and abhorrence, the latter meriting contempt ranging from blistering to indulgent amusement.

Yet human foolishness and stupidity can drive the moralist as mad as human knavery. Certain forms of stupidity assist the perpetration of cruelty and atrocity. We are more than capable of distinguishing between the contempt we feel for a pompous fool and the revulsion we feel for the dim transgressive brute, this in spite of postmodern scholarly attempts to value the dim brute's cruelties as carnivalistic celebration and "empowerings" of the oppressed.[13] For the Jews murdered during carnival, the women raped, the animals set on fire and tormented it would have been small solace that late-twentieth-century scholars would find cause for admiring such "authentic rites," "sites of resistance," or "counter-hegemonic practices." There is a world of difference between the stupidity of the pompous and officious Polonius and the depraved stupidity of the drunken peasant who tortures his horse to death in Raskolnikov's nightmare.

Notice that a considerable number of the vices that prompt disgust—cruelty, hypocrisy, betrayal—tend also to be institutionalized politically and socially. Take hangmen, lawyers, and politicians, for example. All are what might be called necessary evils. Without hangmen and lawyers the judicial system cannot carry out its mission; without politicians public order seems largely unachievable and only imaginable as utopian fantasy. I call these people *moral menials;*[14] they perform functions in the moral order similar to those played by garbagemen and butchers in the system of provisioning, by hod carriers in building, by scavengers and bottom feeders in various ecosystems.[15] Moral menials deal with moral dirt, or they have to get morally dirty to do what the polity needs them to do. And despite the fact that we need to attract people to this kind of labor, we still hold them accountable for being so attracted. No particular individual is forced to be a moral menial. They are seduced by its benefits; they choose to do these labors. Their having so chosen, however, is not what disgusts; their choosing is only cited as a partial justification for blaming them for disgusting us on other grounds.[16]

Moral meniality is remarkably fertile in its disgust-generating capacities. It provides more than one basis for revulsion. At the simplest level, our disgust mingles with envy for how well the culture rewards certain menials: especially the lawyers and the politicians. They raise the ugly specter of easy virtue, of the vulnerability of virtue to a price. Moral meniality inverts the reward system of social meniality. Garbagemen make paltry sums compared to doctors, although it is hardly clear who contributes the most to public health. But moral menials tend to be nicely remunerated, often in direct proportion to the extent to which they make precisely those moral compromises which so often disgust the impartial observer or the seeker of justice.

The vulnerability of virtue, its conniving with vice, the whole notion of necessary evils richly rewarded, links moral meniality to the phenomenology of the disgusting elucidated in the previous chapters. We are disgusted by the fact that our world makes purity transient, vulnerable, and ultimately unmaintainable. The notion of necessary evil and the moral menials who undertake to do it disgusts because it means that the boundaries that separate vice from virtue, good from evil, pure from polluted are permeable, and worse, necessarily permeable. To our disgust, the good is always engaging in unseemly compromises that implicate us. The image of life soup, of ceaseless turmoil seething, of the never ending flux of eating, generating, rotting, and regenerating reproduces features of the moral domain in which evil and slack morals generate the possibility of good and firm morals in others.

We are caught coming and going. For if the necessity of moral compromise disgusts, it is another disgust-eliciting vice not to compromise at all; this is the vice of Puritanism, of inequitable rigidity in the pursuit of principle, which so often ends up winking at cruelty and succumbing to hypocrisy and thus compromising with vice in spite of itself. How appropriate that disgust, which as we saw in Chapter 6 must get its hands dirty to protect us from the disgusting, is itself the passion that fuels our disapproval of those moral menials whose hands, as a necessary consequence of their role, are also dirty.

It is not just that their evils are necessary, it is that the notion of necessary evil so often involves vices that disgust: these are the ordinary vices of hypocrisy (lawyers and politicians), betrayal (politicians), fawning (politicians and lawyers), and cruelty (hangmen and politicians). Indignation seems inadequate to the task of betrayal and cruelty, and not quite appropriate to hypocrisy: disgust has a particular aptness in this terrain. I will make a few brief points about disgust's relation to hypocrisy, which is as a sociological and psychological matter an exceedingly complex vice whose fascinating complexity I will simply brush aside. I will also ignore betrayal, which one might see as a special case of hypocrisy, and postpone cruelty to a later discussion.

What is it about hypocrisy that makes it so appropriate as an elicitor of disgust? When it presents itself as unctuousness, fawning serviceability, and base flattery it proclaims its loathsomeness. So repulsive are these styles that it is hard to believe they could ever gain their ends if they were not assisted by the corresponding vice of vanity and susceptibility to flattery in the other.[17] These traits and practices disgust because we understand them to mimic the forms of the loathsome in the material world.[18] They slither, insinuate, and exude slime and grease. There is an effrontery to the style; one senses one is being mocked by the excessiveness of the display, by its obvious markers of groveling servility.[19]

Embody now our hypocrite not as a physically repulsive Uriah Heep exuding unctuousness but as someone more attractive; change the polyester of the used car salesman for more respectable garb in which seeming virtue is indistinguishable from virtue itself. Sophisticated hypocrisy mimics perfectly the style of virtue. Even more pernicious, as Shklar points out, is that hypocrisy has evolved so that it does not need to assume the trappings of sincerity as a pose, but is often sincerity itself.[20] The calculating hypocrite has been superseded by a newer model who sincerely believes himself virtuous and committed to the opinions he voices: many serviceable flatterers actually believe in the praiseworthiness of their object. Does such seamless hypocrisy disgust as Uriah Heep disgusts or for the same reasons? Or does disgust only respond to the markers of vulgar hypocrisy? Is it, in other words, vulgarity and ineptitude more than hypocrisy which revolts us? Is the mechanism of our moral revulsion, our moral disgust, so shallow?[21]

One of the real costs of hypocrisy of whatever stripe, and especially of the sincere self-deceiving variety, is not just that hypocrites swindle us, make fools of us, and mock principles we feel should be better served; it is that they impose vices on us: distrustfulness, cynicism, and paranoia. They make all virtue suspect; they give us cause to believe no appearance of virtue to be virtuous. These hypocrites are parasites on the moral order and sap the strength of the organism they feed on. But like any parasite they require the long-term viability and virtue of the host organism. In a perverse way the hypocrite has more at stake in seeing virtue thrive than the virtuous person, for the hypocrite depends utterly on most people valuing virtue whereas the virtuous person will remain committed to the cause of virtue whether dwelling amidst the virtuous or the vicious.

Even healthy virtue becomes suspect by its innocent enablement of hypocrisy. Hypocrisy, after all, owes its existence to virtue in general,[22] to the very idea, imagined possibility, and attractiveness of virtue, and no other vice (except perhaps Puritan persnicketiness in an especially perverse way) can make that claim. And that helps account for why hypocrisy disgusts. Like so much else in the realm of the disgusting, it makes us wonder whether fair is foul; it confuses boundaries so that there is no firm point in which we can trust, and it reminds us that the best things come with sickening costly side effects. Is there nothing that can be simply pure? Why must pleasure truck with disgust? Why must virtue enable vice? Mere failure of principle, mere swindling, would leave us indignant. But hypocrisy betrays principle in a way that makes one uncertain about recognizing principle the next time or even recognizing betrayal; it forces upon us the knowledge that there is a greater cost to virtue than the merely personal one measured by the difficulty of its attainment. Virtue imposes the social cost of hypocrisy.

Hypocrisy makes us realize that there can be no best world. Virtue must needs give rise to hypocrisy. And although not all moral menials are called on to be hypocrites, the moral menial reminds us that even the second-best world will still find it necessary to call on people to fill certain roles that the perfectionist in us finds reprehensible. All this imperfection, all this compromise, all this unnerving imperfectibility and contamination of the moral order have genuine disgust-evoking power, for all these things involve the recognition of the inevitable pollution of the pure. One important qualification is in order, however. The viciousness of hypocrisy is not divorced from the moral and political order in which it takes place. Imagine a regime so repressive, corrupt, and unjustifiable that hypocrisy functions to provide a barrier behind which embattled and nearly extinct virtue can be sustained, however weakly. It is tempting to claim that the demonstrable perversity of such regimes is that they manage to turn hypocrisy from a disgusting vice to the last bastion of virtue. Hypocrisy in such a regime, however, though recruited to virtue's cause, is still not itself virtuous for all that. It is still functioning, as usual, menially.

Disgust and Smith's Impartial Spectator

I want to shift gears now and call on Adam Smith for a fuller picture of the workings of disgust in the moral domain. In Smith's *Theory of Moral Sentiments* disgust is part of the emotional arsenal of the impartial spectator. This spectator is the determiner of social and moral propriety, which in Smith's scheme is not just a matter of the right deeds but of right deeds motivated by proper passions properly displayed. The spectator's judgment is less a rational assessment than a reading of the progress of his own sympathetic capacities. The impartial observer knows the actor's sentiments and actions are proper when he "can enter into them" by sympathy. The very failure of the observer to sympathize constitutes his adverse judgment on the propriety of the behavior observed. And this failure of sympathy, depending on the exact nature of the impropriety, can end in disgust. Successful social actors are those who play the impartial observer to their own actions and thus modulate their passions to that pitch which will not embarrass or disgust the observer—will not, that is, prevent sympathy. Depending on the breach in propriety the spectator can feel disgust, contempt, anger, hatred, or other less defined passions of disapproval.[23]

Smith's impartial observer is a fairly fastidious fellow; he does not like improprieties; he is immediately suspicious of anger until he can

discern that it is justified and even then remains skittish about it; he
is a man of refined sensibilities, very reserved and not given to excessive displays of passion (he is almost a parody of the American
view of the British); he is a man of taste, who is capable of pity but
would prefer that pitiable scenes were rather rare. The impartial observer, whether embodied in another person or simply carried within
us as the capacity for social self-monitoring, makes Smith's moral
world primarily one of shame, disgust, and the other wider-ranging
moral sentiments, rather than one of guilt and anger. In his moral
and social order nothing can be worse than to be seen as contemptible,
than to know oneself the elicitor of aversive judgments in impartial
spectators; conversely, nothing can be better than to gain their approbation.

Because we play the impartial observer to others we know how to
play it to ourselves. We thus know that the worst that could befall
us would be to be seen as we in fact see others when they are being
foolish, vile, inept, or disgusting. When we see others in this light
there may be a countervailing *Schadenfreude* that helps make more
palatable the unpleasant sensation of observing others fail badly.[24] But
no such dark pleasure attends our consciousness of our own failings.
When we are the objects of disgust, contempt, or derision, it is not
just the disapproval that hurts but the small delight we suspect that
our discomfiture gives the disapprover; and in telling symmetry, the
pleasure we gain from the approbation of others is enhanced when
we suspect that it causes our approvers some pangs of envy. Their
envy marks the sincerity of their approbation.

Smith recognizes that the observer who prompts our mortifications
need not always be impartial. In fact envy and *Schadenfreude* always
threaten to undermine impartiality,[25] as indeed do social rank and
class. With the failure of impartiality disgust becomes even more
likely in the observer. Consider how the poor person is seen by the
rich. The poor person is subject to double mortification. He is either
invisible because contemptible or visible because disgusting: "The
fortunate and the proud wonder at the insolence of human wretch-
edness, that it should dare to present itself before them, and with the
loathsome aspect of its misery presume to disturb the serenity of their
happiness" (*TMS* 51).

The propriety of the passions is a function of their appropriateness to the conditions eliciting them and, just as important, of the moderation and decorum of their display. The principal actor must modulate the display of his passions to that point at which the sympathies of the observer are engaged, it being understood, by definition, that the observer cannot sympathize with excessive or insufficient displays. Yet only some improperly modulated displays will prompt disgust; others will rather elicit pity, or the kind of loving contempt that manifests itself in finding the other cute or endearing.

Smith divides the passions into groups, each of which affects the course of sympathy and hence the form of propriety differently. Those passions "which take their origin from the body," for instance, elicit little sympathy.[26] The strong expressions of thirst, hunger, and sexual desire "are loathsome and disagreeable." It is not that we cannot sympathize with the distress of famished persons; it is that we do not feel their hunger.[27] Smith's notion of sympathy is not narrowly restricted to pity and compassion, but encompasses the imaginative experience of the other's general experience; it is about the possibility of vicarious sensation, of experiencing *as* the other experiences or should experience: "The true cause of the peculiar disgust which we conceive for the appetites of the body when we see them in other men, is that we cannot enter into them." Even the first-person actor who experiences the longing finds that once it is gratified he can barely understand his prior desire: "the object that excited him is no longer agreeable."

As with food so with sex: "When we have dined, we order the covers to be removed; and we should treat in the same manner the objects of the most ardent and passionate desires, if they were the objects of no other passions but those which take their origin from the body" (28). Once our bodily appetites have been sated we do not want to be reminded of our prior uncontrolled urges. They provide the occasion for embarrassment, shame, and disgust. And the impartial spectator beats us to the punch, sympathizing with the shame and disgust to come, not with the present overwhelming urge. Smith's observation is compelling even when the specter of pornography is raised as proof against it. Pornography does not work by vicarious emotion, but by instilling a first-order passion. Those passions which depend totally on another's bodily sensations embarrass and disgust us and are usually felt as best kept private or decorously suppressed. And as Smith suggests, even when kept private, we would soon be rid of the objects of our sexual passion once sated unless such objects were also the objects of our love.

Disgust figures also in our reaction to the "unsocial passions." These are the passions—anger, resentment, hatred—that accompany contention and dispute, but also are necessary to motivating and doing justice. These passions will "serve rather to disgust" and thus prevent sympathy unless they are accompanied by a narration of the circumstances that evoked them. They need a justifying account to overcome the disgust they naturally elicit (11). Smith's observer is still wary of the unsocial passions even when "they are justly provoked: there is still something about them which disgusts us" (36). This is why, he says, we admire the self-command of the person who restrains and modulates his anger so as not to make a scene. Given the nature of the situations in which these unsocial passions arise, they involve the observer in divided sympathies. Should hatred and anger not be properly modulated, sympathy shifts to the target of these unsocial passions, whose condition we now come to recognize as a "plight." We thus come to sympathize with the hated to the extent that the hater's excessiveness inhibits our sympathies for his claim.

The failure of sympathy, in Smith's theory, doesn't leave the observer at zero affect with sympathy simply blocked. For Smith the failure of sympathy is disapproval, and disapproval often comes bound up with unsocial moral sentiments like the ones the impartial observer finds unsympathetic when present in another: hatred, disgust, and contempt, among others. The observer, however, is a decorous soul and always modulates his disapprobation appropriately. He can do this because of his initial impartiality, which renders him properly passionate, not coldly dispassionate. Sympathy cannot operate dispassionately; it takes its coloring from the emotions sympathized with, and it also is affected by its own limits. That which cannot be sympathized with must have already evoked some form of aversive response, some negative emotion, that prevented sympathy. The judgment of impropriety is *felt*.[28]

Smith's story manifestly does not involve the impartial observer in hidden desires to indulge in the improprieties that disgust him. Those, he would argue, who find the overly joyful Yahoos in beer commercials disgusting do not harbor a desire to be like them. By Smith's account there is no allure in them at all, even in the darkest recesses of the observer's unconscious. The failure to sympathize with their emotional displays and their motivational positions, then, is an unambivalent refusal to let oneself be seen that way.

Yet how does Smith's observer come to the judgment of impropriety unless he in fact imagines himself so acting? The knowledge that he would be seen in the same way as he saw such behavior makes whatever fantasy he constructs about so behaving so unpleasant that he abandons it in disgust. So sympathy is not barred as an absolute matter in those passions that in the end we cannot go along with. The observer imaginatively tests the water and sees himself as others would see him, others who have the same standards he does. Testing the waters, however, is not without risk, the risk of being disgusted (or even fascinated?) by improper passions. As long as the spectator observes action properly motivated and properly displayed he is himself subjected to no temptations or evil imaginings, but as soon as he witnesses impropriety he is himself compromised by the imaginings he must undertake in order to disapprove.

Smith does not take us into the temptations or repressions that might lurk in such negative judgments. His spectator is saved from having a dark side by his requisite impartiality and by the fact that his role is more properly public and social than private and psychological. The impartial spectator makes Smith's morality resemble a shame morality in which one is always under the eye of observers, impartial and otherwise, in a kind of Panopticon in which there are no spaces to hide from the spectator's judgmental vision. Smith has so socialized the morality of motivation that situational improprieties and ineptitudes are almost always morally blamable. They raise a demand for some justifying or excusing account.[29]

According to Smith, excesses in the "social passions"—generosity, kindness, compassion—unlike those in the unsocial passions, do not disgust. The displays of the "too tender mother, the too indulgent father, the too generous and affectionate friend," may be looked upon with "a species of pity, in which, however, there is a mixture of love."

This is disapprobation at its mildest, and the spectator's reaction almost mimics the too indulgent, too tender parent he is observing. That such excessive, indulgent behavior should prompt disgust or "hatred and aversion" would type the person so moved as "the most brutal and worthless of mankind" (40). Smith, we see, for all his reserve had some of the taste of an eighteenth-century "man of feeling" for such sentimental scenes.

One feels, too, that Smith protests too much about those who might find such scenes contemptible or disgusting. Surely excesses in the display of positive emotions can generate disgust in an impartial observer;[30] it is just that such disgust is not mixed with fear and loathing as it is with the unsocial passions, but is mixed with more benign sentiments. Following the theory of disgust I have been articulating, disgust for excesses of the amiable passions is a disgust of surfeit. As with the attractions to sweets and rich foods, the initial view of these sentiments elicits approbation, but overindulgence breeds disgust.

Hating vice and impropriety involves us in types of disapprobation which in some settings must be borne on a suffusion of disgust. To the extent that the moral involves matters of purity and pollution it generally involves disgust.[31] We usually think of a disgust-dominated moral regime as a primitive one of totems and taboos.[32] But as we have seen, the Christian language of sin latched on to disgust with a vengeance, as did in more moderate forms the moral philosophies of Hume and Smith. The disgust of the Scottish philosophers is grounded differently from the Christian one. The form it takes for them, as discussed in Chapter 7, is intimately tied up with the newly emergent concept of good and bad taste. Their disgust made vulgarity a moral issue, and a Marxist might wish to claim that such philosophies were merely supporting a new class-based social order by elevating bourgeois social tastes into moral demands. Jonathan Swift's disgust, in contrast, was still primarily in the old anti-body, antisexual style of Christian asceticism; but it had an added intensity wrought by the civilizing process's expansion of disgust beyond the sexual domain to other bodily matters. The civilizing process also changed the moral valence of poverty. In the earlier Christian ordering poverty could be looked upon as a virtue or at least as an enabler of virtue; the new order's disgust changed that and tended to make poverty a vice or the prime enabler of it.[33]

Disgust is more than just the motivator of good taste; it marks out moral matters for which we can have no compromise. Disgust signals our being appalled, signals the fact that we are paying more than lip-service; its presence lets us know we are truly in the grip of the norm whose violation we are witnessing or imagining. To articulate one's disgust is to do more than state a preference or simply reveal a sensation in our bodies. Even if we are only using the diction of disgust as a fashion of talking, that is, independent of the feeling, we are still stating most emphatically the belief that the norms being referenced by our expression of disgust should be the sort that hold us in their grip.

Let me again have recourse to Hume. When a person calls another an enemy, Hume notes, he speaks the language of self-love and he is understood "to express sentiments, peculiar to himself, and arising from his particular circumstances and situation"; when, however, he calls someone vicious, odious, depraved, "he then speaks another language, and expresses sentiments, in which he expects all his audience are to concur with him."[34] The avowal of disgust expects concurrence. It carries with it the notion of its own indisputability, and part of this indisputability depends upon the fact that disgust is processed so particularly via offense to the senses. It argues for the visibility, the palpability, the concreteness, the sheer obviousness of the claim. Disgust poses less of a problem for intersubjectivity than perhaps any other emotion. When you say you love or that you feel regret I am never quite sure of your inner state in the way I am when you say you are disgusted. The *feelings* of love and regret are not as easily definable as the *feelings* of disgust. When you have the creeps or feel defiled I know what is going on inside you. Disgust thus communicates rather better than most emotions.

Disgust has other powerful communalizing capacities and is especially useful and necessary as a builder of moral and social community. It performs this function obviously by helping define and locate the boundary separating our group from their group, purity from pollution, the violable from the inviolable. It does so also as a consequence of its capacity for being readily experienced vicariously. Disgust, like indignation, is something we experience as much upon hearing and seeing offenses done to another as those done to ourselves.[35] Both emotions seem to compel us to what is often styled as the victim's position. This capacity of disgust and indignation to reach out does not depend on the wronged party also experiencing disgust or indignation; we do not "catch" our disgust from the victim. We play Smith's impartial spectator and experience what we would experience in the other's shoes; that is, in the Smithian scheme, we experience what we judge the wronged person *should* be experiencing. Disgust and indignation unite the world of impartial spectators into a moral community, as cosharers of the same sentiments, as guardians of propriety and purity. These sentiments supply the motivation for punishing certain kinds of offenses.

I would suggest that the reason love lamentably has not had much historical success as the sentiment upon which a moral community can be built is that it cannot be readily entered into by third parties. We can, for instance, readily experience disgust on someone's behalf for their having been defiled or indignation for their having been wronged or harmed, but we cannot readily feel the love or jealousy another enjoys or suffers; those feelings are always personal, *sui generis,* and somewhat incommunicable. We may understand what the lovers are feeling, but we do not *feel* what they are feeling. Should, however, gratitude or love fail to be offered to one who deserves it, we are easily provoked to indignation or disgust for the ingratitude as if we were the wronged party. It may thus be that humankind isn't quite as dispositionally vile as misanthropic moralists would claim. Rather we are stuck with the structures of the emotions as they are given to us. Love, like pride, simply is structured as a rather private emotion which can cause us pleasure and amusement if we see others in its throes, but that pleasure is not vicarious; it is not an imaginative reconstruction of the other's sentiments or of ours as we would imagine them to be if we were in the other's shoes.

The sympathetic identifications borne by disgust do not always, by themselves, clarify the moral order. Consider the relation of disgust to the vice of cruelty. Cruelty generates a double disgust in the impartial spectator, that is, once we recover from the shock it can give.[36] First, the perpetrator is looked on with fear and loathing, with the most intense kind of disgust and horror. Then a second disgust focuses on the degraded victim, whether bloody and disfigured or morally annihilated in the disgrace of having been so abused. Our pity and desire to relieve the suffering of the victim are inhibited by the same emotion that compels us to execrate the person responsible for the plight. Thus does cruelty compromise the impartial observer, who is caught up in such a superfluity of disgust that he is paralyzed. The observer must now come to feel acutely his own inadequacy in the face of such evil. The disgust directed against the violator is raised purely by what we would recognize as moral failure; the disgust directed against the victim, however, imputes moral failing to him as a consequence of his having been rendered ugly, deformed, undignified, and disgusting by victimhood. The victim is held to some moral account for being so degraded unless the victim has the peculiar status we accord to infants and children for whom the demands of dignity are largely suspended. This is some of the cost of disgust's inevitable association with shame. Witnessing another's shame disgusts us. And this is why shaming is such a powerful sanction: shame is the internalization of the spectator's disgust and contempt.

If disgust gets twisted upon itself in the face of cruelty, indignation pushes it back onto the right track. When disgust is operating in tandem with indignation it helps create a kind of supercharged indignation which may be indicated by outrage or something akin to horror. Indignation forces disgust to aid in the cause of justice by motivating action against the offender; without indignation disgust too often withdraws or averts the gaze or is caught in the double bind described in the preceding paragraph. The risk of outrage, however, is that it loses a sense of proportion and drives Smith's impartial observer to disgust at his own excesses. Yet don't wanton cruelties suspend the norms of proportion? Or is it rather that wanton cruelties, by being so disproportionate themselves, are never fully punishable or fully expiatable? Not even the alliance of disgust and indignation is adequate to the task. The ineradicable presence of cruelty thus sinks us into despair and frustration, threatening to consign us in the end to an unhappy and resentful misanthropy.

The Moral Failings of Disgust

Disgust, we have supposed, is the moral sentiment that does the work of disapprobation for the vices of hypocrisy, cruelty, betrayal, unctuousness in all its forms: officiousness, fawning, and cringing servility. It also polices those activities which I have described as the necessary evils of moral meniality and other moral matters of lesser moment: the kind that produce character failings that offend in certain predictable ways such as persnicketiness, fastidiousness, boorish stupidity, among others, but also physical deformity. Are these properly *moral* matters? Disgust has a vice; it is a moral sentiment of extraordinary inclusiveness and does more than register a simple aversion toward the objects of its focus. It degrades them in some moral way. As long as disgust is warring against cruelty and hypocrisy we are delighted to enlist it to our cause, but when it wars against the intrusively annoying or the deformed and the ugly it may clash with other moral sentiments, like guilt and benevolence, that push us in another direction.

"Moral" is one of those frustrating terms that eludes us in the definition even as we think we know what we mean when we use it. The moral can be looked at in a number of ways, some rather narrow, some quite wide ranging. Some try to reduce it to simple statements of this sort: love virtue, hate vice. Others articulate the domain of the moral by reference to specific moral emotions or moral sentiments.[37] Some might thus center morality on any of a number of sentiments: benevolence, respect, guilt, shame, or a specially constituted independent moral sense.[38]

Consider, for instance, Allan Gibbard's attempt to construct an admittedly narrow theory of morality privileging anger and guilt: "Morality looks to the kind of acts for which a person can be to blame. A person is to blame for an act if it makes sense for others to be angry at him . . . and if it makes sense for the person himself to feel guilty for what he has done."[39] Making guilt foundational has a restricting effect on the range of the moral.[40] Guilt's restrictiveness flows from its tie to the voluntary.[41] Guilt makes sense for those (bad) deeds that we chose to do, that we intended to do, and that we had the power to choose not to do. Guilt gives a legal cast to the moral with all the restrictions the idea of *mens rea* brings. Guilt thus underwrites the punishment of culpable actions (and specific omissions) rather than general failings of character. Guilt asks for atonement, some of which is payable simply by the appropriate display of a guilty conscience. The atonement should be in an amount sufficient to assuage the justified anger the offense gave rise to.

Gibbard finds the restriction to intentional wrongs efficient. Guilt does not ask for reformation of an entire person as shame does and as disgust might do, just a change in actions that are within the voluntary control of the wrongdoer. Other distinctly moral sentiments, like shame, humiliation, disgust are, to Gibbard, less discriminating.[42] They ask the offender for too much, often for entire transformations of character, and even for physical transformations such as skin color, gender, body type, age, and state of health, things for which guilt morality says we cannot justifiably be blamed since they are not meaningfully matters of choice.

A morality uniquely dependent on the guilt/anger mechanism, however, does not account for all the blaming we do, all the actions and states that we hold people accountable for. Anger is not the only nor always the chief means of registering disapprobation or making moral claims against those who offend. We need not look to primitive shaming cultures for warrant for a more expansive moral domain in which disgust, contempt, and derision figure prominently. Our own sentiments and our own social interactions provide a myriad of instances. Erving Goffman has described in detail how the ordinary, the routine, and the normal generate social anticipations which we then transform into "normative expectations, into righteously presented demands," into, that is, moral claims on others not to upset the smooth-running routine we feel entitled to count on.[43]

Morality in this setting becomes less a matter of guilt and conscience than of how we impress the people who observe us, supposing their demands on us to be broadly justifiable. This morality is largely a shame morality, in which our good standing depends on achieving and maintaining competence through the whole range of standards by which character is judged. Shame morality is more expansive than guilt morality; it cares about what you are as well as what you do; it cares about what you don't do and what you can't do. More becomes blamable. And because more becomes blamable, correlatively more becomes a matter for honor and pride. Shame morality is not necessarily a bad thing. Let me expand on these issues briefly before returning to disgust.

Being in the presence of others in Goffman's scheme demands of the actors a respect for the setting, for the encounter they find themselves in. They are not to upset the working consensus that such interactions depend upon for smooth functioning except in the most extreme instances and then only in ways that others will come to understand as justified. The very minimal demand imposed by co-presence is not to make undue claims on people's fears or trigger their embarrassment and disgust. One is not to be a cause of alarm or undue concern, which means that for routine activities, such as walking down the street or waiting for a bus, one is to behave so as to be safely disattendable. At a convivial gathering one is not to fall on one's knees and ask others to join in prayer.[44] This is the minimal moral demand in the Goffmanian order: accord to others civil inattention and behave yourself so as to be civilly disattendable by those about you.

This minimal demand of being civilly disattendable, however, is very hard to meet for certain people. Take the beautiful: we do not blame them for their lack of disattendability since they do not elicit our attention by disgust or alarm. They do, however, impose extra demands on our poise and tact, on our abilities to maintain decorum. There is a thin line between the looks of admiration these people have come to expect as their due and importunate gawking. On the other side are the stigmatized: the obese, the disabled, the deformed, the mentally ill, the grotesquely ugly, the criminal,[45] or those who do not qualify for membership in the generous category of "normals."[46] Stigma disrupts the conditions that make for uneventful disattendability. The stigmatized variously generate alarm, disgust, contempt, embarrassment, concern, pity, or fear. These emotions in turn confirm the stigmatized person as one who is properly stigmatized. (Note that both Goffman's and my projects at this point are purely descriptive of how we order the morality of co-presence, not a claim that we should order it that way.)

Strangely enough, it has come to pass that one of the surer markers of our recognition of stigma is our guilt for having recognized it. The stigmatized thus make us feel that we are not properly according them civil inattention, for we are never certain what we are supposed to do in their presence. We suspect we are supposed to act naturally, but in the face of the stigmatized what does that mean? look away? provide assistance? pretend there is nothing unusual? The stigmatized are felt to disrupt the smooth-running social order that normals righteously demand.

In a harsher age there would be little or no guilt on the observer's part for the emotions the stigmatized elicit; in ours there is.[47] First we learn to suffer guilt for mocking. As we become more civilized, guilt subtends the nagging fear that we might mock or deride involuntarily. By degrees, our guilt is reduced to lurking about even as we accord the stigmatized decent treatment. Either we blame our good deeds as being motivated more by guilt than by nobler sentiments such as a respect for persons; or guilt comes in the end to puncture the self-congratulation we indulge in when we do treat stigmatized people decently, treatment which at some level we still feel lies beyond the call of duty. Wonderful of me, isn't it, that I am secure enough to be seen out for lunch with the obese X?

Disgust makes beauty and ugliness a matter of morals. And part of our embarrassment over this unfortunate state of affairs takes the form of arguing that beauty is properly the subject of aesthetics, not ethics or morals, it being understood that aesthetic failings are not to involve the seriousness of consequence that failings in the moral domain should bring. The attempt to constitute a discrete aesthetic domain divorced from the moral might reasonably be understood to be itself a moral claim about the proper content of the moral. It is an attempt to cabin by a fiat of categorization the rather insistent psychological and social tendencies we evince to accord moral significance to beauty and ugliness and to fail to distinguish consistently the good from the beautiful. We have accepted at the discursive level, backed by a sanction of guilt, a distinction between the aesthetic and the moral; yet we are still gripped by other sentiments which continue to manifest themselves in the sense of betrayal we feel when a beautiful person turns out to be mean-spirited or in the sense of grudgingness with which we finally concede the inner beauty of an ugly person when the concession turns out to be warranted.

Our moral world is thus at odds with itself. But it is not a case of opposing morality against immorality or non-morality. Nor is it a case of the despair of relativism. Different moral sentiments of varying reach and intensity generate substantive inconsistencies in the moral order. Gibbard makes a useful distinction here between accepting norms and being in their grip which I have just alluded to in the preceding paragraph; norms we accept are maintained by talk and discussion, by various discursive practices, while those which have us in their grip simply come to dominate our wills.[48] With regard to stigmatized people, norms governing respect for persons which we accept are subverted by norms holding us in their grip whose violation engenders disgust.

The difference between "accepting" and "being in the grip" often comes down to which sentiments support the norm. When a norm is backed by disgust we are in its grip, whereas guilt can be triggered by failure to abide by a norm we accept. The gripping power of norms backed by disgust should temper with a dose of middling reality our delight at exposing the paradoxes of disgust in which the disgusting is also the fascinating, the interest-generating, and even the object of desire. That may well be the case at some level, but nothing quite pays homage to the grip of a norm than literally getting sick at the thought of violating it. Few moral reformers would not prefer having the norms of respect for persons or of commitments to the fundamentally equal value of all humans maintained by disgust despite the paradoxes that come with it than by the weaker moral sentiments that back the discursive acceptance of norms.

Goffman's public order roughly corresponds to the demands made by shame cultures.[49] Guilt and anger still have roles to play in this order but they are luxuries available to those who have preserved their respectability by having passed moral muster in the larger order of shame, derision, contempt, and disgust. And one is seldom as concerned about giving cause for anger as about giving cause for contempt, mockery, or disgust. To anger someone is to be accorded a kind of equality, even a superiority; to be the object of contempt, derision, or disgust degrades oneself relative to the other.

One achieves the minimal respectability of being civilly disattendable by showing respect for the social and moral norms that govern self-presentation. This kind of respectability has to be achieved; it does not simply come with the territory of being human; it comes as a consequence of making a commitment to follow and then in fact following the rules of propriety, rules which subsume the social and aesthetic into a larger moral order. Respect is the homage one pays to the order itself, rather than to individuals. The first condition for a smooth-running social order is respect for it.

There is a certain harshness in this kind of moral ordering that should trouble us. Gibbard captures some of the problem, we saw, by worrying about the lack of discrimination in the moral sentiments of disgust, shame, fear, and embarrassment. It is easy to see the costs of letting disgust and contempt order our moral and social lives without their being subordinated to or constrained by countervailing sentiments and principles. We end up punishing the stigmatized, who may have no justifiable cause for feeling guilt for their stigma, although they often internalize the social judgments of their stigmatization as shame, self-loathing, self-disgust, self-contempt, self-hatred.[50] We fear that disgust and contempt may violate norms of fairness and justice, of a liberal respect for persons; that they may maintain brutal and indefensible regimes.

These are some reasons why we do not and should not accord any one moral sentiment the power to govern all situations in which it may be elicited. We cannot, to adapt Judith Shklar's phrase, put disgust or shame first, but if we, as she proposes, put cruelty first among vices we may not be able to or wish to avoid giving disgust a very big role in our moral regime.[51] What we need are ways of knowing when to trust our disgusts and contempts. But despite their considerable warts contempt and disgust do proper moral work. More strongly, even their warts are moral; it is just that other criteria make us nervous about constituting official Morality that way. Contempt, disgust, and shame rank us and order us in hierarchies; these emotions provide the basis for honoring and respecting as well as for dishonoring and disrespecting.

The view that moral emotions like disgust and contempt are necessary evils does not do them justice; they do much salutary work, if we inhibit their excesses. And we do inhibit them regularly, limiting the scope of their legitimacy by recourse to other norms we accept. We also clip disgust's wings by wisely subjecting the entire moral

regime to certain political and legal constraints that severely circumscribe the actions that can justifiably be taken in consequence of moral
judgment. Even in the informally regulated domain conceded to us
by law and politics to sort out for ourselves we find serious restrictions imposed on the sanctions we can visit upon those who are the
objects of disgust. Thus open mockery or even less malign forms of
shunning are marked as unjustifiable or even illegal. We are left only
with the private experience of our disgust and the suspect pleasure
of a contempt which colors our sense of self-congratulation for being
so much better behaved than the deformity-mocking gods of Olym-
pus.

Probably the greatest homage we pay to our anxiety about condemning those who disgust us is our construction of stories making
the stigmatized blamable in the restricted sense demanded by guilt.
As was touched upon in Chapter 4, we impute to the disgusting a
will to offend. The obese are thus fat because they are unwilling not
to be. We even hold the stigmatized to partial account for those
stigmas that we know, at the level of official knowledge, are not
within their power to change. If we cannot quite blame the blind for
their blindness we get around it by blaming them for not remaining
invisible, for not maintaining disattendability, especially when their
attendability is read as making a demand on us. We expect them to
be enchanted so that a kiss will metamorphose them into princes and
princesses; and when the evil spell proves too durable we blame them
for willing the inefficacy of the magic antidote.

We blame the ill for their sicknesses even as we paradoxically try
to exculpate the guilty by defining them as sick, which in turn will
subject them to blame for being so infected. The muddle-headed
reformers who seek to make crime a matter of illness rather than
culpable intention fail to realize that we do not cease blaming just
because someone is sick.[52] Sickness, we think, is a punishable offense.
AIDS is as blameworthy as leprosy once was. Even mundane illnesses
are blamable, if not as the wages of sin, then as failures to take care
of oneself properly.

We thus work to salve our doubtful consciences about the wide
reach of moral sentiments like shame and disgust by expanding the
reach of guilt. The narrower more constrained morality of Gibbard's

guilt/anger syndrome turns out not to be so narrow at all once we expand the category of the voluntary to include what one is as well as what one does. And if we find too much resistance in subsuming the shameful and disgusting into the domain of guilt, we are still not all that unwilling to punish on the basis of disgust alone. And when we do punish those who disgust us our suspect warrant is provided by the Goffmanian public order: disattendability is a virtue and not being disattendable is a vice for which one can be held to blame.

Not only does disgust blame a little too indiscriminately and make the category of the moral larger than competing principles of justice, benevolence, pity, and fairness think it ought to be; it also has a style of negativeness, a depressed and depressing style that makes us uncomfortable. Compare fiery indignation with dour, phlegmatic disgust.[53] As has been suggested in previous chapters, disgust is very ambivalent about life itself, particularly human life. Life soup, *human* life soup, lies at the core of the disgusting. And that makes disgust unavoidably misanthropic in its cast. Disgust recoils at what we are and what we do, both the voluntary and the involuntary. Indignation, for all its vengeful fury, does not condemn humanity so irrevocably. Once vengeance is taken or justice is done the world is back in order, and the order can very well be an exhilarating one, full of life and possibility. Indignation gives us reasons for living. Disgust gives us reasons for withdrawing. Disgust does its moral work but leaves us feeling polluted by the process.

Disgust is a recognition of danger to our purity. But it is more. The mere sensation of it also involves an admission that we did not escape contamination. The experience of disgust, in other words, does not itself purify us in the way the experience of anger or indignation can. Disgust signals the need to undertake further labors of purification. It is thus that disgust does not do its moral work so as to allow us unambivalent pleasure in our relative moral superiority to the disgusting other. Disgust admits our own vulnerability and compromise even as it constitutes an assertion of superiority. The feeling of contempt, in contrast, is cleaner and more pleasurable. We might see this as one of disgust's moral virtues. Disgust does not move us to condemn for pure pleasure because it always makes us bear some of the costs of condemnation. Disgust never allows us to escape clean.

It underpins the sense of despair that impurity and evil are contagious, endure, and take everything down with them.

Disgust tends to focus its moral work on moral issues that involve the body. Sex, obviously, attracts its attention, but also those bodily failings which indicate insufficient attention to the duty to make the social order as uneventful as it can be. Disgust also is the prime sentiment of disapproval, obviously, of those vices for which idioms of disgust seem to fit so well. Here there is a priority problem. Is the unctuous fawner slimy, greasy, or oily because he disgusts; or does he disgust because that behavior could not so appropriately be described in any other way? Whatever the case may be, there are those vices and offenses for which notions of ugliness, smelliness, sliminess readily apply, and those for which they do not. Hypocrisy, betrayal, cruelty put us in the swamp of the disgusting, and no other moral sentiment seems as well qualified to express our disapprobation.

From the moral sphere we will repair now to the social and political order. Disgust (and contempt), emotions of status demarcation, emotions that assign to lower status those against whom they are directed, have an important role to play in hierarchical societies. Democracy, in contrast, is at ease with neither, but it nonetheless has been able to make a serviceable accommodation with contempt. Disgust, however, still plagues democracy as it continues to motivate class, race, and ethnic divisions. In the next chapter we focus on contempt's political anatomy and distinguish it from that of disgust, postponing until Chapter 10 a fuller account of the politics of disgust.

9

MUTUAL CONTEMPT
AND DEMOCRACY

IN THIS CHAPTER we shift gears to focus more closely on disgust's close cousin contempt and its role in the production and maintenance of social hierarchy and political order. Close as they are and mutually reinforcing in some contexts, disgust and contempt have different political ramifications and it is especially helpful in understanding disgust's role in the political order to compare it with that of contempt. Contempt, it turns out, was assimilable to democracy. In fact, rather than subverting democracy, it assisted it by making generally available to the low as well as to the high a strategy of indifference in the treatment of others. Contempt thus came to underwrite the basic minimal respect for persons so crucial to democracy, the style of tolerance captured by the saying "live and let live." Disgust, as we will see in Chapter 10, is a much more powerful anti-democratic force, subverting the minimal demands of tolerance. In these two chapters I seek to give some idea of how deeply implicated different moral sentiments are in the creation of certain styles of political order.

Contempt and humiliation, contempt and shame, go hand in hand. Actions of our own that should shame us, styles of self-presentation that should humiliate us if we are socially competent enough to recognize our ineptitudes and failings, are those actions and styles that generate and justify the contempt, even the disgust, of others for us. Or, changing the order: another's contempt for or disgust with us will generate shame or humiliation in us if we concur with the judgment of our contemptibility, that is, if we feel the contempt is justified, and will generate indignation and even vengeful fury if we feel it is unjustified. Not that our concurrence will always be sufficient as a matter of justice. We may not concur with the judgment of our contemptibility and simply be behaving obstreperously or incorrigibly, or we may concur with the judgment and be the victim of an unjust social order that deprives us of the ability to make sufficiently autonomous evaluations of our lot in that particular social order. Be that as it may, contempt is clearly a mechanism of ranking people or of contesting relative rankings and as such has an intensely political significance.

Contempt raises a myriad of issues involving the relation of emotions to various social orders, to the justice of those social orders, and to the micropolitics of face-to-face interaction in those social orders. I want to narrow my range here. What I wish to speculate about is the nature of what I will call upward contempt, that is, the contempt the low have for the high; I will then make some suggestions about how this might manifest itself in different social and political regimes: heroic society, the *ancien régime*, and democracy.[1]

By some accounts the notion of upward contempt involves a definitional impossibility. Contempt, after all, is usually captured by the metaphor of "looking down on someone or something" and this metaphor is even physically embodied in the common facial expression of the one-sided smile and the raised head, the partially closed eyes which view the contemptible person askance. But as we shall see, upward contempt has certain stylistic features of its own that distinguish it from the classic style of contempt. Suffice it to say for the present that what I mean to capture is the contempt teenagers have for adults, women for men, servants for masters, workers for bosses, Jews for Christians, blacks for whites, the uneducated for the educated, and so on. Please don't take this to mean that I think all upward contempts are the same, or are triggered by the same conditions. The black, the Jew, the woman, the teenager, the worker, may all share an inferior status, but that does not mean that their inferiority is constituted in the same way. Each oppression has its own particular history and local rules. Some inferior conditions, moreover, are easily escapable (adolescence); some are less so.

Consider this tale of competing contempts. A little while ago I hired a mason to do some work on my house. He was a large beefy man, with several tattoos of the conventional sort: dragons, Vikings, and other over-muscled comicbook-like figures. His jeans were worn low so that when he bent over his rear fissure (oh, the trials of decorum!) was exposed. He looked fairly tough, with the air of someone for whom the receipt of physical pain was not as much a cause of fear as the giving of it was of pleasure. He had already been on the job for a few days when I rode up on my bicycle, backpack on my back, said hello and continued pedaling back to the garage. The mason said to my wife, "He a teacher?"[2] The failure of the "is" to introduce that question captures only some of the contemptuousness of his tone. I went back to make some small talk, comment on the job, and then took my leave.

He and I each have no small amount of contempt for the other. But our contempts are not constructed in quite the same way. His for me is less ambivalent than mine for him, riddled as mine is with conflicting designs and commitments. Consider some of the bases of my contempt for him. First were the tattoos. I took them as signs of his will to vulgarity (or at least of his will to offend types like me). He not only didn't disown them but displayed them proudly. His pride in them reinforced my contempt, for had he been ashamed, then I might have felt embarrassed on his behalf. Or I might still have felt contempt but it would have been a benign contempt, almost undifferentiable from pity and compassion, not the sensation of incredulity mixed with disgust and revulsion the tattoos induced in me.

His physicality, his obliviousness to seeking pain (in my formative years the non-tattooed were always treated to stories about the painfulness of getting tattooed), his lack of concern for or even knowledge of what might offend me might have made me wary, if not quite fearful. I could, without being paranoid, read in his style an affront. He was bigger, stronger, and tougher than I was and between men such assessments count for something. I suppose I could have respected him for his willingness to affront me or for his simply not giving a damn what I thought. But unabashed vulgarity doesn't make it easy to grant even grudging respect on that account. It seems that whatever wariness he generated in me did not go to engendering respect for him; it only undermined certain foundations of respect for myself, as contemptibly unphysical, miserably unmartial. The whole encounter was, as far as the total of respect in the world goes, less than zero-sum.

I should add that my view of the significance of tattooing dates me. Now that middle-class young of both sexes get tattoos the relation between tattoos and notions of vulgarity will undergo some shift. Still the classbound significance of tattoos is likely to survive the recent middle-class attraction to them for some time. There is not much difficulty in discerning the difference between tattoos designed to shock one's parents and those designed to identify with them.

Take the exposure of his backside when he bent over. This produced a contempt that bordered on both amusement and disgust. The amusement was driven by my utter inability to imagine choosing to present oneself in such a fashion; or, if in fact there had been no choosing, by the incomprehensibility of being so oblivious to one's body and presentability. From my point of view he was playing the clownish vulgar mechanic: he was in the mold of Bottom the Weaver or Curly, Moe, and Larry. This is the amusement of contempt, and it reveals an intimate connection between some styles of contempt, disgust, and the comic.

It didn't stop there. On another day he and my wife met each other in a tee-shirt duel: hers read "save endangered mammals" and his had "crack kills" inscribed beneath a cartoon of a human being crushed between the cheeks of a naked backside. His, of course, was meant to be funny, not only in its scatology but by piercing the pretensions of the grave style of a somber and self-consciously concerned citizenry;[3] the perverse result is that my wife's tee-shirt ends up as funny as his. Strange how most of us live so as to justify the not-so-friendly stereotypes others impose upon us.[4]

But this kind of Rabelaisian comic grotesquerie edges toward horror too; it wouldn't take much for this base mechanic to metamorphose into a monster. Horror can be frightening, or it can be repulsive and disgusting.[5] And while contempt can be a kind of defense against a fear of the contemptible, it also bears some close connections with disgust. The same aspects of his style that amused me also came close to disgusting me. In a sense, he was contaminating. The notion of pollution and contamination is part of what disgust brings to the world of contempt.

I hope that readers will suspend their condemnation of the failure of my account to accord with certain pieties that I may actually accept as a matter of political commitment. Before you excoriate me, would you treat this unambivalent expression of contempt by rapper Ice-T to the same condemnation? "Let me tell you something about the masses. You ever watch wrestling? Hulk Hogan and all that, guys jumping off the ropes? And the arena's always packed? Those same people vote, man." I find in Ice-T's espousal of such anti-democratic views a paradoxical emblem of the triumph of democracy, for the contempt of the people that once was a prerogative of high-Toryism is now readily available to everyone.[6]

Ice-T anticipates one of the main points I intend to make in this chapter. But I need to spin things out a little further between the mason and me. At the same time I was having feelings of contempt for him I was also indulging in no small amount of self-contempt, for my lack of physicality, for my certainty that I could not win a fight with him, for my doubts about the social value of what I do, and for my feeling contemptuous of him while at the same time realizing (or supposing) he was utterly untroubled by his contempt for me. Although we both live in the third century of American democracy and liberal democratic political and moral theory, those traditions only seem to undercut my contempt for him, not his for me. For those styles of political, moral, and social thought did much more to delegitimate downward contempt than they did upward contempt.

One could even hazard the suggestion (which I will return to later) that democratic theory does more than free upward contempt from having to make a pretense of hiding itself in the servant's quarters; it actually changes the style of that contempt. And one could further suggest that one of the defining markers that distinguishes upward from downward contempt in democratic societies is the greater likelihood that the downward contempt will be accompanied by doubts of its own legitimacy, whether these doubts be experienced as guilt, shame, or a mere sense of concern. This inkling of self-doubt also makes the downward contemner wonder if his firm sense that the other, in this case the mason, experiences no anxiety at all about his own feelings of contempt for the other, in this case me, is simply another manifestation of the contemner's contempt for the lower classes, seeing them as too insensate to be anxious about anything.

But this is to make my contempt less sure of itself than I actually experienced it, even though my feelings had questionable legitimacy. I actually had to remind myself that he was of equal value with me and of the same dignity. Moreover, he merited respect for the skill he had, and for doing his job well, for which indeed I did respect him. But I can't shake my contempt for what he is independent of his role as a competent mason. The contempt was there with a vengeance, in spite of my lack of confidence about its justifiability. The uneasiness I was suffering from was not liberal guilt. That is the sentiment one feels for being privileged when one doubts the justifiability of one's entitlement to such privilege. My contempt was not so much tinged with guilt or even self-doubt as it was colored by a sense of wonderment that my contempt is so incorrigibly part of me, ineradicable by all the years of official discourse to the contrary. So that although I feel a sense of my own failure to live up to some high-toned principles about human equality, dignity, and value, I also experience a genuine pleasure in thinking myself superior to those I feel contempt for.

The true source of my uneasiness is not my own failure to live up to noble principles that at one level of consciousness I accept and admire, but the more down-to-earth matter that I discerned his contempt for me and feared he might be getting the best of me. It was quite clear to me that the form his contempt took was that he did not care what I thought of him (with a small exception for preferring that I thought he was doing a good job rather than a bad one). He was indifferent to my contempt and I was not indifferent to his. He was unambivalent in his contempt (at least as a conscious matter). To the extent that his contempt was tinged with envy, if any, he reinterpreted the envy as resentment that someone as unprepossessing as I should have such an easy life.

I feel rather confident that I can construct much of his contempt for me not only because he so plainly manifested it but also because I am no stranger to feeling this kind of contempt either, recalling quite well having felt it for the type I have come to be; for even if I like to think myself differentiable from the others he associates me with, I expect him to make no such distinctions, nor am I even confident that my sense that I am distinguishable from those I am grouped with is anything but a delusion. But then am I not simply projecting my self-contempt, making it his contempt for me? I do not want to get lost in this problem except to note a few things: if we are to function competently in this world we have to be reasonably good at discerning the motivations and intentions of others. We do it all the time. To be sure, some of us are better at it than others, and those who are better at it seem to have, over the long haul, a competitive advantage over those who aren't. Those inept at discerning motivation in others are easily swindled; they are also more likely to give offense and thus elicit more hostile reactions than those who are more adept. That still doesn't answer whether I am projecting or not, but it seems that I am no more likely to know whether I am projecting than I am likely to know his motivation. Consider that our therapeutic society seems to depend on an implicit assumption that we are less likely to know ourselves than certain licensed experts are likely to know us.[7]

Furthermore, it may not be as important whether I am right about this particular interaction as that such an interaction seems to make complete social and psychological sense; that is, there is nothing surprising in my account either about my inner states or about his. Nor do I feel it necessary to apologize for an inevitable subjectivity in the account: how, after all, are we to get at motivation without the data of our own inner states? So these qualifications having been made I am confident that he would see me as a feminized male. My build, my bike, my backpack, my profession, mark me as something contemptible in his eyes. I don't work with my hands. Whatever skills I may have are dubiously magical, intangible, never really verifiable. I am a "teacher" in his eyes: a member of a profession he had contempt for as a boy and about which he has never seen any reason to revise the judgment.[8]

If he cared to notice, he might have found it contemptible in me that I cared to have him think me a man like him. He might have discerned that ever so slightly I was aping him back to him. At one level my behavior could be seen as competent and graceful condescension in the eighteenth-century sense of the word.[9] I alter my style in the direction of his in expectation that he will do the same, and we should converge toward the middle, each having compromised out of respect for the encounter if not quite for each other. But he might notice that I was not quite dealing from a position of strength, that, in short, I was trying too hard; to the discerning eye I was somewhat undignified. Here my commitments to democratic egalitarianism only made me a fool in his eyes. I would have been better off to have dealt with him with a kind of cordial aloofness. He unquestionably won the encounter.

His contempt for me, unlike mine for him, was unlikely to have been mingled with horror or disgust. I simply was a matter of indifference to him other than as a source of livelihood. My role was of a one-shot dispenser of money, nothing else. And then there was the suspicion that for all his indifference the culture's determination of status is not without some effect. I belonged by conventional notion to the higher class. I lived in the better neighborhood. This made me, for all my effeminacy in his eyes, less a pollutant in his world than he could be in mine. Though I was contemptibly risible in his eyes, the fact that I was of the higher class made me not have the capacity to pollute. What is the higher in higher class if not the capacity to put more space, real physical space, between yourself and others, to be less polluting even to those who find you contemptible? While one could surely imagine that my unmanliness could disgust him, it, in fact, was not threatening to him at all. I was contemptibly insignificant in his eyes and I could discern this by his cheerful sense of my disattendability. If I had been disgusting, he would not have been so cheerful nor would I have been of such little consequence.

This utterly routine interaction raises many issues, only three of which I will pursue further: (1) the content and mechanics of some varieties of contempt; (2) the particular features of upward contempt that distinguish it from the usual downward contempt; and (3) how social and political arrangements might affect the moral economies of competing versions of contempt.

The Elements of Contempt

"Those things which we neither Desire, nor Hate, we are said to Contemne: Contempt being nothing else but an immobility, or contumacy of the Heart, in resisting the action of certain things." Thus Hobbes in *Leviathan*. Contempt in his formulation looks like indifference. And although this formulation is not unimaginable to us as a species of contempt, it hardly accords with our core notion of contempt. Yet Hobbes is clear that his version of contempt is a passion, not simply the absence of affect.[10] Hume's contempt looks a little more familiar. For him it is a mix of pride and hatred.[11] Pride gives the necessary downward direction and the elevation of oneself in relation to the person contemned; hatred supplies the negative judgment of the other involved in the comparison.

But contempt is much richer than either of these formulations. Seldom, as I have mentioned, is an emotion ever experienced unalloyed with other emotions. It is no easy job, for instance, to separate a pure experience of humiliation from its accompanying despair or indignation; it is difficult to experience jealousy independent of anger, grief independent of frustration. Contempt is especially rich in the protean powers we understand it to have in being able to combine with a multitude of other passions and sentiments. We recognize contempt as a complex which can be made of various admixtures of affect and social style.

Without taking the time to give a rich account of each possible combination, most of us will have no trouble imagining contempt colluding with pity[12] as well as scorn and derision, bemusement as well as smugness; with haughtiness, disgust, revulsion, and horror; with love (as for pets and even children) as well as hatred, indifference, disdain, snubbing, ignoring, sneering, and an array of sentiments which motivate various forms of laughter and smiles: the sardonic, the sarcastic, and the indulgent (again as with pets and children). What is common to all these experiences is one's relation to someone over whom one is claiming some superiority, the very assertion of the claim being identical with the manifestation of contempt. Contempt is itself the claim to relative superiority. This helps explain the nearly polar extremes we suppose for contempt—from pity to disdain, from hate to love, from bemusement to loathing: all these are possible attitudes the higher may assume vis-à-vis the lower.

Whatever the motives and affects that constitute any particular instance of contempt, we should not be surprised to see its styles and meanings intimately connected to the social and cultural setting in which it arises. Rigid hierarchies or societies of clearly marked status will have their contempts tend in one direction while the contempts of democratic culture, or of roughly egalitarian honor cultures, will tend to be constituted in another way.

Take Hobbes's contempt again. It looks like the contempt of complacency, of never doubting your superiority and rank. It is the contempt of the master for the man, the lord for the peasant, the lady for the maid. These lower persons simply do not merit strong affect; they are noticed only sufficiently so as to know that they are not noticeworthy. One can condescend to treat them decently, one may, in rare circumstances, even pity them, but they are mostly invisible or utterly and safely disattendable.[13] We are not unfamiliar with this contempt of complacent indifference even in democratic cultures. It still flourishes in spite of democratic principle in particular contexts in which status is fixed and mobility across rankings is relatively rare. This kind of contempt characterizes the posture of some bosses toward their secretaries and of professionals toward the maintenance staff.

Two qualifiers here. First: I am speaking of one-on-one encounters. It takes extraordinary complacency to ignore large groupings of the low. Such groupings move the contempt of indifference to the realms of terror, horror, and disgust. And this is why societies that depend on the rigid structuring that enables this kind of Hobbesian contempt are careful to regulate the conditions under which the low can assemble. If the superiors feel secure and can indulge complacency, we will see the Hobbesian contempt of indifference; if, however, the groups are at war or for whatever reason the superior finds the lower not safely disattendable, then we might expect differently motivated and constituted contempts as in those which characterize anti-Semitism, racism, and classism, with sexism perhaps marching to a different beat. Here it is not indifference, but loathing, horror, disgust, hatred, cruelty that accompanies and informs the contempt. Second: The indifference that is this kind of Hobbesian contempt depends upon a precise knowledge of where you stand relative to the other and of a corresponding confidence in the disattendability of the other. The country bumpkin who through ignorance fails to understand when he should defer is not showing contempt in this Hobbesian way.[14]

Now change the setting so that we are not confirming or establishing hierarchical relations across large status demarcations but are contending for esteem and standing within a status; in other words, now suppose a basically egalitarian setting. Here we would expect to see a different style of contempt, the one we usually mean when we refer to treating someone with contempt. This is the treatment we give to let others know that they have failed, that they are not measuring up, that they are claiming more for themselves than they can worthily discharge. This is the contempt of the bloodfeuder for the antagonist he has on the run, of the courtier of very refined manners for courtiers of less competence, of the academic for his nonpublishing colleagues. This is not the contempt for the disattendable but for those we might become or have just recently ceased to be. It is more active than Hobbes's contempt, more a part of consciously assumed strategies of interaction. It is the contempt that is the correlative of shaming or humiliating others for their failures to maintain group norms.

This active contempt is part of the system of challenge and riposte in the process of acquisition and maintenance of status. This contempt does more than merely confirm rankings that are already in place, it actually seeks to claim superiority for oneself and to reduce the rank of the other, to establish and confirm new rankings. To be the object of this kind of contempt is, as articulated by a variety of eighteenth-century moralists and social observers, a most serious matter. For Fielding it was crueler than murder.[15] And Lord Chesterfield, ever wary, warns his son that such contempt is so hateful to others that in many instances it is prudent to avoid displaying it:

> However frivolous a company may be, still, while you are among them, do not show them, by your inattention, that you think them so; but rather take their tone, and conform in some degree to their weakness, instead of manifesting your contempt for them. There is nothing that people bear more impatiently, or forgive less, than contempt; and all injury is much sooner forgotten than insult.[16]

These men moved in circles where they felt their esteem and status at risk from a number of directions: from above by those whose favor they sought; from the side by those with whom they competed for the favors of those above; by those upstarts immediately below whose very presence would devalue the position they had already attained. If they could still rest secure among their servants they could not rest secure among the witlings, the coxcombs, the insolent and impudent would-bes.[17]

In this hurly-burly of anxious competition for status everyone made use of contempt, either to maintain rank already achieved, to test whether it had been achieved, or to challenge for its acquisition. So close is the connection between status and contempt that one frequently sees people, inept at reading all the subtle proprieties of contempt's regulation, promiscuously spraying contempt about in the belief that the mere display of it will secure their rank. This is the "insolent contempt," in Chesterfield's phrase, of the upstart who reveals his anxiety about his rank by failing to condescend amiably to decent people who rank beneath him, treating them instead with blistering contempt. This kind of insolent contemptuousness is incessantly pilloried in comedies of manners; these mean fools—of whom we might take Mrs. Elton, in *Emma*, as one of many instances—are too dim to recognize merit, rank, or where they stand in the eyes of real blue blood. But to some extent they can be excused. They have, after all, rightly recognized the general principle: contempt and status are intimately connected. They just have botched all the details.

Under the rubric of contempt lies a complex of strategy, expression, and affect. By way of reprise, the only thing we can say with reasonable confidence is that whatever the precise style of the particular contempt, whether Hobbesian indifference or visceral loathing and disgust, what is being established or confirmed in every instance is relative social and moral value. Contempt is the emotional complex that articulates and maintains hierarchy, status, rank, and respectability. And differentiated status and rank are the eliciting conditions of contempt. So what we have is a kind of feedback loop in which contempt helps create and sustain the structures which generate the capacity for contempt. And there is good reason to believe that the particular style of contempt will be intimately connected with the precise social and political arrangements in which it takes place.

*   *   *

Let me at this point draw out some key distinctions between disgust and contempt. Disgust and contempt have significant points of overlap, to be sure, but they are ultimately different syndromes, each with substantial areas that do not implicate the other. Darwin, as mentioned in Chapter 2, notes that "extreme contempt, or as it is often called loathing contempt, hardly differs from disgust" (253). The contempt that hardly differs from disgust is that contempt which acquires disgust's frequent physiological markers: queasiness, cringing, recoiling. We usually think of disgust as much more visceral than most instances of contempt for the very reason that such physiological markers are generally unexpected in routine contempt and expected in routine disgust. Disgust is bound to metaphors of sensation or it is not disgust; it needs images of bad taste, foul smells, creepy touchings, ugly sights, bodily secretions and excretions to articulate the judgments it asserts; contempt, in contrast, usually makes do with images of space and rank-order or various styles of ridicule and derision: looking down upon or looking askance at, or simply smiling or laughing at.

Consider too our facial expressions. Contempt, like disdain and sneering, is often indicated by a slight uncovering of the canine tooth on one side of the face. This same expression can imperceptibly metamorphose into a smile, which as Darwin notes, "may be real, although one of derision and this implies that the offender is so insignificant that he excites only amusement; but the amusement is generally a pretense" (254). We all know under what circumstances the amusement is a pretense: when the safely contemptible passes over the line into the threatening and disgusting. In that case the show of amusement is a defensive tactic that attempts to mask the confusion revulsion might bring, revealing that one strategy for dealing with disgust is to pretend it is contempt. But the amusement need not be a pretense; it could just as well be a sign of the genuine ridiculousness of certain kinds of contemptibility.

Although the facial expressions for contempt and disgust can often do service on behalf of the other, we usually associate the one-sided upturned lip, the kind of smirking half smile, with contempt, whereas in disgust the upper lip is retracted symmetrically.[18] The half smile is simply not available for disgust (except as I just indicated as a denial of it by claiming that the occasion warrants mere contempt); while the gape with protruding tongue or the outward curl of the lower lip that often accompanies interjections like yuck or ecch is not available to contempt. Most contempt expressions have a kind of one-sidedness to them, whether it be in the half smile, the tilt or turn of the head from the vertical, or the kind of sneer that accompanies the tongue click usually represented in English by "tsk," articulated by drawing the breath inward as the tongue is positioned to make the "ts" sound. Even when the head is tilted back and the eyes cast down in an expression of disdain, the eyes invariably look to the side rather than straight down.[19] Disgust expressions tend toward bilateral symmetry.[20]

The half-smile, the sardonic sneer, the head tilts, that accompany contempt evidence a close connection between contempt and the ironic. One senses the rightness of the coupling of irony with contempt, whereas disgust seems to undo ironic possibility. One does not get queasy or convulsively recoil in irony; disgust is too closely connected with horror to engage in conventional ironies. Of course we can all think of ironies that pervade the domain of the disgusting, but unlike the very presentness of the ironic sense in much contempt, the ironies of disgust are generally available only upon reflection or to third-party observers: it is hard to avoid the sense of the ironic in contempt, hard to experience it in disgust. Indeed it is the very assumption of an ironical attitude toward the object that constitutes the experience of so much contempt. Displays of contempt often have the air of a pose about them.

But not all contempt need act out its ironic aspect so visibly. Consider again that contempt underwrites decorous treatment of others no less than hostility toward them; herein too there is a noted contrast with disgust. You can just as well let others know they stand beneath you with charity and pity as with sneering and aloofness. And the more benevolent forms of contempt let you glow with self-congratulation for treating another who is beneath you respectfully. Decent treatment of one who disgusts you, however, is accomplished in spite of the disgust; not so with contempt. Perversely, then, whereas disgust cannot inform decent treatment of another, certain styles of contempt not only are consistent with the decent treatment of others, they seem to mark the very form of so much of what we call politeness and much of what is thought of as charity.

Contempt and disgust both are key emotions in maintaining rank and hierarchy, but they work in different ways. Contempt marks social distinctions that are graded ever so finely, whereas disgust marks boundaries in the large cultural and moral categories that separate pure and impure, good and evil, good taste and bad taste. Because contempt is implicated in all rankings of people, it can take on many different styles, as we have just seen, depending on the relative ranking of the people involved, their exact social relation to one another, the measure or quality which is being ranked, and the background assumptions of the social and political order. Contempt can thus range from that kind of Hobbesian indifference that judges the complete disattendability of another, to bemusement at clownishness, to the loathing contempt that cannot rid itself of the displeasure caused by the presence of the other. If disgust can overlap with loathing contempt and is in fact not distinguishable from it, disgust has nothing to do with the contempt that is characterized by indifference. The disgusting is always very present to the senses in a way the contemptible need not be. In fact one of the distinctive markers of what I called Hobbesian contempt is the power it has to prevent the contemptible thing from obtruding on our senses, to render it invisible.

Upward Contempt

I would like to suggest that the notion of contempt moving upward is more than just a play on words. It need not be the case that the conventionally lower person is simply experiencing classic contempt based on the conviction that he or she is superior in terms of the particular standard of comparison. I do not dispute that the lower might know himself more intelligent, physically stronger, more moral, better looking than the higher, but the lower need not hold himself superior in some respect to the higher person to experience contempt for him. He only needs to discern that the higher is lower than the level the higher claims for himself.

But even in those instances where the low recognizes his superiority to the high I claim that his contempt will have a different feel, a different style, that properly makes it *upward* contempt. We have already noted some differences: (1) that upward contempt is less likely to be coupled with disgust, that it is thus less concerned with protection from pollution; (2) that in democratic settings upward contempt, unlike contempt proper, is secure in its legitimacy. Upward contempt, in spite of the fact that it allows the lower to claim superiority regarding a particular attribute, does not take place in a vacuum. The persons below know they are below in the eyes of the others, know they are in some sense held in contempt by those others, whereas the higher by the usual conventions of rank can indulge themselves even legitimately in the thought that they are held in esteem, admired, or envied by the lower.

I am painting broadly here and must add a qualification. In the actual micropolitics of any particular encounter all kinds of competing factors may alter the precise style of mutual status adjustment. Given role proliferation, pluralism, and the significance of certain public spaces, the conventionally low may at certain times be able to compete freely as to whose contempt gets styled as reactive and whose as constitutive. For instance, it makes a difference that the mason and I met on my front porch, rather than in a working-class bar. Upward contempt, by my reckoning, always has some consciousness of its own reactiveness. When it ceases to be thus aware we have either the inadvertent offensiveness of the country bumpkin or the open competition for dominance played out among people contesting their relative ranking.

The knowledge of the expected ranking and ordering is not without consequences. This means that upward contempt takes place in a larger setting of power relations that defines its ranges and meanings. If conventional contempt constitutes hierarchy, upward contempt makes for some psychic space for the low. It never loses the sense of its own limits; it knows itself to be secondary, a kind of remedy for the contempt that is rained down on one, never constitutive, always reactive. In other words, no matter how contemptible I may be to the mason I hired, the fact remains that I hired him, not he me. The hiring of someone to do manual labor constructs the relative ranking in favor of the hirer. But when one hires (we don't even say hires, but rather engages, or retains, or sees) a doctor, law-yer, or some other person engaged in some of the more magical (and suspect) professions it is often the hireling rather than the hirer who occupies the higher ranking.

Upward contempt also differs from conventional contempt in at least two more crucial ways. The contempt of the low for the high, unlike conventional contempt, will often be coupled with a distinctive kind of *Schadenfreude*. If the pleasure of normal contempt is often tinged with complacency, self-satisfaction, and smugness, or even with a simple and less culpable delight in one's own superiority or in the sentimentality of pity, the pleasure in upward contempt is seldom separable from the knowledge that the superior you hold in contempt is humiliating himself, is, in short, looking foolish.[21]

Suppose two different bases of contempt for the high. In one the low accept the values the high espouse and resent their incompetence and knavery in failing to adhere to them; in the second the low find the values themselves ridiculous. Take the first case. Occupying the high position is not without its risks. The high have to maintain the standards they claim to uphold or suffer contempt and resentment for failing to maintain them. The contempt for the ineptitudes and knavery of the high finds its perfect expression in satire, an especially bitter and sardonic satire. And the degree of bitterness is directly related to the satirist's own acceptance of the values that the high profess but do not adhere to. Satire, then, to the extent that it involves the lower's exposing and admonishing the higher, is usually the baili-wick not of the utterly disempowered but of the middling and min-isterial sorts: it is the contempt of those who actually have to clean up the messes and implement the policies of those they contemn.[22]

Take now the second type of upward contempt, which simply finds the high's standards of conduct and virtue and the social institutions which maintain them silly, a cause for general mirth. This style is more clearly associated with hierarchical society (but not necessarily so). Here the strategy is not to paint the higher as knaves, but to see them as clowns and fools. This is the feast of misrule. In this setting the standards and virtues of the powerful are meaningless. Only their power matters. The glee, mirth, laughter, the giggles, deny for the moment the forms of constrained deference. To the extent that pomposity is an attribute of institutionalized power there is always an entry for the glee and delight of seeing it punctured.

Kings and lords inoculated themselves somewhat against the risk of punctured pomposity by privileging fools and lower-class jesters who were allowed to ridicule their superiors to their faces. One way to deal with those laughing behind your back is to make them perform some of the same routines before you to defuse most of their danger. The institution of the privileged fool also indicates that the high were in some respects willing and able to see themselves as their inferiors saw them as long as such seeing was on their own terms and in their own spaces. But not all scenes of punctured pomposity occurred during periods set aside for it each year or under privilege accorded to the jester; whenever the contents of a chamber pot fell on a finely dressed lady or whenever a lord tripped over his sword, events conspired to produce an occasion for laughter. Imagine how hard it must have been for the footman to keep a straight face.

Mini-feasts of misrule, therein lies the image of this style of upward contempt. Contrast it with the usual style of downward contempt: sardonic, indifferent, smug, or bemused, but all in all dismissive. Note too that the two styles of contempt can each have their defensive aspects. Downward contempt defends against the possibility of impudence by denying the capacity of the offender to offend; upward contempt tries to carve out spaces of self-respect by making the contemners of one's respectability comic characters.[23]

The contempt of the higher's values and standards of conduct need not only lead to the mirthful contempt of feasts of misrule. Contempt can be the consequence of calculated self-interest that thrives at the expense of a superior whose values make it easy to fleece him. The embezzlements of Chaucer's Manciple and Reeve[24] were the cost of a noble ethic that made work and attention to the balance sheet a contemptible badge of baseness. Masters were hardly unaware that such thieving by their servants went on. They delighted in a comedic literature in which cunning servants outwitted them. You were almost supposed to be cheated by your servants; if you cared enough to put a stop to it you were base, illiberal, and small-minded. In that kind of society your moral standing and self-esteem were still safely independent of what your servants or other lower-status people thought of you.

Upward contempt, as noted earlier, is marked by its reactive quality. It is a payback of sorts, a response to the contempt being rained down from above. I suspect that the style of upward contempt might vary with the style of contempt it is responding to and that the two might be locked together in a circle of mutual elicitation and influence. We might state it broadly thus: Hobbesian contempt, the style of disattending the other, of being indifferent to him or her, characterizes the contempt of the high for the low in rigid hierarchies until we get to democracy, when it becomes available as a style of upward contempt.

In the West before the French Revolution, Hobbesian indifference was largely unavailable to the low as a style of contempt, at least in a form that could evoke anxiety and concern among the high. In that world the public form of upward contempt was feasts of misrule, or the grim laughter (and disgust) of hypocrisy exposed and ineptitude discovered. And one suspects that even these styles of upward contempt were not quite evenly distributed among the various rankings beneath the nobility. Feasts of misrule were for those at the social antipodes of the nobility, while the bitter delight in exposing hypocrisy was more a style, as indicated earlier, of those who were nearer the high, who actually had a chance to observe them closely, but were still contemned by them.

Consider certain broad types of social arrangements and the various contempts that maintain them. The heroic world, those cultures described in epic, cannot tolerate too much upward contempt of the sort that questions the very value of honor itself. Anyone who risks it is put down quickly and the hierarchy is maintained no matter how comical the values on which it is based may look to the underlings. True, Thersites is given his say, but no one responds to the content of his speech; Odysseus's *ad hominem* assault is deemed to dispose of the issue.[25] In the Icelandic sagas Thersites makes a brief appearance in the guise of a poor farmer named Thorkel of Hafratindar. He has the temerity to refuse to warn the hero of an impending ambush because he finds the feuds of the honorable vaguely amusing and proposes instead to have fun from a safe distance watching them kill each other off. His arguments about the absurdity of honor are not dealt with either, except *ad hominem*. He is killed for his disrespectful sense of humor.[26]

Heroic society, however, knows of contempt; it depends upon it. Contempt is the correlative of shame and humiliation. Contempt is what the honorable have the right to show for the less honorable; it is part of the give and take of the acquisition and maintenance of honor. Fear of contempt or shame is what fuels the engine of honor. The literatures of heroic honor only rarely give us a glimpse of those too mean to be part of the competition for honor: Thersites and Thorkel suffer grievously for their contemptuous ridicule of the ethics of honor. Upward contempt of their sort is dangerous and not tolerable. When one laughs at one's superiors one had better make sure it is safely behind their backs unless one has been granted the privilege of the fool or madman.[27]

It is often the case that those one down in the feud, that is, those who have been wronged and have not yet avenged themselves, may defy their opponent, may in fact show contempt for him. This, however, is not upward contempt, for it is bandied around within a group of rough equals, players in the game. The views of true inferiors, that is, of servants, the lowly, the non-players, don't interest the authors—except, in the saga literature, the views of the women. In Iceland the thoughts of the wives, mothers, and daughters of warrior men do count, and they are experts at subjecting their men to blistering contempt for their failings. They are masterly at shaming and humiliating. Yet this too is not upward contempt. The women are charged with voicing the norms of honor. They are upholding the ethic of honor.[28]

For insistent interest in upward contempt we need hierarchies that are not as fluid as those in the rough egalitarianism of honor systems. We need more formal or less mobile hierarchies that assign whole groups to a rank rather than a game in which individuals compete for relative rank. We also need certain instabilities in the confidence with which the hierarchy is maintained. Consider these accounts in the generation or two that precede the French Revolution and then some that follow reasonably soon upon it.

Fielding, in his *Essay on Conversation,* asks us to "suppose a conversation between Socrates, Plato, Aristotle and three dancing masters" (267).[29] The mere posing of the hypothetical suggests the problem: mutual contempt.[30] The "heel sophists would be as little pleased with the company of the philosophers as the philosophers with theirs." What can be done to remedy the situation? Two courses are proposed: raising the lower and lowering the higher. The former is impossible. What must become of "our dancing masters" should Socrates discourse on the nature of the soul, Plato on the beauty of virtue, or Aristotle on occult qualities? "Would they not stare at one another with surprise and . . . at our philosophers with contempt?" The philosophers must condescend to those topics which are mutually intelligible. Here is a vignette in which mutual contempt between high and low is assumed. But note the tone. The dancing masters are no threat to order, only to interesting conversation. Their contempt for Plato and his pals types them as comically contemptible. If the contempt of dancing masters is all that philosophers have to concern themselves with then they are safe indeed.

The dancing master is not some rude mechanic. He is contemptible especially because his skill is one that he gets no credit for having. There are ideologies, among which we might count Christianity, that grudgingly concede virtue to tillers of the soil and to the builders of things, but the dancing master is simply a low abettor of the vanities of the privileged. Rude mechanics and tillers of the soil occasionally produce Wat Tylers and Jack Cades, but no one fears a dancing master, whose position makes him serviceably oily and obsequious. The only basis a dancing master has for laughing behind your back is his dancing skill, and that is what he is paid to impart to you. So if he laughs at your son's ungainliness he only calls into question his own skills as a teacher. This makes his smirking much less pointed than that of your footman or valet de chambre or chambermaid. If one must suffer occasionally the contempt of the low, what better than have it come from the dancing master?

In this world a gentleman is still in control. He is not anxious about the figure he cuts before his servants. He adopts a condescending confident and benevolent style. Thus Lord Chesterfield: "There is a *bienséance* also with regard to people of the lowest degree; a gentleman observes it with his footman, even with the beggar in the street. He considers them as objects of compassion, not of insult; he speaks to neither *d'un ton brusque*, but corrects the one coolly, and refuses the other with humanity" (to his son, June 13, O.S. 1751). Chesterfield's gentleman calmly keeps his money in his pocket. So the *humanity* of his refusal must simply be that he refrains from beating, berating, or ridiculing the beggar. The compassion he shows then does not lead to action designed to ameliorate the beggar's condition. Evidently inaction counts as an improvement since the benchmark expectation is insult, beating, and beratement.

But some fifty years later we have a more anxious world. William Godwin can observe that "In England at the present day there are few poor men who do not console themselves, by the freedom of their animadversions upon their superiors. The new-fangled gentleman is by no means secure against having his tranquillity disturbed by their surly and pointed sarcasms. This propensity might easily be encouraged, and made conducive to the most salutary purposes."[31] In this threatening, panicky post-revolution world we soon begin to observe the nervous anxieties of the proto-modern paranoid who feels that every servant, every inferior, is laughing at him. From the jovial contemplation of shallow dancing masters having contempt for Plato and Aristotle we move to a world in which every encounter with a social inferior holds the prospect of one's own humiliation. Democratic ideals have, if not quite transformed the old style, surely altered expectations and perceptions. Downward contempt becomes less complacent because it now suspects it is being paid back in kind. The high can no longer as easily maintain the Hobbesian contempt of indifference. Only the insentient fool is indifferent to threat. One can pose as indifferent, but this is a strategy designed to veneer fear and gnawing doubts about the figure one cuts in a world all of a sudden much more densely populated. The servants are no longer quite invisible.

William Hazlitt, for instance, sees himself in a constant struggle with servants out to ridicule and humiliate him: "Their betters try all they can to set themselves up above them, and they try all they can to pull them down to their own level. They do this by getting up a little comic interlude, a daily, domestic, homely drama out of the odds and ends of the family failings, of which there is in general a plentiful supply or make up the deficiency with materials out of their own heads."[32] No point in preempting their mockery with kindness: "Any real kindness or condescension only sets them the more against you. They are not to be taken in in that way." Notice again that the style of upward contempt is the style of comedy and drama. And it is not just your own servants who are cheeky and cheat, but "after a familiar conversation with a waiter at a tavern, you overhear him calling you by some provoking nickname" (107).

This is a world in which the once invisible is now monstrous and flexing its muscle. Breaches of deference forebode a world turned upside down so that there can no longer be any complacency in the smallest exchange, even though most of them still pass off with all deference intact and all respectfulness preserved. Hazlitt casts about for strategies to save face. Condescension, humanity, he says, don't work. The low will simply hold you in greater contempt (here writing of dull and low people rather than specifically of servants):

> All the humility in the world will only pass for weakness and folly. They have no notion of such a thing. They always put their best foot forward; and argue that you would do the same if you had any such wonderful talents as people say. You had better, therefore, play off the great man at once—hector, swagger, talk big, and ride the high horse over them: you may by this means extort outward respect or common civility; but you will get nothing (with low people) by forbearance and good-nature but open insult or silent contempt.[33]

Hazlitt is desperate and at loose ends. He is still enough of the world of rank and order that he can suppose pretentiousness is a viable humiliation-avoiding strategy. Or we may see him as a proto-Dostoyevskian underground man in which the defining trait of the new modern order is precisely the inevitability of humiliation, the inevitability of appearing contemptible to those you style yourself as better than. In this kind of world the only safe strategy for the preservation of a virtually unattainable self-esteem is paradoxically to seek humiliation.[34] Be pretentious, put on airs, hector and upbraid your social inferiors, because if you don't they will see you as even more contemptible for being embarrassed about your own superiority.

This is modernity itself: suffering upward contempt, feeling self-loathing, and looking ridiculous to those you fancy yourself better than. Instead of being admired, you are now spurned for your attempts at "democratic condescension" when lordly condescension is what is preferred. We have not quite reached the mason and me, but we are very close. Note too that Hazlitt, and in a lesser way my account of the mason, suggests, in contrast to Nietzsche, that self-consciousness is a function of the high's fears of the low's mockery, rather than a function of the low's resentment of the high.

We are in the midst of big changes here. But just what has changed? Are the low less deferential? Or is it that the same old cheekiness, buffoonery, and cunning are now noticed where once they were safely disattendable? Is the change, in other words, more in the masters than in their lackeys? There were always cheeky servants and swindling stewards. Both provided their superiors with stock characters in the comedies that amused them. What I suspect Hazlitt observes is not his inferiors literally laughing in his face where once they never would have dared, but that now types like him care obsessively about impudence and effrontery. They are panicked in seeing what they were once able to ignore; they even imagine being laughed at when they aren't. They are now actively concerned about how they are seen by their inferiors, and they fear that the earlier strategies of dealing with effrontery are no longer so easily available: caning, whipping, or contemptuously refusing to recognize the affront. It is this concern and this fear that look new. A hundred years earlier Swift can imagine his servants laughing at him, knows in fact that they do, but the tone is not of urgent desperation; it is a slapstick comedy in which servants smirk at their superiors' bowel movements, guffaw at their pratfalls, and waste their lords' estates with their knavery and incompetence. The fear is not of revolution, but of bankruptcy. The master is still the master in spite of his servants' effrontery.[35]

Hazlitt is writing at the outset of a new ordering of assumptions about rank and status. Things, he feels, are in flux. But one wonders if he might not be picking up on something different in style from the usual cheekiness and impudence in the low that was there from Plautus onward.[36] The new democratic order allows for a real inversion of contempts. It is now the low who can indulge a Hobbesian contempt; they can treat their superiors with indifference. The waitperson cares less about you than you do about him or her. Contrast this to how the Manciple's and the Reeve's contempt depended on assiduous concern and attention to their masters, on pleasing them, yes, but also on knowing them better than they knew themselves, on becoming utterly indispensable to them, so as to construct the basis for their planned violations of their masters' trust. These cunning operators could never relax; there was no time when they could be indifferent to their masters. Modern inferiors may need to display obsequiousness in some settings, but these settings are severely restricted. For the most part they don't give a damn and have their own spaces within which they have more important things to worry about: like competing for esteem among their peers.

Tocqueville tells another story in which he contrasts English and American customs of treating strangers. Why is it, he asks, that Americans abroad greet one another but the English do not?[37] The short answer is that the English are nervous wrecks about the security of their rank; hence their distinctive reserve. According to Tocqueville, in England the security of an aristocracy of birth has given way to one of wealth and "the immediate result is an unspoken warfare between all the citizens . . . Aristocratic pride still being a very strong force with the English and the boundaries of the aristocracy having become doubtful each man is constantly afraid lest advantage be taken of his familiarity." In America, by contrast,

> where privileges of birth never existed and where wealth brings its possessor no peculiar right, men unacquainted with one another readily frequent the same places and find neither danger nor advantage in telling each other freely what they think. Meeting by chance, they neither seek nor avoid each other. Their manner is therefore natural, frank, and open. One sees that there is practically nothing that they either hope or fear from each other and that they are not concerned to show or to hide their social position.

It seems that before all this natural frank openness can take place it must be preceded by a judgment that the other person is indeed entitled to such free intercourse.[38] The openness does not precede a determination of who exactly is entitled to it, but itself follows on the ascertainment that one is dealing with a rough equal. Tocqueville is comparing apples and oranges. He compares an Englishman who has yet to judge whether the person he is dealing with is his peer to Americans who have already made that judgment.[39] The Englishman is wary of a person about whose exact rank he is uncertain; the American has that settled already because the place frequented will be a place for his kind of people to frequent.

I am overstating it. There surely was something more open about America for broad ranges of men (and I mean men) when compared with Europe and even the large freedoms of England. The English did and do cut distinctions of rank in much finer gradients than Americans. Yet I would imagine that these natural, frank Americans would quickly settle among themselves who was a man to be reckoned with and who was not, who was to be deferred to and who was not, who was to be respected and who was not, even if this form of respect was less hedged in with formalized conventions than English relations among classes and ranks would be. If the class of people an American admitted as his equals was more broadly recruited than an Englishman's it was rather sharply delimited nonetheless, and those boundaries were maintained as before by contempt, humiliation, and disgust.

Consider further the following extract from a letter a young New Yorker wrote home to his sister in 1852 about his travels in the Caribbean:

Here a black man is as good as a white one . . . They do not hesitate to offer their hands to be shaken. Our washerwoman, sits upon the sofa in the cabin and talks as bold and loud as tho' the ship was hers. A washerwoman in NY, a white one too, would not open her lips or think of sitting down. Nor would she offer to shake hands, as our Antiguan lady washerwoman did, which I politely refused to accept. The English say much against what they call equality in the states. They call it the most disagreeable part of their travels in our country that any man can ride who pays. If they think our equality disagreeable, I think theirs disgusting—for certainly our servants would not offer to shake hands with us, a thing often occurring in Antigua.[40]

I want to make two points about this wonderfully rich passage. One point is the revelation that equality comes in all kinds of sizes and shapes. And that the American size and shape still had plenty of room for rank and status, not only for race and gender as in the young traveler's letter, but we suspect among white men too, even, I would guess, on the egalitarian western frontier.[41] There is English equality and American equality and each style seems to appall the other and provide the basis for competing contempts and disgusts between Americans and the English. And what is it that makes these equalities appalling? The impudence of people clearly designated as inferior. Both equalities want ranks maintained even if the grand theory of ranks has fallen on hard times. The English dislike the fact that American common carriers don't distinguish rank among paying passengers, while the American finds it disgusting that the English allow servants such familiarity as to think to shake hands with their social superiors (one suspects our traveler is mistaking a frontier colonial style for a particularly English style). Upstartism of some sort is as upsetting to Americans as it is to the English, in spite of the polemical point Tocqueville wishes to make. One wonders, by the way, how our young traveler thought it was possible to refuse the washerwoman's hand *politely*. Presumably, he, like Chesterfield to the beggar, assumes an appallingly low benchmark in which caning, raping, or spitting in the face is the norm.

The second point is that Mr. Dudley, the letter writer, shows that any claim about democracy liberating upward contempt to combat the contempt being rained down from above must be accompanied by a much more nuanced and detailed story than I am providing here. Apparently these two opposing contempts established various equilibria at different times and places. The New York washerwoman is still all deference to Mr. Dudley's mind. But is she? She may simply be utterly indifferent to this confident young prig, finding him at best a bore, at worst an annoyance. And what of the black washerwoman in Antigua? Why assume with Mr. Dudley that she is simply too dense to understand the effect of her lack of deference on the young American man? She may very well be putting him on, exposing him to a very heavy dose of a more broadly comic contempt, rendering him the pretentious fool. It is not as if Mr. Dudley was able to ignore her. Quite the contrary. He thought she was really worth writing home about.

Mr. Dudley and the Antiguan washerwoman are engaged in a battle of mutual contempts; they are struggling over rank and deference.[42] Darwin and the native of Tierra del Fuego, as I described them in Chapter 1, were engaged in a battle of mutual disgusts; the issues that divided them were primarily ones of purity and pollution. Still, the interactions have significant points in common. Both tell of white outsiders dealing with and moved to tell about interactions with darker natives, and both involve what in the eyes of the white person are impermissible touchings. Dudley and the washerwoman's combat takes place against a background of the politics of equality, of ex-slave or daughter of slaves meeting a facsimile of the enslaver; the black woman appears to be delighting in what she must know will be perceived as effrontery, while from Dudley's point of view she has forgotten herself and had better "remember" him in the sense that word had in the world of service and rank. These two are not total strangers; each lives in a social world in which the other plays a part.

The interaction between Darwin and the native, for all its intriguing complexity, is much simpler as a social matter than Dudley's interaction with the washerwoman. These are two men, both utter strangers, without much history giving added complexity to their interaction (such in any event is inferable from the manner in which the account is narrated). Even though it would be fashionable to see colonialism rearing its head here no less than in the Antiguan case, Darwin's interaction with the "native" strikes me as more stripped of history and macro-political concerns; it is about otherness pure and simple, the simple fact of strange difference and how it is experienced, about what lies on the other side of the bounds of purity. It is not so much concerned about regulating a social interaction that already is embedded in an elaborate code of regulation.

*   *   *

I conclude by restating my broad claim. Democracy doesn't destroy the conditions for contempt. In spite of the language of equality we still recognize statuses, classes, and ranks that establish hierarchies. We can, in other words, still safely mark many instances of contempt as upward or conventionally downward. While some contempts surely represent competing claims for dominance as in the style of contempt among rough equals in heroic society, others relatively easily map onto the styles of contempt discoverable in rigidly hierarchical societies. Democracy, far from undoing the basis for contempts of high and low, simply makes it possible for the low to add to the styles of upward contempt they already had in the old order.

If the dominant form of upward contempt was and still is largely that of making the superior look ridiculous, either by feasts of misrule or by satirical exposure of the hypocrisy and incompetence of the superior, it became possible with role proliferation, role division, and democratic assumptions simply to be indifferent, to find more than enough space for oneself in which the superior is disattendable and simply doesn't matter much. The low now have available to them the Hobbesian contempt of just not caring to attend to their superiors, and it is this which does so much to engender anxieties in the superior, for the superior cannot fathom that he or she could be so utterly disattendable.

And what possible strategy is there to oppose to such indifference? Ignoring it? That is simply to battle his indifference with your feigned indifference. Caning is no longer permissible and firing and not hiring are severely circumscribed. Some of the high may indulge in egalitarian experiments in the style of Brook Farm in the nineteenth century or of the type that Tom Wolfe parodied in *Radical Chic & Mau-Mauing the Flak Catchers* in the twentieth. But these experiments seemed to exacerbate snobbism and competing contempts, rather than undo the basis for them.[43] It just might be that the mutuality of contempt is much of what pluralistic democracy is all about. What democracy has done is arm the lower with some of the contempts that only the high had available to them before. Every person is now entitled to think his vote undervalued in comparison with those of all those contemptible others with whom democracy has lumped him. This is no small achievement. It is much of what makes democracy so different from the old order.

10

ORWELL'S SENSE
OF SMELL

IN THE PREVIOUS CHAPTER I distinguished two main types of contempt: the conventional one that created and maintained the official social orderings and rankings, that is, the contempt the high have for the low; and another, upward contempt, which the low feel for the high. I hypothesized a historical connection between upward contempt and the general internalization of democratic ideals, that democracy in some sense enabled the low by legitimating their contempt for the high and delegitimating to some degree the privilege of the high to express their contempt for the low. In other words, the claim was that democratization involved changes in the propriety of certain emotions. The proper terrain of contempt was shifting. The high still felt contempt for the low, to be sure, but they now had to suffer minor guilts, anxieties, or self-doubts for feeling so. We confined our attention largely to issues of class and located the key shifts in the emotional economy to have begun in earnest in the late eighteenth and early nineteenth centuries, as evidenced in writers like Hazlitt, Tocqueville, Godwin, and others, all of whom recognized the revolutionary consequences of expanding the right to express contempt to those previously only the object of it. Class and rank were the categories first under assault, but the process could not be contained.

The same process has expanded to include hierarchies based on race, ethnicity, gender, physical and mental handicap, sexual orientation, and the whole array of other groupings the new identity politics has given birth to. In each case the move is only narrowly for equal rights; the battle is for changes in the emotional economy. It demands, as a first step, that the high no longer be presumptively entitled to indulge in Hobbesian contempt, the contempt which renders the contemptible invisible, the confident and complacent contempt of utter indifference. Although often couched in terms of gaining respect, the battle of the low is more realistically one of seeking to change the kinds of contempt that they must suffer. The low, I suppose, can demand to be respected. That is commonly a refrain in liberation movements of this sort. But gaining the respect of those whose contempt takes the form of not even seeing you means first getting their attention. And attention need not bring respect at all; disgust or more intense forms of contempt are just as likely. The demand to be respected is itself often received with contempt. Respect does not usually come on demand; it must be earned.[1]

The fear is that the high, even when the world is turned upside down, will never stop seeing the low as usurpers and upstarts, vulgar and contemptible. The better strategy for attaining rough equality may be to undo the basis for the *complacency* of the high's contempt, if not the contempt itself. Make the high know that their contempt is matched by the low's contempt for them. The battle is to have the high come to recognize the contemptible figure they cut before the low; the realistic goal, or maybe just the unintended consequence, is to create the conditions of democracy by equalizing access to publicly acceptable manifestations of contempt. In any event, it is much easier to show contempt than to elicit respect.

The mechanism by which this shift in the array of contempts comes about is not just a matter of the strategies adopted by the low. Their work is often done for them by defectors from the high who seek to advance the interests of the low, even to teach them that they are victims if they have yet to acquire that knowledge or have suppressed it. The defector's own self-contempt, shame, and self-loathing provide a model for new contempts the low can add to the contempt that observing the foolishnesses of the high had always provided them. Whatever the mix of mechanisms, the high come to suspect the way the low are looking at them (or not looking at them), and indeed the low begin to confirm the worst anxieties of the high, as we saw in the previous chapter in Hazlitt's fear of the mockery he believed the low were directing at him.

Once the high find themselves the objects of the same styles of contempt that they felt were their prerogative alone, we not only have a different emotional terrain, but a different political one as well. The high's serene and secure contempt either gives way to a more anxious contempt that tries to efface itself in acts of charity or in various attempts at mingling with the low, or it takes the opposite course and adopts a more visceral contempt that traffics with disgust and is openly aversive and hostile. The low's form of contempt changes too. Once only expressible by secretive laughing behind the master's back and in privileged feasts of misrule, it now can also adopt the style the high can no longer confidently muster. It is less that truckling is transformed into truculence than that, more and more frequently, the higher classes simply become disattendable, the cause for no special concern to the low. A rather somber view of democracy and pluralism this is—a grid of competing contempts, variously styled—but distinctly recognizable and perhaps even a necessary starting point for a minimally basic respect for persons. After all, this equality of contempts is not a bad thing; in my view democracy (a good thing) depends upon it; it is some (necessary?) part of what a real working equality must mean.

When the conventional contempt of the upper classes becomes less certain of its warrant, when the lower classes are no longer invisible or safely disattendable, when they constitute rather intrusive sources of concern and anxiety, then, as I just indicated, contempt reconstitutes itself in a different form. No longer quite capable of complacent indifference, it moves toward horror, loathing, fear, hatred, and disgust. Recall my confrontation with the mason in the preceding chapter. There I noted that the lower, as determined by the dominant conventions and mechanisms of hierarchy, are polluting in a way that the higher, for all their hypocrisy and contemptibility in the lower's eyes, are not. Because the low are defiling they elicit disgust, as well as the lighter forms of contempt that may be tinged with either pity or amusement at what is perceived to be their clownishness. Clownish or invisible is what the contemptible are when they do not constitute a threat; disgusting is what they are when they do. The threat need only be perceived; it need not, by some independent measure, be real. Jews, for instance, by their very existence, were considered threatening by Christians regardless of their power, numbers, or location. And, similarly, the case could be made that men perceive women to be more threatening, more uncanny, the less official power they have.

I want to examine more closely the role of disgust in maintaining social and political hierarchy. This topic was something of an obsession of George Orwell's and formed the central theme of his *The Road to Wigan Pier*. Orwell has a just claim to be the best essayist in English since Hazlitt, a person with whom he shares more than trivial affinities. Along with Swift and Hazlitt, Orwell evidences a "curious mixture of grit and fastidiousness,"[2] the latter trait making them suitable authorities for many of the claims I have been making in this book.

The very matter-of-fact Orwell is the twentieth century's real poet of disgust, not the self-indulgent writers of sex and sexuality, sadism and masochism, pornography and criminality, not the likes of Genet or Bataille. There is little pose or pretense in Orwell's disgust; no cheap thrills, no Nietzschean posturing. Like Swift, he was incessantly tormented by uglinesses and bad smells, and for both these fastidious souls disgust probably outweighed indignation as the moral sentiment of choice. Yet unlike Swift he fought against his super-supersensitivities before succumbing to them: he thus lived as a tramp among tramps. When gathering materials for *Wigan Pier* he lodged chez Brooker (of which more anon), a tripe shop doubling as a lodging house of incredible squalor. He overcame his fastidiousness sufficiently to sleep and eat in such settings, but the images of disgust were indelibly imprinted on his consciousness; more than that, they formed his consciousness. Disgust organized much of his social and moral world. In Richard Hoggart's words, disgust was a quality that "Orwell never lost and which was partly (but not wholly; he was also *by nature* fastidious) socially-acquired . . . He could *smell* his way through complex experiences."[3]

The Road to Wigan Pier was to have been a study of working-class conditions in the industrial north midlands in the midst of the miseries of the general economic collapse of the mid-thirties. The book was commissioned by his publisher, Victor Gollancz, who undertook to publish it for the Left Book Club, of which he was one of the organizers. What Gollancz got was not what he commissioned, which prompted him to write a foreword distancing himself from the book and warning members of the book club what they were in for. What they got was a two-part essay: the first part being a description of working conditions largely consistent, in spite of its quirks, with the author's brief; the second, however, being an extended and personalized essay on disgust and its relation to class.

Disgust, for Orwell, was what stood in the way of socialism's success. More particularly, the question was not only how a sensibility like Orwell's was to overcome the revoltingnesses of the working classes but also how anyone could overcome the repulsiveness of those middle-class types who were drawn to the socialist cause, whom he characterizes as bearded fruit-juice drinkers, nudists, sandal-wearers, nature cure quacks, pacifists, feminists, and food cranks.[4] A food crank is a vegetarian, "a person willing to cut himself off from human society in hopes of adding five years on to the life of his carcass" (175). Orwell, remember, is arguing *for* some vague notion of democratic socialism, not against it. But the problem is that real people and their assaults on one's senses and sensibilities get in the way of loftier ideals.

Before you can favor socialism, says Orwell, "you have got to take up a definite attitude on the terribly difficult issue of class" (121). The verb "take up" suggests an optimism that is immediately rejected. One "takes up," it turns out, pretty much the attitude that was instilled in one as a member of a particular class. His argument is directed, as will become evident, to the middle and upper classes. It is the higher whose attitudes on the class issue will make it next to impossible for them to embrace socialism; the attitudes of the working class, to the extent they matter at all, will not interfere unless the offensiveness of the middle-class types drawn to socialism—the fruit-juice drinkers and sandal wearers—drives them away.

The upper-class attitude toward the "common" people is one of "sniggering superiority punctuated by bursts of vicious hatred" (124). Orwell supposes that this attitude trickled up to the upper classes from that segment of the middle class that occupies the marches at the border between lower and middle, where the distinction between classes was less a matter of means than of manner and manners. These embattled middle-class people are consumed with keeping up appearances and not sinking among the low with their "coarse faces, hideous accents and gross manners." The hatred was sometimes justified given that working-class kids attacked you, "set on you five or ten to one." But it was not that they beat you up. "There was another and more serious difficulty," and it holds the

> real secret of class distinctions in the West—the real reason why a European of bourgeois upbringing, even when he calls himself a Communist, cannot without a hard effort think of a working man as his equal. It is summed up in four frightful words which people nowadays are chary of uttering, but which were bandied about quite freely in my childhood. These words were: *The lower classes smell.* (127)

The qualifier of limitation to "the West" is not made in the pusillanimous qualifying style of the nervous academic. Orwell's prose is remarkable for eschewing hedges. He means that people smell worse in the West than in the East.[5] The Burmese, we learn later, among whom Orwell spent five years, were not "physically repulsive." Though they had a distinctive smell, the smell did not disgust him. He records that the Asians believe Europeans smell somewhat like corpses but does not draw the relativizing conclusion that such beliefs might lead to, because he seems to think the Asians might be more fastidious about these matters than even he is himself (141–142).

The nastier point being made explicitly is that "our" working classes smell worse than coolies in the Empire. It is thus much easier to be anti-imperialist than a socialist. And in fact the second part of *The Road to Wigan Pier* is an account of Orwell's move toward socialism as an expiatory action for the guilt of having participated in the evils of imperialism in Burma. Much of his expiation took the form of forcing himself to endure disgust, to use his fastidiousness as a way of mortifying his flesh, in certain respects not unlike Catherine of Siena.[6] Once the guilt had been assuaged, however, the smells remained and his fastidiousness reemerged invigorated rather than overcome.

The crucial thing is that smell is "an impassable barrier:" "For no feeling of like or dislike is quite so fundamental as a *physical* feeling.

Race-hatred, religious hatred, differences of education, of tempera-
ment, of intellect, even differences of moral code can be got over;
but a physical repulsion cannot. You can have an affection for a
murderer or a sodomite, but you cannot have an affection for a man
whose breath stinks—habitually stinks, I mean." It does not matter
that one is brought up to believe the working classes "ignorant, lazy,
drunken, boorish and dishonest; it is when he is brought up to believe
they are dirty that the harm is done" (128).

Orwell is careful at first to say that the stench of the working
classes is a middle-class *belief,* but it soon becomes clear that it is a
belief he himself holds and that it may not be unjustified.[7] Sane persons, after all, cannot usually continue to maintain beliefs they *know*
are untrue. "Meanwhile, *do* the 'lower classes' smell? Of course, as
a whole, they are dirtier than the upper classes . . . It is a pity that
those who idealise the working class so often think it necessary to
praise every working class characteristic and therefore to pretend that
dirtiness is somehow meritorious in itself." Their smell, however, is
not their fault. They are dirty by necessity, not by choice: "Actually,
people who have access to a bath will generally use it" (130).

His target is not just the working classes. It is those self-hating
bourgeois who idealize them because they don't have middle-class
habits: "I have known numbers of bourgeois Socialists, I have listened
by the hour to their tirades against their own class, and yet never,
not even once, have I met one who had picked up proletarian table-
manners. Yet, after all, why not? Why should a man who thinks all
virtue resides in the proletariat still take such pains to drink his soup
silently? It can only be because in his heart he feels that proletarian
manners are disgusting" (136).

No one escapes the force of the satire. Working-class manners are
so disgusting as to make disgusting hypocrites out of the middle-
class socialists who support the proletarians. Middle-class self-hatred,
it is revealed, cannot overcome the revulsion of slurped soup. And if
Orwell excuses himself from hypocrisy by admitting his disgusts and
by having at least attempted to overcome them by living as a tramp,
he still must posture as a crank himself to get away with the polemic.
The passage provides testimony indeed to the strength of the civilizing process's hold on Orwell and the middle class in general: table

manners are now sufficient to stop political movements dead in their tracks. The civilizing process captured the middle classes, made them what they are. Yet the lamentable fact is that the process ran up against an impenetrable barrier: the proles' refusal to give up their vulgarity.

There is genuine frustration being expressed here. Orwell suggests that if only the working class would civilize itself he would undertake, in contrast to the manner in which the aristocracy reacted to the civilizing of the bourgeoisie, to give them a still target to shoot at. Once you learn, he seems to say, to eat without slurping, wash regularly, and pronounce your aitches I will not further refine the code of manners so as to re-distance myself from you. But it is clear that if distinctions are going to be erased they will only be erased by the working class moving in the direction of middle-class manners rather than the other way around. He cannot imagine that slurping, not bathing, and not keeping a tidy home could ever be preferable to and less revolting than keeping a tidy home, bathing, and not slurping.

And he is right; relativism, like socialism, cannot overcome slurped soup. The working-class family that cultivates bourgeois manners is likely to be held in contempt by their fellow proles, but the new habits themselves are unlikely to disgust. If there is disgust it is for the affectation, not for the way of eating. Among the middle classes, however, the acquisition of soup slurping and chewing with one's mouth open would prompt disgust. The rule we have discerned still governs: the high do not constitute a polluting threat to the low in the way the low do to the high. There are two mechanisms at work that make this so: a socially contingent one which simply defines the high as non-polluting and the low as polluting, and a more essentialist one in which some things carry with them distinctly lower probabilities of being disgusting than other things. The non-smelly are simply less likely to disgust than the smelly, as is the quiet eater less likely than the noisy eater.

In Part II of *Wigan Pier,* the working class's smells, unpronounced aitches, and slurped soup are raised in service of Orwell's ridicule of the egalitarian pretenses of middle-class socialists. In Part I there is no such polemic, just unmediated disgust. Any doubts expressed in Part II about the justifiability of middle-class beliefs concerning working-class uncleanness have already been resolved long before in Part I at the Brookers'. Orwell is a master at descriptions of revolting squalor. His accounts of food preparation in a large Parisian hotel in *Down and Out in Paris and London* or the sour filth and dinginess of the preparatory school in "Such, Such were the Joys" imprint themselves on the memory, but none so indelibly as the Brookers. Orwell stayed there while in Wigan, sharing cramped sleeping quarters, which "stank like a ferret's cage," with three other lodgers. Nothing in the main living quarters was ever cleaned. At the dining table, Orwell would "get to know individual crumbs by sight and watch their progress up and down the table from day to day" (7). The Brookers sold tripe, black tripe, "grey flocculent stuff" crawling with black beetles. Reality sometimes has a way of making itself allegory; how else to explain the attraction of the Brookers to tripe? Orwell descended into the living hell of England's lower intestinal tract; the road to Wigan Pier necessitates passing through a figural bowel that is the Brookers' tripe shop.

Mr. Brooker was a sour man and "astonishingly dirty." Since Mrs. Brooker played the invalid, Mr. Brooker was responsible for preparing the food. "And like all people with permanently dirty hands he had a peculiarly intimate, lingering manner of handling things" (8). He insisted on cutting and thinly buttering each lodger's bread, which he handed to them imprinted with the black mark of his filthy thumb (15). This was no ordinary dirty thumb: it was usual to observe Mr. Brooker "carrying a full chamber-pot which he gripped with his thumb well over the rim" (12). Mrs. Brooker, on the other hand, would lie around, "a soft mound of fat and self-pity," and complain endlessly about no one coming to the shop. Orwell is dismayed that they could not understand that last year's flies dead on their backs in the shop window were not good for business. Mrs. Brooker ate constantly and would wipe her mouth on her blankets or on strips of newspaper which she would then crumple and throw on the floor. The details mount and Orwell does not let us escape without inviting us to several meals taken in the Brookers' company.[8] He finally leaves when he discovers a full chamber-pot under the breakfast table.

Disgust, we are made to feel, cannot avoid the moral implications that come with it. As we saw in Chapter 8, disgust generally moralizes what it touches. Mere description of the Brookers casts blame, mostly on them but also in part on the world that generates them. It makes loathing them inescapable; the outward signs of filth are read as accurate mirrors of rotting and disgusting souls.

> In the end Mrs. Brooker's self-pitying talk . . . revolted me even more than her habit of wiping her mouth with bits of newspaper. But it is no use saying that people like the Brookers are just disgusting and trying to put them out of mind. For they exist in tens and hundreds of thousands; they are one of the characteristic by-products of the modern world . . . It is a kind of duty to see and smell such places now and again, especially smell them, lest you should forget that they exist; though perhaps it is better not to stay there too long. (17)

Why would anyone want to join up with the Brookers without first demanding that the Brookers transform themselves into something at least worthy of pity? To be pitiable, we see, is a sign that one has escaped the realm of the disgusting, if not the realm of contempt. The Brookers are beneath pity because they are beneath contempt.[9]

When trying to tweak middle-class socialists Orwell can suppose that the working class would be clean if dirt weren't forced upon them, but the Brookers deprive him of such comforting thoughts. Too many like them have a will to filth: "The squalor of these people's houses is sometimes their own fault . . . Even if you [are poor] there is no *need* to have unemptied chamber-pots standing about in your living room" (60). Yet he is still able to distinguish among the working class. He can muster genuine pity for the lot of those who still give some indication to him that they are suffering, and suffering because of the costs that such squalor has for the possibility of their own dignity. For these he can construct moving accounts in which their dignity is repurchased by their shame.

But to construct such an account Orwell still has to overcome his sense of smell. And thus it comes as no surprise that his most moving image of the despair of the poor is of a scene he witnesses through the windows of a railway car mercifully taking him away from Wigan. It is the face of a young woman, her youth blasted by the harsh life of poverty, wearing "the most desolate, hopeless expression

I have ever seen" as she kneels "in the bitter cold on the slimy stones of a slum backyard, poking a stick up a foul drain-pipe" (18). Pity is enabled and disgust prevented by the intervening glass and by the receding position from which he observes the events. He thus neither has to smell the odors nor to hear the aitchless accents that would mar her plaint. Sympathy is best elicited in the middle distances. Too close and romanticization is defeated by the uglier side of reality; too far and one's attention is not engaged.

Critics have generally dismissed Orwell's discussion of class as naive, even mean-spirited.[10] They are wrong. From my perspective he is well within the tradition of Adam Smith, who recognizes that an account of class, rank, or social hierarchy must be thin indeed unless accompanied by an account of the passions and sentiments that sustain it. Eliminate his own desire to tweak and offend from the exposition and what remains is a serious meditation on the connection of emotions, particularly disgust, to the creation and maintenance of class hierarchy. Disgust may not be necessary to all rank orderings, but it appears as an insistent feature in some of our most common social orderings. It figures in class, caste, race, religion, and gender. Christians, whites, the upper classes, and men have all complained through the centuries, often obsessively, about the smells of Jews, nonwhites, workers, and women.[11] For instance, Felix Fabri, a fifteenth-century friar on a pilgrimage to Jerusalem, wonders why the Saracens would allow Christians admittance to their public baths. The reason, he tells us,

> is said to be that the Saracens emit a certain horrible stench, on account of which they use continual ablution of diverse sorts, and since we have no stench, they do not mind our bathing with them. This indulgence they do not extend to Jews, who stink even worse; but they are glad to see us in their baths, for even as a leper rejoices when a sound man associates with him, because he is not despised, and because he hopes that because of the sound man he himself may gain better health, so also a stinking Saracen is pleased to be in the company of one who does not stink.[12]

Saracens, Jews, and lepers are all polluting and thus they must stink. Stenches are differentiable and correspond exactly to the level of danger afforded. Jews and lepers are thus more polluting than Saracens while Christians in this context cannot smell. This is the same man who preserved for us the account of his companions throwing chamber pots at each other on shipboard (see Chapter 7). In that setting a new ordering takes place and presumably our pilgrim will come to notice that some of the people on board, though Christian, will smell worse than others.[13] "We have no stench" makes no claim that individual Christians don't smell, it is only a claim that no Christian smells by virtue of his Christianity. What is being denied is the existence of a group stench and no more. And of course he is right as long as he remains a Christian in a unified Christian social and moral regime. So secure is Fabri in his belief that he imputes its confirmation to the Saracens. They thus bathe because they know they stink, even on their own turf where they are the dominant group. The logic of this strikes us as strange indeed, for one suspects that the claim is less that Christians do not bathe because they do not smell, than that they must be clean and have no smell because they do not bathe.

These kinds of group stenches come with group membership.[14] And to the extent that one could distance oneself from the group or adopt a special status one's stench would proportionally subside. The stench of Jews, as noted earlier, could thus be washed away by baptism; that of women by chastity, and so on. It is not just the high who believe in the stench of the low. The low come to believe it of themselves or, if they cannot quite smell it, they suspect that others can. Orwell believed he smelled when he occupied the lowest rung of the pecking order as a scholarship student in his preparatory school, his family being without the means to pay full tuition:

> I had no money, I was weak, I was ugly, I was unpopular, I had a chronic cough, I was cowardly, I smelt. The picture, I should add, was not altogether fanciful. I was an unattractive boy. Crossgates soon made me so, even if I had not been so before. But a child's belief in its own shortcomings is not much influenced by facts. I believed, for example, that I "smelt," but this was based simply on general probability. It was notorious

that disagreeable people smelt, and therefore presumably I did so too.[15]

One wonders if the heavy use of colognes and aftershaves by lower-class men is a reflex of these beliefs. Their belief is that one cannot smell bad if one smells good, but in fact this is a misreading of the code that governs the relation of smell to class. The true rule is that one does not smell bad if one does not smell. So the aftershave, sure enough, begins to stink.[16] Good smells can be a cause for suspicion, mistrusted as a mask or a veneering covering something that needs to be hidden.[17] We cannot trust our own sense of smell to discover that we smell bad; we know only too well that we get used to ourselves and that as fastidious as we may be we cannot quite trust our capacity to discern how we smell to others. So those low who care enough about how they are seen by the high come to mistrust their senses and admit "the general probability" that they smell. Like one's beauty and one's social and moral standing, so one's smell seems to be in many ways a creation of the other.

I said "in many ways." Some smells nature selected for their aversiveness; they are offensive in essence. Skunks gained an evolutionary advantage by having a musk that was objectively offensive to a wide range of species, was difficult to become inured to, and retained its force largely independent of context. Yet our senses, even our olfactory sense, are manipulable and markedly affected by our beliefs. Many bad odors become reasonably acceptable when knowledge of their origin is suppressed. The same odor believed to come from strong cheese is much more tolerable than if thought to emanate from feces or rank feet. Presumably the mark of cheap perfume is in who is wearing it, just as beauty is often simply what the lowly aren't; so that when the low were thin and malnourished corpulence was beautiful, and when the poor became fat the aesthetic quality of thinness shifted signs. Jews, blacks, or workers smelled as a matter of principle. Whether they really smelled or not, a stench would be imputed to them and presumably suggestion and wishful thinking made it so. These low engendered undeniable disgust and revulsion, so smell they must.

These beliefs were governed by remarkably rich context-sensitive rules that suspended the stench in particular settings. The Jewish physician, the black woman who nursed the white child and cooked the food, were not deemed contaminating even as (or because) they were allowed intimate contact. The stench was in abeyance and was smelled only when the time was threatening to be out of joint, or when the low were considered in general as an undifferentiated mass, or when the low were acting in ways that did not explicitly admit deference or inferiority. This knowledge of the social-structural nature of polluting powers was available before Mary Douglas. Thus a writer for the *Atlantic* in 1909 can note that while no Negro

> is allowed to travel in a Pullman car between state lines or to enter as a guest a hotel patronized by white people, the blackest of Negro nurses and valets are given food and shelter in all first-class hotels and occasion neither disgust nor surprise in the Pullman cars ... The black nurse with a white baby in her arms, the black valet looking after the comfort of a white invalid, have the label of their inferiority conspicuously upon them.[18]

The stench of the low seems to bear a direct relation to the anxiety they generate in the high. When out of place they smell; when safely in place they do not.

Orwell knows well enough that one's official odor was a function of being lowest on the totem pole independent of the "truth" of one's smell. That, after all, was why he knew he "smelt" at Crossgates. But this knowledge brought Orwell little solace for two reasons. Just because an odor might be socially constructed does not mean it is not there. Even if the smell was invented, thrust into the situation by the high, that did not make the smell go away. It was still there as long as the structures that gave rise to it were. Moreover, the working classes might actually smell, independent of upper-class beliefs and wishes. The proles might have rescued the whole issue from the threats of relativism by actually stinking. Orwell suspected such was the case and he sought somehow to confirm it even though he knew he was in the grip of beliefs that would impute a stench to them anyway. Hence lodging with the Brookers, who provide the Platonic form of the disgusting, the pure thing. We learn that he had left perfectly decent accommodations among some unemployed miners to stay in the tripe shop.[19] He sought the Brookers out. They would make for a better story and they would also allow him to keep, it seems, some rather cherished beliefs. His nose knew that they were like skunks, not merely made so by their structural position in some grid of pollution and purity.

No wonder Orwell is pessimistic about the class issue, when so many of the very people whose interests he sincerely champions revolt him at some deep level. There will always be classes, he feels, as long as a group insists on living in a way that will objectively offend even those sympathetic to it. Classlessness, socialist equality, must depend on eliminating the conditions of this kind of social disgust. Classes held in place by disgust will be immediately restored by disgust unless people like the Brookers are civilized and clean up. Therein lies the one small cause for hope. Unlike skunks the Brookers do not need their musk; they can be taught to abandon it, and it is in their interest to do so.

There is wit in all this. *Wigan Pier* is half an attempt to overcome and half a confession of his failure to overcome a certain snobbishness. Prior to his sojourn in Burma, Orwell openly admits, he was "both a snob and a revolutionary," having spent "half the time in denouncing the capitalist system and the other half in raging over the insolence of bus-conductors" (140–141). But he runs up against disgust and so must end up reclaiming, if not quite his snobbishness, his commitment to the virtues of middle-class tastes and attitudes, which he is stuck with anyway because they are what he is; they constitute his identity:

> It is easy for me to say that I want to get rid of class-distinctions, but nearly everything I think and do is a result of class-distinctions. All my notions—notions of good and evil, of pleasant and unpleasant, of funny and serious, of ugly and beautiful— are essentially middle-class notions; my taste in books and food and clothes, my sense of honour, my table manners, my turns of speech, my accent, even the characteristic movements of my body, are the products of a special kind of upbringing and a special niche about half way up the social hierarchy . . . To get

outside of the class-racket I have got to suppress not merely my
private snobbishness, but most of my other tastes and prejudices
as well. I have got to alter myself so completely that at the end
I should hardly be recognizable as the same person. (161)

To transform himself so is more than he is willing to do, or more
than he could ever do even if willing. In his typical confrontational
style he notes that very few people who rail against class distinctions
really want to abolish them: "Every revolutionary opinion draws part
of its strength from a secret conviction that nothing can be changed"
(158). Those fruit-juice-drinking middle-class socialists can wish for
a classless society only if they romanticize the working class. "Let
them get into a fight with a drunken fish-porter on Saturday night,
for instance—and they are capable of swinging back to the most
ordinary middle-class snobbishness" (163). Orwell can hardly blame
the middle-class socialist for his revulsion at the drunken fish porter;
what he finds blameworthy is the hypocrisy in pretending that there
can ever be merit in such vulgar behavior as opposed to the genuine
virtues of middle-class values: civility, privacy, cleanliness of body,
decorum, democracy, and non-intrusive manners. These things are
no mean historical achievement.

Once we discount the effects of Orwell's desire to shock and sen-
sationalize and of his middle-class commitment to things like table
manners, cleanliness, and decorous restraint, we are still left with
some powerful social theoretical points. Besides anticipating Bourdieu
in many ways, Orwell understands that it makes a difference just how
a social norm holds us in its grip. That it is disgust tightening the
grip raises a different set of problems than if it were hate, fear, pity,
concern, a sense of duty, or even some of the milder versions of
contempt doing the work. It matters that the low are repulsive rather
than merely laughable, disgusting rather than invisible.

Orwell's position is that disgust has a firmer hold on us, that it is
more basic to our definition of self, than most other passions. Our
very core, our soul, is hemmed in by barriers of disgust, and one
does not give them up unless one is in love or is held at the point of
a gun. In fact, the claim seems to be that the core or the essence of
one's identity can only be known as a consequence of which passions

are triggered in its defense. Disgust's durability, its relative lack of responsiveness to the will, suits it well to its role as the maintainer of the continuity of our core character across social and moral domains. Our durable self is defined as much by disgust as by any other passion. Disgust defines many of our tastes, our sexual proclivities, and our choices of intimates. It installs large chunks of the moral world right at the core of our identity, seamlessly uniting body and soul and thereby giving an irreducible continuity to our characters.

I am exaggerating somewhat. There are disgusts that deal with frills and trivialities too; the overstatement, however, helps capture the elusive distinction between how contempt maintains rank and how disgust does. Contempt, I claimed earlier, has an ineradicable irony to it and doesn't undo the bases for concern, care, pity, love or kindness and indeed often is necessary to them. Disgust, in contrast, is less benign for the lower in the pecking order. It works to prevent concern, care, pity, and love. Here is the crucial difference between these very close cousins: contempt denies being threatened or operates by pretending that no threat exists; disgust necessarily admits the existence of danger and threat. Disgust can thus lead to disproportionate responses; it often seeks removal, even eradication of the disgusting source of threat. But there is an ambivalence in the desire to eradicate. Like those we hate, those who disgust us define who we are and whom we are connected with. We need them too— downwind.

I have argued that contempt, far from being inimical to democracy, seemed in the end greatly to assist its project, as long as the possibilities for contempt were fairly equally distributed among groupings in the polity—as long, that is, as upward contempt in the dismissive style was available to the low. Disgust is a different matter entirely. It does not admit of equitable distribution, and it works against ideas of equality. It paints a picture of pure and impure. And the compromises it makes across those lines are by way of transgression as sin, lust, or perversion. Hierarchies maintained by disgust cannot be benign; because the low are polluting they constitute a danger; a policy of live and let live is not adequate. Look at "live and let live." Is it not the fundamental principle of pluralistic democracy? Does it not embody a pure sentiment of contempt equitably distributed? The

252 THE ANATOMY OF DISGUST

problem, however, is that democracy not only worked to ensure the equitable distribution of contempt across class boundaries but also produced the conditions that transformed the once benign complacent contempt or indifference of the upper classes into a more malign and deeply visceral disgust.

When disgust maintains social hierarchy its movement is not outward from some physical core disgust to more metaphorized moral and social domains. This disgust starts in the moral and social domains and moves toward concretizing itself in smells, cringes, and uglinesses. Once, however, the loathing of the lower orders ends in the perception of their odor there is a temptation to see a distinctly sexual, sometimes genderized twist to the style of the subordination. This can work itself out in various ways. Orwell goes rather against the grain by excusing women from smelling. He only complains of the odor of working-class men.[20] In fact, to the extent he recognizes the lower males as feminized their odor distinctly improves. Thus his Burmese menservants who dressed him did not revolt him by their touch as an English manservant would have: "I felt toward a Burman almost as I felt toward a woman." And then he admits that the Burmese had a distinctive smell but it never disgusted him (142).

Except for Mrs. Brooker, English working-class women, recall, fare much better than their revolting men; they can be the objects of pity and solicitude because Orwell takes care to maintain respectfully safe distances. His stinking workers do not smell like women at all; their odor is distinctly base and distinctly masculine; it is the reek of sweat, dirt, and excrement, not of menstruation and intercourse. Orwell recognizes that sex is implicated in class hierarchy in a way that assumes, not the feminization of working-class men, but rather their very masculine designs on higher women. Sex is what ultimately defeats middle-class solicitude and admiration of lower-class people. Dickens, Orwell notes, can genuinely admire the virtuous and lowly Pegottys, but it is conditioned on their marrying their own kind. Should lower men aim too high the novelist's "real feelings on the class question" come out. "The thought of the 'pure' Agnes in bed with a man who drops his aitches [Uriah Heep] . . . really revolts Dickens."[21]

Subordination takes different forms, and the odors that the high perceive emanating from the low may well take on different casts depending on the social and cultural bases for that particular hierarchical arrangement. A common reductionist move resorted to more and more frequently is to make sexual and gender hierarchy provide the basic model for all hierarchical arrangements. By this account, to be subordinated is, by definition, to be feminized; that the low should then begin to smell would be consistent with the inveterate misogynistic constructs that make women reek of sex and sexuality. The gender model is better at explaining certain styles of hierarchy than others. It does much better with anti-Semitism than with class and some forms of race hatred. The Jew is not threatening as a male but in the way of females. His fabled sexual prowess and voracious sexual appetite work to feminize not masculinize him, in the sense that he is capable of copulating continuously without the usual restorative delays. The *foetor judaicus* was partly the smell of filthy lucre and feces, but also partly the smell of menstrual blood, a belief sustained by the convergence of Christian male fears of Jews, circumcision, and women.[22]

So far so good. But the feminization of the worker and perhaps the black man has to be marked rather differently if it is to be found at all. One suspects rather that what stinks about workers and blacks is their threatening style of masculinity: sweat and excrement, the smells of lowliness and toil. These men are hardly feminized in their subordination; in fact their manner and smell reveal the feminization of the men above them. The model the civilized and dominant males use to subordinate the male worker is to make him childlike, not womanlike, a move that has the effect of transforming the civilized male into mother as much as into father. The trouble, one perceives, is that the gender game can be played to generate any result one wishes to reach.

The smell of Jews owed little to the civilizing process and its lower thresholds of disgust over bodily matters. Jews smelled to Christians before Christians used forks and handkerchiefs, before the notion of good and bad taste had become current. The advance of civility and refined taste, however, did help somewhat to transform the coarse but bearable odor of the peasant into the more dangerous odor of the urban worker who bore more than his share of the stench of

NOTES

WORKS CITED

INDEX

NOTES

1. Darwin's Disgust

1. *The Expression of the Emotions in Man and Animals* 256–257.
2. Disgust comes to English via French via Latin: dis (a negative prefix) + gustus (taste).
3. See Susan Miller, "Disgust: Conceptualization, Development and Dynamics," 295; see Freud, *Three Essays* II 177–178.
4. See, among others, the works of Tomkins, Izard, and Rozin in the list of Works Cited.
5. The moral aspects of disgust have only very recently been recognized in academic psychological literature. See Haidt, McCauley, and Rozin, "Individual Differences in Sensitivity to Disgust," and Haidt, Rozin, et al., "Body, Psyche, and Culture." In the Freudian account disgust is distinctly moral or at least does much the same work as morality; Freud makes reaction formations a trinity of disgust, shame, and morality; see *Three Essays* II 177–178.
6. Wierzbicka argues for the distinctiveness of the notions of revulsion, repulsiveness, and disgust ("Human Emotions," 588–591). Disgust, she supposes, refers to ingestion of, revulsion to contact with, and repulsiveness to proximity to the offensive entity. She underestimates the generality and easy interchangeability of these concepts. Disgust melds notions of ingestion, contact, and proximity.
7. *Purity and Danger,* to be discussed more fully in Chapter 3.
8. Susan Miller, "Disgust Reactions," 711.
9. See letter to Fliess, Nov. 14, 1897, Masson ed., 280. See also *Three Essays* I 160–162, II 177–178; *Civilization and Its Discontents* 99–100n1.
10. Angyal, "Disgust and Related Aversions."
11. Ibid., 394–395, 397.
12. Disgust had appeared, in the intervening time, in lists of the primary emotions but received no more than cursory attention. See variously Plutchik, *The Emotions* and *Emotion: A Psychoevolutionary Synthesis;* Tomkins, *Affect, Imagery, Consciousness;* Izard, *The Face of Emotion;* McDougall, *Introduction to Social Psychology.*
13. Susan Miller produced a thoughtful and sensible article—"Disgust: Conceptualization, Development and Dynamics"—in the practicing analytic tradition.

Finding both food-ingestion and reaction-formation theories too narrow, she argues that disgust includes a considerable range of responses roughly organized around a notion of riddance. Disgust functions as an organizer of experience into good and bad, inside and outside the self. A follow-up essay ("Disgust Reactions") is devoted more narrowly to disgust's role in specific therapeutic cases, primarily in cases of counter-transference. Julia Kristeva's discussion of abjection has implications for much of the domain of the disgusting, especially as these things are played out in the semiotics of pollution; see *Powers of Horror*. Outside of S. Miller, Kristeva, and Rozin the work is limited and of questionable value; e.g., Galatzer-Levy and Gruber, "What an Affect Means: A Quasi-Experiment about Disgust."

14. See Rozin, Haidt, and McCauley, "Disgust," 584.

15. See Haidt, McCauley, and Rozin.

16. One senses a delightfully wicked wit underlying Rozin's work that even the grim formal constraints of academic psychological writing cannot quite suppress. Imagine the barely suppressed glee that must have accompanied crafting imitation dog feces out of peanut butter and smelly cheese and then offering it along with (sterilized) grasshoppers to toddlers.

17. For able reviews of the various theories of emotions see the philosophers Lyons, *Emotions* 1–52, and de Sousa, *The Rationality of Emotion* 36–46. For a review of psychological theories see Plutchik, *Emotion: A Psychoevolutionary Synthesis* 1–78, and more recently Ellsworth, "Some Implications of Cognitive Appraisal Theories of Emotion." Anthropological theories are discussed by Lutz and White, "The Anthropology of Emotions"; see also the discussion by the cultural psychologist Richard A. Shweder in "Menstrual Pollution, Soul Loss, and Emotions." For a review of the sociological literature see Thoits, "The Sociology of Emotions."

18. See, e.g., Tomkins, "Affect Theory," 377, for the view that disgust would be only an auxiliary drive mechanism if it were limited to its defensive functions in controlling intake of food.

19. See de Sousa, 36, for the idea that emotions are characterized by "level-ubiquity." They function as physiological, psychological, and social phenomena.

20. Much of the recent philosophical interest in the emotions can be seen as a continuation of Hume's project to complicate the reason/passion distinction and then to reevaluate the passions positively relative to reason.

21. Rozin and Fallon, 32. Notions like the plenitude of grace try to overcome this deeply held conviction that the impure is much more powerful than the pure. But the exceptional nature of grace merely underscores the underlying sense that only the truly exceptional can do battle with the most routine types of pollution. The deck is still stacked in favor of degradation by the low rather than elevation by the high.

22. Hobbes in *Leviathan* and Spinoza construct such schemes.

23. Johnson and Oatley, "The Language of Emotions" and "Basic Emotions, Rationality, and Folk Theory."

24. Ekman, "An Argument for Basic Emotions"; Izard, *Human Emotions*.

25. E.g., Plutchik; also Tomkins.

26. See the references in the preceding three notes; cf. Ortony and Turner, "What's Basic about Basic Emotions?"

27. Thus Johnson and Oatley, "Basic Emotions," but surely one could propose that disgust is a particular kind of fear, the fear of contamination? I do not wish to take the time to critique each of these theories; none strikes me as satisfactory. Some of their failings are recited in Ortony and Turner; also Turner and Ortony, "Basic Emotions."

28. William James (2.1097) takes a view similar to this, as do by implication many appraisal theorists; see Smith and Ellsworth, "Patterns of Cognitive Appraisal in Emotion."

29. On the serviceability and content of our folk psychology see Gordon's discussion of Hebb's experiment in *The Structure of Emotions* 1–20; see also D'Andrade, "A Folk Model of the Mind" and "Some Propositions about the Relations between Culture and Human Cognition;" for a defense of the ultimate psychological reality of our emotion categories see Johnson and Oatley, "Basic Emotions." Compare, however, Kagan, "The Idea of Emotion in Human Development."

30. I am being much too hasty about complex issues that have provoked a lot of discussion across a wide range of disciplines. But I do not wish to get bogged down in the problems of relativism and universalism. One common view is that it is easier to understand cultures nearer to us culturally than those farther away. The difference in, say, the frequency of bathing between Germans and Americans does not distance Germans from us to the same extent that headshrinking and cannibalism among the Jibaro might separate them from us; see, e.g., B. Williams, *Ethics and the Limits of Philosophy* 159–167. But is this always true? Sometimes our attitude to the vastly different is less demanding because they are so different and we are more willing to indulge their ways by allowing our imaginations to construct relativizing and hence justifying accounts for them. The Dominican friar of the sixteenth century might thus have been more disgusted by a Protestant than by a New World Indian.

31. Chevalier-Skolnikoff, "Facial Expression of Emotion in Nonhuman Primates"; see Rozin, Haidt, and McCauley, 578.

32. The distinction between distaste and disgust is made by Rozin: the former is motivated by sensory factors, whereas disgust involves ideational factors like contagion and contamination; see Rozin and Fallon, 24. I might not like the flavor of almond extract but I do not find it disgusting. Others might find green peppers and hot peppers unpleasant to eat, but not disgusting for being unpleasant.

33. The contagious and magical qualities of disgust substances are discussed by Rozin, Millman, and Nemeroff, "Operation of the Laws of Sympathetic Magic in Disgust," and Rozin and Nemeroff, "The Laws of Sympathetic Magic," drawing ultimately on Angyal, 395.

34. Rozin, Hammer, et al., "The Child's Conception of Food"; Rozin, Fallon, and Augustoni-Ziskind, "The Child's Conception of Food." Judging by the experience of my own children the range seems much too conservative. Those researchers who believe facial expressions of an emotion are the emotion itself

claim that emotions like disgust, interest, and distress are fully operational at birth; see Izard, "Emotion-Cognition Relationships and Human Development." Shweder, Mahapatra, and Miller's research ("Culture and Moral Development," 183) shows that by age five children are already capable of expressing distinctive culturally appropriate judgments about what is morally right and wrong. To make these appropriate judgments, they argue, moral sentiments like empathy, shame, and disgust must also be in place.

35. The evidence is ambivalent. The wild boy of Aveyron certainly had distaste for some foods, and although sniffing at anything without aversion, he was not reported to have been coprophagic. See Jean Itard, *The Wild Boy of Aveyron*.

36. See Susan Miller's treatment of the developmental phases of disgust; "Disgust: Conceptualization, Development and Dynamics," 297–299.

37. "Such, Such were the Joys," 22.

38. I am making no grand claim here about a theory of moral development, but the view I am advancing is contrary to the unsustainable Piagetian and Kohlbergian theories of cognitive and moral development; see the critique by Flanagan, *Varieties of Moral Personality* 181–195. My views largely track those of Shweder, Mahapatra, and Miller, 183–194, who show, in an American sample, that competence in matters of convention and local situation, to the extent these can meaningfully be distinguished from the moral, develop later than more generalized moral principles.

39. If we take incest as a set of rules governing appropriate marriage partners then we can imagine that fear or a sense of duty, shame, or guilt could sustain the norm as well as disgust. If, however, we take incest as a set of rules governing permissible sexual partners then we will suspect that disgust would play the dominant role. Even the denizens of Roman Egypt who preferred brother-sister marriage had rules preventing father-daughter and mother-son marriages. Shweder, Mahapatra, and Miller, 188, offer nine candidates for moral universals across adult populations (the sample included Brahmins, Untouchables, and middle-class Americans): these were keeping promises, respect for property, fair allocation, protecting the vulnerable, reciprocity-gratitude, and taboos against incest, arbitrary assault, nepotism, and arbitrariness. Some of these, e.g., a norm of reciprocity and taboos against incest and arbitrariness, strike me as more likely than others to be universal. Others seem downright implausible. Nepotism hardly raised eyebrows in the pre-modern western world in which careers open to talent were the exception rather than the rule. Would all these virtues and vices be sustained by the same moral sentiments? Incest seems a prime candidate for being maintained mainly by disgust, but most violations of deeply held norms are capable of eliciting disgust under conditions that show the violator depraved, hypocritical, arbitrary, or cruel.

40. A plausible claim can be made that those coprophagic rites reported in various societies are always liminal rituals where the very act of eating feces marks the activity as symbolic, ritualistic, and violative of the normal. See Greenblatt's discussion in "Filthy Rites" and Angyal (399–403) explaining away Bourke's material.

41. See Kristeva, 71: "Polluting objects fall, schematically, into two types: excremental and menstrual. Neither tears nor sperm, for instance, although they belong to the borders of the body, have any polluting value." Tears true, but sperm? I am not quite sure how she means to circumscribe her discussion here to make the exclusion of sperm less absurd. I argue in Chapter 5 that sperm is one of the most polluting of all substances.

42. Some "exceptions" work rather to confirm the general rule, as when the practice is meant to mark transgressive behavior. Greenblatt's point about the coprophagic ritual in "Filthy Rites" is that it was largely undertaken to horrify the white Indian agents, missionaries, and anthropologists. Edmund Leach ("Magical Hair," 156) comes close to accepting that certain substances are nearly universally impure: "Everyone knows that impurity attaches itself indiscriminately both to the genital-anal region and to the head. The most typically impure things are faeces, urine, semen, menstrual blood, spittle, and hair." On the possibility of universal elicitors of various emotions see Shweder, "Menstrual Pollution," 243–244.

43. See Herdt, "Sambia Nosebleeding Rites"; Evans-Pritchard, *The Nuer* 30; and Bourke, *Scatologic Rites* 4–6.

44. "Filthy Rites," 60.

2. *Disgust and Its Neighbors*

1. Gibbard, *Wise Choices, Apt Feelings* 126–127.

2. On fear being opposed by lust as well as anger see Mandeville, *Fable of the Bees,* Remark R. The justness of the fear/anger opposition, as indeed of the love/hate opposition, is open to dispute. I suggest that in some ways love is more opposed to disgust than to hate. Aristotle opposed confidence to fear (*Rhetoric* II.5). Precisely what emotion will suitably oppose another depends on context and the criterion of judgment. Sometimes the opposition is generated by comparing the actions the emotions motivate, sometimes by comparing the types of objects the emotions seek, sometimes by the structural mechanics of the emotions.

3. As in Hume, *Treatise* II.i.

4. Plutchik, *Emotion* 135–137, 160.

5. See Harré's discussion of iterated emotions (e.g., anger at being angry, disgust at being disgusted) and nested emotions (e.g., guilt at being happy) in "Embarrassment," 200.

6. Some claim that emotions are mixable in the way that colors are; see Plutchik (*Emotion* 160–165). Others dispute the usefulness of the analogy; see the discussion in Ortony and Turner, 329.

7. It can be disputed whether compounds of emotions aren't in fact quick alternations among them. Those who believe that, say, fear and disgust are primary hardwired emotions would be compelled to argue that a blend of them is really a blurring of quickly alternating fears and disgusts, not some true compound called horror; see Ekman, "An Argument for Basic Emotions."

8. On the relation of emotions to color see D'Andrade, "Some Propositions," 73–74; and Johnson, Johnson, and Baksh, "The Colors of Emotions in Machiguenga." These experiments suggest that the emotional significance of colors is remarkably stable across cultures. Just as sliminess may be more likely to be disgusting than non-sliminess, so blue is more likely to be associated with sadness than with happiness.

9. Rozin, Haidt, and McCauley, 575. Presumably the distinction is meant to capture the role disgust plays in defending purity. But it comes at the cost of misrepresenting the complexity of both disgust and fear.

10. The close relation between disgust and horror is also noted by S. Miller, "Disgust: Conceptualization, Development and Dynamics," 303; Darwin, in contrast, suggests that horror combines dread and hate (304–305) and is often elicited by the contemplation of great pain or torture. One of the twenty-three subjects to whom Darwin showed a picture of the horror expression identified it as disgust. It has been suggested that the combination of disgust and fear produces shame or prudishness (Plutchik, *The Emotions* 118, *Emotion* 162). This is simply an inadequate description of shame. We may fear being shamed, but fear is not a constituent of shame.

11. See Solomon, "The Philosophy of Horror," 125–126: "In fear, one flees . . . In horror, on the other hand, there is passivity, the passivity of presence. One stands (or sits) aghast, frozen in place . . . Horror is a spectator's emotion, and thus it is especially well-suited for the cinema and the visual arts."

12. See, for example, *Alien I, The Invasion of the Body Snatchers,* and even *Ghostbusters,* in which ghosts are in the habit of "sliming" people. See Clover's discussion of "possession" films such as *The Exorcist* in *Men, Women, and Chain Saws* 65–113. The horror movie genre is complex and admits of various subgenres. There are slasher and splatter films, monster films, vampire films, possession films, each of which engages slightly different aspects of the disgusting. Some horror films more properly truck with terror rather than disgust: these are the films featuring all-too-human stalkers (usually male) stalking all-too-human victims (usually female). See also Carroll, *The Philosophy of Horror* 17–24, who notes disgust as a necessary component of the horror genre. The horrifying in Carroll's regime involves fears of contamination by the impure (27–28): "it is crucial that two evaluative components come into play: that the monster is regarded as threatening *and* impure. If the monster were only evaluated as potentially threatening, the emotion would be fear; if only potentially impure, the emotion would be disgust. Art-horror requires evaluation both in terms of threat and disgust."

13. Mild disgust seems to fade by degrees into vaguely felt anxiety.

14. See the discussion in Angyal, 406–408, who is characteristically perceptive. Carroll (42) would distinguish between genres he calls art-horror and art-dread (the "art" is meant to distinguish the emotion raised by knowingly fictional depiction from "real" occasions of horror and dread). Art-horror, as previously noted, must as a formal matter engage disgust, while art-dread engages the uncanny.

15. See Rozin, Millman, and Nemeroff; also Rozin and Nemeroff.

16. Castration is fetishized in the Freudian and Lacanian orders in different ways. For Freud, castration anxiety is about really losing the male generative apparatus; for Lacan and others, castration becomes a foundational image used to indicate losses, lacks, and separations that help differentiate subject from object. See Silverman, *The Acoustic Mirror* 13–22, for a devastating internalist critique of both Freud's and Lacan's castration theories from a feminist perspective.

17. Freud, "History of an Infantile Neurosis," 82–85. Uncanniness inheres not only in the revival of repressed infantile complexes but also "when primitive beliefs which have been surmounted seem once more to be confirmed." But then the gain achieved by that small non-reductive move is reclaimed for reduction in the next sentence: "primitive beliefs are most intimately connected with infantile complexes" ("The Uncanny," 249).

18. Horror, contempt, castration, and female genitalia are all bound together in Freud's misogynistic account. Horror is posed as a peculiarly male emotion centered on the fear of castration, which fear makes the female genitalia horrifying since the sight of them suggests that castration is no mean threat. The combination of the fear and the sight of female genitalia "permanently determine the boy's relations to women: horror of the mutilated creature or triumphant contempt for her" ("Some Psychical Consequences of the Anatomical Distinction between the Sexes," 252). Thus too the horror of Medusa's head, which recalls castration and is itself an image of "the terrifying genitals of the Mother" ("Medusa's Head," 274). Freud offers as irrefutable proof of "the existence of the castration complex . . . fright at the sight of the female genital" ("Fetishism," 155).

19. Regarding the maleness of the belief: Haidt, McCauley, and Rozin found that women were consistently more sensitive to disgust across six of the seven domains tested. The one in which women were less sensitive (and distinctly so) was sex. With regard to food, animals, excreta, hygiene, among others, they were more sensitive than men.

20. See Kamir, *Stalking.*

21. For a recent discussion of *accidie* and melancholy see Harré and Finlay-Jones, "Emotion Talk across Times," 220–233; see also the account of the rise of boredom in Spacks, *Boredom* 7–23.

22. Michael Ignatieff's term "moral disgust" is an attempt to capture yet another style of despair which approximates some features of *tedium vitae*. Moral disgust references the frustration, irritation, anger, that attend the failure of one's own good intentions. For Ignatieff the disgust is not itself moral, it is rather disgust at the failures of one's own moral action to have any effect. It is a kind of moral withdrawal. See "The Seductiveness of Moral Disgust," 83.

23. Orwell, "Inside the Whale," 230.

24. See Duclos et al. and Levenson et al. The concept of posing or pretending gives a pejorative turn to what we could more positively call training, role playing, drill, and practicing. The lawyer trying her first case, the surgeon doing her first operation, the adolescent first in love are all adopting certain poses of competence and knowledge that have yet to become "second nature." Also see Strack et al.,

detailing an experiment in which people gripped a pen either with their teeth to engage smile muscles or with their lips to engage frown muscles and then judged cartoons. Those gripping the pen with their teeth found them funnier.

25. Sartre, *La nausée.*

26. Freud also grants the melancholic special perspicacity but usually in regard to his own inner states; "Mourning and Melancholia," 246. The best treatment of melancholy's connection to the intellectual life remains Burton's; see "Democritus to the Reader" in *The Anatomy of Melancholy.*

27. See Taylor and Brown, "Illusion and Well-Being" and Flanagan's critique in *Varieties of Moral Personality* 315–332.

28. Plutchik, *Emotion* 157. Plutchik argues that once emotions become less intense they also become less distinguishable as they converge to a zero point of affect-lessness. As they grow more intense they grow more distinguishable. But are rage and loathing, his intense versions of anger and disgust, more differentiable from each other than anger and disgust? The argument could be made that they are closer than their primaries are.

29. Darwin, 253.

30. I take up the issue of the difference between disgust's and contempt's facial expressions in Chapter 9.

31. Psychologists have wavered on the distinguishability of disgust and contempt. Those who argue for the existence of basic emotions sometimes include contempt on the list or collapse contempt with disgust. See Ekman and Friesen, "A New Pan-cultural Facial Expression of Emotion"; Izard, *The Face of Emotion* 236–245. Tomkins, *Affect, Imagery, Consciousness,* starts by distinguishing them on the basis of taste (disgust) and smell (contempt) but then collapses them in the remainder of his discussion; see Rozin, Lowery, and Ebert, "Varieties of Disgust Faces and the Structure of Disgust," 871.

32. There is a voluminous literature on shame in anthropology, philosophy, and psychology, as well as, more recently, in the suspect psychology of self-help. I discuss shame in some detail in *Humiliation*, chs. 3–5, and supply a fuller bibliography there. On the philosophical side recent excellent treatments are available in Gibbard, 136–140, Taylor, *Pride, Shame and Guilt* 53–84, and Williams, *Shame and Necessity;* for recent anthropological discussions see the essays assembled in Gilmore. The essays in the classic collection edited by Peristiany are still well worth consulting. On the long-vexing distinction between shame and guilt see Williams, *Shame and Necessity* 88–94, Gibbard, 137–140, and Piers and Singer, *Shame and Guilt.* See further Chapter 8, note 49.

33. S. Miller, "Disgust Reactions," 721: "Disgust is also a response to the failure of shame."

34. See Frijda, *The Emotions,* who grounds his theory of the emotions on the action tendencies of the particular affect.

35. To the extent that the idea of an unconscious emotion makes sense it is easier to imagine unconscious hatred than unconscious disgust. The notion of unconscious disgust does not make sense to me. Although I think the idea of unconscious

emotions may ultimately be defensible I am not always sure what is being claimed by the notion. The psychobabble of the self-esteem movement asks us to get in touch with our anger, our hatred, our love. But if we are not conscious of our anger can that unconscious anger really be anger? Anger needs an object; it is not an aimless affect, likewise love and hate. See Freud, "The Unconscious," 177: "It is surely of the essence of an emotion that we should be aware of it, i.e., that it should become known to consciousness. Thus the possibility of the attribute of unconsciousness would be completely excluded as far as emotions, feelings, and affects are concerned."

36. Plutchik, *Emotion* 162, lists indignation as a mix of disgust and anger. This strikes me as simply wrong.

37. In "Clint Eastwood and Equity" I discuss in some detail the difference between conceiving of justice as making the wrongdoer *pay for* his wrong and as making the wronged person *pay back* the wrongdoer for having been wronged.

38. Cruelty comes in different varieties and is not always easy to get a fix on, but all manifestations of it seem to elicit more than indignation. Note that cruelty, unlike violence, encompasses depraved and callous omissions as well as brutal commissions. Some may wish to distinguish the cruelty of the vulgar pogrom from those types of cruelty which have an effete and dandyish cast to them. (I am unwilling to make that much moral distinction between loutish cruelty and sophisticated dandyish cruelty, although the two may be rather differently motivated; it is not always clear that we are more disgusted by sophisticated cruelty than by the vulgar version.) Yet another sort of cruelty claims the warrant of self-interest and reason of state rather than the warrant of pleasure; Machiavellian cruelty has the less blamable motive of prudence and the general benefit of securing public order. Is the prince who issues cruel commands cruel or rather more appropriately described as callous? Is cruelty only what takes place at the point of pain? Surely the callous prince should not escape execration and punishment, but will he elicit disgust as much as the torturer whose work he commissions? Note too that indignation allows for the infliction of pain upon and degradation of wrongdoers. Does this become cruel because it prompts the joys of revenge? These are vast problems; for a beginning one may wish to consult Walzer, "Dirty Hands"; Nagel, "Ruthlessness in Public Life"; Scarry, *The Body in Pain;* Collins, "Three Faces of Cruelty"; and Shklar, *Ordinary Vices.*

39. Chaucer, "Prologue to the Miller's Tale," A3176–3182. "And so whoever does not want to hear it turn the page and choose another tale . . ."

3. *Thick, Greasy Life*

1. I don't mean to upset biologists by still dividing life into two kingdoms, plant and animal, rather than the five or so that have come to be accepted in the more than three decades since I took biology in high school. I stick with the binary division simply because it more accurately reflects the folk categories upon which our notion of disgust draws its imagery, style, and substance.

2. See Bynum's description of the literature of late antiquity regarding the horror of death and putrefaction: "Death was horrible, not because it was an event that ended consciousness, but because it was part of oozing, disgusting, uncontrollable biological process"; *The Resurrection of the Body* 113.

3. It was not just decaying vegetation that generated life; decaying flesh was just as productive. Recall Hamlet's revolting images linking sex, rot, and fecundity (to Polonius): "For if the sun breed maggots in a dead dog, being a good kissing carrion—Have you a daughter?" (2.2.181–182). For the historical pedigree from Aristotle onward of spontaneous generation from decaying matter see Hankin, "Hamlet's 'God Kissing Carrion'." (As an aside: the "good kissing" of the quote is the reading of both the good quarto and the folio; "God kissing" is Warburton's eighteenth-century emendation.)

4. I am taking issue here both with Angyal, 396, and with Rozin and Fallon, who follow him in denying the capacity of vegetable matter to disgust.

5. The multiple senses of rankness as excessive growth and then as excessively strong and foul odors seem partly responsible for a minor crux in the textual tradition of *Hamlet*. The "fat weed that roots itself in ease" is the reading of the quartos, while the folio substitutes "rots" for "roots." On the association of maternal sexuality, fecundity, rankness, and death in *Hamlet* see Adelman, *Suffocating Mothers* 17.

6. See Rozin, Haidt, and McCauley.

7. Angyal, 397; Dumont, *Homo Hierarchicus* 59–61.

8. Douglas, *Purity and Danger;* Julia Kristeva restates and reformulates Douglas's position seeking to root its structuralism within the diction of her particular brand of feminist depth psychology and semiotic theory. For her, abjection, which is not quite disgust, is explained as that which "disturbs identity, system, order. What does not respect borders, positions, rules. The in-between, the ambiguous, the composite" (4).

9. One could argue that these substances may come with their meanings supplied by another conceptual grid that is simply trumping the grid that is organizing the relevant social structure. Freudians would argue that the foundational grid with the massive gravitational force is none other than Freudian theory. But might it not be that Freudian theory itself shows the effect of having come into the gravitational field of sperm, menstrual blood, and excrement and has never escaped orbiting them? I am not arguing that these nearly universal contaminants exist independently of our understandings of them as contaminants. One of the purposes of this book is to show just how richly overdetermined the disgusting is socially, culturally, morally, physically, but ultimately never far removed from human sensory perception and the horror of the flux about us.

10. See Douglas's discussion, 36–40, 55–57, and Leach, "Anthropological Aspects of Language."

11. See Stallybrass and White's (143–146) illuminating account of the symbolic load borne by rats after the public health movement succeeded in putting urban sewers underground in the nineteenth century. Rats, again in accord with the Douglasian model, became ambiguous creatures transgressing "the boundaries that separated

the city from the sewer, above from below." Their account shows nicely how the rats' marginality is constituted differently depending on the historical moment. Yet they seem untroubled by the rat's capacity to be marginal no matter what the operative scheme, whether in times with underground sewers or in times without them. The rat, like feces, seems to be somewhat independent of structure. For Freud rats have the capacity to be uncanny as well as disgusting as he construes their significance in the fantasies of Rat Man; see "Notes Upon a Case of Obsessional Neurosis," 215n2.

12. Compare the opossum, which though ratlike does not have the rat's disgust-generating powers; we think opossums almost cute in their playing dead, their having a pouch, and their comical imitation of looking as if they are wearing a rat costume. The cuteness of marsupials shows that not all category transgressions will pollute or be dangerous. Douglas needs more than just the notion of not fitting, because only certain kinds of not fitting are upsetting.

13. Leviticus 11.41.

14. Rozin and Fallon, 28; Rozin, Haidt, and McCauley, 584. See also Angyal, 395: disgust is "a specific reaction to waste products of the human and animal body."

15. On the Brahmin restrictions see Dumont, 137–142.

16. See the discussion in Flandrin, "Distinction through Taste," 273–274: "the key distinction was no longer between aristocrats, who ate game and fowl, and bourgeois, who ate gross meats, but between the nobility and bourgeoisie, which ate the good cuts of meat, and the common people, who ate the *bas morceaux*, the low-grade cuts." Compare in our own culture how the eaters of pork rinds and pork roast, of tenderloin, sirloin, round, chuck, and sausages, are not evenly distributed across the social hierarchy.

17. By employing edible here to indicate all foods which we could profitably eat independent of culturally generated prohibitions I do not mean to deny that in the end culture defines what will be eaten.

18. Note that the use of the word "harvest" to describe the reduction of living animals to dead ones strikes some as disgusting. Images of slaughter evoke disgust, but the harvest euphemism utterly fails to eliminate any of the disgust inherent in slaughter and manages to add new sources of disgust by virtue of its suspected dishonesty and hypocrisy. Eviscerating cadavers to get organs is not a pretty picture either, but it gets even more disgusting when it is thought of as harvesting. Euphemisms are supposed to do better than that. Why is it that the harvest euphemism fails to euphemize whereas ones like Kleenex and restroom are more successful? The issue has only partly to do with the moral stakes of the euphemism. It also has to do with how the euphemism works. Kleenex and restroom do not attempt to degrade their referent. In some sense there is no way the referent could be further degraded. Such is not the case with "harvest," in which the euphemism attempts to prettify its referent by degrading it. It thus works against itself in a way restroom and Kleenex do not.

19. There has been a tendency over the last three centuries to disguise the living origins of the meat we eat. Since the eighteenth century, culinary practice has moved in the direction of reducing the butchered animal to steaks and chops

before it gets to the table (and among Americans before it is even put out for sale), rather than bringing it in whole to be carved in the presence of the diners. The transition has not been complete. Fowl can still be carved at the table even though some of them can look strangely like newborn babies, and fish can still be served whole although some restaurants remove the heads because they offend the fastidious. Norbert Elias would make such fastidiousness part of the civilizing process (see Chapter 7); the psychologists of disgust, Rozin in particular, might argue that civilization is merely giving us the means to repress that about which we always were ambivalent anyway. Elias would accept a precultural aggressive bestiality, the others a precultural anxiety about bestiality.

20. Our belief that it matters what the animals we eat eat seems to derive from a more inclusive belief that if we are what we eat then they must also must be what they eat and so we in turn are what they eat. See Rozin and Fallon, 27; and especially Rozin and Nemeroff, 214–216, and Nemeroff and Rozin, who provide experimental evidence for the continued power of the belief that we are what we eat.

21. Angyal, 409, in one of his few lapses, argues that animals offend because they defecate and that we are thus careful to eat those animals whose feces is least revolting. In his view this explains our preference for eating herbivores rather than carnivores.

22. Leviticus 11.2–41; see Douglas's attempt to organize the various Levitical dietary prohibitions under the general principle that cleanness in animals is a function of their conforming fully to their class; *Purity and Danger* 55. Cf. Kristeva, 90–112. Structural anthropology claims that the position of the particular item within the larger grid of meanings will determine its edibility. The view is that we are likely to eat animals according to the same broad principles that govern marriage. The permissible and hence non-disgusting lies in the middle regions as middle is determined by the symbolic and social structures ordering the society. Disgust governs the extremes. Tambiah, "Animals Are Good to Think and Good to Prohibit"; Leach, "Anthropological Aspects of Language."

23. See Douglas, 54, presenting the views expressed in Samuel R. Driver's biblical commentary (1895).

24. Philo quoted in Douglas, 44.

25. Orwell, in an attempt to outdo Swift, proposes just such a reduction: "all our food springs ultimately from dung and dead bodies, the two things which of all others seem to us the most horrible"; "Politics vs. Literature," 4.222.

26. I have not dealt with the argument that food-restriction rules, especially those of Leviticus, are public health measures designed to prevent disease. This view has been so thoroughly discredited as to be relegated to a footnote. Some research on animal phobias, subscribing to a simplistic evolutionary and functional model, still takes this line. It argues that avoidance of disease explains our disgust for animals from which there is no fear of attack, such as slugs, roaches, newts. Why avoidance of disease should make us more likely to be revolted by a newt than by a cat is not explained. See the works whose lead authors are Davey, Matchett, and Webb in the list of Works Cited.

27. Hallpike, "Social Hair," assembles cross-cultural evidence to show a nearly universal symbolic meaning that long hair and hairiness in general signify unconstrained animality.

28. Cf. Haidt, Rozin, et al.: "we fear recognizing our animality because we fear that, like animals, we are mortal." The fear does not explain the disgust. We might as individuals fear death, but the disgust is motivated by impatience with life. Death is only part of the reason it is so messy to live.

29. See Goffman's essay "Territories of the Self" in *Relations in Public*.

30. Goffman distinguishes three types of self-violation (ibid., 52-56): self-befoulments, in which one uses one's own bodily contaminants to pollute the pollutable parts of the self; self-debasements, in which the source of the contaminant is someone else; and self-exposures, which manifest themselves variously by improper attire, excessive displays of public grief, or indecorous self-revelations, the kind one frequently endures on airplane flights from the person in the next seat. The first two always disgust others and indeed are usually intended to do so. The third type—self-exposures—can also elicit disgust, but usually stops at embarrassment. See also my discussion of humiliation rituals in *Humiliation* 161-165.

31. The image of the skin as being nothing more than a sack filled with excrement was common in moral writing well through the Renaissance and is still much alive as anyone who has done some deep cursing can confirm. Thus Thomas Nashe: "In a damnable state are you, o yee excrementall vessels of lust" (*Christs Teares over Jerusalem* [1593] 77v). See Bynum, *Resurrection of the Body* 61. See Gerald of Wales, *Gemma Ecclesiastica*, II.iv. Gerald tells us that Alexander the Great asked Dionysius three questions: What was I, what am I, and what will I be? Answer: "vile scum, a sack of shit, food for worms."

32. Body hair is not general to the entire human species. It shows considerable variation by race.

33. See Bartlett, "Symbolic Meanings of Hair in the Middle Ages"; Hallpike, "Social Hair"; and Leach, "Magical Hair."

34. In the Middle Ages, for women loose hair indicated the status of being unmarried, bound hair meant the bonds of marriage; loose hair again could indicate grieving. Among us the significances of bound vs. loose are more informally coded but coded nonetheless in a way that bears clear marks of descent from pre-modern meanings. The humiliation ritual of cutting off an enemy's hair and beard has been employed widely across cultures, from Samson, to Merovingian Gaul, to the American West.

35. *Sachsenspeigel, Landrecht* I.xlii, cited in Bartlett, 44.

36. Freud believed the fetishization of hair and feet was linked with "coprophilic pleasure in smelling which has disappeared owing to repression. Both the feet and the hair are objects with a strong smell which have been exalted into fetishes after the olfactory sensation has become unpleasurable and been abandoned"; *Three Essays* I 155n3.

37. Hair, along with mud and dirt, is considered trivial and undignified by Parmenides in his dialogue with Socrates; *Parmenides* 130c-d. Socrates denies they could

have a form; "in these cases, the things are just the things we see; it would surely be too absurd to suppose that they have a form."

38. See Phyllis Rose, *Parallel Lives* 54–56.

39. Darwin in several instances in his discussion of facial expressions references the performances of his infant children. He notes that at age five months one of his children made a classic expression of disgust at a piece of cherry put in his mouth. The baby stuck his tongue out and shuddered, but Darwin doubted he felt real disgust.

40. Rozin, Hammer, et al. "The Child's Conception of Food."

41. T. S. Eliot, "The Love Song of J. Alfred Prufrock."

42. Swift and Eliot's vision, it should be said, is given more than a slight assist by a loathing of sex and deep consequent misogyny. Swift, more honest and courageous than Eliot in these matters, does not stop with woman but turns the same sensitive eye (and nose) to all mankind. Gulliver recalls that Lilliputians were disgusted by his skin (II.1). One wonders if Swift's sensitivity was possible before the civilizing process had proceeded as far as it did. Montaigne reports that the Emperor Maximilian I (reigned 1493–1519) was fastidious about his person too, although not to the point of distraction; "Our Feelings Reach Out Beyond Us," *Essays* 11.

43. Ovid seemed no less fastidious about female hairiness and advised women thus: "How nearly did I warn you that no rude goat find his way beneath your arms and that your legs be not rough with bristling hairs!" *The Art of Love* 3.193–195.

44. Just as Ovid advised women to shave their legs and armpits so he counseled men to make sure no nasal hairs were visible. *The Art of Love* 1.521. Men who removed the hair from their legs, however, he thought to be overdoing it (1.506).

45. The insight is Goffman's; see *Relations in Public* 49.

46. My son Louie, at age four, offered during his bath the observation that since one's insides never get washed they are very dirty. The hostile reader might discern a chip off the old block.

47. The commonplace theme of truth obscured by veils or darkened glass will lead the optimist to suspect that beauty lies behind the veil; the pessimist will suspect excrement. See, e.g., Victor Hugo's treatment of sewers in *Les Miserables* (V.ii), in which they constitute the truth which the fair city veils.

4. The Senses

1. In his translation of the *Iliad* Alexander Pope felt it necessary to footnote the description of Hera's bathing and anointing with oil (14.185ff): "The Practice of Juno in anointing her Body with perfumed Oils was a remarkable part of ancient Cosmeticks, tho' entirely disused in the modern Arts of Dress. It may possibly offend the Niceness of modern Ladies; but they who paint so artificially ought to consider that this Practice might, without much greater Difficulty, be reconciled to Cleanliness."

2. Cf. Sartre: "If we are to establish consciously and clearly a symbolic relation between sliminess and the sticky baseness of certain individuals, we must appre-

hend baseness already in sliminess and sliminess in certain baseness"; *Being and Nothingness* 771.

3. Imagine too the amount of cultural work that would have to be done to make low better than high, down better than up. See Shweder, "Menstrual Pollution," 253, 261.

4. The viscous, Douglas would argue (38), is anomalous because neither solid nor liquid. Douglas's account, it should be said, remains strangely unmotivated. Disgust barely appears. It is all cold structure and its consequences. Inner states of individual actors are not her concern and so committed is she to her anti-psychological account that she does not simply ignore the emotions but seems to suggest they have no role at all in maintaining the structures of purity and pollution. See her discussion on p. 124.

5. "Slime is the agony of water . . . Water is more fleeting, but it can be possessed in its very flight as something fleeing. The slimy flees with a heavy flight which has the same relation to water as the unwieldy earthbound flight of the chicken has to that of the hawk . . . Throw water on the ground; it *runs*. Throw a slimy substance; it draws itself out, it displays itself, it flattens itself out, it is *soft;* touch the slimy; it does not flee, it yields." *Being and Nothingness* 774–775. Sartre's tour de force on slime includes animadversions on the sticky also. Stickiness and sliminess horrify because they erase the distinction between subject and object (777).

6. I indicated in the preceding chapter a dissatisfaction with the Douglasian account that makes the impure a matter of anomaly, disorder, and failure to fit. The disgusting usually fits quite well; it just fits at the bottom end of the grid, from which vantage point it threatens all above it. The deconstructive point could be made against Douglas, which is that the anomaly holds the key to ordering the structure opposed to it. What she calls the structure is in fact a lesser included structure in a wider one which opposes the anomalous to that which fits.

7. See Freud, "The Antithetical Meaning of Primal Words."

8. OED s.v. clean, a.

9. The similarity of the sacred and the unclean as united in the notion of taboo was a commonplace of late nineteenth-century anthropology. Douglas rejects that view, but it has a certain attractiveness. See Douglas, 7–28. Holiness, like the polluting, is characterized by contagion; thus the power of the King's touch and other kinds of holy healing powers. But if holiness were ever as contagious as pollution both holiness and pollution would have been put out of business long ago. Recall from Chapter 1 the asymmetrical effects of a teaspoon of sewage added to a cask of wine compared to a teaspoon of wine added to a cask of sewage.

10. Kristeva, 2–3.

11. We all know that texture is an important element in the palatability of food, technically a matter of touch not taste. Thus the difference between pasta *al dente* and pasta boiled into a mass of slimy squish.

12. See Rozin, " 'Taste-Smell Confusions.' "

13. Psychological research has shown that the association between smells and their

verbal descriptions is weak. See Engen, "Remembering Odors and Their Names." See also the discussion in Rindisbacher, 10–20. On olfaction in general see Engen, *The Perception of Odors* and *Odor Sensation and Memory*.

14. Attempts to provide a qualitative lexicon for smell and taste, as for instance among wine connoisseurs, strikes the non-initiated as either silly or pretentious.

15. On the language-destroying capacity of pain see Scarry.

16. "The Lady's Dressing Room," vv. 99–116, *Poetical Works* 479. Swift was preceded by Ovid who, in his *Remedia Amoris*, advised that when all else failed the sovereign remedy for killing one's passion was to "lurk in hiding while the girl performed her obscenities and saw what even custom forbids to see" (vv. 437–438 in *The Art of Love and other Poems*).

17. Or it may be that Swift is confusing defecation and coitus, production and reproduction, anuses and vaginas. See below, note 23.

18. Freud, "History of Infantile Neurosis," 63. See also Kundera, *The Unbearable Lightness of Being* 245–246: "Spontaneously, without any theological training, I, as a child, grasped the incompatibility of God and shit and thus came to question the basic thesis of Christian anthropology, namely, that man was created in God's image—and God has intestines!—or God lacks intestines and man is not like Him. The ancient Gnostics felt as I did at the age of five. In the second century, the great Gnostic master Valentinus resolved the damnable dilemma by claiming that Jesus 'ate and drank, but did not defecate.' Shit is a more onerous theological problem than is evil. Since God gave man freedom, we can, if need be, accept the idea that He is not responsible for man's crimes. The responsibility for shit, however, rests entirely with Him, the Creator of Man."

19. "Cassinus and Peter," vv. 117–118, *Poetical Works* 531.

20. "The Lady's Dressing Room," vv. 129–130, *Poetical Works* 480.

21. "Strephon and Chloe," vv. 233–234, *Poetical Works* 525.

22. Swift makes the connection between creative thought and excremental vapors explicit in *The Mechanical Operation of the Spirit*, in which Norman O. Brown has argued he anticipates entirely Freud's theories of sublimation; see Brown, 192–193.

23. The male confusion of the anus and the vagina is a central feature in the Freudian construct; see, e.g., "History of an Infantile Neurosis," 78–79. The confusion is a commonplace in the Viking world also; see further Chapter 5, note 27.

24. Gerald of Wales tells of a young nun's desire for an old monk named Gilbert. She confessed her desire to him. He cured her by giving a public sermon about resisting fornication in which he stripped and revealed his naked body, "hairy, thin, scabby and horrid . . . The woman was by that remedy totally cured of her carnal desires" (*Gemma Ecclesiastica* II.17).

25. *Civilization and Its Discontents* 99–100n1. Freud was not the only sex researcher at the time to be interested in the relation between noses and female genitalia. His correspondent Wilhelm Fliess published a book on the subject: *Die Beziehungen zwischen Nase und weiblichen Geschlechtsorganen in ihrer biologischen Bedeutung dargestellt* [The relations between the nose and the female sexual organs portrayed in their biological significance].

26. Freud also dealt with these issues earlier, discussing them briefly in two letters to Fliess of Jan. 11 and Nov. 14, 1897; see also the footnote added in 1910 to *Three Essays* I 155n2.

27. This is the view presented in the text to which Freud appended the footnote.

28. *Civilization and Its Discontents* 105–107n3.

29. For a thoughtful treatment of this same text from a feminist perspective see Kahane, "Freud's Sublimation: Disgust, Desire and the Female Body."

30. Freud earlier had recourse to the image of superseded gods becoming demons in his discussion of the "double" in his essay "The Uncanny," 236.

31. Latin *mephitis*, "a noxious, pestilential exhalation from the ground."

32. Montaigne, "Of Smells," *Essays* 228.

33. The Freudian story of the nose was put to very strange use (and without irony) by Horkheimer and Adorno. They suggest that anti-Semitism is in part caused by Christian resentment of the Jews' closer association to the primitive, the bestial, which is indicated by Jewish big noses. That the Jews seem so at home with and casual about their noses means they can accomplish with effortlessness what Fascists must contrive with staged festivals. See *Dialectic of Enlightenment* 179–186.

34. Vision (and hearing) are usually understood in aesthetic philosophy as higher senses, smell (and taste) as lower. The problem with smell is it is too immediate, not allowing for reflection, only sensation. Touch is ambivalent. Kant puts it high, Hegel low. See discussion and citations in Rindisbacher, 17–18.

35. See also Dante's *Purgatorio* 19.33.

36. Engen, *Odor Memory* 79–80.

37. See Gross and Levenson; Levenson et al.; and Strack et al.

38. *Lear* 1.1.16. In Elizabethan English "fault" is slang for the female genitalia; see Astington, " 'Fault' in Shakespeare." For Shakespearean puns on fault, fall, and *foutre* see Adelman, 23–26, 105.

39. Recall the fire and brimstone sermon in Joyce's *Portrait of the Artist,* part III, which is as fine a performance in the tradition of Hell as sewer, sin as stench, as there is.

40. See OED s.v. stink v. 2a: "Now implying violent disgust on the part of the speaker; in ordinary polite use avoided as unpleasantly forcible."

41. See Elias, *History of Manners* 203, who links the devaluation of smell as against vision to the civilizing process, not as Freud does to the organic development of upright posture.

42. Newman, *Theism* 164, "Cleanliness," vv. 82–88. Unlike John Henry, Francis Newman found solace in Unitarianism.

43. Compare the slang collocation for sexual intercourse "bumping uglies."

44. Recall the feelies, movies allowing for more than just visual and aural stimulation, in Huxley's *Brave New World*.

45. Farts, interestingly, do not appropriately belong on this list. Their sound has been almost totally assimilated to the comic order. Their smell, however, still belongs firmly in the world of disgust.

46. Is it just images of Hitlerian ranting and goosestepping soldiers that makes

German sound uglier than French? I think Hitler has pretty much made it impossible to make a judgment about the sound of German without such images intruding.

47. See de Sousa's discussion, 279–280: "Imagine a man whose habitual sound of laughter is a cackle or a giggle: would you like your daughter to marry him?"

48. Can music disgust? How about Muzak versions of your favorite music? Music you hate can drive you crazy, torture you, but does it disgust you? I would suppose that the expert is indeed disgusted by forms he loathes. And surely it makes sense to think of loathing music. But isn't there something quite different about aversions to music you hate and aversions caused by disgusting sights and sounds? Hateful music is a torture, a torment; it does not have the same feel as disgust.

49. Darwin prints a picture of a man recoiling with his hands extended in a gesture of "yuck, get that thing away." Plate 5, figs. 2, 3.

50. There may be a different developmental story to tell. A facial expression of disgust was already in place in my son Hank at six weeks. He rejected a pacifier forced into his mouth with a distinct disgust expression, although the aversion he was expressing would not have been disgust as we know it. Nevertheless this expression does precede the cringe, which an infant of that age simply lacks the coordination to carry out and the visual references and competence to understand what could reasonably elicit it. There is no doubt that the expression originates as a way of expelling offensive things from the mouth and is later generalized to register aversion to offenses discerned by other senses.

5. Orifices and Bodily Wastes

1. Cf. Freud. "The Uncanny," 231. It was not an infrequent practice for third- and fourth-century Christians and pagans to castrate themselves or seek castration. And though the zeal of types like Origen shock us, their actions are not quite so inconceivable to us as they would be had they chosen to blind themselves instead. See Peter Brown, *The Body and Society* 168–169, and Rousselle, *Porneia* 121–128.

2. The eyes can even be perceived as sexual organs to the extent that in humans it is they that first discern the desirable and are important in maintaining desire once initiated. See the preceding chapter on Freud's discussion of vision's displacement of olfaction in the process of desiring.

3. Not all tear-like emissions from the eye are immune to disgust. They must be tears to qualify. As soon as watery emissions from the eye cannot be described as tears they get redesignated as watery discharge, a sign of unhealthy eyes. Thus tears caused by cold weather or hot food are pure, but discharges that accompany certain flus and colds are polluted by their association with illness.

4. Sunglasses have among their many virtues the capacity of letting the eye see without itself being seen.

5. I am of course making no claim as to the moral justifiability of our general cultural views on these matters; I am only remarking their existence. The political

movements that have been organized over the last decades to remove the stigma from stigmatizing conditions like blindness and deafness are to be commended for forcing us to do the work of destigmatizing them. The work that must go into the attempt at transforming such views, however, is indirectly a tribute to their tenacity and strength.

6. Earwax is ambiguous. Snot and saliva clearly are produced in non-skin areas inside the body envelope, but earwax is produced by skin. Earwax is ill-mannered sweat that didn't have the sense to evaporate discreetly. The disgustingness of earwax also varies by race. Asians tend to produce dry flakes rather than the pasty stuff produced by most whites and blacks; see Overfield, *Biologic Variation in Health and Illness*.

7. Posset: to curdle, formed from the noun describing a drink made by curdling milk, but also in dialect used to refer to the curdled milk vomited by babies. See OED, s.v. posset 2. Eager: vinegar. Tetter barked: barked as a tree with eruptions, here suggesting syphilis.

8. See Herdt's description of Sambian nosebleeding rites.

9. Painful penetrations of the orifices mark the action as torture, as cruel, as perverse. A stake in the heart is one thing, an ice pick in the ear or up the nose another. Killing in a way that disgusts marks a certain improper moral stance and thus even has implications for legal punishment and claims of justification and excuse.

10. There is much situational variation with the rules governing the discharge of snot and saliva. Athletes, for instance, are allowed to blow it out and spit, baseball players having made this a distasteful rite of membership in their guild.

11. From Homilia XIV, *De mulieribus et pulchritudine,* quoted by Gerald of Wales writing in the late twelfth century, *Gemma Ecclesiastica* (tr. Hagen, 140).

12. See Payer, *The Bridling of Desire* 29.

13. See "Du Chevalier qui Fist Parler les Cons," in Hellman and O'Gorman, *Fabliaux* 105–121. Female genitalia have taken to writing as well as speaking in the non-ironic presentations of certain French feminists; see, e.g., Luce Irigaray's *The Sex Which Is Not One*. For further discussion of the relation of mouths and vaginas in the medieval French fabliaux see Burns, "The Prick Which Is Not One." We need not have recourse to Old French fabliaux to make the claim; one film critic, drawing on the psychoanalyst Ernest Jones, argues that classic American cinema makes the female voice, not just the mouth, stand for the vagina; see Silverman, 67–71. See also Laqueur, 36–37.

14. See Bynum, *Resurrection of the Body* 111.

15. Siker: surely; moste: must; han: have; "Wife of Bath" vv. 465–466. Middle and early modern English supported delightful punning possibilities that followed the Wife in playing suggestively with the homophony of lickerous (tasty, gluttonous, but also lecherous), lecherous (also meaning tasty and gluttonous in some instances), and lick. See OED s.v. lickerous and lecherous. The double and triple entendres were possible because Middle English borrowed two dialect versions of Old French *lecheros,* one from the northern dialect yielding lickerous, the other from the central dialect yielding lecherous.

16. "The Pardoner's Tale," v. 527.

17. Among the Brahmins, saliva, even one's own, is especially contaminating. A Brahmin who inadvertently touches his fingers to his lips should bathe or change his clothes. See Douglas, 33. Eating is so fraught with danger that it is better done alone or among a few safe people and then only with great circumspection: "meals are not those pleasant conversational gatherings with which we are acquainted: they are technical operations which leave room for only a limited margin of freedom" (Dumont, 139).

18. See Rozin and Fallon, 26, on the mouth as a staging area.

19. Of course I am stating our rules; certain South American Indian tribes make an alcoholic beverage out of masticated bitter manioc roots, chewed by the women and then spit into a vat to ferment.

20. Women are more careful in their regulation of these things than men and are more likely than men to be disgusted by non-sexualized excreta; see Templar et al.; also Haidt, McCauley, and Rozin.

21. Allport, 43; see also Leach, "Magic Hair," 157, regarding the magical quality of detached objects such as cut hair, feces, saliva.

22. "Strephon and Chloe," vv. 235–244, *Poetical Works* 525.

23. The more interesting question is whether he gains status to the extent that the other loses it. One Icelandic saga notes, for instance, that though the penetrated had the worse of it, the penetrator didn't have it so good either; see *Bjarnar saga hítdœlakappa* ch. 17. See further Clover, "Regardless of Sex"; Gade, "Homosexuality and the Rape of Males"; and Meulengracht Sørensen, *The Unmanly Man.*

24. See Bersani, "Is the Rectum a Grave?"

25. The word was still in general use in the sense of anus until the twentieth century, when it became rarer, seeming at last to have completed the journey to learned euphemism. See OED s.v. fundament, 3.

26. Notice how the Freudian view of feces as child and child as feces links up with the ascetic tradition in which adult humans are seen as dung or sacks of excrement.

27. Carol Clover notes that Old Norse had no separate word for vagina that could not also be used for anus. And it is in insults to males that the terms for vagina are most frequently attested. Clover's argument implies that the male anus was primary in the Old Norse world and that the vagina was understood merely as a variant of it. The condition of one's anus thus bore an intimate connection to one's standing in the moral order. See Clover, "Regardless of Sex," 375–378.

28. See Douglas, 3.

29. Andrew Marvell, "To his Coy Mistress," vv. 27–29. Quaint is a long-standing euphemism for the female genitalia.

30. It is almost too trite to observe that women are blamed both for denying (and enticing) male desire by being overly protective (in the desiring male's view) of virginity and also for ending male desire in an access of disgust by overly indulging (again in the male's view) their own desire. The contrast in the Shakespearean order is between Isabella of *Measure for Measure* and Gertrude of *Hamlet;* for a discussion in a sophisticated psychoanalytic vein of how these two views

of women influence the critical and interpretive histories of the two plays see Jacqueline Rose, "Sexuality in the Reading of Shakespeare."

31. One needn't delve too deeply into the anthropological literature or the ascetic literature of the Christian West to discover evidence of the belief in semen as a pollutant. Pornography has been interpreted to have its cheap thrills depend on the polluting nature of semen: "in pornography to ejaculate is to *pollute* the woman" (emphasis in original; Andrea Dworkin, *Intercourse* 187).

32. See the Penitential of Cummean 2.15–16 (7th century); the Penitential of Theodore 1.8.8 (7th century), in McNeill and Gamer, 104, 192. The status of semen in prelapsarian paradise challenged the ingenuity of theologians as did the problem of what Edenic copulation would have been like. They ultimately tamed its dangerousness by reducing the ardor of the sex act. Having accepted that procreation obtained in paradise, they gave semen its place; even though it was considered a superfluity at the level of the individual, it was not so considered at the level of the species. Sweat and mucus were banished, however, as were, according to Albert the Great, spontaneous emissions and menstruation. Copulation would give sufficient pleasure to give adequate incentive to undertake it, but not so much pleasure as to undo reason, although the theologians show a marked disparity as to just how much pleasure it would take to undo reason in paradise where presumably reason would come better prepared for the demand being made of it. See the discussion in Payer, 26–34, and the comic discussion of these issues in Kundera, *The Unbearable Lightness of Being* 246–247.

33. *The Anatomy of Melancholy* I.2.2.4. Too much venery was also believed to cause blindness, which, following the imagistic suggestions of *Lear*, would reduce one to smelling one's way through the world; see the discussion and references in Adelman, 295–296.

34. John Wilmot, Earl of Rochester, "A Ramble in St. James Park," v. 118, c. 1672; *Complete Poems* 40.

35. Rousseau, *Confessions* II, pp. 72–73.

36. The similarity of sperm and phlegm was a commonplace in ancient Greek medical literature; see Laqueur, 35.

37. Thomas Nashe, *Christs Teares Over Jerusalem* (1593), 78v.

38. Recall the study noted in Chapter 2, note 19, in which women were found to have lower sensitivities to disgust in the sexual domain (but were more sensitive throughout all other domains tested).

39. Our construction of gender still reproduces in some key ways the ancient Galenic opposition of males as dry and females as wet.

40. I am perhaps underestimating the fear of catheterization, which has a specialized life in medical procedure and torture chambers and in fears and fantasies of both.

41. Recall Hamlet again. Part of his disgust with life, fecundity, and death is captured by a certain instability and flux in language which becomes his linguistic trademark: the pun. See Margaret Ferguson's discussion of puns as they mix and mingle love and death, animality, corpses, and spirit in her "Letters and Spirits."

42. Vision has a special role in the organization of shame, but to the exclusion of

the other senses. See Taylor, *Pride, Shame, and Guilt;* and Wurmser, *The Mask of Shame.*

6. Fair Is Foul, and Foul Is Fair

1. "It is during this period of total or only partial latency that are built up the mental forces which are later to impede the course of the sexual instinct and, like dams, restrict its flow—disgust, feelings of shame and the claims of aesthetic and moral ideas"; Freud, *Three Essays* II 177. See also Freud, "Character and Anal Erotism," 171: Reaction-formations "are actually formed at the expense of the excitations proceeding from the erotogenic zones, and they rise like dams to oppose the later activity of the sexual instincts."

2. See the important letter to Fliess of Nov. 14, 1897: "To put it crudely, the memory [of excitations of the sexual zones abandoned with upright posture, viz. oral and anal] actually stinks just as in the present the object stinks; and in the same manner as we turn away our sense organ (the head and the nose) in disgust, the preconscious and the sense of consciousness turn away from the memory. This is *repression.*"

3. At times Freud explicitly remarks that such dams are not products of education and culture but are organic and developmental; *Three Essays* II 177. The evidence of feral children not having these dams would not disprove this since we could construct a developmental story that would still need cultural triggers and socialized inputs to prime the latent organic capacity. Elsewhere Freud admits to certain conventional constraints on such dams; ibid. I 151.

4. This raises some problems if we define an emotion by the actions it gives rise to, as Frijda does. Disgust repels, but then triggers interest in the very fact of repulsion that works against its aversive aspects.

5. The notion that pleasure and disgust are intimately connected is rather a commonplace, it being a subset of the frequent observation that any concept seems to compel the contemplation and even the experience of its opposite. Hume's statement will stand for hundreds of instances: "The more exquisite any good is, of which a small specimen is afforded us, the sharper is the evil, allied to it; and few exceptions are found to this uniform law of nature. The most sprightly wit borders on madness; the highest effusions of joy produce the deepest melancholy; the most ravishing pleasures are attended with the most cruel lassitude and disgust; the most flattering hopes make way for the severest disappointments." Hume, *The Natural History of Religion* § xv.

6. Kant finds no ambivalence in disgust. It is that which no artifice can make bearable. "Fine art shows its superiority precisely in this, that it describes things beautifully that in nature we would dislike or find ugly . . . There is only one kind of ugliness that cannot be presented in conformity with nature without obliterating all aesthetic liking and hence artistic beauty: that ugliness which arouses *disgust*" (emphasis in original); *Critique of Judgment* § 48, p. 180.

7. Freud tries to have his disgust two ways without formalizing how this complicates

disgust seen merely as a barrier. His disgust is not just a reaction formation but also functions to attract on its own.

8. Kristeva, 1.

9. See, e.g., Dostoyevsky, *Notes from Underground* I.iv, for a discussion of the social dynamics of tooth pain.

10. "The Most Prevalent Form of Degradation in Erotic Life," 213.

11. *Three Essays* I 152. Compare the formulation of the relation of disgust to libido in the letter to Fliess of Nov. 14, 1897.

12. Gerald of Wales, *Gemma Ecclesiastica* II.18. The idea of prohibition producing desire is frequently observed. The story of the Fall implicates it and moralists advert to it as a given of human psychological organization; see, e.g., Hume, *Treatise:* "We naturally desire what is forbid, and take a pleasure in performing actions, merely because they are unlawful" (II.iii.4, p. 421). Freud notes the obsessive thinking about sexuality that characterized certain styles of asceticism. For a deeply sympathetic and informed account of the early centuries of Christian asceticism and its particular views of the body see Brown, *The Body and Society*. For more satiric observations see Kundera, *The Incredible Lightness of Being* 247.

13. "Cette vie est un hôpital où chaque malade est possédé du désir de changer de lit . . . Il me semble que je serais toujours bien là où je ne suis pas." *Petits Poëmes en Prose* 48: "N'importe où or du monde (Anywhere out of the world)."

14. Sourness, I argued earlier, does not disgust. The parable uses sourness to stand for any sensation unpleasant enough to repel desire. Nothing in the parable depends on its being sourness that impels the aversion; it could just as well be rottenness, which is indeed disgust evoking. For the fox sourness was a thought unpleasant enough to kill desire; for others thoughts of rottenness would be required to do the necessary work.

15. On disgust as a defense see S. Miller, "Disgust: Conceptualization, Development and Dynamics," 295.

16. One wonders whether the transgressive delight such jokes have for children will survive under the marketing onslaught of snot candy and chewing gum boogers. For a brief introduction to these products see Don Oldenburg, "Great Expectorations: 'Boogerman' Rides a Yucky Tide of Gross-Out Marketing for Kids," *Washington Post* (April 4, 1995), E5.

17. There are some small exceptions in which shame is experienced vicariously, but even these are usually construable as a first-order experience of one's own loss of status because of one's association with the person on whose behalf one is experiencing shame. See my discussion in *Humiliation* 155–156.

18. Linda Hutcheon in commenting on Bakhtin notes the paradox inherent in carnivalistic parody in the "authorized transgression of norms"; *A Theory of Parody* 74. See also Stallybrass and White, 12–19.

19. John Waters in *Pink Flamingoes* takes coprophagia beyond pure talk and beyond comedy perhaps. Waters is being comic; Divine, the actor who eats dog feces, is being psychotic.

20. Greenblatt, in opposition to Bakhtin, notes that Rabelais is better understood not as an example of a pure release from public constraint but rather as someone

whose humor is already parasitical on a newly emerging fastidiousness; "Filthy Rites," 68. Bakhtin's account is strangely pious in its celebration of the grotesque body and makes little room for disgust. The energy of Rabelais need not come from releasing the energy held behind dams of disgust; it could as well come from breaches in norms of deference to the powerful and religious; but then how to explain the fact that in his account so much of the misrule takes the form of an excremental and excretory celebration? Rabelais is much more in the grip of disgust norms than Bakhtin's wishful thinking would have him be. His humor often depends on it; otherwise his celebration of the body becomes banal, as in the "hard-body" American way, or as in recent scholarly obsessions with "the body."

21. See *Civilization and Its Discontents* 100n1. Montaigne makes excrement an image of our faults and inverts Erasmus's claim that everyone loves the smell of his own dung: "If we had a good nose, our excrement ought to stink worse to us inasmuch as it is our own"; "Of the Art of Discussion," *Essays* 710.

22. See Freud, "History of an Infantile Neurosis," 84.

23. On disgust and appetite curbing see Knapp, "Purging and Curbing."

24. It is not only habitual indulgence in satisfaction of the appetites that prompts disapproval and raises the objection of *over*-indulgence. Nearly any satisfaction of the appetites that distracts the actor from duty or from other valued activities puts him arguably into the realm of the "too much."

25. Our notion of the extent to which foods can cloy is subject to variation. When I was growing up a breakfast of bacon and eggs was considered hearty even if somewhat high in calories. Now someone feels polluted for eating the same thing. Clearly the threshold at which grease began to cloy was higher then. But that doesn't mean that anything thought to be unhealthy would have the capacity to cloy. That is a peculiar function of rich, oily, and sweet foods, not just of our sense of their health value.

26. The starting point is Paul's first letter to the Corinthians. See the sensitive contextualized reading of this foundational text for clerkly attitudes regarding chaste marriage in Brown, *The Body and Society* 44–57.

27. Notice how nicely this image reproduces the feel of the passage discussed in Chapter 3 from *The Duchess of Malfi* in which humans as luxurious plum trees draw horseleeches who sate themselves and then drop off.

28. Tourneur, *Revenger's Tragedy* 1.3.

29. *Hamlet* 3.4.185.

30. See *Revenger's Tragedy* 1.1.

31. "The Most Prevalent Form of Degradation in Erotic Life," 214.

32. I focus on male Don Juanism rather than female Wife of Bathism because it is Freud's take on surfeit, wine, and women that I am glossing. The somewhat partial account of desire here reflects, I hope, Freud's prejudices rather than my own.

33. See Elster, *Sour Grapes* 121, who draws a distinction between addicting substances and sexual love. The former leads to ever greater demands for consumption, the latter to ever less. He is assuming a monogamous relation it seems and not dealing with Don Juanism.

34. See Chapter 5, note 32.

35. See Haidt, McCauley, and Rozin.

36. I have used the translation of this essay as it appears in the Collected Papers, preferring that version to the Standard Edition's "On the Universal Tendency to Debasement in the Sphere of Love."

37. Again recall the vulgar euphemism "bumping uglies."

38. See Stallybrass and White, 156–169, who draw on Swan, "Mater and Nannie," to question Freud's making the nurse and serving girl a displacement for the mother, rather than vice versa. The Oedipus complex is a way of keeping the object of desire in the appropriate class, even at the expense of flirting with the incest taboo, rather than letting the desired object be found among the lower classes.

39. With the Freudian account of incest it is instructive to compare another. Consider two of the four reasons Thomas Aquinas offers as justification for prohibiting incest: "The second reason is that blood relations have to live closely together. Were they not debarred from sexual intercourse the opportunities presented would make it too easy, and their spirits would be enervated by lust . . . A fourth reason: . . . since a man has natural affection for his own kin, were this to be charged with sexuality, it would be set ablaze and rage in libidinousness against chastity." *Summa Theologica* 2a2ae. 154.9 (trans. vol. 43, p. 239). It is a marvel how innocently this reproduces what Freud supposed could only be buried in the deepest recesses of the unconscious. And perhaps we owe the openness of these thoughts to Thomas's celibacy, for only a sexual innocent would be so freed of the repressive powers of the incest taboo as to be able to think that one's sisters would be as attractive as the more mysterious and unknown women down the street.

40. See the discussion of the polluting powers of semen in Chapter 5.

41. Self-degradation, it seems, occurs nonetheless, for the sexual act itself is felt to be generally degrading: "at the bottom of his heart he too regards the sexual act as something degrading, which soils and contaminates not only the body" (211). The soiling of his own body in the sexual act, however, is not treated here as a source of pleasure to him, but as the reason why he is dangerous to the women he has tender feelings for. Because sex is degrading one must spare the true objects of desire and find pleasure in the degradation of those who seem by virtue of their class to be suitable objects for the degrading sensual feelings.

42. In one study involving the sexual practices and fantasies of 72 subjects only one reported being aroused by disfigurement in others; Eve and Renslow, "Private Sexual Behaviors," 100. Compare our attitude toward the moral stature of those who seek out the deformed and ugly for sexual release with our attitude toward those who are able to remain loyal to a severely disfigured mate or, as an initial matter, to ignore such disfigurement for love.

43. Julien Sorel in Stendhal's *The Red and the Black* may be the first example.

44. Jesus's love by this account is maternal, and this was recognized in some medieval devotions; see Bynum, "Jesus as Mother."

45. Again see Haidt, McCauley, and Rozin, whose study showed that women are more disgust sensitive than men in all tested domains except the sexual (see

Chapter 2, note 19). Yet when it comes to the disgusting tasks of childrearing women strike men as tougher, less sensitive to disgust than men. But might not the strength of mother-love be better explained by postulating women's greater ability to overcome disgust? Women seem much more able than men to overcome disgust in the interests of love and devotion even if it is granted that their initial sensitivity to disgust is likely to be higher than men's across the relevant domains. The study purported to measure present disgust, not the capacity to overcome disgust no matter what the initial level. The test does allow the conjecture that certain unpleasant chores conventionally associated with motherhood may be harder for women to get acclimated to than they would be for men. But one wonders to what extent the study's result would have been affected had the women polled been mothers rather than thoroughly middle-class college sophomores.

46. Witnessing sex of course can produce arousal as well as disgust. Or more precisely, witnessing can simply reproduce the ambiguities between attraction and aversion we have been dealing with all along.

47. An entire social theory of public behavior expanding on the theatrical metaphor is offered with his usual perspicacity by Goffman in *The Presentation of Self in Everyday Life*.

48. See also Vlastos (52): "Constancy of affection in the face of variations of merit is one of the surest tests of whether or not a parent does love a child. If he feels fond of it only when it performs well, and turns coldly indifferent or hostile when its achievements slump, then his feeling for the child can scarcely be called *love*." Is this kind of unconditionality a necessary feature of non-parental love? Is it even a necessary feature of parental love? Parental love is surely indulgent and forgiving, but it still is tested by failures in merit without it being less love for experiencing itself put upon and tested.

49. See generally Elias, *History of Manners*, whose argument comes close to suggesting such covariance. I mean to suggest something rather different from the largely discredited arguments in Ariès's *Centuries of Childhood* and Stone's *Family, Sex, and Marriage* that would attribute to the seventeenth century the origins of our style of familial love.

7. *Warriors, Saints, and Delicacy*

1. The claim I am making is a little more problematic for the sagas than for the other texts mentioned in that the heroic saga style was also used to chronicle events nearly contemporaneous with their writing. But that does not undercut the claim, for the writing of the sagas coincided with the end of the political and social culture which made such a style of feud and honor possible. See my *Bloodtaking and Peacemaking* and Andersson, *The Problem of Icelandic Saga Origins*.

2. When the heroic ethic is in our midst we seldom find it a cause for celebration, condemning it instead as primitive, lawless, and egoistic when it is played out in criminal subcultures or in inner-city ghettos. Narrative representations of life in the 'hood do not invoke nostalgia although they still elicit a nervous awe we accord to people who accept the grimmest demands of honor.

3. On the sexual nature of these insults see Meulengracht Sørensen, *The Unmanly Man;* Gade, "Penile Puns"; and Clover, "Regardless of Sex."

4. *Þorgils saga ok Haflíða* ch. 10.

5. On farts see Gade's discussion in "Einarr Þambarskelfir's Last Shot" and Andersson and Miller, *Law and Literature in Medieval Iceland* 184n110.

6. One qualification: the reluctance of the heroic style to dwell on feeling does not mean the accounts don't bristle with emotion barely repressed or that these people don't have reasonably complex inner lives. See my *Humiliation* ch. 3 and "Deep Inner Lives."

7. See *Egils saga* ch. 78.

8. Guests have the capacity to impose obligations every bit as noisome as one's enemies do. The rarity of mentions of *dreita inni* admits of some conjectural explanation. It depends, for one thing, on having privies that one has to go outside to get to, an arrangement that *Laxdæla* indicates was getting rarer. The other mention takes place in 1198, a mere forty years before the writing of *Laxdæla;* see *Íslendinga saga* ch. 7. In any event, the *Laxdæla* author thought it necessary to explain that back "then" when the events narrated in the saga were taking place (c. 1005) houses had a different arrangement than in 1240, when *Laxdæla* was written.

9. Cf. *Eyrbyggja saga* chs. 4, 9, where defecation was prohibited in a sacred place. Those opposed to the family controlling the sacred ground officially commenced hostilities by violating the stricture.

10. *Prests saga Guðmundar góða* ch. 18.

11. Southern, *The Life of St. Anselm* 57–58.

12. See Erasmus's description of behavior in an inn quoted in Elias, *History of Manners* 72.

13. Cited in *Middle English Dictionary* (hereafter MED) s.v. abhominacioun, n. This quote comes from an English text of the early fifteenth century but reflects commonplaces in the Latin tradition from centuries earlier.

14. "Pardoner's Tale," vv. 948–955: "You would make me kiss the seat of your old pants and swear it were the relic of a saint, even though it was smeared by your anus. But by the cross which Saint Helen discovered, I wish I had your balls in my hand in stead of relics or a reliquary. Let's cut them off; I will help you carry them; they shall be enshrined in a hog's turd."

15. Benton, *Self and Society* 104.

16. "ad requisita naturæ consesserat" in *Guibert de Nogent* 83.

17. From the *Brunswick Court Regulations* cited in Elias, 131.

18. From *Galateo*, by Della Casa, cited in Elias, 131.

19. Those who still cling hard to the indefensible view that norms of disgust are matters of hygiene and disease avoidance should take note that it is better to suffer dirty hands than to remind the company of what had dirtied them by washing.

20. We now have an inverse romanticization of thinking all pre-Enlightenment behavior vulgar in the extreme.

21. See Fabri, 155.

22. Mary Douglas (124), arguing from Indian evidence, suggests that it is easy to be

casual about the physical presence of contaminants on an individual level as long as public and hierarchy-ordering ritual purities are maintained.

23. My account draws extensively from Moore, *The Formation of a Persecuting Society*—a provocative essay that refreshingly cuts through the reverence with which medievalists have come to treat the twelfth century.

24. Moore, 60.

25. Moore, 64. The only effective deodorant for the *foetor judaicus*, the Jewish stench, was baptism; see Richards, *Sex, Dissidence and Damnation* 102.

26. See Barber, "Lepers, Jews, and Moslems."

27. *Philosophical Dictionary* 7:114 (cited in Gilman, *Sexuality* 87).

28. See Gilman, 41–42, and the sources cited therein.

29. See my discussion of Fabri's account of Jewish stench in Chapter 10.

30. See the instances of supposed Jewish excremental desecrations of Christian holy objects recorded by Little, *Religious Poverty* 52–53. Chaucer's "Prioresse's Tale" links Jews, lucre, excrement, and Christian blood into a mean-spirited tale in devotion of the BVM; see Fradenburg's illuminating discussion.

31. Little, 52–55.

32. Fear of cannibalism was also implicated in the doctrine of the resurrection of the body, a doctrine intimately associated with disgust of putrefaction. See Bynum, *The Resurrection of the Body*. It also figured complexly in some of the more brutal styles of colonialism; see Taussig, "Culture of Terror," 489–497, esp. n77.

33. I have included the "were to" in brackets to translate the subjunctive form of "see" in the original: sige; Wycliffe, *Elucidarium* 25: (c. 1400) cited in *MED* s.v. abhorren.

34. See the "child-host" miracle plays of the later Middle Ages, in which the actual body of the Christ-child is eaten instead of the communion wafer. These were part of a campaign to shore up belief in the Real Presence in the face of Lollard attack. See Sinanoglou, "The Christ Child as Sacrifice." I do not think it far-fetched to see a common associational thread linking transubstantiation and the blood libel against Jews in which it is supposed that Jews needed Christian blood for Passover matzah, the same Passover ceremony at which Christ embodied himself in matzah.

35. From Orderic Vitalis cited in Moore, 61.

36. I quote, having modernized the spelling, from a 1609 English translation of the Latin *Vita;* Raymundus de Vineis, *The Life of Sainct Catharine of Siena* pt. II, ch. 11, 152–167. Catherine and the style of holy self-abasement she exemplifies have received much attention in the last fifteen years. See, e.g., Bell, *Holy Anorexia;* and Bynum, *Holy Feast and Holy Fast*.

37. Bynum reads Catherine's sucking on Jesus's side, correctly I think, not in a psychosexual way but as just what it purports to be: a taking of nourishment. See Bynum, "The Body of Christ in the Later Middle Ages." And focusing on drinking from Christ's wound rather than from the cancerous breast of the woman she was nursing allows Bynum to argue that there is a strong late medieval tradition that does not see the body as evil, but as humanizing, as a source of sustenance more than a locus of sin and corruption. Ibid. 116–117.

38. The particular styles of devotion that Bell associates with holy anorexia, it should be noted, begin in the early thirteenth century just when the Real Presence becomes dogma. See Bell, 215ff.

39. Compare, however, Cooper's *Dictionary of Practical Surgery* II 316: "Pus has a sweetish, mawkish taste." Pus tasting had passed from the bailiwick of saints to that of medical researchers. One wonders if in this description of the taste of pus we are not seeing the sense of taste influenced greatly by the knowledge of the nauseating and disgustful thing being tasted. Urine drinking, never quite as unthinkable as pus drinking, is, according to *Newsweek* (Aug. 21, 1995, p. 8), becoming somewhat of a trend among devotees of holistic healing.

40. Irrational behavior may make good strategic sense, but its effectiveness depends on others thinking it is not undertaken because it has strategic advantages. These advantages must come as unintended consequences. A reputation for being crazy may help you in bargaining settings where a reputation for pretending to be crazy would not. See Schelling, 21–42.

41. See Ranum's account of Mme Mondonville in "The Refuges of Intimacy," 241–242; annoyed at having been sickened while cutting the vermin-infested hair of a wounded soldier she was tending, she decided to put the hair in her mouth out of devotion to Jesus. This is in the middle of the seventeenth century.

42. Not to be outdone, Swift has several performances in the "anti-painting" genre that are a triumph of disgust-eliciting mean-spirited misogyny. See, e.g., "The Progress of Beauty," *Poetical Works* 172.

43. Plus ça change: on women's magazines advising women to spread semen on their faces to enhance their complexions see Dworkin, 187.

44. On the link of Jews to leprosy and syphilis see Gilman, 85–87.

45. Bell, 43.

46. Trevisa Barth. 81b/b (c. 1398), cited in MED s.v. abhominacioun, n.

47. See OED s.v. abominable.

48. "and lothly for to here (hear):" see MED s.v. loth, adj., 2a.

49. *The Owl and the Nightingale,* v. 354 (early thirteenth century) uses wlate to indicate the nausea of surfeit: "Overfulle maketh wlatie." Elsewhere it is used to indicate the proper response to sin; see OED s.v. wlate.

50. H. Buttes, *Dyets dry dinner,* London, 1599; cited in OED s.v. loathe v. 3.

51. It is not uncommon for words, over time, and even synchronically in related forms, to mean themselves and their opposites. See Freud, "The Antithetical Meaning of Primal Words."

52. See Ariès, *The Hour of our Death* 29–92.

53. See Wierzbicka, "The Semantics of Interjection."

54. By 1400 rank can mean loathsome, but its most distinctively pejorative senses are not firmly in place until the sixteenth century.

55. Cf. Braunstein, "Toward Intimacy," 610–615, who in an attempt to uncover the particular kind of sensuality of medieval French romance argues for a lower ranking of visual images in late medieval literature as a consequence of uncorrected bad eyesight. He finds more pleasant images devoted to smell, hearing, and taste. His focus is sufficiently narrow that he is able to ignore the danger-

ousness of gluttony and lust that is so prominent in more hortatory literature, but that also creeps into the less flesh-hating world of romance.

56. *Summa,* 2a2æ.148.5: "delectationes tactus."

57. Bourdieu, *Distinction* 486–491.

58. See OED s.v. disgust sb. and *Robert,* s.v. dégoût.

59. The argument is attractive but perhaps too neat. Dictionaries show taste as the sense of the appropriate, harmonious, and beautiful lagging behind the appearance of disgust the word by some fifty years (in both English and French). The lag is not sufficient to undo the argument made here, for in both languages before disgust came into the lexicon taste already had been expanded to describe the mental perception of any preference. Disgust would thus have indicated aversions to anything not in accord with one's preferences, not just to food.

60. The social historian J.-L. Flandrin wonders whether "the ideas of good and bad taste developed first in the culinary or in the artistic and literary domain"; ("Distinction through Taste," 300). He finds inconclusive evidence pointing both ways but suggests that it may have been the cooks who first so aestheticized food production as to make possible the metaphorical extension of taste into non-culinary domains.

61. See Jaeger, *The Origins of Courtliness.* See also van Krieken's critique in "Violence, Self-Discipline."

62. "Religion, the belief in the punishing or rewarding omnipotence of God, never has in itself a 'civilizing' or affect-subduing effect. On the contrary, religion is always exactly as 'civilized' as the society or class which upholds it"; *History of Manners* 200. One notes Elias's restriction of religion to matters of belief rather than as an institutionalized regime. He supposes the utter subservience of religion to some prior society that religion in no way helped constitute, but merely reflects.

63. Elias anticipates Mary Douglas's dismissal of the argument by hygiene; see Chapter 3, note 26. Hygiene has nothing to do with preferring forks to spoons, obviously, nor for objections to eating organ meat or snails, etc.

64. By the end of the seventeenth century there are very explicit poetic performances by men, consciously in the Ovidian tradition, advising women and urging them to keep clean so as not to kill Eros in men by disgusting them. An especially vulgar performance was penned by John Wilmot, Earl of Rochester c. 1680, of which I provide one verse:

> Fair nasty nymph, be clean and kind,
> And all my joys restore
> By using paper still behind
> And spunges for before.

From "Song," vv. 5–8, *Complete Poems* 139. Note the early mention of toilet paper. Congreve, too, undertook a verse translation of Book III of Ovid's *The Art of Love,* and one discerns, in a way ignored by Elias, that classical models could serve to reeducate Europeans on bodily cleanliness. Notice the directness with which Congreve renders Ovid's admonishment to women to depilatorize their legs, among other things, noted earlier (Chapter 3, note 44):

> I need not warn you of too pow'rful Smells,
> Which, sometimes Health, or kindly Heat expels.
> Nor, from your tender Legs to pluck with Care
> The casual Growth of all unseemly Hair.

William Congreve, *Ovid's Third Book of the Art of Love* vv. 248–251; see also Pope's querulous advice to women in his note on anointing, quoted in Chapter 4, note 1.

Mary Wollstonecraft, writing in the 1790s, undertakes to advise women on proper cleanliness in matters of defecation and menstruation. The demands of decorum put her to extraordinary feats of circumlocution, obliquity, obscurity, and desperate euphemism. Defecation is unsurprisingly "that business . . . which ought never to be done before a fellow creature." But consider the number of words it takes her simply to advise women not to talk about their periods: "I could proceed still further, till I animadverted on some still more nasty customs, which men never fall into. Secrets are told where silence ought to reign; and that regard to cleanliness, which some religious sects have perhaps carried too far, especially the Essenes, amongst the Jews, by making that an insult to God which is only an insult to humanity, is violated in a beastly manner. How can *delicate* women obtrude on notice that part of the animal economy, which is so very disgusting? And is it not very rational to conclude, that the women which have not been taught to respect the human nature of their own sex in these particulars, will not long respect the mere difference of sex in their husbands? After their maidenish bashfulness is once lost, I, in fact, have generally observed that women fall into old habits, and treat their husbands as they did their sisters or female acquaintance" (*Vindication of the Rights of Woman* 235–236).

65. *Treatise* III.iii.4, p. 611. The same paragraph appears nearly verbatim later in his *An Enquiry Concerning the Principles of Morals* 104.

66. For the notion that cleanliness comprehended the condition of one's linen more than one's body see Revel, 189.

67. Consider the discussion of the history of cleanliness and its change in meaning in Francis Newman, who is so thoroughly a product of the civilizing process that he can propose that ancient taboos were genuinely concerned with public health in the nineteenth-century style (*Theism* 163: "Cleanliness," vv. 14–32):

> With excellent reason then did ancient religion judge,
> In denouncing with authority every such negligence as a sin,
> And in driving away from the public throng (sacred or civil)
> Every leper or unclean person who might spread a dangerous taint.
> But when religion urged Cleanliness so authoritatively,
> That it could not be more authoritative for Justice and Truth,
> And zeal for ceremonies spread, and men made display of Holiness
> By various outward purity, forgetting the inward man
> Then the precepts of cleanliness became disguised and mistaken:
> And one class of men extolled ceremonial purity
> As of celestial value,—the more artificial the more divine,—
> And despised foreign virtue, which neglected such precepts;

While another class of men decried ceremonial purity,
And reproved all religious enforcement of cleanliness,
As confounding inward holiness with the fictitious outside:
Nay, reversing asceticism, many marvellously went forward
Into admiration of filthiness and of bodily neglect,
As denoting the true saint, raised above things earthly,
Bent to renounce or to humiliate all that vulgar minds cherish.

68. See Dumont, 60–61: "The etiquette of purity corresponds in one way to what we call culture or civilization, the less punctilious castes being regarded as boorish by the more fastidious."

69. Recall that purity is not invariably linked to disgust. All disgust raises an idea of purity, but not all purity need be sanctioned by disgust. Guilt, shame, a sense of duty can maintain purity rules as well, although not as aggressively.

70. It has even been argued that the means to urinate and defecate in an acceptably private manner is a necessary precondition of autonomy and freedom; see Waldron, "Homelessness and Freedom," 320–321. The interpenetration of the civilizing process and the rise of liberal political theory makes for some strange conjunctions and disjunctions. With the civilizing process the content of a minimal human dignity expands to include a private place to excrete. The civilizing process makes it harder (or at least more expensive) to accord minimal dignity just at the time such dignity takes on foundational importance in political theory.

71. The Weberian account in which the history of the West is one in which bureaucratic rationality claims ever greater terrain and finally succeeds in disenchanting the world is greatly complicated, even seriously undercut, by the account we have constructed for disgust. The entire civilizing process depends on disgust's imbuing greater portions of the social order with uncanny and magical power, the power to pollute and revolt us.

72. "Looking Back at the Spanish Civil War," *Essays* 196.

73. On the distinction between manners and morals see Harré, "Embarrassment," and Goffman, *Behavior in Public Places* 209.

8. The Moral Life of Disgust

1. *Works* 3:24.

2. Johnson was not narrowly monkish about what constituted vice. Like Mandeville he defended the benefits of luxury. For Johnson on Mandeville, see *Life of Johnson* April 15, 1778, Chapman ed. 947–948.

3. I am not here defending the emotivist position, which I do not generally accept. I merely note that as a social matter emotions that tend to do moral work are often understood to involve a moral judgment whenever they work. Even though moral sentiments may not be properly congruent with what we would call moral judgments, it is not clear that any but analytic philosophers can consistently maintain the distinction; see Gibbard, 129–131, 147–150. Notice that moral sentiments like disgust will let us blame things that our moral judgment says we

should not and that conversely there are times when our moral judgment says we should disapprove of things which seem to elicit very little aversion in us at all.

4. Nashe, *Christs Teares over Jerusalem* 83r. Recall variously *Les Miserables, Our Mutual Friend,* and Orwell's "Such, Such were the Joys."

5. Vices (and virtues) are often treated as if they were traits of character, and I am eliding traits and vices here, but I wish to make no claim as to their synonymy. On this issue and other related ones see Flanagan 280–292.

6. *Enquiry* 90n1.

7. The fastidious person disgusts by hypersensitivity to the disgusting, the boor by hyposensitivity to it, but they both have the capacity to disgust by bringing the disgusting to bear in situations where a more finely attuned sensibility would have avoided intimations of it.

8. Hume, *Enquiry* 75–76. I do not wish my claims to be dependent on the presence of the word disgust. I have fastened on passages in which it is used but not exclusively. Disgust is hard to gloss with precision in these passages. It is clearly a stronger term than disapprobation or aversion; but depending on the context it can indicate various intensities of aversion from mere distaste to contempt, hatred, loathing, and revulsion.

9. Compare Montaigne on stupidity: "Stupidity is a bad quality; but to be unable to endure it, to be irritated and chafed by it, as happens to me, is another sort of malady which is scarcely less troublesome than stupidity"; "On the Art of Discussion," *Essays* 704.

10. The misogyny that makes the dumb blonde an object of sexual desire involves us more in the prevalent forms of degradation of erotic life and the complex interpenetrations of disgust and sex that we touched on in Chapter 6.

11. *Enquiry* App. iv, 157. His thoughts are more moderately expressed in the *Treatise:* "Let a man have the best intentions in the world, and be the farthest from all injustice and violence, he will never be able to make himself be much regarded, without a moderate share, at least, of parts and understanding" (III.iii.4, p. 607). Hume saw fit to reproduce the same passage in the *Enquiry* (159) as part of an appendix. Note that it is not mere lack of intelligence that Hume finds disgusting; it is stupidity coupled with the lack of self-knowledge regarding one's limits. It is the fool, the person who thrusts his stupidity upon you, that elicits his disgust. On Hume's theory of virtue see Baier, *A Progress of Sentiments* 198–219.

12. Hume's lack of charity here embarrasses Baier, one of his most admiring commentators; see Baier, "Moralism and Cruelty."

13. The academic celebration of carnival, the canonization of Bakhtin's *Rabelais,* and the elevation of Georges Bataille from obscurity are cases in point. For a friendlier and insightful critique of this style of academic writing see Desan.

14. We might also wish to include deicides, prostitutes, and moneylenders in our list of moral menials, but each raises special problems that would lead us too far afield. The Jew is doubly cast as a moral menial trafficking in necessary evil, not only as a killer of Christ but also as a moneylender. As a deicide he performs the necessary function that inaugurates Christianity, thus in Christian eyes mak-

ing the fall from Eden a fortunate fall. As a moneylender he assists capital formation and prevents the economy from grinding to a halt. But the complicated history of anti-Semitism raises intractably difficult problems that have little to do with the brief points I wish to make about moral meniality.

As for prostitution, we have come to think it an evil but not a necessary one. In the nineteenth century it was argued that prostitution was necessary to sustain marriage and the virtue of proper women by affording "decent" men a class of women to whom they were to restrict their predations. On this matter our Puritanism is in some ways more thoroughgoing than the nineteenth-century variety, and that is probably a good thing too. Unlike lawyers and politicians, prostitutes elicit pity as much as disgust. They benefit from the low expectations that misogyny and sexist assumptions have for the moral possibility of women in general. Notice too that though the hangman is clearly a moral menial, the soldier and the policeman usually manage to avoid being so designated. The atrocities and brutalities they commit from time to time are generally understood to be egregious rather than routine, whereas the perfidy of lawyers and politicians is understood to be business as usual.

15. Moral philosophers have been drawn to the problems raised by the divergence of so-called professional morality and common morality. As these themes impinge on the politician see the excellent contributions by Walzer and Nagel; with regard to lawyers see Williams, "Professional Morality and Its Dispositions," 264.

16. Compare the unemployed person who is also blamed for choosing his condition even though the proper running of the economy requires 3–6 percent unemployment. Although the unemployed can be seen as necessary evils they are not understood to be moral menials. There is a general and insistent unwillingness to believe that unemployment is as necessary and inevitable as politicians and lawyers; moreover, we are incapable of conceiving of the unemployed's lack of employment as a *task*, however morally menial the condition may be. We extenuate the blame we attribute to the lawyer and politician because we really believe them to be necessary and we can understand them to be "laboring." The lawyer and the politician are fulfilling a moral function, though distasteful and menial; the unemployed are perceived as just that, unemployed, doing no work whatsoever, not even morally menial work, even though experts know that they are no less necessary than lawyers. It is not that the public benefits derivable from vices like gluttony and sloth have not been celebrated, but their celebration depends on their practitioners being sufficiently wealthy so as to have the means to provide employment to others to abet their luxury. The unemployed of the lower orders have yet to find their Mandeville; on the history of the idea that vices confer public benefits see Hirschman, *The Passions and the Interests*.

17. The used car salesman plays on the fact that his style is so off-putting that people will close the deal just so they can escape.

18. Again see Sartre's discussion of sliminess: Chapter 4, notes 2 and 5.

19. Is it possible for someone to praise a superior without the praise taking on all the attributes of flattery? Must he only praise the superior to third parties and

out of the praised one's hearing? Even the superior who praises the inferior can be fishing for compliments. Managing praise without taking on the appearance of unctuousness, of false-seeming, or of flattery is not always easy.

20. See Shklar, *Ordinary Vices* 58: "The naive hypocrite hides acts and beliefs that he knows to be wrong. His conscience may even trouble him. That is why he resorts to subterfuge to quell his own guilt as well as to escape censure from other people. The new hypocrite simply adjusts his conscience by ascribing noble, disinterested, and altruistic intentions to all his behavior. He is the sole instructor of his own conscience."

21. I prefer to leave these questions open, but I wish to note that the hypocrisy that comes attended with all the signs of unction and sleaze will disgust in the way vile disgusting matter does; the hypocrite whose exterior is not disgusting, whose style is utterly charming, or whose hypocrisy is supported by self-deceiving sincerity will still evoke disgust with all its unpleasant sensations *on the first discovery of his failing,* when it will be coupled with a sense of betrayal. We may be readier to forgive the hypocrite whose style avoids the obvious markers of calculation or vulgarity, but we also may come to dread his presence. We may reinterpret his charm as false and end in making it as revolting as if it had come with all the trappings of obvious calculation or vulgarity.

22. See La Rochefoucauld, Maxim 218: "Hypocrisy is the homage vice renders to virtue."

23. Smith is clear that disapprobation is experienced in many different forms depending on the particular breach of propriety; *TMS* 325.

24. See my discussion in *Humiliation* 134–174 and in "I can take a hint" on the discomforts occasioned by watching failure and ineptitude and its close connection with comedy, amusement, and entertainment.

25. Smith is embarrassed by this psychological obstruction to impartiality. "When there is no envy in the case" is almost a refrain in his exposition. He is also somewhat embarrassed by the "malice in mankind" which finds others' little uneasinesses a source of diversion for us; *TMS* 42, 44–46. My own sense of *Schadenfreude* is that this "malice" is permissible, if not admirable, only with regard to others' *little* misfortunes and that we use the term *Schadenfreude* specifically to indicate the pleasure that another's *minor* misfortunes grant us. Pleasure in another's major misfortunes is truly malicious and hateful.

26. *TMS* 27–28. Smith divides the passions into five groups. I am not going to take the space to go through these systematically, but restrict myself to a few points Smith makes that are narrowly relevant to our themes.

27. Note that one of the ways we come to sympathize with the distress of desperate hunger is by partially suspending our disgust and replacing it with awe when we hear that people in severe duress resorted to eating bugs, drinking urine, or eating their dead companions. Our disgust is not totally suspended, however. For our sympathy with their plight depends on our recognition of the disgust they had to overcome to drink urine and eat insects or their dead companions. The plight we sympathize with is not hunger but having to eat such things because of hunger.

28. The emotions that prevent sympathy will always be negative ones of various degrees of intensity and dangerousness. Sometimes the failure of sympathy is a moral failing in the observer. When sympathy fails to accord with joys that the observer should sympathize with, it leaves him "ashamed of [his] own envy" (*TMS* 44).

29. Goffman follows Smith in this regard. Interactional impropriety in Goffman always requires an accounting either by an attempt at justification or by apology. Goffman's account, as rich as it is, lacks the beauty that Smith is able to provide via the vehicle of the impartial spectator's sympathy.

30. Smith's sentimentality does not extend to excessive displays of the selfish passions, grief and joy: "We are disgusted with that clamorous grief, which without any delicacy calls upon our compassion with sighs and tears and importunate lamentations" (24). He reserves special rage for indecorous displays of joy. Anyone who has suffered the painful embarrassment of watching televised locker-room celebrations or fans celebrating a championship will sympathize with Smith: "the man who skips and dances about with that intemperate and senseless joy which we cannot accompany him in, is the object of our contempt and indignation" (44). Smith's sentimentality is reserved for those dyadic displays of love and generosity in which the observed person's excessive display is not self-referential.

31. Purity is not completely congruent with the moral to be sure; purity pretends to admit of no compromises, while working morality can have no such pretenses. However, they share enough common ground that disgust must perforce join the moral.

32. See Gibbard, 271.

33. Recent work in psychology has shown that disgust is a frequent marker of moral claims across a wide range of cultures. Haidt and his colleagues observe that although there are cross-language differences in the semantic domains for disgust words, it is still abundantly clear that socio-moral disgust is not a quirk of English; see Haidt, Rozin, et al.

34. *Enquiry* 110–111.

35. Hobbes goes further and defines indignation as "anger for a great hurt done to *another*" (*Leviathan* I.6, emphasis supplied).

36. Cruelty can be so unbelievably appalling that disgust can be postponed until we recover our ability to make discernments. This demonstrates that although disgust is visceral it is still very thought-dependent. Shock is distinctly more immediate than disgust.

37. There are, of course, ways of defining the moral that do not directly involve moral sentiments. Some philosophers think of morality as the terrain for the resolution of dispute and conflict, a matter of rights. See, e.g., Philippa Foot, 208.

38. See, e.g., Hutcheson, "An Inquiry Concerning Moral Good and Evil," §§ 303–309.

39. Gibbard, 293. See D'Arms and Jacobson's extended critique of Gibbard's formulation. What of those situations, they ask, in which it makes sense to feel

guilty while thinking you have not done wrong or when you could not be justifiably an object of others' anger?

40. Compare Baier's similar formulation involving slightly different emphases: "Morality is the culturally acquired art of selecting which harms to notice and worry about, where the worry takes the form of bad conscience or resentment"; *Postures of the Mind* 263.

41. In spite of legal and moral philosophical efforts to restrict guilt to the voluntary, it is not rare to feel responsible for our involuntary actions. We thus feel it necessary to apologize or excuse ourselves when we inadvertently bump into someone. See the discussion in Williams, *Shame and Necessity* 92–94 and Gibbard, 297.

42. See Gibbard, 297.

43. Goffman, *Stigma* 2. I draw promiscuously on Goffman in the discussion that follows: see *Relations in Public, Interaction Ritual, Behavior in Public Places*, and *The Presentation of Self in Everyday Life*.

44. The example comes from Kant and is discussed in Taylor, *Pride, Shame, and Guilt* 70.

45. Note that though the criminal is made such within the confines of the legalized guilt/anger system, once convicted the criminal enters the stickier shame system. He may serve his time, but we still hold him polluted unless he is willing to do much more than merely serve his time. We expect major characterological transformations. Guilt systems attempt to bring closure to incidents by boxing time in very small units. One is not to look too far before the act in question; and once he makes atonement one is to forget he ever did the punishable deed. These are nearly impossible psychological demands on the rest of us.

46. The term is Goffman's; *Stigma* 6.

47. Consider, for instance, how the gods laugh at Hephaestus's lameness or how Homer and the Greek multitudes mock Thersites' physical deformity which to them is more than a sign of an inner moral failure, but is itself a moral failure; see the *Iliad* 1.586–600 and 2.211–221 and the discussion in Lincoln, 27–32. Note, too, Nietzsche's remark about Socrates' ugliness: "In origin, Socrates belonged to the lowest class: Socrates was plebs. We know, we can still see for ourselves, how ugly he was. But ugliness, in itself an objection, is among the Greeks almost a refutation" ("The Problem of Socrates," ch. 3, in *Twilight of the Idols*).

48. Gibbard, 55–82.

49. Much of my *Humiliation* is devoted to showing that the morality of honor/shame and the emotions that support that moral economy still govern wide ranges of our social existence. Gibbard (136ff) rather ingeniously finesses the difficulty of the shame-guilt distinction by pairing each, shame or guilt, with the emotion in the second party it is a response to. Thus shame is a response to derision and contempt, guilt a response to anger, and since anger and contempt are easily distinguishable the shame/guilt distinction can piggyback on the easy distinguishability of anger and contempt. The shame/guilt distinction has been rightly and roundly criticized; see among others, Piers and Singer. Yet despite the cri-

tique the distinction between shame and guilt cultures still has a rough heuristic value.

50. Notice that even shame morality in practice allows certain stigmatized persons to be accepted with limited privileges if they are willing to adopt certain roles reserved for them. The blind are accepted and honored as musicians, the fat as good humored, the Jew as physicians and scientists, the black as athletes and performers. And monumental efforts at self-overcoming are honored, but all these strategies pay homage to the order that generates the stigma.

51. Shklar, *Ordinary Vices* 7–44.

52. See Samuel Butler's classic account of blamable sickness in *Erewhon*.

53. Notice how the old Galenic humors capture the difference of "feel" of various moral sentiments.

9. Mutual Contempt and Democracy

1. James Scott in his *Domination and the Arts of Resistance,* as his title suggests, deals with the styles of resistance the lower take with regard to the higher, but his chief focus is on societies with institutionalized slavery, untouchability, or racial domination. His discussion only indirectly alludes to the emotional force motivating the "hidden transcripts" of the disempowered. It largely assumes that resentment, indignation, and fear mark the style. Contempt makes only a rare appearance (e.g., pp. 2, 199). Many of Scott's points are anticipated by Baumgartner, "Social Control from Below." See Hochschild, *The Managed Heart,* for an ethnography of the psychological costs of emotion management among flight attendants, which for its many virtues underestimates, I think, the strategic resources the attendants have in their repertoire.

2. He thereby demonstrates his competence in deciphering the codes of class and the distinctions that mark class; see generally Bourdieu, *Distinction.*

3. Presumably he was not aware of how funny his tee-shirt was to us, given the irony that his most salient feature for us was *his* killer crack.

4. For a good treatment of class, sexuality, and vulgarity see Kipnis, "(Male) Desire and (Female) Disgust."

5. See Solomon, *The Passions* 292, who asks us to imagine a cockroach, then a six-foot cockroach. On the grotesque the obligatory cite is Bakhtin, *Rabelais and His World.*

6. John Anderson, "Ice-T's Role Reversal," *Newsday* (March 3, 1991), Pt. II, p. 3. Ice-T's views on democracy reduplicate those of such conservative anti-democrats as Edmund Burke.

7. Hebb, as early as 1946, made the stronger claim that such observers need not be experts, but that the observer's position has natural advantages in monitoring key behavioral and contextual aspects of emotion which are not available to the subject. See Hebb, "Emotion in Man and Animal," 101.

8. Notice how the type of work he does will affect the content of his contempt for me. As a mason he prides himself on having a skill which is not easily acquired by others without years of training. If, however, he were simply providing a

lawn service, he might look at the very fact that I have hired him as an indication of my moral failing.

9. To show gracious affability to one's inferiors; to eschew for the nonce certain privileges of rank.

10. See *Leviathan* I.6.

11. *Treatise* II.ii.10, pp. 390–393. Hume's sense of hatred does not always carry with it the same intensity as our usage does; the word can be used to indicate a generalized aversiveness.

12. See Hume, *Enquiry* 84: "The misfortunes of our fellows often cause pity, which has in it a strong mixture of good-will. This sentiment of pity is nearly allied to contempt, which is a species of dislike, with a mixture of pride."

13. Tocqueville discusses the inability of sympathy to cross wide separations of class as between lord and peasant in *Democracy in America* II.iii.1. And for Adam Smith's belief that moral regard for others depends on a rough egalitarianism see *TMS* 55. See the discussion in Herzog, *Without Foundations* 215.

14. Consider, however, that the superior may blame the lower for not recognizing under what circumstances certain forms of deference should be due. The lower's ignorance would not excuse his offense but simply reveal a reckless disregard of the obvious. A swift caning might be considered appropriate instruction.

15. "An Essay on Conversation," 251, 262.

16. To his son October 9, O.S. 1746. This sentiment is repeated in about ten other letters almost verbatim. Also: "Wrongs are often forgiven, but contempt never is. Our pride remembers it for ever" (July 1, 1748, to his son).

17. "Of all the Fops in Nature, none are so ridiculously contemptible as the Would-bees." London Mag. I.240, cited in OED, s.v. would-be, B. sb.

18. Le Brun, "Conférence sur l'expression des passions," combines hatred and contempt by depicting bilateral upper lip extension. He provides no example of the one-sided smile. Darwin gives us a one-sided lip raise in a sneer, but no picture of the one-sided smile (ch. 10, plate 4). The exact nature of the contempt expression and the question of its universality have generated much recent debate among those who hold to the view that facial expressions are the chief definers of emotion. See Ekman and Friesen, "A New Pan-cultural Facial Expression of Emotion"; Izard and Haynes; and Ekman and various co-authors' debates with Russell. For an excellent critique of this point of view see Neu, "A Tear Is an Intellectual Thing."

19. See the expression of the woman in Plate V in Darwin, opposite p. 254.

20. On disgust expressions see Rozin, Lowery, and Ebert.

21. Upward contempt can also make use of the self-loathing of the lower (if present) to augment contempt for the high. Thus in certain instances of upward contempt the pleasure of the lower is not quite separable from the knowledge that the superior he holds in contempt is at least in some respects lower even than he himself is; lower, in other words, than the low.

22. "Satire is an unwilling tribute to power; but it also implies the recognition of a certain inevitability in the thing satirized, a lack of any constructive alternative"; Southern, *The Making of the Middle Ages* 154. To the extent that the high are

hypocrites the satire is also suffused with disgust, but the disgust is not sufficient to render the high socially polluting. Since the satirist accepts the principles of the present order his disgust is constrained so as not to undo that order. He will still defer but with utter contempt for those of the high whose conduct works to undermine the legitimacy of the social order by their depravity and incompetence.

23. The feast-of-misrule style of upward contempt is plainly not Nietzsche's value-transforming *ressentiment,* although the satiric and moralizing style of upward contempt has clear resemblances to it; see *Genealogy of Morals* I.10.

24. The Manciple's skills in thievery were especially noteworthy because, as steward of the temple housing the best lawyers in England, he was able to fleece his masters; in other words, he fleeced the fleecers. And of the Reeve it is said that "His lord wel koude he plesen subtilly, / To yeve and lene [give and lend] hym of his [the lord's] owene good" (*Canterbury Tales,* A569–588, 612–613).

25. *Iliad* 2.214–282; see the discussion of the scene in Lincoln, 21–34.

26. *Laxdæla saga* chs. 49, 52.

27. Note that Thersites tries to gain such privilege by playing the clown. It is denied him.

28. For more on the remarkable women of the Icelandic sagas see my *Bloodtaking and Peacemaking* 212–213 and the citations listed there.

29. Throughout the eighteenth century the dancing master is a stock figure of contemptibility who is surpassed in that unenviable category only by hairdressers. See the entertaining account of the significance of late-eighteenth-century references to the latter in Herzog, "The Trouble with Hairdressers."

30. Fielding was also drawn to the topic of mutual contempt in his *Covent-Garden Journal* (Sat. Aug. 29, 1752, no. 61). In this delightful entry he supposes all contempt to be matched by the equivalent contempt in the contemnee. "Contempt is, generally at least, mutual, and that there is scarce any one Man who despises another without being at the same Time despised by him, of which I shall endeavour to produce some few Instances . . .

"Lady Fanny Rantun, from the side Box, casting her Eyes on an honest Pawnbroker's Wife below her, bid Lady Betty her Companion take Notice of that Creature in the Pit: 'did you ever see, Lady Betty,' says she, 'such a strange Wretch: how the aukward Monster is dressed!' The good Woman at the same Time surveying Lady Fanny, and offended perhaps, at a scornful Smile, which she sees in her Countenance,—whispers her Friend.—'Observe Lady Fanny Rantun. As great Airs as that fine Lady gives herself, my Husband hath all her Jewels under Lock and Key, what a contemptible Thing is poor Quality!'

"Is there on Earth a greater Object of Contempt than a poor Scholar to a splendid Beau; unless perhaps the splendid Beau to the poor Scholar!"

Still we note that these mutual contempts do not inspire fear in the higher if it is even clear who the higher is. These are people jostling for preeminence in a more complex world in which it is not clear who should defer to whom. These are manifestly not examples of the servant contemning the master in repayment for the master's contemning him.

31. Godwin, *Enquiry Concerning Political Justice* I.5, p. 42.

32. Hazlitt, "On the Knowledge of Character," (1821), 105.

33. Hazlitt, "On the Disadvantages of Intellectual Superiority," (1821), 188.

34. I discuss humiliation-avoidance strategies at length in *Humiliation*. The general observation is that the risk of humiliation inheres in pretension, but that so dolorous is the social world that pretensions of some sort are never completely avoidable. Thus the despairing strategy of Dostoyevsky's underground man to seek out humiliation so as to have it on his own terms.

35. See Swift, *Directions to Servants*.

36. The virtue of *mansuetudo* (mildness and restraint) was evidenced in the hagiographies of the saintly court bishops of the tenth and eleventh centuries by having them endure the surliness of servants without becoming enraged; see the discussion in Jaeger, 37–40. Cicero points to the contrast of Ajax and Odysseus, the latter being so capable of restraint that he could endure insults from slaves and maidservants when it was in his interest to do so; *De officiis* 1.113. The Thersites episode in the *Iliad* shows, however, that when it was in his interest to berate the impudence of the low he did not restrain himself.

37. *Democracy in America* II.iii.2.

38. Making reference to how thriving upward contempt is in America, Weber paints a bleaker picture more in line with my argument: "As late as the early 1900's the author inquired of American workers of English origin why they allowed themselves to be governed by party henchmen who were so often open to corruption. The answer was, in the first place, that in such a big country even though millions of dollars were stolen or embezzled there was still plenty left for everybody, and secondly, that these professional politicians were a group which even workers could treat with contempt whereas technical officials of the German type would as a group 'lord it over' the workers." *The Theory of Social and Economic Organization* 391–392.

39. If the English were nervous wrecks with regard to one another abroad it was because they were very secure in their standing as against the natives of the land they were in. It was the other way with Americans, whose anxiety about their standing with the natives of European countries drove them into one another's arms when in fact they might not at all have been so driven at home without first having acquired knowledge as to the person's respectability.

40. Letter of Thomas C. Dudley, a young ship's purser from Yonkers, New York, to his sister Fanny, 16 June 1852, in the Dudley collection at the Clements Library, Ann Arbor.

41. Tocqueville is aware that there are forces establishing ranks in America, even making for new aristocracies; e.g., *Democracy in America* II.ii.20.

42. If his battle with the washerwoman is one of competing contempts, his battle as an American against the English puts Dudley to saying he is disgusted by the English type of equality: "If they think our equality disagreeable, I think theirs disgusting." He is showing the English that he can be more than their match when it comes to disapprobation. If theirs is moderate, his will be intense, and how better to show intensity than by rhetorical and strategic recourse to disgust. Their equality is disgusting rather than contemptible not just because disgust

carries more force (it is not clear that it would in this setting), but because his selection of "disgusting" registers a kind of deference to the power of the English that this defensive American still feels deeply. Contemptible they are not to him for they are not insignificant. The disgusting are never quite as easily dismissible as the contemptible.

43. See especially Hawthorne's profound treatment in *The Blithedale Romance* of the psychological anguish that attended cross-class mingling in the Brook Farm experiment.

10. Orwell's Sense of Smell

1. I am glibly treating respect here as if it were obvious what it is. A reasonable delineation would involve a book as long as this one. Presumably the basic minimal respect for persons that is the cornerstone of the liberal political order need not be earned, nor does it exist in any meaningful equilibrium with contempt. Since it comes with the territory of being human it offers no basis for approbation or self-esteem. Imagine, as Nozick (243) points out, the ridiculousness of saying: Hey, I am really something—I have an opposable thumb. The respect for another *as a human being* is a thin notion indeed. But the general claim for respect is usually also a claim for something more than that, something involving merit and rank. For a recent attempt to formulate a content for respect see Gibbard, 264–269.

2. George Steiner, *New Yorker*, March 1969, reprinted in Meyers, 366.

3. Hoggart, "George Orwell and 'The Road to Wigan Pier,' " 73–74.

4. Remarkable how the list in the thirties passed without change to the sixties and pretty much unmodified to the nineties.

5. While I do not wish to confirm or deny Orwell on this matter, it is the case that many Asians (and American Indians) tend to be without or have fewer odor-producing apocrine sweat glands, the main source of underarm and genital perspiration odor, than either blacks or whites; see Overfield 15.

6. Orwell is explicit that his tramping and voluntary assumption of the lowest poverty were undertaken to expiate the guilt of his imperial service; see *Wigan Pier* 148–150.

7. See Patai, *The Orwell Mystique* 81–82.

8. With Orwell's treatment of the Brookers compare Hawthorne's treatment of Silas Foster in *The Blithedale Romance*. Hawthorne's narrator cannot quite hide his revulsion at the rustic Foster's table manners; disgust manages to break through his desperate commitment to accept Foster as his equal even as he must struggle to find him honorable in spite of his unwiped mouth: "Grim Silas Foster, all this while, had been busy at the supper-table, pouring out his own tea, and gulping it down with no more sense of its exquisiteness than if it were a decoction of catnip; helping himself to pieces of dipt toast on the flat of his knife-blade, and dropping half of it on the table-cloth; using the same serviceable implement to cut slice after slice of ham; perpetrating terrible enormities with the butter-plate; and, in all other respects, behaving less like a civilized Christian than the worst

kind of an ogre. Being by this time fully gorged, he crowned his amiable exploits with a draught from the water-pitcher, and then favored us with his opinion about the business in hand. And, certainly, though they proceeded out of an unwiped mouth, his expression did him honor" (ch. 4, p. 658). On the snobbism and other anxieties of cross-class mingling in the Brook Farm experiment see Packer, 466–470. But the peasant vulgarity of Silas Foster is distinctly less threatening than the vulgarity of the urban proletariat.

9. Note that the expression "beneath contempt" usually relegates the object so described to the realm of the disgusting.

10. See Rai, *Orwell and the Politics of Despair* 68; Wollheim, "Orwell Reconsidered"; Raymond Williams is less severe in *Culture and Society* 288.

11. Depending on the hierarchy the smell has different associations and meanings, but the broad claim here survives the local variations.

12. Fabri, 439–440.

13. See Braunstein, 613–615.

14. See Thomas Browne's attack on the proposition that Jews stink in *Pseudodoxia Epidemica*, IV.10, p. 174: "Now the ground that begat or propagated this assertion, might be the distasteful averseness of the Christian from the Jew, upon the villainy of that fact, which made them abominable and stink in the nostrils of all men. Which real practice and metaphorical expression, did after proceed into a literal construction; but a fraudulent illation."

15. "Such, Such were the Joys," 37–38.

16. See Montaigne, "Of Smells," *Essays* 228.

17. On the New Age move to change all this by odor therapy see Klein, "Get a Whiff of This," who is an advocate.

18. Ewing, "The Heart of the Race Problem," 395.

19. See the account of Bernard Crick and his informant quoted in Rai, 68: "We found him," an old miners' leader told Crick, "perfectly clean and decent lodgings. Most people had more time to clean when out of work and had prided themselves on it. He left them after a while for no good reason and went to that hole."

20. See Patai, 80–86.

21. "Charles Dickens," 76, 78.

22. Recall the belief that Jewish men menstruated noted in Chapter 7.

WORKS CITED

Adelman, Janet. *Suffocating Mothers: Fantasies of Maternal Origin in Shakespeare's Plays, Hamlet to the Tempest.* New York: Routledge, 1992.

Allport, Gordon W. *Becoming: Basic Considerations for a Psychology of Personality.* New Haven: Yale University Press, 1955.

Andersson, Theodore. *The Problem of Icelandic Saga Origins.* New Haven: Yale University Press, 1964.

Andersson, Theodore, and William Ian Miller. *Law and Literature in Medieval Iceland.* Stanford: Stanford University Press, 1989.

Angyal, Andras. "Disgust and Related Aversions." *Journal of Abnormal and Social Psychology* 36 (1941): 393–412.

Ariès, Philippe. *The Hour of Our Death.* Trans. Helen Weaver. New York: Knopf, 1981.

Aristotle. *The "Art" of Rhetoric.* Trans. John Henry Freese. Loeb Classical Library, no. 193, 1926. Cambridge, Mass.: Harvard University Press, 1982.

Astington, John H. " 'Fault' in Shakespeare." *Shakespeare Quarterly* 36 (1985): 330–334.

Baier, Annette C. "Moralism and Cruelty: Reflections on Hume and Kant." *Ethics* 103 (1993): 436–457.

———. *Postures of the Mind: Essays on Mind and Morals.* Minneapolis: University of Minnesota Press, 1985.

———. *A Progress of Sentiments: Reflections on Hume's* Treatise. Cambridge, Mass.: Harvard University Press, 1991.

Bakhtin, Mikhail. *Rabelais and His World.* 1965. Trans. Helene Iswolsky. Bloomington: Indiana University Press, 1984.

Barber, Malcolm. "Lepers, Jews, and Moslems: The Plot to Overthrow Christendom in 1321." *History* 66 (1981): 1–17.

Bartlett, Robert. "Symbolic Meanings of Hair in the Middle Ages." *Transactions of the Royal Historical Society,* 6th ser., 4 (1994): 43–60.

Baudelaire, Charles. *Petits Poëmes en Prose.* Ed. Robert Kopp. Paris: José Corti, 1969.

Baumgartner, M. P. "Social Control from Below." In *Toward a General Theory of Social Control,* 2 vols. Ed. Donald Black. New York: Academic Press, 1984, 1: 303–345.

Bell, Rudolf M. *Holy Anorexia*. Chicago: University of Chicago Press, 1985.

Benton, John F., ed. *Self and Society in Medieval France: The Memoirs of Abbot Guibert of Nogent* (1064?–c. 1125). Trans. C. C. Swinton Bland. New York: Harper and Row, 1970.

Bersani, Leo. "Is the Rectum a Grave?" *October* 43 (1987): 197–222.

Boswell, James. *Life of Johnson*. Ed. R. W. Chapman, rev. J. D. Fleeman. Oxford: Oxford University Press, 1970.

Bourdieu, Pierre. *Distinction: A Social Critique of the Judgment of Taste*. Trans. Richard Nice. Cambridge, Mass.: Harvard University Press, 1984.

Bourke, John G. *Scatologic Rites of All Nations*. Washington, 1891.

Braunstein, Philippe. "Toward Intimacy: The Fourteenth Century and Fifteenth Century." *A History of Private Life*, vol. 2: *Revelations of the Medieval World*. Ed. Philippe Ariès and Georges Duby. Cambridge, Mass.: Harvard University Press, 1988, 535–630.

Brown, Norman O. *Life Against Death: The Psychoanalytical Meaning of History*. Middletown, Conn.: Wesleyan University Press, 1959.

Brown, Peter. *The Body and Society: Men, Women, and Sexual Renunciation in Early Christianity*. New York: Columbia University Press, 1988.

Browne, Thomas. *Pseudodoxia Epidemica; or, Enquiries into very many received tenents and commonly presumed truths*. 3rd ed. London, 1658.

Burns, E. Jane. "This Prick Which Is Not One: How Women Talk Back in Old French Fabliaux." In *Feminist Approaches to the Body in Medieval Literature*. Ed. Linda Lomperis and Sarah Stanbury. Philadelphia: University of Pennsylvania Press, 1993, 188–212.

Burton, Robert. *The Anatomy of Melancholy*. 1624. Ed. Floyd Dell and Paul Jordan-Smith. New York: Tudor, 1938.

Bynum, Caroline Walker. "The Body of Christ in the Later Middle Ages: A Reply to Leo Steinberg." In *Fragmentation and Redemption: Essays on Gender and the Human Body in Medieval Religion*. New York: Zone Books, 1992, 79–117.

———. *Holy Feast and Holy Fast: The Religious Significance of Food to Medieval Women*. Berkeley: University of California Press, 1987.

———. "Jesus as Mother and Abbot as Mother: Some Themes in Twelfth-Century Cistercian Writing." In *Jesus as Mother: Studies in the Spirituality of the High Middle Ages*. Berkeley: University of California Press, 1982, 110–169.

———. *The Resurrection of the Body in Western Christianity, 200–1336*. New York: Columbia University Press, 1995.

Carroll, Noël. *The Philosophy of Horror or Paradoxes of the Heart*. New York: Routledge, 1990.

Chaucer, Geoffrey. *The Works of Geoffrey Chaucer*. 2nd ed. Ed. F. N. Robinson. Boston: Houghton Mifflin, 1957.

Chesterfield. *Lord Chesterfield: Letters*. Ed. David Roberts. Oxford: Oxford University Press, 1992.

Chevalier-Skolnikoff, Suzanne. "Facial Expression of Emotion in Nonhuman Primates." In *Darwin and Facial Expression: A Century of Research in Review*. Ed. Paul Ekman. New York: Academic Press, 1973, 11–90.

Clover, Carol J. *Men, Women, and Chain Saws: Gender in the Modern Horror Film.* Princeton: Princeton University Press, 1992.

———. "Regardless of Sex: Men, Women, and Power in Early Northern Europe." *Speculum* 68 (1993): 363–388.

Collins, Randall. "Three Faces of Cruelty: Towards a Comparative Sociology of Violence." *Theory and Society* 1 (1974): 415–440.

Congreve, William, trans. *Ovid's Art of Love.* Book III. London, 1709.

Cooper, Samuel. *A Dictionary of Practical Surgery.* 6th London ed. New York, 1830.

D'Andrade, Roy. "A Folk Model of the Mind." In *Cultural Models in Language and Thought.* Ed. Dorothy Holland and Naomi Quinn. Cambridge: Cambridge University Press, 1987, 112–148.

———. "Some Propositions about the Relations between Culture and Human Cognition." In *Cultural Psychology: Essays on Comparative Human Development.* Ed. James W. Stigler, Richard A. Shweder, and Gilbert Herdt. Cambridge: Cambridge University Press, 1990, 65–129.

D'Arms, Justin, and Daniel Jacobson. "Expressivism, Morality, and the Emotions." *Ethics* 104 (1994): 739–763.

Darwin, Charles. *The Expression of the Emotions in Man and Animals.* 1872. Chicago: University of Chicago Press, 1965.

Davey, Graham C. L. "Characteristics of Individuals with Fear of Spiders." *Anxiety Research* 4 (1992): 299–314.

Desan, Suzanne. "Crowds, Community, and Ritual in the Work of E. P. Thompson and Natalie Davis." In *The New Cultural History.* Ed. Lynn Hunt. Berkeley: University of California Press, 1989, 47–71.

de Sousa, Ronald. *The Rationality of Emotion.* Cambridge, Mass.: MIT Press, 1987.

Douglas, Mary. *Purity and Danger: An Analysis of the Concepts of Pollution and Taboo.* London: Routledge and Kegan Paul, 1966.

Duclos, Sandra E., James D. Laird, Eric Schneider, and Melissa Sexter. "Emotion-Specific Effects of Facial Expressions and Postures on Emotional Experience." *Journal of Personality and Social Psychology* 57 (1989): 100–108.

Dumont, Louis. *Homo Hierarchicus: The Caste System and Its Implications.* Trans. Mark Sainsbury. 1966. Chicago: University of Chicago Press, 1970.

Dworkin, Andrea. *Intercourse.* New York: Free Press, 1987.

Egils saga Skalla-Grímssonar, ed. Sigurður Nordal. Íslenzk Fornrit, vol. 2. Reykjavík: Hið Íslenzka Fornritafélag, 1933.

Ekman, Paul. "An Argument for Basic Emotions." *Cognition and Emotion* 6 (1992): 169–200.

Ekman, Paul, and Wallace V. Friesen. "A New Pan-cultural Facial Expression of Emotion." *Motivation and Emotion* 10 (1986): 159–168.

Ekman, Paul, Maureen O'Sullivan, and David Matsumoto. "Confusions about Context in the Judgment of Facial Expression: A Reply to 'The Contempt Expression and the Relativity Thesis.'" *Motivation and Emotion* 15 (1991): 169–176.

———. "Contradictions in the Study of Contempt: What's It All About? Reply to Russell." *Motivation and Emotion* 15 (1991): 293–296.

Elias, Norbert. *The History of Manners.* Trans. Edmund Jephcott. Vol. 1 of *The Civilizing Process.* 1939. New York: Urizen, 1978.

———. *Power and Civility.* Trans. Edmund Jephcott. Vol. 2 of The Civilizing Process. 1939. New York: Pantheon, 1982.

Eliot, T. S. *Complete Poems and Plays, 1909–1950.* New York: Harcourt, Brace, 1952.

Ellsworth, Phoebe C. "Some Implications of Cognitive Appraisal Theories of Emotion." *International Review of Studies on Emotion* 1 (1991): 143–161.

Elster, Jon. *Sour Grapes: Studies in the Subversion of Rationality.* Cambridge: Cambridge University Press, 1983.

Engen, Trygg. *Odor Sensation and Memory.* New York: Praeger, 1991.

———. *The Perception of Odors.* New York: Academic Press, 1982.

———. "Remembering Odors and Their Names." *American Scientist* 75 (1987): 497–503.

Evans-Pritchard, E. E. *The Nuer: A Description of the Modes of Livelihood and Political Institutions of a Nilotic People.* Oxford: Oxford University Press, 1940.

Eve, Raymond A., and Donald G. Renslow. "An Exploratory Analysis of Private Sexual Behaviors among College Students: Some Implications for a Theory of Class Differences in Sexual Behavior." *Social Behavior and Personality* 8 (1980): 97–105.

Ewing, Quincy. "The Heart of the Race Problem." *Atlantic Monthly* 103 (1908): 389–397.

Fabri, Felix. *The Book of Wanderings of Brother Felix Fabri.* c. 1484. Trans. Aubrey Stewart. In Palestine Pilgrims' Text Society, vols. VII-X. London, 1893–1897.

Ferguson, Margaret W. "*Hamlet:* Letters and Spirits." In *Shakespeare and the Question of Theory.* Ed. Patricia Parker and Geoffrey Hartman. New York: Methuen, 1985, 292–309.

Fielding, Henry. *The Covent-Garden Journal and A Plan of the Universal Register-Office.* 1752. Ed. Bertrand A. Goldgar. Middletown, Conn.: Wesleyan University Press, 1988.

———. "An Essay on Conversation." 1743. In *Miscellaneous Writings,* vol. 1, 243–277. *The Complete Works of Henry Fielding.* Ed. William E. Henley. New York: Croscup and Sterling, 1902, 243–277.

Flanagan, Owen. *Varieties of Moral Personality: Ethics and Psychological Realism.* Cambridge, Mass.: Harvard University Press, 1991.

Flandrin, Jean-Louis. "Distinction through Taste." In *A History of Private Life,* vol. 3: *Passions of the Renaissance.* Ed. Roger Chartier. Cambridge, Mass.: Harvard University Press, 1989, 265–307.

Foot, Philippa. "Utilitarianism and the Virtues." *Mind* 94 (1985): 196–209.

Fradenburg, Louise O. "Criticism, Anti-semitism, and the Prioress's Tale." *Exemplaria* 1 (1989): 69–115.

Freud, Sigmund. "The Antithetical Meaning of Primal Words." 1911. In *The Standard Edition of the Complete Psychological Works of Sigmund Freud.* Ed. James Strachey. London: Hogarth Press, 1953–1974 [hereafter *S.E.*]. 24 vols. 11, 155–161.

———. "Character and Anal Erotism." 1908. *S.E.* 9, 169–175.

———. *Civilization and Its Discontents.* 1930. *S.E.* 21, 59–145.

————. *The Complete Letters of Sigmund Freud to Wilhelm Fliess, 1887–1904.* Ed. and trans. Jeffrey M. Masson. Cambridge, Mass.: Harvard University Press, 1985.

————. "Fetishism." 1927. *S.E.* 21, 149–157.

————. "History of an Infantile Neurosis." 1918. *S.E.* 17, 3–123.

————. "Medusa's Head." 1922. *S.E.* 18, 273–274.

————. "The Most Prevalent Forms of Degradation in Erotic Life." In *Collected Papers.* Ed. Joan Riviere and J. Strachey. 1912. The International Psycho-Analytical Library 4. London, 1924–50, 203–216.

————. "Mourning and Melancholia." 1915. *S.E.* 14, 239–258.

————. "Notes Upon a Case of Obsessional Neurosis." 1909. *S.E.* 10, 153–318.

————. "Some Psychical Consequences of the Anatomical Distinction between the Sexes." 1925. *S.E.* 19, 243–258.

————. *Three Essays on the Theory of Sexuality.* 1905. *S.E.* 7, 125–245.

————. "The Uncanny." 1919. *S.E.* 17, 218–256.

————. "The Unconscious." 1915. *S.E.* 14, 161–215.

Frijda, Nico H. *The Emotions.* Cambridge: Cambridge University Press, 1986.

Gade, Kari Ellen. "Einarr Þambarskelfir's Last Shot." *Scandinavian Studies* 67 (1995): 153–162.

————. "Homosexuality and Rape of Males in Old Norse Law and Literature." *Scandinavian Studies* 58 (1986): 124–141.

————. "Penile Puns: Personal Names and Phallic Symbols in Skaldic Poetry." In *Essays in Medieval Studies: Proceedings of the Illinois Medieval Association.* Ed. John B. Friedman and Patricia Hollahan. Urbana: University of Illinois Press, 1989, 57–67.

Galatzer-Levy, Robert M., and Mayer Gruber. "What an Affect Means: A Quasi-Experiment about Disgust." *Annual of Psychoanalysis* 20 (1992): 69–92.

Gerald of Wales (Geraldus Cambrensis). *Gemma Ecclesiastica.* Ed. J. S. Brewer. Opera 2. Rerum Britannicarum Medii Aevi Scriptores (Rolls Series), vol. 21. London, 1862. (Trans. John J. Hagen, *Gemma Ecclesiastica.* Davis Medieval Texts and Studies, vol. 2. Leiden: Brill, 1979).

Gibbard, Allan. *Wise Choices, Apt Feelings: A Theory of Normative Judgment.* Cambridge, Mass.: Harvard University Press, 1990.

Gilman, Sander L. *Sexuality: An Illustrated History.* New York: John Wiley, 1989.

Gilmore, David D., ed. *Honor and Shame and the Unity of the Mediterranean.* A special publication of the American Anthropological Association, no. 22. Washington, 1987.

Godwin, William. *Enquiry Concerning Political Justice.* 2 vols. London, 1793. Rpt. Woodstock Books, 1992.

Goffman, Erving. *Behavior in Public Places: Notes on the Social Organization of Gatherings.* New York: Free Press, 1963.

————. *Interaction Ritual: Essays in Face-to-face Behavior.* Chicago: Aldine, 1967.

————. *The Presentation of Self in Everyday Life.* Garden City, N.Y.: Doubleday, 1959.

————. *Relations in Public.* New York: Basic Books, 1971.

WORKS CITED   305

————. *Stigma: Notes on the Management of Spoiled Identity.* New York: Simon and Schuster, 1963.

Gordon, Robert M. *The Structure of Emotions.* Cambridge: Cambridge University Press, 1987.

Greenblatt, Stephen J. "Filthy Rites." In *Learning to Curse: Essays in Early Modern Culture.* New York: Routledge, 1990, 59–79.

Gross, James J., and Robert W. Levenson. "Emotional Suppression: Physiology, Self-report, and Expressive Behavior." *Journal of Personality and Social Psychology* 64 (1993): 970–986.

Guibert de Nogent: Historie de sa vie (1053–1124). Ed. Georges Bourgin. Paris: Alphonse Picard, 1907.

Haidt, Jonathan, Clark McCauley, and Paul Rozin. "Individual Differences in Sensitivity to Disgust: A Scale Sampling Seven Domains of Disgust Elicitors." *Personality and Individual Differences* 16 (1994): 701–713.

Haidt, Jonathan, Paul Rozin, Clark McCauley, and Sumio Imada. "Body, Psyche, and Culture: The Relationship between Disgust and Morality." In *The Cultural Construction of Social Cognition.* Ed. G. Misra. New York: Sage, forthcoming.

Hallpike, C. R. "Social Hair." *Man* 4 (1969): 256–264.

Hankins, John E. "Hamlet's 'God Kissing Carrion': A Theory of the Generation of Life." *PMLA* 64 (1949): 507–516.

Harré, Rom. "Embarrassment: A Conceptual Analysis." In *Shyness and Embarrassment.* Ed. W. Ray Crozier. Cambridge: Cambridge University Press, 1990, 181–204.

Harré, Rom, and Robert Finlay-Jones. "Emotion Talk across Times." In *The Social Construction of Emotions.* Ed. Rom Harré. Oxford: Basil Blackwell, 1986, 220–233.

Hawthorne, Nathaniel. *The Blithedale Romance.* 1852. New York: Library of America, 1983, 629–848.

Hazlitt, William. *William Hazlitt: Selected Writings.* Ed. Ronald Blythe. Harmondsworth: Penguin, 1970.

Hebb, Donald O. "Emotion in Man and Animal: An Analysis of the Intuitive Processes of Recognition." *Psychological Review* 53 (1946): 88–106.

Hellman, Robert, and Rickard O'Gorman, ed. and trans. *Fabliaux, Ribald Tales from the Old French.* New York: Thomas Y. Crowell, 1966.

Herdt, Gilbert. "Sambia Nosebleeding Rites and Male Proximity to Women." In *Cultural Psychology: Essays on Comparative Human Development.* Ed. James W. Stigler, Richard A. Shweder, and Gilbert Herdt. Cambridge: Cambridge University Press, 1990, 366–400.

Herzog, Don. *Without Foundations: Justification in Political Theory.* Ithaca: Cornell University Press, 1985.

————. "The Trouble with Hairdressers." *Representations* 53 (1996): 21–43.

Hirschman, Albert O. *The Passions and the Interests: Political Arguments for Capitalism before Its Triumph.* Princeton: Princeton University Press, 1977.

Hochschild, Arlie Russell. *The Managed Heart: Commercialization of Human Feeling.* Berkeley: University of California Press, 1983.

Hoggart, Richard. "George Orwell and 'The Road to Wigan Pier'. " *Critical Quarterly* 7 (1965): 72–85.

Horkheimer, Max, and Theodor W. Adorno. *Dialectic of Enlightenment*. Trans. John Cumming. 1944. New York: Continuum, 1994.

Hume, David. *An Enquiry Concerning the Principles of Morals*. 1751. La Salle, Ill.: Open Court, 1966. Rpt. from 1777 ed.

————. *The Natural History of Religion*. 1757. In *David Hume: On Religion*. Ed. Richard Wollheim. Cleveland: Meridian, 1963, 31–98.

————. *A Treatise of Human Nature*. 1739–1740. Ed. L. A. Selby-Bigge; 2nd ed. P. H. Nidditch. Oxford: Clarendon, 1975.

Hutcheon, Linda. *A Theory of Parody: The Teachings of Twentieth-Century Art Forms*. New York: Methuen, 1985.

Hutcheson, Frances. "An Inquiry Concerning Moral Good and Evil." 1725. In *British Moralists 1650–1800*. Ed. D. D. Raphael. Oxford: Clarendon Press, 1969, 261–299.

Ignatieff, Michael. "The Seductiveness of Moral Disgust." *Social Research* 62 (1995): 77–97.

Irigaray, Luce. *This Sex Which Is Not One*. Ithaca: Cornell University Press, 1985.

Itard, Jean. *The Wild Boy of Aveyron*. 1801. In Lucien Malson, *Wolf Children and the Problem of Human Nature*. New York: New Left Books, 1972.

Izard, Carroll E. "Emotion-Cognition Relationships and Human Development." In *Emotions, Cognition, and Behavior*. Ed. Carroll E. Izard, Jerome Kagan, and Robert B. Zajonc. Cambridge: Cambridge University Press, 1984, 17–37.

————. *Human Emotions*. New York: Plenum, 1977.

————. *The Face of Emotion*. New York: Appleton-Century-Crofts, 1971.

Izard, Carroll E., and O. Maurice Haynes. "On the Form and Universality of the Contempt Expression: A Challenge to Ekman and Friesen's Claim of Discovery." *Motivation and Emotion* 12 (1988): 1–16.

Jaeger, C. Stephen. *The Origins of Courtliness: Civilizing Trends and the Formation of Courtly Ideals, 939–1210*. Philadelphia: University of Pennsylvania Press, 1985.

James, William. *Principles of Psychology*. 3 vols. Cambridge, Mass.: Harvard University Press, 1981.

Johnson, Allen, Orna Johnson, and Michael Baksh. "The Colors of Emotions in Machiguenga." *American Anthropologist* 88 (1986): 674–681.

Johnson, Samuel. *The Rambler*. 1750–1752. Ed. Walter Jackson Bate and Albrecht B. Strauss. In *Works of Samuel Johnson*, vol. 3. New Haven: Yale University Press, 1963.

Johnson-Laird, P. N., and Keith Oatley. "Basic Emotions, Rationality, and Folk Theory." *Cognition and Emotion* 6 (1992): 201–223.

————. "The Language of Emotions: An Analysis of a Semantic Field." *Cognition and Emotion* 3 (1989): 81–123.

Kagan, Jerome. "The Idea of Emotion in Human Development." In *Emotions, Cognition, and Behavior*. Ed. Carroll E. Izard, Jerome Kagan, and Robert B. Zajonc. Cambridge: Cambridge University Press, 1984, 38–72.

Kahane, Claire. "Freud's Sublimation: Disgust, Desire and the Female Body." *American Imago* 49 (1992): 411–425.

Kamir, Orit. *Stalking: History, Culture and Law.* SJD dissertation. University of Michigan Law School, 1995.

Kant, Immanuel. *Critique of Judgment.* 1790. Trans. Werner S. Pluhar. Indianapolis: Hackett, 1987.

Kipnis, Laura. "(Male) Desire and (Female) Disgust: Reading *Hustler.*" In *Cultural Studies.* Ed. L. Grossberg et al. New York: Routledge, 1992, 373–391.

Klein, Richard. "Get a Whiff of This: Breaking the Smell Barrier." *The New Republic* 212 (1995): 18ff.

Knapp, Peter H. "Purging and Curbing: An Inquiry into Disgust, Satiety and Shame." *Journal of Nervous and Mental Disease* 144 (1967): 514–534.

Kristeva, Julia. *Powers of Horror: An Essay on Abjection.* Trans. Leon S. Roudiez. New York: Columbia University Press, 1982.

Kundera, Milan. *The Unbearable Lightness of Being.* New York: Harper and Row, 1984.

Laqueur, Thomas. *Making Sex: Body and Gender from the Greeks to Freud.* Cambridge, Mass.: Harvard University Press, 1990.

La Rochefoucauld. *Maximes.* 1659. Ed. Jacques Truchet. Paris: Flammarion, 1977.

Laxdæla saga, ed. Einar Ól. Sveinsson. Íslenzk Fornrit, vol. 5. Reykjavík: Hið Íslenzka Fornritafélag, 1934.

Leach, Edmund R. "Anthropological Aspects of Language: Animal Categories and Verbal Abuse." In *New Directions in the Study of Language.* Ed. Eric H. Lenneberg. Cambridge, Mass.: MIT Press, 1964, 23–63.

——. "Magical Hair." *Journal of the Royal Anthropological Institute of Great Britain and Ireland* 88 (1958): 147–164.

Le Brun, Charles. "Conférence sur l'expression des passions." 1668. Rpt. in *Nouvelle revue de psychanalyse* 21 (1980): 96–109.

Levenson, Robert W., Paul Ekman, and Wallace V. Friesen. "Voluntary Facial Action Generates Emotion-specific Autonomic Nervous System Activity." *Psychophysiology* 27 (1990): 363–384.

Lincoln, Bruce. *Authority: Construction and Corrosion.* Chicago: University of Chicago Press, 1994.

Little, Lester K. *Religious Poverty and the Profit Economy in Medieval Europe.* Ithaca: Cornell University Press, 1978.

Lutz, Catherine, and Geoffrey M. White. "The Anthropology of Emotions." *Annual Review of Anthropology* 15 (1986): 405–436.

Lyons, William. *Emotions.* Cambridge: Cambridge University Press, 1980.

Mandeville, Bernard. *The Fable of the Bees or Private Vices, Publick Benefits.* 1732, 6th ed. Ed. F. B. Kaye. 2 vols. Oxford: Clarendon Press, 1924. Rpt. Liberty Press, 1988.

Marvell, Andrew. *The Poems of Andrew Marvell.* Ed. Hugh MacDonald. London: Routledge and Kegan Paul, 1952.

Matchett, George, and Graham C. L. Davey. "A Test of a Disease-Avoidance Model of Animal Phobias." *Behaviour Research and Therapy* 29 (1991): 91–94.

McDougall, William. *An Introduction to Social Psychology*. Boston: Luce, 1921.

McNeill, John T., and Helena M. Gamer, trans. *Medieval Handbooks of Penance*. New York: Columbia University Press, 1938.

Meulengracht Sørensen, Preben. *The Unmanly Man: Concepts of Sexual Defamation in Early Northern Society*. Trans. Joan Turville-Petre. Odense: Odense University Press, 1983.

Meyers, Jeffrey, ed. *George Orwell: The Critical Heritage*. London: Routledge and Kegan Paul, 1975.

Middle English Dictionary. Ed. Hans Kurath and Sherman M. Kuhn. Ann Arbor: University of Michigan Press, 1952—.

Miller, Susan B. "Disgust: Conceptualization, Development and Dynamics." *International Review of Psychoanalysis* 13 (1986): 295–307.

———. "Disgust Reactions: Their Determinants and Manifestations in Treatment." *Contemporary Psychoanalysis* 29 (1993): 711–735.

Miller, William Ian. *Bloodtaking and Peacemaking: Feud, Law, and Society in Saga Iceland*. Chicago: University of Chicago Press, 1990.

———. "Clint Eastwood and Equity." In *In Law in the Domains of Culture*. Ed. Austin Sarat and Thomas Kearns. Ann Arbor: University of Michigan Press, 1997.

———. "Deep Inner Lives, Individualism, and People of Honour." *History of Political Thought* 16 (1995): 190–207.

———. *Humiliation: And Other Essays on Honor, Social Discomfort, and Violence*. Ithaca: Cornell University Press, 1993.

———. " 'I can take a hint': Social Ineptitude, Embarrassment, and *The King of Comedy*." *Michigan Quarterly Review* 33 (1994): 322–344.

Milton, John. *John Milton: Complete Poems and Major Prose*. Ed. Merritt Y. Hughes. New York: Odyssey Press, 1957.

Montaigne, Michel de. *The Complete Essays of Montaigne*. Trans. Donald M. Frame. Stanford: Stanford University Press, 1958.

Moore, R. I. *The Formation of a Persecuting Society: Power and Deviance in Western Europe, 950–1250*. Oxford: Basil Blackwell, 1987.

Nagel, Thomas. "Ruthlessness in Public Life." In *Mortal Questions*. Cambridge: Cambridge University Press, 1979, 75–90.

Nashe, Thomas. *Christs Teares over Jerusalem*. London, 1593.

Nemeroff, Carol, and Paul Rozin. " 'You are what you eat': Applying the Demand-Free 'Impressions' Technique to an Unacknowledged Belief." *Ethos* 17 (1989): 50–69.

Neu, Jerome. " 'A Tear Is an Intellectual Thing.' " *Representations* 19 (1987): 35–61.

Newman, Francis W. *Hebrew Theism*. 1858, 2nd ed. London, 1874.

Nietzsche, Frederich. *On the Genealogy of Morals*. 1887. Trans. Walter Kaufmann and R. J. Hollingdale. New York: Vintage, 1967.

———. *Twilight of the Idols*. 1889. In *The Portable Nietzsche*. Ed. and trans. Walter Kaufmann. New York: Viking, 1954, 463–563.

Nozick, Robert. *Anarchy, State, and Utopia*. New York: Basic Books, 1974.

Ortony, Andrew, and Terence J. Turner. "What's Basic about Basic Emotions?" *Psychological Review* 97 (1990): 315–331.

Orwell, George. "Charles Dickens." 1939. In *George Orwell: A Collection of Essays*. San Diego: Harcourt Brace, 1981, 48–104.

———. *Down and Out in Paris and London*. 1933. New York: Harcourt Brace, 1950.

———. "Inside the Whale." 1940. In *George Orwell: A Collection of Essays*. San Diego: Harcourt Brace, 1981, 210–252.

———. "Looking Back at the Spanish Civil War." 1943. In *George Orwell: A Collection of Essays*. San Diego: Harcourt Brace, 1981, 188–210.

———. "Politics vs. Literature: An Examination of *Gulliver's Travels*." 1946. In *Collected Essays, Journalism and Letters of George Orwell*. Ed. Sonia Orwell and Ian Angus. London: Secker and Warburg, 1968. Vol. 4, 205–223.

———. *The Road to Wigan Pier*. 1937. New York: Harcourt, Brace, 1958.

———. "Such, Such were the Joys." 1947. In *George Orwell: A Collection of Essays*. San Diego: Harcourt Brace, 1981, 1–47.

Overfield, Theresa. *Biologic Variation in Health and Illness: Race, Age, and Sex Differences*. Menlo Park, Calif.: Addison-Wesley. 1985.

Ovid. *The Art of Love and other Poems*. Trans. J. H. Mozley. Loeb Classical Library, vol. 232. Cambridge, Mass.: Harvard University Press, 1929.

Packer, Barbara L. *The Transcendentalists*. In *The Cambridge History of American Literature*, vol. 2, 1820–1865. Ed. Sacvan Bercovitch. Cambridge: Cambridge University Press, 1995, 329–604.

Parmenides. Trans. F. M. Cornford. In *The Collected Dialogues of Plato*. Ed. Edith Hamilton and Huntington Cairns. New York: Pantheon, 1961, 920–956.

Patai, Daphne. *The Orwell Mystique: A Study in Male Ideology*. Amherst: University of Massachusetts Press, 1984.

Payer, Pierre J. *The Bridling of Desire: Views of Sex in the Later Middle Ages*. Toronto: University of Toronto Press, 1993.

Peristiany, J. G., ed. *Honour and Shame: The Values of Mediterranean Society*. Chicago: University of Chicago Press, 1966.

Piers, Gerhart, and Milton B. Singer. *Shame and Guilt: A Psychoanalytic and Cultural Study*. 1953; New York: Norton, 1971.

Plutchik, Robert. *The Emotions: Facts, Theories, and a New Model*. New York: Random House, 1962.

———. *Emotion: A Psychoevolutionary Synthesis*. New York: Harper and Row, 1980.

Pope, Alexander. *The Iliad of Homer*. London, 1715.

Rai, Alok. *Orwell and the Politics of Despair*. Cambridge: Cambridge University Press, 1988.

Ranum, Orest. "The Refuges of Intimacy." In *A History of Private Life*, vol. 3: *Passions of the Renaissance*. Ed. Roger Chartier. Cambridge, Mass.: Harvard University Press, 1989, 207–263.

Raymundus de Vineis. *The Life of Sainct Catharine of Siena*. English trans. John Fen, 1609. London: Scholar Press, 1978.

Revel, Jacques. "The Uses of Civility." In *A History of Private Life*, vol. 3: *Passions of the Renaissance*. Ed. Roger Chartier. Cambridge, Mass.: Harvard University Press, 1989, 167–205.

Richards, Jeffrey. *Sex, Dissidence and Damnation: Minority Groups in the Middle Ages*. London: Routledge, 1991.

Rindisbacher, Hans J. *The Smell of Books: A Cultural-Historical Study of Olfactory Perception in Literature*. Ann Arbor: University of Michigan Press, 1992.

Rose, Jacqueline. "Sexuality in the Reading of Shakespeare: *Hamlet* and *Measure for Measure*." In *Alternative Shakespeares*. Ed. John Drakakis. New York: Methuen, 1985, 95–118, 229–231.

Rose, Phyllis. *Parallel Lives: Five Victorian Marriages*. New York: Knopf, 1983.

Rousseau, Jean-Jacques. *The Confessions*. 1781. Trans. J. M. Cohen. Harmondsworth: Penguin, 1953.

Rousselle, Aline. *Porneia: On Desire and the Body in Antiquity*. Trans. Felicia Pheasant. Oxford: Basil Blackwell, 1988.

Rozin, Paul. " 'Taste-Smell Confusions' and the Duality of the Olfactory Sense." *Perception and Psychophysics* 31 (1982): 397–401.

Rozin, Paul, and April E. Fallon. "A Perspective on Disgust." *Psychological Review* 94 (1987): 23–41.

Rozin, Paul, April E. Fallon, and MaryLynn Augustoni-Ziskind. "The Child's Conception of Food: Development of Categories of Rejected and Accepted Substances." *Journal of Nutrition Education* 18 (1986): 75–81.

Rozin, Paul, Jonathan Haidt, and Clark R. McCauley. "Disgust." In *Handbook of Emotions*. Ed. Michael Lewis and Jeannette M. Haviland. New York: Guilford, 1993, 575–594.

Rozin, Paul, Larry Hammer, Harriet Oster, Talia Horowitz, and Veronica Marmora. "The Child's Conception of Food: Differentiation of Categories of Rejected Substances in the 1.4 to 5 Year Age Range." *Appetite* 7 (1986): 141–151.

Rozin, Paul, Laura Lowery, and Rhonda Ebert. "Varieties of Disgust Faces and the Structure of Disgust." *Journal of Personality and Social Psychology* 66 (1994): 870–881.

Rozin, Paul, Linda Millman, and Carol Nemeroff. "Operation of the Laws of Sympathetic Magic in Disgust and Other Domains." *Journal of Personality and Social Psychology* 50 (1986): 703–712.

Rozin, Paul, and Carol Nemeroff. "The Laws of Sympathetic Magic: A Psychological Analysis of Similarity and Contagion." In *Cultural Psychology: Essays on Comparative Human Development*. Ed. James W. Stigler, Richard A. Shweder, and Gilbert Herdt. Cambridge: Cambridge University Press, 1990, 205–232.

Russell, James A. "The Contempt Expression and the Relativity Thesis." *Motivation and Emotion* 15 (1991): 149–168.

———. "Negative Results on a Reported Facial Expression of Contempt." *Motivation and Emotion* 15 (1991): 281–291.

———. "Rejoinder to Ekman, O'Sullivan, and Matsumoto." *Motivation and Emotion* 15 (1991): 177–184.

Sartre, J.-P. *Being and Nothingness*. 1943. Trans. Hazel E. Barnes. New York: Washington Square, 1992.

———. *La nausée*. Paris. Gallimard, 1938.

Scarry, Elaine. *The Body in Pain: The Making and Unmaking of the World*. New York: Oxford University Press, 1985.

Schelling, Thomas C. *The Strategy of Conflict*. Cambridge, Mass.: Harvard University Press, 1960.

Scott, James C. *Domination and the Arts of Resistance*. New Haven: Yale University Press, 1990.

Shakespeare. *The Complete Works*. Ed. Alfred Harbage et al. Baltimore: Penguin, 1969.

Shklar, Judith. *Ordinary Vices*. Cambridge, Mass.: Harvard University Press, 1984.

Shweder, Richard A. "Menstrual Pollution, Soul Loss, and the Comparative Study of Emotions." In *Thinking through Cultures: Expeditions in Cultural Psychology*. Ed. Richard A. Shweder. Cambridge, Mass.: Harvard University Press, 1991, 241–265.

Shweder, Richard A., Manamohan Mahapatra, and Joan G. Miller. "Culture and Moral Development." In *Cultural Psychology: Essays on Comparative Human Development*. Ed. James W. Stigler, Richard A. Shweder, and Gilbert Herdt. Cambridge: Cambridge University Press, 1990, 130–204.

Silverman, Kaja. *The Acoustic Mirror: The Female Voice in Psychoanalysis and Cinema*. Bloomington: Indiana University Press, 1988.

Sinanoglou, Leah. "The Christ Child as Sacrifice: A Medieval Tradition and the Corpus Christi Plays." *Speculum* 48 (1973): 491–509.

Smith, Adam. *The Theory of Moral Sentiments*. 1759. Ed. D. D. Raphael and A. L. Macfie. Oxford: Clarendon Press, 1976.

Smith, Craig, and Phoebe C. Ellsworth. "Patterns of Cognitive Appraisal in Emotion." *Journal of Personality and Social Psychology* 48 (1985): 813–838.

Solomon, Robert C. *The Passions: The Myth and Nature of Human Emotion*. 1976. Notre Dame, Ind.: University of Notre Dame Press, 1983.

———. "The Philosophy of Horror, or, Why Did Godzilla Cross the Road?" In Solomon, *Entertaining Ideas*. Buffalo: Prometheus Books, 1992, 119–130.

Southern, R. W., ed. and trans. *The Life of St. Anselm, Archbishop of Canterbury by Eadmer*. London: Thomas Nelson, 1962.

———. *The Making of the Middle Ages*. New Haven: Yale University Press, 1953.

Spacks, Patricia Ann Meyer. *Boredom: The Literary History of a State of Mind*. Chicago: University of Chicago Press, 1995.

Stallybrass, Peter, and Allon White. *The Politics and Poetics of Transgression*. Ithaca: Cornell University Press, 1986.

Sterne, Laurence. *Tristram Shandy*. Ed. James A. Work. Indianapolis: Odyssey Press, 1940.

Strack, Fritz, Leonard L. Martin, and Sabine Stepper. "Inhibiting and Facilitating Conditions of the Human Smile." *Journal of Personality and Social Psychology* 54 (1988): 768–777.

Swan, Jim. "Mater and Nannie: Freud's Two Mothers and the Discovery of the Oedipus Complex." *American Imago* 31 (1974): 1–64.

Swift, Jonathan. *Directions to Servants.* 1745. Ed. Herbert Davis. Oxford: Basil Blackwell, 1959.

————. *Gulliver's Travels.* 1726. Ed. Martin Price. Indianapolis: Bobbs-Merrill, 1963.

Swift: Poetical Works. Ed. Herbert Davis. London: Oxford University Press, 1967.

Tambiah, S. J. "Animals Are Good to Think and Good to Prohibit." *Ethnology* 8 (1969): 423–459.

Taussig, Michael. "Culture of Terror—Space of Death: Roger Casement's Putumayo Report and the Explanation of Torture." *Comparative Studies in Society and History* 26 (1984): 467–497.

Taylor, Gabriele. *Pride, Shame, and Guilt: Emotions of Self-Assessment.* Oxford: Clarendon Press, 1985.

Taylor, Shelley E., and Jonathan Brown. "Illusion and Well-Being: A Social Psychological Perspective on Mental Health." *Psychological Bulletin* 103 (1988): 193–210.

Templer, Donald I., Frank L. King, Robert K. Brooner, and Mark D. Corgiat. "Assessment of Body Elimination Attitude." *Journal of Clinical Psychology* 40 (1984): 754–759.

Thoits, Peggy A. "The Sociology of Emotions." *Annual Review of Sociology* 15 (1989): 317–342.

Thomas Aquinas. *Summa Theologiæ.* Blackfriars ed. New York: McGraw-Hill, 1964.

Tocqueville, Alexis de. *Democracy in America.* Trans. George Lawrence; ed. J. P. Mayer. Garden City, N.Y.: Anchor, 1969.

Tomkins, Sylvan S. *Affect, Imagery, Consciousness,* vol. 2: *The Negative Affects.* New York: Springer, 1963.

————. "Affect Theory." In *Emotion in the Human Face.* Ed. Paul Ekman. 2nd ed. Studies in Emotion and Social Interaction. Cambridge: Cambridge University Press, 1984, 353–381.

Tourneur, Cyril. *The Revenger's Tragedy.* 1607. In *John Webster and Cyril Tourneur.* New York: Hill and Wang, 1956.

Turner, Terence J., and Andrew Ortony. "Basic Emotions: Can Conflicting Criteria Converge?" *Psychological Review* 99 (1992): 566–571.

van Krieken, Robert. "Violence, Self-discipline and Modernity: Beyond the 'Civilizing Process.'" *Sociological Review* 37 (1989): 193–218.

Vlastos, Gregory. "Justice and Equality." In *Theories of Rights.* Ed. Jeremy Waldron. Oxford: Oxford University Press, 1984, 41–76.

Waldron, Jeremy. "Homelessness and the Issue of Freedom." *UCLA Law Review* 39 (1991): 295–324.

Walzer, Michael. "Political Action: The Problem of Dirty Hands." *Philosophy and Public Affairs* 2 (1973): 160–180.

Ware, Jacqueline, Kamud Jain, Ian Burgess, and Graham C. L. Davey. "Disease-Avoidance Model: Factor Analysis of Common Animal Fears." *Behaviour Research and Therapy* 32 (1994): 57–63.

Webb, Katie, and Graham C. L. Davey. "Disgust Sensitivity and Fear of Animals:

Effect of Exposure to Violent or Revulsive Material." *Anxiety, Stress, and Coping* 5 (1992): 329–335.

Weber, Max. *The Theory of Social and Economic Organization.* Trans. A. M. Henderson and Talcott Parsons. New York: Free Press, 1947.

Webster, John. *The Duchess of Malfi.* 1623. In *John Webster and Cyril Tourneur.* New York: Hill and Wang, 1956.

Wierzbicka, Anna. "Human Emotions: Universal or Culture-Specific." *American Anthropologist* 88 (1986): 584–594.

———. "The Semantics of Interjection." *Journal of Pragmatics* 18 (1992): 159–192.

Williams, Bernard. *Ethics and the Limits of Philosophy.* Cambridge, Mass.: Harvard University Press, 1985.

———. "Professional Morality and Its Dispositions." In *The Good Lawyer: Lawyers' Roles and Lawyers' Ethics.* Ed. David Luban. Totowa, N.J.: Rowman and Allanheld, 1983, 259–269.

———. *Shame and Necessity.* Berkeley: University of California Press, 1993.

Williams, Raymond. *Culture and Society, 1780–1950.* New York: Harper and Row, 1958.

Wilmot, John. *The Complete Poems of John Wilmot, Earl of Rochester.* Ed. David M. Vieth. New Haven: Yale University Press, 1968.

Wollheim, Richard. "Orwell Reconsidered." *Partisan Review* 27 (1960): 82–97.

Wollstonecraft, Mary. *A Vindication of the Rights of Woman.* 1792. Harmondsworth: Penguin, 1975.

Wurmser, Léon. *The Mask of Shame.* Baltimore: Johns Hopkins University Press, 1981.

INDEX